NEW INTERNATIONAL
BIBLICAL COMMENTARY

Old Testament Series

NEW INTERNATIONAL BIBLICAL COMMENTARY

GENESIS

JOHN E. HARTLEY

Based on the New International Version

© 2000 by Hendrickson Publishers, Inc.
P. O. Box 3473
Peabody, Massachusetts 01961–3473

First published jointly, July 2000, in the United States by
Hendrickson Publishers and in the United Kingdom by the
Paternoster Press, P. O. Box 300, Carlisle, Cumbria CA3 0QS.
All rights reserved.

Printed in the United States of America

First printing — August 2000

Library of Congress Cataloging-in-Publication Data

Hartley, John E.
    Genesis / John E. Hartley.
       p. cm. — (New International biblical commentary. Old
  Testament Series; 1)
    Includes bibliographical references and indexes.
    ISBN 1–56563–211–7 (paper)
    1. Bible. O.T. Genesis—Commentaries. I. Title.
  II. Series.
    BS1235.3 .H37   2000
    222′.11077—dc21   00–023013
                                              CIP

ISBN 1–56563–211–7 (U.S. softcover)
ISBN 1–56563–578–7 (U.S. hardcover)

British Library Cataloguing in Publication Data
A catalogue record for this book is available
from the British Library.

ISBN 0–85364–722–4 (U.K. softcover)

In memory of my parents
Mary E. and Walter Hartley
for their loving support

Table of Contents

The Primeval Narrative (Gen. 1:1–11:26)

The Abraham Narrative (Gen. 11:27–25:18)

The Jacob Narrative (Gen. 25:19–36:43)

The Joseph Narrative (Gen. 37:1–50:26)

Foreword
New International Biblical Commentary

As an ancient document, the Old Testament often seems something quite foreign to modern men and women. Opening its pages may feel, to the modern reader, like traversing a kind of literary time warp into a whole other world. In that world sisters and brothers marry, long hair mysteriously makes men superhuman, and temple altars daily smell of savory burning flesh and sweet incense. There, desert bushes burn but leave no ashes, water gushes from rocks, and cities fall because people march around them. A different world, indeed!

Even God, the Old Testament's main character, seems a stranger compared to his more familiar New Testament counterpart. Sometimes the divine is portrayed as a loving father and faithful friend, someone who rescues people from their greatest dangers or generously rewards them for heroic deeds. At other times, however, God resembles more a cruel despot, one furious at human failures, raving against enemies, and bloodthirsty for revenge. Thus, skittish about the Old Testament's diverse portrayal of God, some readers carefully select which portions of the text to study, or they avoid the Old Testament altogether.

The purpose of this commentary series is to help readers navigate this strange and sometimes forbidding literary and spiritual terrain. Its goal is to break down the barriers between the ancient and modern worlds so that the power and meaning of these biblical texts become transparent to contemporary readers. How is this to be done? And what sets this series apart from others currently on the market?

This commentary series will bypass several popular approaches to biblical interpretation. It will not follow a *precritical* approach that interprets the text without reference to recent scholarly conversations. Such a commentary contents itself with offering little more than a paraphrase of the text with occasional supplements from archaeology, word studies, and classical theology. It mistakenly believes that there have been few insights into the Bible since Calvin or Luther. Nor will this series pursue an *anticritical* approach whose preoccupation is to defend the Bible against its detractors, especially scholarly ones. Such a commentary has little space left to move beyond showing why the Bible's critics are wrong to explaining what the biblical text means. The result is a paucity of vibrant biblical theology. Again, this series finds inadequate a *critical* approach that seeks to understand the text apart from belief in the meaning it conveys. Though modern readers have been taught to be discerning, they do not want to live in the "desert of criticism" either.

Instead, as its editors, we have sought to align this series with what has been labeled *believing criticism.* This approach marries probing, reflective interpretation of the text to loyal biblical devotion and warm Christian affection. Our contributors tackle the task of interpretation using the full range of critical methodologies and practices. Yet they do so as people of faith who hold the text in the highest regard. The commentators in this series use criticism to bring the message of the biblical texts vividly to life so the minds of modern readers may be illumined and their faith deepened.

The authors in this series combine a firm commitment to modern scholarship with a similar commitment to the Bible's full authority for Christians. They bring to the task the highest technical skills, warm theological commitment, and rich insight from their various communities. In so doing, they hope to enrich the life of the academy as well as the life of the church.

Part of the richness of this commentary series derives from its authors' breadth of experience and ecclesial background. As editors, we have consciously brought together a diverse group of scholars in terms of age, gender, denominational affiliation, and race. We make no claim that they represent the full expression of the people of God, but they do bring fresh, broad perspectives to the interpretive task. But though this series has sought out diversity among its contributors, they also reflect a commitment to a common center. These commentators write as "believing critics"—scholars who desire to speak for church and academy, for academy and church. As editors, we offer this series in devotion to God and for the enrichment of God's people.

ROBERT L. HUBBARD JR.
ROBERT K. JOHNSTON
Editors

Acknowledgments

Engagement with a book of the Bible over several years produces a strong sense of inner joy and peace. Genesis is particularly delightful to study because of its interesting narratives, the orientation it gives to God's program for humanity, and its recounting the roots of the people of God. Therefore, I express my deep gratitude to Robert Johnston and Robert Hubbard, the general editors of this series, for inviting me to write this volume, for their encouragement along the way, and for significant suggestions on improving the volume.

I wish to express my thanks to several who have read the entire manuscript and offered helpful suggestions, particularly Mrs. Lark Rilling, Mr. Timothy Finlay, and Mr. Doug Brown. I am grateful to several colleagues who have read portions of the commentary and provided significant feedback. In addition, I wish to thank the editorial staff of Hendrickson Publishers and especially Shirley Decker-Lucke for their diligent labor in enhancing this volume. I wish to thank my wife, Dorothy, for her hard work in typing this work with the various changes. I heartily thank the administration of Azusa Pacific University for a sabbatical and other resources that fostered the production of this volume. Certainly I am indebted to the vast array of scholarship that has brought much insight into the meaning of the passages in this great book; a portion of this indebtedness will be indicated along the way and in the additional notes.

Abbreviations

AB	Anchor Bible
ABD	*Anchor Bible Dictionary*
Akk.	Akkadian
Ant.	Josephus, *Antiquities*
Aqht	Tale of Aqhat
Arab.	Arabic
Aram.	Aramaic
BA	*Biblical Archaeologist*
Ber. Rab.	Bereshit Rabba
Barn.	*Epistle of Barnabas*
BETL	Bibliotheca ephemeridum theologicarum lovaniensium
Bib	*Biblica*
BJRL	*Bulletin of the John Rylands University Library of Manchester*
BR	*Biblical Review*
BSac	*Bibliotheca sacra*
BTB	*Biblical Theology Bulletin*
BZAW	*Beihefte zur Zeitschrift für die alttestamentliche Wissenschaft*
ca.	circa
CBQ	*Catholic Biblical Quarterly*
CBQMS	Catholic Biblical Quarterly Monograph Series
cf.	compare
ch(s).	chapter(s)
ConBOT	Coniectanea biblica: Old Testament Series
E	Elohist
1 En.	*1 Enoch*
ed(s).	editor(s)
Eng.	English
f.	following
fem.	feminine
FOTL	Forms of the Old Testament Literature

Gk.	Greek
GKC	*Gesenius' Hebrew Grammar*
Hb.	Hebrew
HSM	Harvard Semitic Monographs
HTR	*Harvard Theological Review*
IEJ	*Israel Exploration Journal*
Int	*Interpretation*
IRT	Issues in Religion and Theology
ISBE	*International Standard Bible Encyclopedia,* revised edition
ITC	International Theological Commentary
J	Yahwist
JAAR	*Journal of the American Academy of Religion*
JANESCU	*Journal of the Ancient Near Eastern Society of Columbia University*
JAOS	*Journal of the American Oriental Society*
JB	Jerusalem Bible
JBL	*Journal of Biblical Literature*
JEA	*Journal of Egyptian Archaeology*
JJS	*Journal of Jewish Studies*
JNSL	*Journal of Northwest Semitic Languages*
Joüon	*Grammar of Biblical Hebrew*
JSOT	*Journal for the Study of the Old Testament*
JSOTSup	Journal for the Study of the Old Testament: Supplement Series
KJV	King James (Authorized) Version
lit.	literal
LXX	Septuagint
Macc.	Maccabees
MT	Masoretic Text
NEB	New English Bible
NICOT	New International Commentary on the Old Testament
NIV	New International Version
NJPS	*Tanakh: The Holy Scriptures: The New JPS Translation according to the Traditional Hebrew Text*
NRSV	New Revised Standard Version
NT	New Testament
OBO	Orbis biblicus et orientalis
OBT	Overtures to Biblical Theology
OT	Old Testament

P. Šeb.	*Palestinian Shevi'it*
P	priestly writer
pl.	plural
RSV	Revised Standard Version
Sam. Pent.	Samaritan Pentateuch
ScrB	*Scripture Bulletin*
SJT	*Scottish Journal of Theology*
Syr.	Syriac
Tg.	Targum
T. Benj.	*Testament of Benjamin*
TDOT	*Theological Dictionary of the Old Testament*
Tg. Cant.	*Targum on Song of Solomon*
ThWAT	*Theologisches Wörterbuch zum Alten Testament*
ThZ	*Theologische Zeitschrift*
TJT	*Toronto Journal of Theology*
TOTC	Tyndale Old Testament Commentaries
trans.	translated by
TT	*Theology Today*
TynBul	*Tyndale Bulletin*
Ugar.	Ugaritic
v(v).	verse, verses
Vg.	Vulgate
vol.	volume
VT	*Vetus Testamentum*
WBC	Word Biblical Commentary
WTJ	*Westminster Theological Journal*
ZAW	*Zeitschrift für die alttestamentliche Wissenschaft*

Introduction

Title

The word Genesis comes from the Greek *genesis*, "birth, origin." The Hebrews called the book by its first word, *bere'shith*, "in the beginning." Genesis, of course, is about beginnings—specifically the beginning of the earth and the beginning of the people of God. Its purpose is to present the deep roots of Israel's lineage by recounting those key episodes in the primeval time that set the stage for God's calling Abraham to become the bearer of the promises. These promises set into motion God's program for bringing blessing to all peoples. The promises would thus overcome the curses God had placed both on the earth and on aspects of human existence because of human wickedness. The core of Genesis is found in the narratives about Israel's ancestors Abraham, Jacob, and Joseph. Many other figures, such as Sarah, Isaac, Rebekah, Leah, Rachel, and Judah also play key roles in the narratives.

Structure and Composition

The book of Genesis contains two major divisions: the first consists of primeval narrative, which provides a global setting for the ancestral narratives by presenting the major events and their consequent curses that have profoundly influenced the course of all human life (1:1–11:26), and the second consists of the ancestral narratives, in which the Abraham, Jacob, and Joseph narratives show the ways God counters the curses (11:27–50:26). In the primeval narrative Adam and Eve eat the forbidden fruit, which leads to their expulsion from the garden; human violence increases, which leads to the great flood; Ham shames Noah, which leads to the curse on Canaan; and numerous peoples plan to build a common culture at Shinar (Babylon), which leads to God's confusing their speech and scattering them. Then, in the three narratives that make up the ancestral narratives, God counters these curses. He creates a people who will worship only him and provides a way for all the nations to find blessing through this people. God calls Abraham to leave Haran and go to Canaan and backs up the call with several promises that Abraham's descendants will become a great nation. In Canaan, God promises to give Abraham's descendants that land as their heritage. These descendants move about Canaan believing that God will give this land to their children and that their children will multiply into a nation. The narrative then describes the growth of Abraham's seed into seventy persons who must go to Egypt in order to survive a terrible famine in Canaan. Genesis closes with all the descendants of Abraham's grandson Jacob living in Egypt and looking forward to their return to Canaan and possession of the land God promised to their great ancestor.

Toledoth Formula

Genesis has ten clearly marked sections, five each in the primeval and ancestral narratives. Each section is headed by a *toledoth* passage (in the first section the formula stands at 2:4a, see comments). The *toledoth*, a Hebrew noun from the root *y-l-d* "to bear," often identifies a list of descendants of a person or the lead members of a clan. The genealogy may be short (e.g., 11:27–32), or it may name several generations (e.g., 5:1–32). These lists often were the official record of a family's lineage and frequently function as an introduction to a section. Sometimes notes about births and/or deaths or anecdotes became attached to a genealogy. Given the variety in the material identified by *toledoth*, this Hebrew term is translated by several English words, as "genealogy," "generations," "account," "family history," and "ancestral narrative." Usually this formula heads a section by identifying the father of the major figure in that section.[1]

The *toledoth* formulas in Genesis establish the generations from Adam to Joseph, thereby connecting the seed of Abraham to both the primeval generations and the created order. They also locate the seed of Abraham among the nations in general and the peoples of Canaan in particular. Here are the ten formulas:

Primeval Narrative

  1. The generations of the heavens and the earth
     (1:1–4:26)
  2. The generations of Adam (5:1–6:8)

3. The ancestral narrative of Noah (6:9–9:29)
4. The generations of Noah's sons (10:1–11:9)
5. The genealogy of Shem (11:10–26)

Ancestral Narratives

6. The ancestral narrative of Terah (11:27–25:11)
7. The genealogy of Ishmael (25:12–18)
8. The ancestral narrative of Isaac (25:19–35:29)
9. The genealogy of Esau (36:1–43)
10. The ancestral narrative of Jacob (37:1–50:26)

Sometimes a *toledoth* formula heads a genealogy of names (e.g., numbers 5 and 7). Other times it provides a brief family lineage as an introduction to a narrative of that person's son (e.g., number 6). The final editor has placed each *toledoth* strategically as the heading to the following narrative.[2] These *toledoth* sections tie the book together and place all the narratives into a genealogical framework. They probably had a separate origin from the narrative material.

Like the Mesopotamians, the Israelites zealously preserved genealogies. But while Mesopotamian genealogies established the right of kings to rule, the Israelite genealogies in the primeval narrative of Genesis present the lineage of the natural descendants from Adam to Noah and from Noah to Terah for the purpose of showing the interconnection of all people from the earth's beginning. The primeval narrative gives no emphasis to status or rulership; each descendant has value by bearing the image of God. Because of God's blessing (1:28; 9:1), humans increase rapidly to form clans, tribes, and nations. The genealogies in the ancestral narratives identify the position and inheritance of the members of the seed of Abraham.

The Structures of the Four Narratives of Genesis

Structurally, the two major divisions of Genesis are divided into four narratives. The first division is made up of the primeval narrative (1:1–11:26). The second division, the ancestral narratives, is made up of the Abraham narrative (the *toledoth* sections covering the families of Terah and Ishmael; 11:27–25:18), the Jacob narrative (the *toledoth* sections covering the families of Isaac and Esau; 25:19–36:43), and the Joseph narrative (the *toledoth* section of Jacob's family; 37:1–50:26).[3] The material in each of these narratives has been artfully arranged with balance and symmetry in mind. The organizing principle for the Abraham and Jacob narratives is palistrophic (chiastic). A palistrophe is the arrangement of material in a V-shaped pattern so that material in each step moving in toward the center mirrors material on the corresponding step moving out from the center. For example:

> A The Outer Frame
> > B The Inner Frame
> > > C The Core Story
> > B' The Inner Frame
> A' The Outer Frame

The center itself may or may not be mirrored, and there may be as many steps as an author desires.

The Primeval Narrative. The prominent themes in the primeval narrative are human transgression/divine punishment and God's mercy. The primeval narrative has eleven units; the first six are organized in a palistrophe and the remaining six (the middle unit, A*, is shared) are set in two parallel panels of three units each.[4]

Thus the pattern of the primeval narrative is as follows:

> A Creation (1:1–2:4a)
> > B The making of the garden of Eden, human disobedience, and God's judgment (2:4b–3:24)
> > > C_1 The genealogy of Cain, fratricide, contributions to culture, and Lamech's boasting of multiple murders (4:1–24)
> > > C_2 The genealogy of Seth (ten generations) and the worship of Yahweh (4:25–5:32)
> > B' The increase of wickedness (6:1–8)
> A* The flood (uncreation; 6:9–8:22)
> > B_1* God's covenant of the rainbow (9:1–17)
> > > C_1' Noah's genealogy, his contribution to culture, and Ham's transgression (9:18–29)
> A_1' The Table of Nations (re-creation; 10:1–32)
> > B_2 Human rebellion in building the Tower of Babel (11:1–9)
> > > C_2' The genealogy of Shem (ten generations; 11:10–26)

In discussing the organizational pattern of each of the four narratives in Genesis, accounts with similar themes standing in parallel position are marked by ' (for example A, A'), accounts with contrasting themes standing in parallel position, being antithetical, are marked by * (such as in A, A*), and accounts standing in parallel position that treat different topics while sharing a theme or issue in common are noted by a numerical subscript (as in C_1, C_2, C_3).

In this discussion we shall call the palistrophic pattern (1:1–8:22) the first segment and the parallel sequence (6:9–11:26) the second segment. Materials in the second segment modulate themes in the first segment. The fulcrum between the two segments is the account of the flood (A*), since it belongs to both patterns. The whole is united by the movement from creation (A) to chaos or uncreation (A*) to re-creation (A'). Although the earth God creates is very good (A), human society becomes so violent that God has to judge the inhabited earth with a cataclysmic flood (A*), returning the earth to a state of chaos similar to its existence at the beginning (1:2). After the flood the restored earth is repopulated, as attested in the Table of Nations (A'; ch. 10).

In the B position of the first segment are accounts of human rebellion: human disobedience in the garden of Eden (B) and the intolerable increase of wickedness on earth (B'). In the B position of the second segment are God's covenant of peace symbolized by the rainbow (B_1*) and the account of the Tower of Babel (B_2), which expands the theme of human rebellion found in all B positions. In B two people disobey God; in B_2 an entire city-state opposes God's desire. Rather than dispersing, they gather in Shinar and undertake a massive building project to promote their own fame. Their actions bring God's judgment, just as the rapid increase of violence in society in B' move God to bring about the flood. While the account of God's covenant of peace (B_1*) does not recount any deed of human wickedness, it highlights God's covenant relationship with humans and thus expands on the (implied) covenantal relationship between God and humans, which was initiated in the garden of Eden (B). Furthermore, the report of God's covenant of peace (B_1*) is antithetical to the report of the increase in human wickedness (B'); nevertheless, these two accounts share a concern for all humanity. This antithesis, heightened by also being in a B position, lets the picture of God's grace stand out against the dark background of human wickedness.

Genealogies stand at the center of both segments, all in C position: Cain's (C_1) and Seth's (C_2) are in the first segment; Noah's (C_1') and Shem's (C_2') are in the second segment. Cain's and Noah's genealogies contain reports of wicked deeds and cultural achievements. The cultural contributions of Cain's offspring foster the development of civilization; the contribution of Noah's offspring brings humans refreshment and relaxation, corresponding to the meaning of his name, "rest." The second genealogy in both segments has ten generations: from Seth to Noah (C_2) and from Noah to Terah (C_2'). Thus Genesis presents epochs of ten generations on each side of the flood.

There are six accounts of humans disobeying God, and all except the third are followed by the consequential judgment. In B the first human pair eats the fruit that God has forbidden, and God expels them from the garden after pronouncing a curse against an aspect of their being (3:1–24). In C_1 Cain commits fratricide, and God curses him (4:8–12). Lamech boasts of his willingness to kill wantonly (4:23–24). Society becomes characterized by increasing violence, and God brings a great flood to wipe out this wickedness (6:1–7:24). In C_1' Ham acts shamefully toward his father, and Noah curses Canaan (9:20–27). In B_2 humans brazenly go against God's design by assembling in Shinar and setting out to build a city and a tower to promote their own fame, and God confuses their language so that they will disperse throughout the earth (11:1–9).

By contrast, God in four acts of mercy takes steps to make life more tolerable for humans under divine curse. In Eden God gives Adam and Eve garments made from skins to provide them protection against the harsher environment outside the garden (B; 3:21). God puts a mark on Cain's forehead to prevent an avenger from killing him (C_1; 4:15). God gives Noah plans to build an ark in order to deliver his house and representatives of all the animals from the flood (A^*; 6:13–21). God puts the rainbow in the sky as a sign that there will never be another cataclysmic flood (B_1^*; 9:8–17). These acts of mercy assure us that God cares for the well-being of humans despite their proneness to do wrong.

The Abraham Narrative (Gen. 11:27–25:18). Against the universal background of the primeval narrative (1:1–11:26) stand the patriarchal narratives. The first of these begins with God's calling Abraham to leave his father's household and go to the land that God will show him. God bolsters this call with several promises to work through Abraham's seed to establish his kingdom on earth. Through Abraham's seed God unleashes a blessing that is the antidote to those curses God pronounced as judgments on human rebellion (chs. 1–11). Through this great nation all the families of the earth (listed in the Table of Nations, ch. 10) may find blessing. In promising to give Abraham a great name *(shem)*, God is providing an honorable path to a lasting reputation *(shem)*. Lasting fame, therefore, comes from walking with God in faith, rather than from building earthly monuments that are subject to decay and destruction. Abraham's fame continues to this day: Jews, Arabs, and Christians all celebrate him as their father.

The Abraham narrative is organized as a palistrophe:

A The family history of Terah (11:27–32)
   B Abram obeys God by moving to Canaan (12:1–9)
      C_1 Sarai in Pharaoh's harem (12:10–20)
      C_2 Abram's success and Lot's separation from Abram (13:1–18)
         D Abram rescues Lot (14:1–24)
            E_1 God makes a covenant with Abram (15:1–21)
            E_2 God informs Hagar of the birth of Ishmael (16:1–16)
            E_1' God renews the covenant with Abraham (17:1–27)
            E_2' God informs Sarah of the birth of Isaac (18:1–15)
         D' Abraham intercedes for Sodom and Lot's deliverance (18:16–19:38)
      C_1' Sarah in Abimelech's palace (20:1–18)
      C_2' Ishmael and Hagar expelled from Abraham's household and Abraham's success, leading to a covenant with Abimelech (21:1–34)
   B' Abraham obeys God by binding Isaac (22:1–19)
A' Genealogy of Nahor (22:20–24)

Following this palistrophic pattern, five entries bring the Abraham narrative to a close:

a The burial of Sarah in the Cave of Machpelah (23:1–20)
b Finding a bride for Isaac (24:1–67)
c Abraham's children by Keturah (25:1–6)
d The death and burial of Abraham (25:7–11)
e Ishmael's children (25:12–18)

The core narratives about Abraham are framed by the genealogies of his relatives in Haran—Terah (A) and Nahor (A'). At the center is God's covenant with Abraham, inaugurated (E_1) and renewed (E_1'). The key verse positioned just before God enters into covenant with Abraham (E_1) defines Abraham's relationship with God: Abraham believes Yahweh, and Yahweh credits it to him as righteousness (15:6). Closely linked to both covenantal ceremonies are the announcements of the births of Abraham's sons: Ishmael (E_2) and Isaac (E_2').

In the B positions stand two amazing examples of Abraham's complete obedience to God. At God's command Abraham leaves his father's household at Haran and travels to Canaan (B). Near the end of his life he follows God's instructions by binding Isaac and laying him on an altar as proof of his unconditional obedience to God (B').

After Abraham arrives in Canaan, he faces several trials. The accounts of these trials stand in positions C and D. Twice Abraham faces the threat of losing Sarah to a foreign king: to Pharaoh in Egypt (C_1) and to Abimelech in Gerar (C_1'). Twice Abraham's success is acclaimed. After he returns to Canaan from Egypt, there is a description of his wealth and his peaceful movement through the land (C_2). On the other side, there is the account of Abimelech's making a covenant with Abraham because of Abraham's success (C_2'). Twice Abraham suffers the sorrow of separation as the means to overcome intense conflict in his household. In order to end the quarreling between his shepherds and Lot's due to the increasing size of their flocks, he and Lot separate (C_2). After the birth of Isaac, Sarah, impelled by jealousy of Hagar and Ishmael as well as by her desire to protect Isaac, demands that Abraham expel Hagar and Ishmael from the household (C_2'). After Lot settles in Sodom, Abraham has to rescue him from harm on two occasions. The first time he undertakes a military excursion to free Lot, who has been taken captive by the kings of the East (D). The second time, on the basis of Abraham's righteousness, divine messengers deliver Lot from the conflagration of the cities of the plain (D'). Lot is last seen living in a cave as a recluse with his daughters. Thus Lot serves as a foil that emphasizes Abraham's obedient faith all the more.

Two dimensions of the picture of Abraham deserve mention. First, Abraham is portrayed as a sheik or a chief (king). In the second millennium B.C. there were many kings in Canaan, ruling over city-states. While Abraham does not have a city-state, he is portrayed as being on a par with these kings. He has access to and visits the courts of Pharaoh, king of Egypt, and Abimelech, king of

Gerar. The settlement Abraham received from the latter places him on the same level as this king. When Abraham goes to the elders of Hebron to buy a plot of land, they receive him with the deference accorded a chief (ch. 23). Abraham's ability to muster a military force (14:14–16) shows that he is in the same league with other princes in Canaan. Thus Abraham is numbered among the leaders or kings of Canaan.

Second, Abraham is portrayed as a prophet. God explicitly identifies Abraham as a prophet to Abimelech (20:7). Abraham exercises that role by praying for Abimelech's household (20:17) and by interceding for Sodom (18:16–33). Psalm 105:12–15 describes the patriarchs as prophets. Also, Abraham is characterized as a prophet in receiving the word of Yahweh. The formula "the word of Yahweh came to . . . " (*hayah debar-yhwh 'el*) in 15:1 (see v. 4) is used by many prophets to give their words authority (e.g., Jer. 1:4, 11, 14; 2:1; Ezek. 1:3; 3:16; 6:1; 11:14). Not long after the word of the Lord comes to Abraham, God causes a deep sleep to fall on him and in that sleep reveals to him the destiny of his people (15:13–16). Even Abraham's response to God's orders in leaving Haran is similar to a prophet's call: after leaving home, he follows God wherever he leads (one may consider the calls of Amos [Amos 7:14–15] and Elisha [1 Kgs. 19:19–21]).

The Jacob Narrative (Gen. 25:19–36:43). The palistrophic pattern in the Jacob narrative is as follows:

    A Births of Jacob and Esau (25:19–34)
        B Interlude: Isaac's conflicts with the people of the Negev (26:1–35)
          C Jacob steals Esau's blessing (27:1–28:9)
            D Jacob's heavenly vision at Bethel (28:10–22)
              E Jacob joins Laban's house in marriage (29:1–30)
                F The increase of Jacob's family (29:31–30:24)
                F' The increase of Jacob's flocks (30:25–43)
              E' Jacob departs from Laban's house with family and flocks (31:1–55)
            D' Jacob wrestles with a heavenly "man" at Peniel (32:1–32)
          C' Jacob's reconciliation with Esau (33:1–16)
        B' Interlude: Jacob's conflict with the people of Shechem (33:17–34:31)
    A' Birth of Joseph and Jacob's return to Bethel (35:1–22a)

There follow three supplemental pieces:

    a List of Jacob's sons (35:22b–26)
    b Burial of Isaac (35:27–29)
    c Genealogy of Esau (36:1–43)

Within its overall palistrophic pattern, the Jacob narrative consists of three cycles: Jacob's years at home (25:19–28:9), Jacob's stay in Haran with his uncle Laban (29:1–32:2), and Jacob's settling in Canaan (33:1–35:29). Accounts of Jacob's encounter with God serve as transitions between the cycles (28:10–22 and 32:22–32). In the first two cycles, Jacob's journey is marked by persistent scheming to advance himself. In the third cycle, with a new name (Israel), Jacob places his trust in God instead of deceitful schemes.

Two birth reports frame the Jacob narrative. At the opening Rebekah gives birth to twins, Esau and Jacob (A), and at the close Rachel dies giving birth to Benjamin (A'). Two interludes, in B position, interrupt this narrative and add an element of suspense to its dramatic movement. The first interlude presents vignettes about Isaac's conflicts over wells in the Negev (B). The second recounts the conflict between the people of Shechem and Jacob's children, leading to the pillage of Shechem (B'). Both interludes treat the theme of relations between the promised seed and the local population. In both accounts a Gentile seeks to take a daughter of the elect line as a wife, and the children of Abraham negotiate alliances with the local inhabitants: Isaac with Abimelech of Gerar (B), and Jacob's clan with the citizens of Shechem (B').

Jacob's dealings with Esau stand in C position. In his early manhood he steals his father's blessing from Esau (C). Twenty years later he is reconciled with his brother in the Transjordan (C'). Jacob is full of fear of his brother Esau during his two encounters with God. On the first occasion he flees from home because Esau has sworn to kill him, and he has a dream at Bethel, in which God promises to protect him (D). On his second encounter with God, Jacob is exceedingly apprehensive about the impending meeting with Esau before reentering Canaan. When he is at Peniel Jacob wrestles with "a man," possibly the angel of the Lord, throughout the night (D'). Jacob perseveres in that struggle until God blesses him with a new name, Israel. Jacob's encounters with God (D, D') frame his sojourn in Laban's household (E, F, E', F₁'), and his success in gaining numerous children and a large flock stands at the center (F and F') of the narrative. Despite the efforts of Laban to outwit his son-in-law, Jacob prospers because of God's blessing.

The opening vignette in which Rebekah gives birth to twins sets the tone for the Jacob narrative. The two fetuses struggle so fiercely in her womb that she almost despairs of life. When she gives birth Jacob grabs his brother's heel, trying to prevent him from being the firstborn, but Esau prevails. As a result, his parents give Jacob a name that means, "heel grabber, finagler." As his name indicates, he tends to use deceit to advance his cause. At Peniel, Jacob is transformed from a deceiver to Israel, that is, "one who wrestled with God and prevailed."

Jacob's reconciliation with Esau is symbolic of the change in his character. After Peniel, Jacob faces many setbacks without resorting to deception to advance his own purpose. Rather, he displays patience and forbearance in the face of four tragic situations. (a) Simeon and Levi pillage the city of Shechem, employing such a dishonorable ruse that Jacob is disgraced before the local tribes. (b) Reuben shames Jacob by lying with Bilhah, his concubine. (c) His sons cruelly deceive him by making him believe that his favorite son Joseph has been killed. He mourns the loss of Joseph for years, unaware that his beloved son is really alive. (d) Jacob grieves over Simeon's imprisonment in Egypt when his sons have told the Egyptian overseer too much. Thus Jacob, who inflicted pain by deception in the prime of his life, in his later years suffers great sorrow as the victim of many harsh deceptions. Nevertheless, he earnestly desires to see God's promises to Abraham fulfilled in his children.

Fragments of the last section of the Jacob narrative have been woven into the end of the Joseph narrative. It is clear that this material comes from the Jacob narrative because it contains the sort of dramatic, direct encounters with God that characterize Jacob's meetings with God (46:1–4). These sorts of encounters are not typical of Joseph, who is guided by God's providential control over events in his life.

The Joseph Narrative (Gen. 37:1–50:26). The Joseph narrative differs from the other sections in that it is a coherent story with a well-developed, suspenseful plot, whereas the other major narratives consist of self-standing accounts loosely strung together by a dominant theme; the latter lack a tightly developed plot. The author of the Joseph narrative has artfully constructed the scenes so that they revolve around the conflict between Joseph and his brothers and build the suspense. The powerful climax is Joseph's revelation of his identity to his brothers. In addition to being the story of Joseph, this last segment of Genesis is also the continuation of the story of Israel's patriarchs.

In this narrative the primary social setting shifts from that of wandering shepherds in the Canaanite hills to the complex urban environment of Egypt's capital. The importance of possessing wisdom also comes to the fore. Wisdom equips Joseph with various skills such as interpreting dreams, providing insightful advice, developing a program to address a national crisis, skillfully administering a high governmental office, and working shrewdly to achieve reconciliation with the estranged members of his own family.

A palistrophic pattern of two levels frames the Joseph narrative.

A Jacob's favoritism of Joseph and his brothers' increasing hatred (37:1–36)
  B Interlude: Judah settles in Adullam (38:1–30)
    C Joseph's rise and fall in Potiphar's house and imprisonment (39:1–20a)
      D Joseph's anguish in prison (39:20b–40:23)
        E Joseph's interpretation of Pharaoh's dreams, saving Egypt (41:1–57)
    C' Joseph's brothers purchase grain in Egypt and Simeon is in bondage (42:1–38)
      D' Joseph's brothers' anguish while buying grain in Egypt (43:1–45:28)
        E' Jacob and his family migrate to Egypt, saving the family (46:1–47:12)
  B' Interlude: Joseph's skill in administrating for Egypt (47:13–31)
A' Jacob blesses Joseph's sons, Ephraim and Manasseh (48:1–22)

In the outer frame in A position are accounts of Jacob's favoring Joseph. When Joseph is a young man, Jacob gives him an elegant cloak (A). Then at the end of his life Jacob makes Joseph his principal heir by elevating Ephraim and Manasseh to the level of his own children (A'). Between this outside frame and the core drama are two interludes (B). The first is a story of Judah's settling in Adullam (B).[5] The second is a description of Joseph's administration of the famine (B'). Each of these interludes pictures one of the chosen seed living among Gentiles.

While a palistrophic pattern frames the core of the Joseph narrative, the central drama (39:1–47:12) consists of two acts, each having three scenes.[6] In each act the main characters have their hopes shattered, go through a time of agonizing distress, and then experience a dramatic reversal of fortunes under God's guidance. In the first act (C, D, E) Joseph rises in Potiphar's house to chief administrator. He is undermined by Potiphar's wife, who falsely accuses him of attempted rape. This leads to his imprisonment (C). There he spends several months in discouragement (D). God directs a course of events that leads to Joseph being summoned to appear before Pharaoh. He skillfully interprets Pharaoh's dreams, and, taking advantage of the moment, he astutely advises Pharaoh on a strategy that will enable Egypt to survive the coming hard famine (E). In a dramatic move Pharaoh invests Joseph with full authority over his house. From that high post Joseph is able to save Egypt from the devastation of the seven-year famine. In the second act (C', D', E') Joseph's brothers go through several experiences that parallel Joseph's journey at significant points. After several good years in Canaan, the terrible famine forces them to go to Egypt to buy grain. There the head of agriculture harasses them, falsely accusing them of spying. In order for them to take grain back to their families in Canaan they must leave Simeon behind in prison (C'). In the ensuing months there are several heated discussions in Jacob's household about returning to Egypt for more grain. At last Jacob relents, and the brothers leave for Egypt with Benjamin. On this journey they are very apprehensive about the safety of their youngest brother. After they arrive in Egypt, Joseph puts them through a series of perplexing, agonizing incidents (D'). Then, in one of the most dramatic moments in Scripture, Joseph makes known his identity to his brothers. Afterward he has all of his father's house resettle in Egypt in order that he might save them from the hard famine (E').

God no longer appears in epiphanies in the Joseph narrative, nor does the angel of Yahweh meet and converse with humans. Rather, God, the distant sovereign and Lord of all nations, directs affairs and situations on earth from the heavenly realm for both Abraham's seed and the Egyptians. When God communicates more directly, it is in dreams.

Dreams are a unifying motif in the Joseph narrative. At the outset Joseph has two dreams, which he describes to his family. These dreams foreshadow Joseph's rise to power, and they also fuel his brothers' hatred toward him. In prison Joseph interprets the dreams of two high officials from Pharaoh's court. This incident leads to Joseph being summoned to explain to Pharaoh the meaning of his dreams. Joseph's boyhood dreams are fulfilled when Pharaoh appoints him as head of agriculture.

Another motif found throughout the Joseph story is that of clothes; in this story they carry great symbolic force. The robe Jacob gives Joseph expresses his deep love for him and possibly expresses his anticipation that he will be head of the family (37:3). But this outer garment becomes the focus of his brothers' jealousy, and after they sell Joseph it is their means of persuading Jacob, without words, that Joseph has been accidentally killed (37:33). Jacob mourns this loss by tearing his clothes (37:34). In Potiphar's house, when Joseph flees seduction by Potiphar's wife, she catches and keeps his tunic (39:12). She then uses it as evidence of his attempted sexual assault and has Joseph thrown into prison (39:13, 15, 16, 18). When Joseph is taken from the prison to appear before Pharaoh, he is first given a change of clothes (41:14). After elevating Joseph to high office, Pharaoh gives him fine linen garments (41:42). Later, when Joseph introduces himself to his brothers, he gives Benjamin five festival garments to express his joy at being reunited with his full brother (45:22). Thus garments symbolize love, social status, bonding, and authority in the Joseph narrative—as well as betrayal.

Yet another recurring motif is that of going down to Egypt. Joseph is taken to Egypt (A), the brothers go down to Egypt to buy grain twice (C' and D'), and Jacob goes down to Egypt with his entire clan (E').

Accounts of the deaths and burials of Jacob and Joseph bring the ancestral age to an end:

> a Jacob's last testament (49:1–28)
> > b Jacob's elaborate funeral (49:29–50:14)
> a' Full reconciliation of Joseph and his brothers (50:15–21)
> > b' Joseph's death and burial (50:22–26)

These four units stand in an alternating a:b pattern. In position a are Jacob's last testament concerning all twelve of his sons and the account of Joseph's reconciliation with all of his brothers. These two units are about all of Jacob's twelve sons, looking forward to their developing into a tribal league. In position b are the accounts of Jacob's elaborate funeral and Joseph's death. Thus Genesis ends in anticipation of the way that God will fulfill the promises to Abraham by giving the birth to the nation Israel.

This supplementary material plays an important role by explaining how the seed of Abraham ended up in Egypt and by giving the Israelites who lived for centuries as slaves in Egypt hope of their eventual deliverance from this bondage: Jacob's last testament looks to the settlement of the tribes in Canaan; Jacob is buried in Canaan, not Egypt, signaling that the destiny of his seed is to be realized in Canaan; and Joseph gives the clan a symbol that they will return to the promised land by having them swear that they will carry his bones out of Egypt when they leave. Genesis thus concludes with all of Jacob's sons living together in harmony in Egypt.

The Joseph story serves many additional functions. It vividly illustrates the troubles caused by tribal jealousies and proves that a strong leader, one who believes that God orchestrates all events toward fulfilling his promises to Abraham, can overcome such jealousy. Therefore, the twelve tribes must work together to survive the hardships of nature and the political power of the nations. The narrative also teaches that God can influence the mightiest empires like Egypt to support the continuance of Abraham's seed. That is, God directs events so that Gentile nations play a beneficial role in Israel's destiny.

These final chapters of Genesis, furthermore, lay the foundation for the leadership role that the tribe of Judah will play in Israel. Of Jacob's sons Judah is highlighted in the account of his pitching a tent among the Canaanites in the low hills south of Bethlehem (ch. 38), the very area that his descendants will come to inherit. In the crises caused by the terrible famine, Judah emerges as the leader in guiding Jacob's clan. Then Jacob, in his last testament, depicts Judah as a prosperous, strong, victorious, enduring leader who is praised and revered by his brothers (49:8–12). Chapter 38 tells the extraordinary circumstances that led to the birth of the twins, Perez and Zerah, to Judah by Tamar. This is significant in that David was the tenth generation from Judah through Perez (Ruth 4:18–22). Thus, these chapters show that God will fulfill the promises made to Abraham through the tribe of Judah (Gen. 12:1–3).

Composition of the Book

Having reviewed the structure of Genesis, we next consider the way these accounts were assembled to make the book of Genesis. In addressing this topic we enter the arena of speculation.

The distinctive literary features of the various accounts suggest that most of them rose independently,[7] while the structure of the narratives about each patriarch attests that an editorial hand has skillfully compiled them. The composition of a gospel may serve as a pattern for understanding the formation of Genesis. An author collected the narratives and teachings of Jesus, drawing on both written and oral sources, and then organized them into a gospel (see Luke 1:1–4). It is possible that in a similar way, one or more editors collected the traditions about Abraham and Jacob and organized them into two narratives, according to a palistrophic pattern. This pattern was chosen for its artistry, because it makes it easier to memorize the material, and for the additional insights it provides into the spiritual meaning of these stories. Then that editor or another one likely collected and arranged the primeval accounts as a prologue to the ancestral accounts. Finally, an editor worked the Joseph narrative into the Jacob narrative and the account of Judah in the Shephelah (ch. 38).

Who were these editors? Since the text of Genesis does not address this issue, we have to use our imagination. The first candidate is Moses, for he had the training, the interest, and the time—during the years the Israelites were camped near Kadesh Barnea—to do the work. Assuming that the ancestral stories, at least in oral form, go back to the time of the patriarchs, recounting them would have played a major role in giving identity and hope to the Israelites in Egyptian bondage. Moses and the Israelites knew these stories as we can see when God reveals himself to Moses as the God of Abraham, Isaac, and Jacob (Exod. 3:6) and when God directs Moses to identify him in this way to the Israelites (Exod. 3:16). This divine self-identification would have no meaning if the Israelites did not know these ancestral accounts. Moses' imprint may be seen in the Abraham narratives. Abraham's first journey through Canaan, including a trip to Egypt because of famine, parallels Israel's coming to Egypt, its bondage, and its release. Moreover, the frequency of the occurrence of the name Yahweh throughout the Abrahamic narrative could have come from Moses. As the person who received that name in its fullness (Exod. 3:13–15), Moses would have been intent on demonstrating that the God Yahweh, who spoke to him at Sinai, was the same God as El Shaddai, who had called and led Abraham.

After Moses, the editorial work may have continued until the finalization of the Pentateuch. Some work may have been done during the time of the judges, as suggested by the materials in Genesis that foreshadow that time. For example, the sayings about the majority of the tribes in Jacob's testament (ch. 49) correspond with the time of the settlement. Other material in Genesis points to editorial activity during the days of the united monarchy. Editors during the rise of the Davidic dynasty would have been particularly interested in the accounts of Judah's settling in the Shephelah of Judah and of his having children by Canaanite women (ch. 38). The description of Judah's prowess as a warrior and his long-lasting rule over his brothers in Jacob's testament also coincides with David's ascendancy as ruler (49:8–12). Furthermore, the emphasis on the prosperity and success of Joseph and his sons at the end of Genesis (48; 49:22–26) accords with the prominence of the Joseph tribes in northern Israel during the rise of the monarchy. Also the joint prominence given to the Joseph tribes and to Judah in the Joseph story accords well with David's incorporating northern Israel with Judah to form a united monarchy that continued under Solomon. Consequently, the narrative of Joseph may have been edited by the wisdom school at the time of Solomon, for under Solomon there was great interest in international wisdom and diplomacy—indeed, one of his wives was an Egyptian princess. The inclusion of the Joseph narrative finalized the formation of Genesis. It is important to remember that the editors who developed Genesis did not invent these accounts of the patriarchs. Their task was to collect, arrange, and order them into the book known as Genesis, and the result is a masterful document of origins that orients the people of God to God's design in creating the earth and in forming one nation to be his own people.

The Religion of the Patriarchs

The religion of the patriarchs and their understanding of God is reflected in their names for God, their prayer, the sorts of altars, sacrifices, and vows they made, and their covenant relationship with God. These can also be seen in the relationship each patriarch had with God. The variety in these relationships provides various models of faith for those who walk with God.

The God of the Fathers

The names patriarchs used for God are a chief source of our understanding of their relationship to God. These names demonstrate that they had a close relationship with God.

The patriarchs frequently identified God as "the God of one's father." Often one of the fathers is named. Only those living after Abraham speak of God in this way; Joshua 24:2-3 tells us that before Abraham left Haran to follow God, he and his family were polytheists. In conversation between family members the title "the God of one's father" usually occurs without a personal name. Jacob spoke of God in this way to his wives (31:5), and so did Jacob's sons in a letter to Joseph (50:17). Addressing Jacob, Laban said that during the night he had received a word from the God of "your" father (31:29; see 43:23). In Jacob's last testament, "your father's God" occurs among a list of divine titles: the Mighty One of Jacob, Shepherd, the Rock of Israel, and Shaddai (49:24-25).

In other references to the God of one's father, one or more of the fathers is named. This fuller form appears for the first time in God's self-identification to Isaac as the God of his father Abraham (26:24). God again used this title when he met Jacob at Beersheba (46:3). In Jacob's dream at Bethel, however, God used a fuller title, "I am Yahweh, the God of your father Abraham and the God of Isaac" (28:13). Later, in his earnest prayer for help because of his impending meeting with Esau, Jacob addressed God with this title, though without the name Yahweh (32:9). On another occasion Jacob made sacrifices to "the God of his father Isaac" (46:1). When Jacob entered into a border covenant with Laban, he identified God as the God of his father Abraham and the Fear of Isaac (31:42). Laban, however, spoke of God as "the God of Abraham and the God of Nahor, the God of their father" (31:53).

The title "God of the father(s)" meant that God was the personal protector deity of the clan. God was thus attached to the clan, not to a specific shrine, and could then accompany the clan in its migrations. The ancestors praised this God for guiding them and for protecting them (31:42; 32:10; 35:3). In Genesis this title for God was also tied to the surety of the promises God gave to Abraham.

El Shaddai

The primary name for God among the ancestors was El Shaddai, that is, God Almighty or God All Sufficient (17:1). In Genesis, El generally occurs with Shaddai, but Shaddai often occurs alone as in 49:25; in places such as Numbers 24:4, 16; and frequently in Job (e.g., 5:17; 6:4, 14).[8] These data suggest that Shaddai became a name for God. Besides Yahweh, it is the most common name for God in the ancestral narratives. It occurs always in speech and never in the narrative frame, which tells us that it belongs to the story's oldest oral stage. Otherwise a late editor would have changed the divine name to one commonly used after Israel became a people. God identified himself by this name both to Abraham (17:1) and to Jacob (35:11, confirmed in 48:3). On two occasions a patriarch used this name in a prayer for the safe return of children about to go on a journey to a foreign land: Isaac enjoined El Shaddai to bless Jacob his son (28:3); and Jacob prayed that El Shaddai might bring both Simeon and Benjamin back to him from Egypt (43:14). Shaddai then had the ability to protect the children of promise in a foreign land. This name also occurs in the list of names at the end of Jacob's testament, being parallel to "your father's God" (49:25).

Other Divine Names in Genesis

The other ancient name for God is El. In Genesis various epithets are joined to El: El Elyon ("God Most High"; 14:18–22), El Roi ("God Who Sees [Me]"; 16:13), El Olam ("the Eternal God" or "God of Ancient Days"; 21:33), and El Bethel ("the God, Bethel"; 35:7). In fact, El does not stand without an epithet or a defining clause in Genesis.[9] Jacob named the altar he erected on the land he bought near Shechem El Elohe Israel, that is, El, who is the God of Israel (33:20). Jacob was identifying El as his own God, the God of Israel.[10] This name thus identifies El as the God of the fathers, making the patron of the clan the highest God.[11]

The Name Yahweh

An important and controversial question is whether or not the patriarchs knew God by the name Yahweh. The key verse in this debate is Exodus 6:3: "I appeared to Abraham, to Isaac and to Jacob as El Shaddai, but by my name Yahweh I did not make myself known to them." Taking this verse literally, many scholars hold that the name Yahweh was introduced to Moses at Sinai. Supporting this position is the remarkable fact that none of the personal names in Genesis include the divine element Yahweh. Furthermore, no god with this name appears in any of the pantheons of the Levant (i.e., those countries bordering the eastern Mediterranean).[12] Other scholars have argued, however, that the idea of knowing in this verse refers not to factual knowledge but rather to the experience of God in the full significance of that name. From the context of Exodus 6:3–9, it is evident that a definitive element in Yahweh's self-identification is that he is the God who keeps covenant. Since none of the patriarchs ever gained title to the land God promised, they never fully experienced Yahweh as the covenant-keeping God. The coming generations would realize the fulfillment of that promise and thus truly know Yahweh, the one who keeps covenant. Based on the evidence available, the possibility that the patriarchs were acquainted with this name is slight. If they did know it, it was not prominent for them.

Why, then, does the name Yahweh occur so frequently in the ancestral narratives? Its presence may be attributed to the effort of the editor(s) to demonstrate conclusively that the God of the fathers was truly Yahweh, who had revealed himself at Sinai. Since most English versions translate Yahweh as LORD, I have used Yahweh in the commentary in order that readers might have a greater sense of the occurrences of this divine name in Genesis.

Devotion to God

The ancestors showed their devotion to God in many ways, perhaps most notably by addressing God directly in prayer. Abraham, for instance, did not hesitate to put a bold complaint to God. When God appeared to him in a vision and spoke words of encouragement, Abraham took the occasion to express his keen disappointment that he still did not have a son (15:1–3). To lift the curse of infertility brought upon King Abimelech's house when Sarah was taken into his harem, Abraham prayed for the king and his realm (20:7, 17–18). When he learned what God intended to do to Sodom and Gomorrah, Abraham earnestly entreated God on behalf of Sodom, asking that it be spared from destruction (18:16–33). God listened patiently to Abraham's repeated petitions, showing that he was open to the pleas of his servant, even though he did not always grant all requests.

Other personages in Genesis also prayed for help and direction in dealing with difficult situations. Abraham's trusted servant displayed great devotion in his search to find a wife for Isaac. During his journey he asked God for specific guidance (24:12–14), and God answered his prayer. He praised God in response, informing others how God had led him (24:26–27, 42–44, 48–49, 52).

When Rebekah, Isaac's wife, continued to be barren after many years of marriage, Isaac petitioned God that she might conceive. God answered his prayer and Rebekah became pregnant (25:21). During her pregnancy Rebekah became so distressed by the continual jostling of the babies in her womb that she took a trip to a shrine to get an explanation from God. There God gave her a specific word about the destiny of the children in her womb.

Leah also prayed for God to give her children and the love of her husband. Her prayers are visible in the reasons she gave for the names of her children—for example, Reuben, because God "has seen my misery" (29:32), and Simeon, because God "heard that I am not loved he gave me this one too" (29:33). The statement that God heard Leah and she became pregnant (30:17) supports this interpretation.

Rachel and Jacob provide additional examples of people praying for help. Rachel prayed for children, and the text says that God heard her and opened her womb (30:22) and she became pregnant with Joseph. Jacob, filled with fear at his impending meeting with Esau, prayed the longest prayer in Genesis (32:9–12).

Another way that the patriarchs expressed their devotion to God was by building altars or erecting pillars. As Abraham traveled through the land he built several altars, bearing witness to his confidence that the promised land would be given to his seed (12:7–8; 13:18). The account of his first journey through Canaan emphasizes the building of these altars (12:7–8, 13:4). Rather than seeking out an established shrine in the vicinity, he established his own place of worship when he built an altar between Bethel and Ai. The manner of identifying this place in the narrative makes it clear that Abraham stayed on the outskirts of local settlements. All that we know of what he did at these altars is that he called on the name of Yahweh at the altar he built near Bethel (12:8; 13:4). Isaac also called on the name of Yahweh at the altar he built at Beersheba (26:25). "Calling" includes praying to God, but it may mean more, possibly offering up one or more animals in sacrifice.

Jacob erected pillars to mark places where he met God. After his dream of the stairway rising to heaven he set up a pillar at Bethel and anointed it (28:18). When he returned to Bethel, God appeared to him; again he set up and anointed a pillar (35:14). Jacob erected or built an altar near Shechem (33:20) and then at Bethel, where he wanted to worship the God who had appeared to him on his flight from Canaan and who had led him safely back to the promised land (35:6–7).

In spite of the fact that there are only a few references to a patriarch making a sacrifice, it may be assumed that the patriarchs regularly offered sacrifices on the altars they set up. In one sacrifice specifically described, God directs Abraham to sacrifice several animals—a heifer, a goat, a ram, a dove, and a young pigeon—for sealing the covenant between them (15:9). Another sacrifice is made on Mount Moriah, when God provides Abraham a ram to offer up as a whole burnt offering in place of his beloved son Isaac (22:13–14). The reference to Jacob stopping at Beersheba on his way to Egypt and making sacrifices (46:1–4) supports the possibility that many more sacrifices occurred than are specifically mentioned. A sacrifice was normally a part of a covenant ceremony, and in the hill country Jacob made a sacrifice for his clan after swearing to the pact between himself and Laban (31:54).

Since the narrator does not tie any of these acts of worship to a specific time, there is no evidence that the patriarchs followed a cultic calendar. There is no emphasis on their keeping the Sabbath or seeking out a priest for making a sacrifice. They displayed their devotion to God either spontaneously or in response to directions from God. Furthermore, there are no references to the patriarchs making pilgrimages. Only Jacob's journey to Bethel in order to worship the God who had appeared to him there years earlier (35:1–7) approximates the idea of a pilgrimage. However, there is no mention of anyone else making a journey to this sanctuary at a particular time.

The patriarchs also made vows and paid tithes. Abraham paid a tithe of the spoil taken from his defeat of the kings of the East to Melchizedek (the priest-king of Salem; 14:20). After receiving a dream at Bethel, Jacob made an elaborate vow that included a commitment to pay a tithe to God on his return to Canaan (28:20–22). Either intuition or tradition taught these men that they needed to honor God's lordship over their possessions by giving a tenth to God.

Covenant Relationship

After Abraham had acted on God's orders by leaving Haran and traveling through Canaan, God came to him and formalized their relationship with a covenant (15:7–21). While Abraham was in a deep sleep, God, symbolized by a smoking fire pot and a blazing torch, passed between the halves of the sacrificed animals (15:17). God was thus making a unilateral covenant with Abraham's seed and committing himself never to break it. This covenant ceremony emphasizes that Abraham's seed will receive the promised land (15:13–16, 18–21). Later God renewed the covenant (ch. 17). On this occasion God stipulated that everyone who identified with Abraham, including servants, had to be circumcised as a sign of the covenant (17:9–14) and that every male of the promised seed was to be circumcised on the eighth day.

These ancestral accounts, therefore, played a vital role in the orientation of Israel as the people of God by recounting their roots and providing the program for their existence in the promises God made to Abraham. As R. Moberly says, "Israel as a nation in its land cannot understand itself simply on its own terms but must relate itself to God's dealings with the patriarchs" (*The Old Testament of the Old Testament: Patriarchal Narratives and Mosaic Yahwism*. [OBT; Minneapolis: Fortress, 1994], p. 141).

Furthermore, Abraham's journey served as a paradigm for the early Israelites. The narrator captures this role of Abraham's journey in God's self-introduction to Abraham before the first covenant ceremony. God says, "I am Yahweh, who brought you out of Ur of the Chaldeans" (15:7). This self-introduction is patterned after the one in the Sinaitic covenant: "I am Yahweh your God, who brought you out of Egypt, out of the land of slavery" (Exod. 20:2). Abraham's leaving Ur parallels Israel's leaving Egypt; each exodus interprets the other. Furthermore, God's covenant with him parallels God's entering into covenant with Israel at Sinai. During the covenant ceremony with Abraham God told him what his seed would experience before entering the promised land. Abraham was able to understand what God told him because of his experiences in Egypt (12:10–20). They would live as strangers in a foreign land; they would become slaves, but God would punish that nation; and they would come out with great possessions (15:13–14). Abraham's experiences in Egypt served as a pattern to help the early Israelites understand how God was leading them.

Jacob's experiences with God also foreshadowed the nation's struggle to serve God. Often Israel as a nation used politically and economically deceitful strategies to advance its position among the nations and to promote its prosperity. When its wealth increased, the nation, like Jacob, erected better pillars (Hos. 10:1). Israel, like Jacob, who wrestled with God until his name was changed to Israel, needed to have an encounter with God in which it would have a change of character (Hos. 12:2–6). Thus

Hosea drew on Jacob's experiences with God in an effort to motivate Israel to repent of its deceptive ways and realign itself with God as did its ancestor.

Joseph's journey was a paradigm of God's guiding Israel through times of success and times of oppressive hardship in order that it might be the leader for bringing salvation to the families of the earth (Gen. 50:20). God's leading is grounded in the covenantal promises made to the patriarchs (12:1–9).

The Historical Witness of the Ancestral Accounts

I wish to argue for the reliability of the patriarchal narratives in reporting the origin of Israel as God's people. First, I shall identify the character and intent of the ancestral accounts. Second, I shall look at correspondences between the customs of the ancestors and those common in Upper Mesopotamia and Canaan in the Middle-Late Bronze Age (ca. 2100–1200 B.C.). Third, I shall make a comparison between these biblical texts and various kinds of literature from the ancient Near East near the beginning of the second millennium B.C. Fourth, I shall assess the character of these narratives in relationship to each other and to the rest of the Pentateuch.

The Character and Intent of the Ancestral Accounts

First, the ancestral accounts in Genesis may be classified as family history, that is, stories about the origin and destiny of Abraham's descendants for four generations. These narratives consist of reports of births, marriages, domestic relationships, travelogs, and acts of devotion to God. Furthermore, these accounts have been preserved as Scripture and focus on God's role in the lives of those who were the bearers of God's program for bringing blessing to all the families of the earth. This last point is crucial, for it is the primary reason that the record of Abraham's family has survived through the centuries.

The emphasis on God's role in these accounts, however, produces a major tension between the orientation of the ancestral narratives and the type of material accepted by secular historians as history. As a guiding principle, such historians rule out God as a factor because there are no empirical criteria for evaluating claims of divine activity. Thus they quickly discount the worth of these accounts for writing a history of that early age. The highest purpose of Genesis, however, is to reveal how God worked in affairs on earth from creation to the forming of a special people who worshiped God through the line of Abraham. The significance of this revelation for those who accept it is dependent upon God's actual involvement in the events and lives of Israel's ancestors.

There are other differences between these accounts and a history written according to the current standards of social science. The narratives in Genesis do not seek to explore the social, economic, political, and religious setting; yet such information is at the core of a typical history. Furthermore, when a narrative in Genesis recounts a transaction between one of Abraham's seed and the local inhabitants, it usually does not pursue the repercussions of that transaction. For example, Abraham purchased a field from a Hittite of Hebron; however, Genesis makes no further reference to these Hittites. The reader has no knowledge of how this agreement affected either the citizens of Hebron or the offspring of Abraham. Describing such impact is a central task of a contemporary historian, but it was of no concern to the ancient narrator. Moreover, the editor(s) did not peg these accounts to any historical points of reference that are currently known; thus Genesis cannot be easily tied to the known history of that era. This makes finding external data to confirm the testimony of these patriarchal accounts improbable. However, while the accounts in Genesis were not composed according to the current standards of history as a social science, this difference in approach does not exclude them from serving as reliable witnesses to what they tell us about the patriarchs. Awareness of these differences in approaches alerts us that we should not read these accounts as historical biography, for their intention is far different. On the other hand, A. Millard's insightful comment offers perspective at this point: "Let all who read remember that the patriarchal narratives are our only source for knowledge of the earliest traditions of Israel, that traditions can be correct reflections of ancient events, and that they do not pretend to be textbooks of ancient near-eastern history or archaeology" ("Methods of Studying the Patriarchal Narratives As Ancient Texts," in *Essays on the Patriarchal Narratives* [ed. A. Millard and D. Wiseman; Winona Lake, Ind.: Eisenbrauns, 1983], p. 51).

Since Genesis does not establish connections between the patriarchs and other personages and events that we know about from the ancient Near East, scholars have proposed a wide range of dates for the patriarchs, including sometime around the twenty-sixth century B.C. (Freedman), the nineteenth century B.C. (Albright), and the fourteenth century B.C. (Gordon). Any suggested date for the era of the patriarchs must be a working proposal. I place Abraham roughly at the end of the twenty-first century B.C. based on the time references in four texts: Exodus 12:40, which says that the sojourn of Israel in Egypt lasted 430 years; 1 Kings 6:1, which places the building of the temple 480 years after the exodus; Genesis 25:7, which reports that Abraham lived 175 years; and Genesis 35:28–29, which informs us that Isaac survived his father by a little more than one hundred years. Since many of these numbers have symbolic force, they cannot be used to arrive at a precise date for any figure in Genesis. Taking them in a general sense leads to placing Abraham sometime near the turn of the millennium in the twenty-first century B.C. and to placing the arrival of Jacob's clan in Egypt sometime in the first half of the second millennium B.C.

The Cultural Information in the Ancestral Accounts

Second, in assessing the historical value of these accounts it is important to compare the information found in them with what we know of the cultures of Upper Mesopotamia and Canaan during the Middle Bronze Age. Throughout the twentieth century, the findings of archaeologists have increased immensely our knowledge of the Levant, that is, the area bordering the eastern Mediterranean, in the Middle Bronze Age. The numerous tablets that have been uncovered at sites such as Mari, Nuzi, and Ugarit are especially valuable. Those who were at the forefront of these discoveries, particularly Cyrus H. Gordon, William F. Albright, and E. A. Speiser, pointed out many similarities between customs witnessed to in these texts and the customs of the patriarchs—particularly regarding marriage, adoption, and inheritance—and created reconstructed readings. In the second half of the twentieth century, scholars restudied these parallels and found that many of the reconstructed readings of the ancestral narratives were not accurate. For example, Albright's view that Abraham was a merchant caravaneer traveling between Damascus and Egypt on a donkey has not withstood scrutiny. What later scholars found wanting were the imaginative reconstructions that had forced alien categories on the ancestral narratives, not the content of the biblical texts themselves. Furthermore, in dealing with the cultural setting of the ancestors we need to keep in mind that the amount of information we possess about the Middle Bronze Age in Upper Mesopotamia, though vastly increased, is still small and fragmented in comparison to the length of that era and the size of Mesopotamia. Even more limiting is the fact that our information about Canaan at this time is minuscule.

Despite these limitations, however, several significant correlations may be made between the ancestral narratives and the customs of the ancient Near East in the centuries around 2000 B.C. Following is a list of eight correlations that support placing the patriarchs in this era:[13] (a) Many names, including Serug, Nahor, and Jacob-El, have been attested in Mesopotamian documents dated around 2000 B.C. (b) Several names in Terah's lineage are associated with the moon—Terah, Milcah, Sarai, and Laban—suggesting that these ancestors worshiped the moon god. This is in accord with their being associated with Ur of the Chaldeans and Haran, both centers of moon worship. (c) Key names in Genesis, including Ishmael, Isaac, and Jacob, are constructed on the pattern of Amorite personal names of the early second millennium B.C. While names in this pattern also appear later, the preference for this pattern waned considerably after the Bronze Age. (d) The names of Abraham, Isaac, and Jacob are at home in this era, and they do not occur later in Scripture. (e) The social organization of pastoralists at Mari provides models that illuminate relationships witnessed to in Genesis, especially the dealings of Laban and Jacob. (f) In the nineteenth century B.C. Haran was a vibrant trade center. (g) El was the chief god of the Canaanites during the Middle Bronze Age, but in the Late Bronze Age Baal displaced El as their most popular god. This point becomes more weighty in that there are no references to Baal in Genesis. (h) The ancestors interacted with the inhabitants of several city-states in Canaan, including Shechem, Hebron, Gerar, Salem, Sodom, and the cities of the plain. Such was the political organization in Canaan in the second millennium as attested in sources like the Tell el-Amarna texts. By the first millennium these cities were governed under various central governments, including those of the Philistines, Moabites, and Edomites.

The Joseph narrative contains many details that support its historicity in terms of what is known of Egyptian culture: (a) There are Egyptian terms in the narrative, including '*akhu* ("reeds," 41:2); *ye'or* ("Nile," 41:1); *shesh* ("fine linen," 41:42); *khartom* ("magician," 41:8); and '*abrek* ("make way or bow down," 41:43). (b) Some characters have Egyptian names, including Potiphar,

Potiphera, Asenath, and Zaphenath-Paneah. (c) The imagery in Pharaoh's dreams is typical of Egypt. Egyptians valued cattle very highly. Fat, sleek cattle grazing in the dense reed grass growing along the Nile, especially in the canals of the Delta, is a typical scene from Egyptian art. Egypt was famous for the high quality of grain produced in the fertile soil along the Nile. The height of the Nile's flooding, which both watered and fertilized the land along its banks, varied from year to year and determined the abundance of each harvest. (d) Egyptian documents attest that the chief cupbearer and the chief baker were two officials in Pharaoh's palace. The cupbearer, having close access to the Pharaoh, had higher privileges and was entrusted with special tasks. Although the chief baker was more distant, his position was important, for Egyptians loved baked goods. Ancient records indicate that the Egyptians had dozens of different kinds of breads and cakes. This accords with the baker's describing the basket on his head as containing "all kinds of baked goods" (40:17). (e) The apprehension of the butler and baker after their dreams, increased by their lack of access to an expert interpreter, reflects Egyptian attitudes toward dreams. One of the skills of the learned Egyptian priests was dream interpretation. (f) Joseph's shaving before his meeting with Pharaoh (41:14) is in accord with Egyptians' being clean shaven, whereas most Asiatics had beards. (g) The presence in Egypt of numerous Semitic peoples from Canaan and Syria, known to the Egyptians as Asiatics, is well attested. In some eras they were numerous, especially when the Hyksos rose to power about 1650–1540 B.C. (h) An Egyptian document from the eighteenth century B.C. proves that Asiatics were hired as domestic help and that some rose to high, trusted positions. (i) The description of Pharaoh's installing Joseph in high office corresponds to Egyptian practice; particularly Pharaoh's giving him a signet ring, linen clothes, a gold chain, an Egyptian name, and a chariot with a defined position in the royal procession (41:41–45). Pictures of such investitures have been found in royal tombs. (j) The emphasis on flocks and herds grazing in the Delta agrees with Egyptian practice. (k) Reference to mummification for Jacob and Joseph is decidedly Egyptian. (l) According to his obituary, Joseph died at the age of 110, the ideal length of life for Egyptians. These points indicate a second-millennium B.C. setting, but they do not allow for a closer dating since the Egyptians followed these practices over several centuries.[14]

Literary Style of the Ancestral Accounts

Third, we may learn of the character of these narratives by comparing their literary style with the various genres from the ancient Near East of the first half of the second millennium B.C., including chronicles, epics, sagas, legends, historical epics, and short tales. From such a comparison we discover that these narratives stand out as straightforward, concise, cryptic accounts (K. Kitchen, *The Bible in Its World: The Bible and Archaeology Today* [Downers Grove, Ill.: InterVarsity, 1977], pp. 61–65) whose intent is to report what took place. Outside of references to God, the embellishments in these accounts are few when compared with the literature of that age.

In considering these accounts as having historical value, however, a secular mind chafes before supernatural references such as visions, angels, a human wrestling with a spirit, and fire and brimstone falling from heaven on wicked cities. But these kinds of references do not automatically discount the general accuracy of what an ancient text reports. A comparison with texts of the early second millennium B.C. from Israel's neighbors shows that the claims of the biblical reports are more believable, giving us confidence that they are reports of what took place, rather than literary creations.[15] We must keep in mind that this kind of data has been included because the primary goal of these accounts is to inspire faith in God and give identity to the people of God.

The Character of the Ancestral Accounts Compared to That of the Pentateuch

Three internal arguments support the credibility of these ancestral accounts. First, the distinctive literary styles of the narratives of the three patriarchs suggest that each narrative originated independently. It can also be demonstrated that accounts within a given narrative had independent origins (e.g., the detailed, report style of Gen. 14 is unique to the book). In this light it may be postulated that the editor(s) who put Genesis together took over ancient accounts, many of them perhaps having been passed down from the time of the ancestors. If this is the way Genesis was compiled, then we can assume that these various accounts are fairly accurate—at least for materials composed before the development of modern historical research—since they were written close to the time of the events they describe.

Second, inconsistencies and gaps in information in the three narratives may indicate that the editor(s) did not significantly alter or add to the material they found in the ancient accounts. They did not remove references to the foibles and failures of the main characters. For example, they kept both accounts of Abraham's identifying his wife as his sister, even though it casts Abraham in an unfavorable light. Neither did the editors fill in glaring gaps in information. For example, the lack of any reference in chapter 24 to Abraham after his trusted servant returned to Canaan with Rebekah is puzzling. One way to explain this omission is to postulate that Abraham died while the servant was in Haran. However, the timeline that can be reconstructed for Abraham indicates that he lived thirty-five years after Rebekah came to Canaan. No attempt is made to close this gap in the information, indicating that the editors were reluctant to enhance accounts handed down to them. The editors did not supply highly desirable information that had been lost. For example, they did not compose an account about Abraham's death nor did they even mention Rebekah's, a lacuna made noticeable by the accounts of Sarah's burial (ch. 23) and of Jacob's elaborate funeral (50:1–14). The lack of narratives about Isaac is troubling, but none were made up to fill this gap. These holes and rough edges increase our confidence in their accuracy, for it is the tendency of humans in retelling an incident to inadvertently make contradictions and omit important information. To say it another way, a fully consistent report is likely either a contrived report or a fictional account. Conversely an account with gaps and difficulties is considered more reliable, for it reflects the tendency of a storyteller close to an event to leave out details that a later audience needs for understanding, for that teller assumes that the immediate audience has a certain awareness of the situation being described.

The third internal argument in support of the credibility of these ancestral accounts is the vast differences in the worship practices and moral attitudes of these ancestors from those of the nation Israel, particularly regarding marriage relations, alliances with Canaanites, inheritance practices, and religious customs and beliefs. These differences indicate that the ancestral accounts were composed before these practices developed into those of the nation Israel. For example, the kinds of marriages the patriarchs entered into are at odds with the cultic and legal practices found in Exodus 25 through Deuteronomy 34. Abraham was married to his half-sister, but that kind of relationship was banned according to the laws in Leviticus 18:9, 11; 20:17. Jacob married sisters (29:21–30), but the law prohibited such practice (Lev. 18:18). Judah, David's ancestor, took a Canaanite wife, but such practice was forbidden in the law (Exod. 34:13–16; Deut. 7:2–3). Even though the law restricted Israelites from making alliances with the peoples of Canaan (Exod. 34:12), Abraham and Isaac both entered into a covenant with Abimelech, king of Gerar (21:22–32; 26:26–33). Jacob honored Joseph by adopting his two sons as his own so that they would be heirs equal to his own children; thus Joseph received a double portion of the inheritance. Jacob also elevated Ephraim, the younger son, over Manasseh, a practice forbidden by Deuteronomy 21:15–17.

Some of the patriarchs' religious practices differed from those of later Israel as well. Jacob set up many pillars. Those pillars, technically known as *matsebot*, were stones of various sizes erected for a variety of reasons, such as to mark sacred places or to commemorate the place where something important happened. Such stones could be unadorned or engraved with a picture, such as hands lifted up to the moon. Because such pillars were used by the Canaanites in their worship of many gods, the law required that the Israelites smash all pillars they found (Exod. 23:24; 34:13; Deut. 7:5; 12:3) and condemned worship sites on hills and under spreading trees (Deut. 12:2). However, Abraham built his first altar near the great tree of Moreh at Shechem (12:6–7), and he lived for many years at the great trees of Mamre, where he also built an altar (13:18). At Beersheba he planted a tamarisk tree and then worshiped El Olam (21:33). Some later traditions were so embarrassed by the accounts of Abraham's worshiping near trees that they altered the reading of some texts to remove this embarrassment. For example, *Targum Onkelos* replaced great tree(s) with "plain, valley" (12:6; 13:18; 14:13; 18:1; also 35:8; R. de Vaux, *The Early History of Israel* [trans. D. Smith; Philadelphia: Westminster, 1978], p. 286). Nonetheless, the editor(s) of Genesis left these accounts in, indicating that they were viewed with respect.

The view of God in Genesis differs markedly from that in the rest of the Pentateuch, where God is a holy and jealous God, a devouring fire (Deut. 4:24; Exod. 20:5; 34:14). In Genesis there is little emphasis on the holiness of God, although the idea may appear in the divine title "Fear of Isaac" (31:42). In Genesis God is the intimate guardian of the clan and Lord of the nations. God appears and speaks to the ancestors, giving a word of encouragement or direction. The people in the ancestral narratives have different encounters with God than do the Israelites who met God at Sinai, and these different experiences shape their differing views of God.

Given these three internal arguments, it is difficult to imagine that one or more authors who lived centuries later would have had the inclination, let alone the skill, to compose stories about Israel's ancestors living and worshiping so differently than prescribed by the Sinaitic law. It is even harder to imagine that such stories would have been so widely accepted as to become part of the canonical tradition if they were first introduced in the exilic or early postexilic eras. Jews at that time, especially those living among Gentiles, were emphasizing their distinctive customs in order to establish their own identity and would have been unlikely to adopt stories in which their ancestors behaved like the Gentiles, had those stories not been genuine and ancient.

The preceding discussion provides a basis for accepting the ancestral accounts in Genesis as reliable witnesses about Israel's ancestors, that is, as an acceptable source of historical information even when there is no collaborating witness. Conclusive external evidence for the existence of any figures in Genesis may never be found, for migratory shepherds living outside urban centers left few traces of their existence. Nevertheless, that these ancestors of Israel did live is vital to those who have faith in the God of Abraham.

These ancestral narratives serve a high theological purpose in teaching that the one true God shows concern for the well-being of all peoples by choosing Abraham as the agent through whom God would bring blessing to all families of the earth. However, if these accounts in Genesis are only literary inventions, the God pictured in them becomes merely the figment of human imagination. If God is no more than a product of human imagination, then humans live devoid of any divine help for dealing with the gigantic issues that potentially threaten their existence. As J. Goldingay says, "While the historicity of the events is not a sufficient evidence of the truth of the narrative's interpretation, it is a necessary evidence of its truth. . . . If they are not fundamentally factual, the ancestral narratives have sense but not reference" ("The Patriarchs in Scripture and History," in *Essays on the Patriarchal Narratives,* p. 29). Although the date of Israel's ancestors cannot be precisely assigned, there is sufficient internal and external evidence to believe with confidence that these ancestral narratives recount the experiences of real people.

New Testament Connections

For New Testament believers, both the primeval narrative and the ancestral narratives are crucial. The primeval narrative provides a basis for understanding why Christ's atoning work was effective for all peoples everywhere, not only for the Jews. The patriarchal narratives are also vital to the New Testament, for the promises God gave Abraham are fulfilled in Jesus. That is, Jesus brought to all humanity those blessings God had promised to Abraham, thereby making Abraham the father of all those who believe in Jesus by faith (Gal. 3:29). As a result, the new seed of Abraham also functions as an agent of blessing for all the families of the earth.

These ancestral stories served the early church as a powerful apology for its new ways of worship and for the new thinking about how a person relates to God. Paul supported his radical teaching that God requires only faith, not works, in order to gain salvation by showing how Abraham's righteousness was the result of faith, not works (Gal. 3:6–18; Rom. 4). Furthermore, prior to the giving of the law and the setting up of the tabernacle, Israel's ancestors followed God wholeheartedly and worshiped him directly wherever they chose (Acts 7:2–53). They needed neither a priest nor a shrine for seeking God. In the same way, Christians may worship God anywhere. They no longer have to observe the ancient practices such as circumcision and ritual purity. As the result of the work of Christ, all believers are priests. They pray directly to God and minister God's grace to others. God's presence accompanies them as they move about, just as God was with the patriarchs wherever they went.

The patriarchs are also models of how persons, both Jew and believer in Christ, relate to God. Abraham is the exemplar of those who obey God, trusting God to fulfill what he has promised. Abraham displayed great generosity many times. After the death of his nephew's father, he reared Lot and took him along to Canaan. When the size of their respective herds required that they separate, Abraham deferred to Lot to choose the direction he preferred to go. This is remarkable in that Abraham, the elder, had been Lot's guardian. Abraham declined gaining personal wealth from the spoil taken from the kings of the East. Abraham did not want any human to be able to boast about making him rich (14:22–23).

Abraham trusted God throughout his life, even though his hope that God would give him a legitimate heir through Sarah stretched to the breaking point as they advanced in age. After Isaac was born, Abraham did not hold back his only beloved son from God. Out of obedience he bound Isaac and laid him on the altar in order to offer him up as a whole burnt offering. In this act Abraham displayed his submission to God's will.

Jacob offers a different model. He strove for self-exaltation until God fought with him and his character was changed. He was so zealous to be the chosen one that he used cunning means to make sure that he gained the position of firstborn. Nevertheless, God appeared to Jacob at crucial times, directing his course. These encounters were dramatic for Jacob and caused him to face his vulnerability. Despite his drive to promote himself, Jacob had a deep longing to serve God, as is evidenced by his not asking God for concessions in these encounters. He dealt with God boldly and directly, even bargaining with God. At Peniel he wrestled all night until his opponent gave him a blessing by changing his name (32:22–30).

Joseph is the paradigm of a wise person who trusts God through all circumstances in life—the darkest times and the times of abundance. The only direct communication he had from God were the two simple dreams he had in his youth. Thereafter, he pursued the tasks he was given energetically and skillfully, trusting God to direct the affairs in his life for the highest good.

As a truly wise person Joseph lived by the fear of the Lord (Prov. 1:7; 9:10). He did not yield to folly, nor was he seduced by the pleasures of sexual allurement (Prov. 2:16–19; 7:6–23). When he complained, he did so quietly in hopes of improving his situation. Wisdom equipped Joseph to counsel kings (Prov. 8:14–16). Years later, when Joseph saw his brothers in Egypt, he directed a sequence of incidents in order that there may be full reconciliation between them. At times he was hard on his brothers, but he showed that he had overcome the bitterness caused by their cruelty. His attitude was revealed when he named his firstborn Manasseh, and he said, "God has made me forget all my trouble" (41:51). After he made himself known to his brothers, he had to convince them that they could trust him. He encouraged their trust by his insightful words: "Do not be distressed and do not be angry with yourselves for selling me here, because it was to save lives that God sent me ahead of you" (45:5). Years later, Joseph reassured his troubled brothers that he would not take vengeance on them, saying, "Don't be afraid. Am I in the place of God? You intended to harm me, but God intended it for good to accomplish what is now being done, the saving of many lives" (50:19–20). Proverbs 19:21 captures Joseph's conviction: "many are the plans in a man's heart, but it is the LORD's purpose that prevails." Joseph lived always trusting in God's leading.

In these stories the patriarchs sometimes erred and even did wrong. The text does not cover up their failures or the way they made matters worse when they did not wait for God to act (e.g., when Abraham took Hagar as a concubine, when both Abraham and Isaac misled people by introducing their wives as their sisters, or when Sarah was cruel to Hagar). The ancestors bore the responsibility for their errors, but they did not let their failures keep them from following God. Consequently, they were moral giants despite their stumbling, especially when they are compared with characters such as Cain, Lamech, or the citizens of Babel. The patriarchs persisted in seeking God until he fulfilled his promises. Their failures raise our estimation of them because we see them as real people who vacillated between trust and action as they walked with God. Since trust in God won out in their lives, their stories motivate us to persevere despite our failures, keeping our eyes focused on God.

Notes

1. There are two variations to this pattern. The first *toledoth* is placed at the end of the creation account (2:4a), forming an *inclusio* with the heading to that account (1:1). This particular *toledoth* formula is also unique in that it recounts the "genealogy" of a thing rather than a person, namely, of the heavens and the earth. Nevertheless, it still identifies the first section of Genesis (1:1–4:26). The other variation is the presence of two *toledoth* formulas in the genealogy of Esau (36:1, 9). The editor of Genesis may have kept both to indicate that he drew on two different sources for these genealogies. Given their proximity and the single topic of ch. 36, they are considered here to mark one section of Genesis.

2. In a few sections material usually included in a *toledoth* has been placed throughout the section. For example, from the *toledoth* of Isaac (25:19–35:29) the report of the births of Esau and Jacob comes at 25:25–26, the note about Isaac's age at their birth at 25:26c, and the account of

Isaac's death at 35:27–29. But this variation is the exception. For a discussion of the role of these *toledoth* formulas in the compilation of Genesis from a conservative viewpoint see D. Garrett, *Rethinking Genesis: The Sources and Authorship of the First Book of the Pentateuch* (Grand Rapids: Baker, 1991), pp. 91–106.

3. The Jacob narrative does not really end with the start of the Joseph narrative, for material from the Jacob tradition is found in chs. 46–50.

4. In describing these structural patterns in Genesis I draw on the work of G. Rendsburg, *The Redaction of Genesis* (Winona Lake, Ind.: Eisenbrauns, 1986); he in turn builds on the solid work of M. Fishbane (*Text and Texture: Close Reading of Selected Biblical Texts* [New York: Schocken, 1979], pp. 40–62).

5. The account of Judah's settlement Adullam, which is in the Shephelah, the lowlands east of Bethlehem, is an interlude in the Joseph narrative and has a role similar to that of the interludes in the Jacob narrative. On the surface this account appears disjunctive to the Joseph story, but a closer look at the details and motifs in the story reveals many connections between it and the following account of Joseph in Egypt (see the introduction to Gen. 38).

6. Rendsburg argues that even the entire section is organized as a palistrophe (*Redaction of Genesis,* pp. 79–97), but his identification of the sections seems somewhat forced.

7. The assumption is that certain features so characterize an author's style as to distinguish the writings of that author from those of others. For example, the creation account (1:1–2:4a) presents an abundance of information economically by recounting in a carefully structured pattern what God did on each day of creation. The account of the garden of Eden, however, is a narrative that achieves penetrating insight into the human dilemma of pain, alienation, and death through brief exchanges between actors and the skillful use of symbols. It is also the only account in Genesis that uses the divine name Lord God (Yahweh Elohim). The story of the deluge has a distinctive structure formed around two chronological systems. An unusual density of wordplays and alliterations distinguish the narrative of the Tower of Babel (11:1–9). These sorts of distinctive features of various accounts attest that they probably existed independently before they were assembled in this collection.

Similarly, it is possible to demonstrate that many of the individual accounts within the Abraham and Jacob narratives originated independently. In contrast, the Joseph narrative is a whole, marked by the same literary style up to the insertion of material from the Jacob traditions.

8. This divine name is part of two names among the ancestors found in Numbers: Zurishaddai (1:6) and Ammishaddai (1:12).

9. El was the supreme God in the Canaanite pantheon. He was known as a kind, wise, yet salacious deity, and many epithets exalt him.

Several scholars equate El in the biblical texts with the Canaanite El, but it is possible that the preference in Genesis for identifying the God of the ancestors as El Shaddai was to place some distance between the God of the fathers and the Canaanite El.

10. Once Jacob used the anomalous name *pakhad Yitskhaq* (possibly "the Fear of Isaac," 31:42; cf. 31:53).

11. El forms a part of several names in the patriarchal narratives, including Eliezer (15:2), Ishmael (16:11), and Bethuel (22:22–23).

12. *Yahweh* or *yahu* is an element in Amorite personal names. Whether it is a name or a verbal element is debated (F. Cross, *Canaanite Myth and Hebrew Epic: Essays in the History of the Religion of Israel* [Cambridge, Mass.: Harvard University Press, 1973], pp. 62–65). Also, some scholars equate the element *ia* in some Northwest Semitic names with Yahweh, but this seems unlikely since Yahweh as a God is not known outside Israel.

13. M. Selman identifies thirteen points of correlation between the ways of the patriarchs and customs attested in the Middle Bronze Age in "Comparative Customs and the Patriarchal Age," in *Essays on the Patriarchal Narratives,* pp. 134–38.

14. Some details in the Joseph narrative, including similarities to themes in Proverbs as noted above, have led scholars who are knowledgeable about Egyptian culture and history to conclude that the author was from Canaan and that this story was edited during the time of Solomon (R. de Vaux, *The Early History of Israel* [trans. D. Smith; Philadelphia: Westminster, 1978], pp. 301, 307–10).

15. The lack of embellishment of the fantastic in the patriarchal narratives is further demonstrated by the way these stories are retold in later literature, including Pseudo-Philo's *Liber Antiquitatum Biblicarum* and the *Book of Jubilees.* These later writers tend to smooth out many of the disjunctives found in Genesis. The fact that these disjunctives have been left in Genesis further indicates that the editors who collected and arranged the accounts of the patriarchs preserved them essentially as they found them. That is, they did not touch up or adjust the accounts so that they would fit together smoothly and be free of seemingly conflicting details.

§1 The Creation of the Earth (Gen. 1:1–2:4a)

Genesis opens with the account of creation, which is as profound as it is simple. It focuses on the way God ordered the earth. The text addresses the heavens only as they have an impact on life on earth.

The purpose of this account is threefold. First, it teaches essential facts about the way God ordered the world so that humans might understand their place and role in creation. Second, it leads us to praise God as the wise, all-powerful Creator. Third, it preempts the deification of any created elements or forces regardless of their splendor.

The text presents the process of creation in six frames called days. Each frame follows a fixed pattern that begins with "and God said" and concludes with "And there was evening and there was morning . . .". Within each frame God gives a command, sometimes stating the reason behind it. The report of the accomplishment of the command follows. God defines the purpose of what came into being, evaluates it, and in certain cases blesses it. The repetition of this structure echoes God's careful ordering of the cosmos, while the scarcity of detail about how God created fosters our sense of wonder at the marvelous creation. In the process of creating, God was involved with the world in many ways: speaking, creating, making, naming, evaluating, deciding, caring for, pondering, blessing, and resting.

The focus of the six days alternates between time and space. Time is central to the activities of days one, four, and seven, while spatial aspects of creation are addressed in days two, three, five, and six. Furthermore, the ordering of each of the first three days corresponds to what is created on days four through six. The light-giving bodies of day four correspond to the origin of light on day one. On days five and six God fills the space defined on days two (sea/air) and three (land) with the appropriate life forms.

A number of literary features point to God's creation of humans on the sixth day as the goal of creation. (a) This day receives the longest coverage. (b) Only before making humans does God take counsel. (c) Humans are created in the image of God. (d) Three of the seven occurrences of the nodal term "create" *(bara')* occur with humans. (e) God pronounces a blessing on humans, and (f) God invests them with authority over other members of the created order. Three features give the seventh day secondary emphasis: first, its pattern is different from that used for the other days; second, God rests; and third, God declares it holy.

This account gives God's people the proper orientation to the created world. There are five ideas that are crucial to this orientation. (a) God entrusts humans, who bear God's image, with stewardship of the earth. (b) God has set boundaries within which the various dimensions of the created order fulfill their purposes. (c) God assigns tasks and responsibilities to various members of creation; for example, the lights in heaven establish times and seasons. (d) No member of the created order is a deity. (e) In resting on the seventh day God provides a regular period of time for humans to enjoy the beauty of the created order. This orientation serves to counter false worldviews, including dualism, astrology, nihilism, and any philosophy that devalues human life (D. Kidner, *Genesis: An Introduction and Commentary* [TOTC; Downers Grove, Ill.: InterVarsity, 1967], p. 57).

There are numerous explanations for the relationship of 1:1–2 to the account of the six days of creation. We will consider four of them. The first is the gap theory or the restitution theory, popularized by the Scofield Bible, which takes verse 1 as the report of the original grand creation. In that world evil became so rampant that God had to destroy it. Verse 2 describes the results of that destruction. After an undetermined span of time God recreated the earth as recounted in the six days of creation. This theory is appealing in that it provides the eons required by some geological interpretations of the earth's formation. It also provides an age for the existence of extinct creatures like dinosaurs, which are otherwise unaccounted for in Scripture. This interpretation, however, stumbles over the grammar of verse 2, which is not structured as an independent sentence in sequence to verse 1. Moreover, this theory leaves much to be desired in that the grand creation is recounted in a single short verse while several verses describe the restructuring of the world. Furthermore, there is no other scriptural support for this position.

A second theory, chaos before creation, holds that the matter with which God began to create (i.e., "the chaotic water") was completely raw material that lacked any order. Those who hold this position translate the first three verses: "When God began to create . . . —the earth being unformed and void—God said . . ." (NJPS). This translation finds support in the way most ancient accounts of creation, including the Babylonian Creation Epic and the account of the garden of Eden (Gen. 2:4b–3:24), begin. The structure of the days of creation runs counter to this theory. The consistent pattern used for each day of creation tells us that verses 1–2 are not an integral part of the first day of creation (vv. 3–5). That is, these first two verses stand apart from the report of what God did on the first day of creation.

A third view, the initial chaos theory, understands verse 2 to describe the raw material that came into existence as a result of God's initial creative act reported in verse 1. That is, after making the raw materials, God went about ordering the cosmos from these raw materials as recounted in verses 3–31. This view, found in the early versions, has received wide support throughout the centuries. It falters, however, before the intolerable tension between the cosmic order depicted in verse 1 and the chaos described in verse 2. In addition, a comparison of the language of verse 1 with the language used to describe God's making/creating in six days indicates that it is incorrect to interpret the wording of verse 1 as describing a specific creative act.

A fourth position takes verse 1, "God created the heavens and the earth," as the heading to the account of creation (1:3–2:4a). That first sentence then came to possess concrete meaning only after the completion of creation. Verse 2 is a circumstantial clause about the unorganized state of matter before God began to create. A description of disorganized matter before speaking of creation accords with the ancient practice of beginning an account of origins by describing that which did not yet exist (2:4b–7).

By juxtaposing verse 2 with verse 1, the author highlights a key theme of Scripture, the polarity between cosmic order and chaos. God created by organizing chaos into cosmos. In so doing, however, God did not eliminate the two key elements of chaos, water and darkness. Their presence accounts for the ebb and flow between abundance and want, blessing and curse. This movement is at the core of human experience. In particular, when Israel keeps the covenant throughout the OT, God blesses nature so that the land yields abundantly. But when Israel forgets the covenant, God unleashes curses that cause nature to languish, resulting in deprivation and hardship.

This movement between abundance and want is evident in the material that follows creation (chs. 1–11). God placed humans in a lush garden. But after they rebelled, God expelled them from the garden, and once east of Eden humans had to work the stubborn soil hard to produce their food. Then, when human society became dominated by violence, God brought judgment by wiping out almost all humans by the cataclysmic flood (6:9–8:22). In that judgment God returned the earth to a chaotic condition similar to that described in verse 2.

This movement between blessing (cosmos) and curse (chaos), which is formalized in the blessings and curses of the Sinaitic covenant (Lev. 26; Deut. 27–28), also became a major theme in eschatological passages. God's final judgment was sometimes described as the *un*creating of the cosmic order (Isa. 34:8–15; Jer. 4:23–26). When God finally creates a new heaven and a new earth (Isa. 65:17–25; 66:22–23) his lordship will be further established. Therefore, the juxtaposition of cosmos (v. 1) and chaos (v. 2) grounds the interplay between abundance and want in God's lordship over order and chaos.

An obstacle to this fourth position is that it seems to allow for the preexistence of matter. However, only the brevity of the creation account creates this impression. Ancient authors did not employ literary techniques for addressing complex issues from many perspectives. They focused on central issues without encumbering their documents with disclaimers. The focus here is on God's sovereignty over the dynamic movement between cosmos and chaos, so as to discount pagan cosmogonies as a valid way of understanding the world's origin. As a result, the theme of creation out of nothing was not addressed because it was not an issue. Nevertheless, the wording of this account does not conflict with the idea of creation *ex nihilo,* which is taught in other Scriptures (e.g., Prov. 8:22–31). In addition, the heading "God created the heavens and the earth" meant for the ancients that God created the earth described in verse 2.

1:1 / In the beginning God created the heavens and the earth. In Hebrew this sentence consists of seven words, mirroring the seven days of creation. "In the beginning" marks the start of time on earth. This is confirmed by the process of creation being presented in a sequence of days and by the creation of light first in order to mark the flow of time in days and nights (1:3–5). **God** (*'elohim*) is the generic term for the one deity. It is used so frequently that it virtually functions as a name. Its plural form conveys the multiplicity and self-sufficiency of God. That is, God, who is superior to all the gods, embodies in himself the qualities of all the gods that make up a pantheon. The OT uses "create" *(bara')* restrictively: only God serves as its subject, and the material out of which something is made is never mentioned. The terms "the heavens" and "the earth," being at opposite ends of the spectrum, stand for the totality of what God created. "Universe" is another possible translation for this phrase, but the ancient view of the cosmos was so different from today's view that this English term would convey more than the ancient author intended.

1:2 / A description of the earth prior to God's giving it form follows, in preparation for recounting the stages of creation and especially for the ordering that took place on the first three days: **the earth was formless and empty, darkness was over the surface of the deep.** "Earth" stands in an emphatic position, signaling that it is the primary focus of this account. In Hebrew "earth" signifies the area where humans live, dry land, and the land of Israel. But in this verse "the earth"—being formless, empty, and covered with water—refers to that which held the potential for becoming land.

Darkness, symbolic of a lifeless void, covered "the deep" *(tehom)*, that is, the primordial ocean. In many ancient Near Eastern myths the primordial deep was the locus of those gods who opposed the gods of order. For example, in the Babylonian Creation Epic the goddess Tiamat, who personified the primordial salt waters, set up a rebellious government in opposition to the heavenly assembly. Only after Marduk, a mighty god of the fourth generation, defeated her was he elevated to be the ruler of the gods. Afterward Marduk ordered the cosmos. In Genesis, however, the deep is an essential element in the cosmos, not a deity. The Creator God exists independently from and transcends all matter. There is no indication that God faced any opposition either before or during the process of creation. Nevertheless, this reference to the deep conveys the latent potential for forces that could be aroused to oppose God's rule and wreak havoc on earth.

The Spirit of God was hovering over the waters. Hebrew *ruah* is used for both "wind" and "spirit." "Hover" or "soar" *(r-kh-p)*, however, is not a verb used with wind; it is used here to compare the Spirit's activity with a bird. The Spirit was circling above the water to make sure that the deep did not oppose God. Manifest as wind, the Spirit was thus in control of these chaotic elements, for it could drive the water wherever it wished. Further, the presence of God's Spirit symbolized the potential of cosmic order and life that could be produced from these formless elements.

1:3–5 / The words **God said** mark off the stages of creation, conveying that God created by the word. God's words were not empty, for the Spirit, who was present over the waters, empowered God's words, bringing into being what God had spoken (A. Kapelrud, "Die Theologie der Schöpfung im Alten Testament," *ZAW* 91 [1979], pp. 165–66). The wording of Psalm 33:6, 9 supports this claim: "By the word of Yahweh were the heavens made, their starry host by the breath of his mouth . . . For he spoke, and it came to be; he commanded, and it stood firm." The parallel in this psalm between "word" and "breath" (v. 6) communicates that God's Spirit was the energy empowering God's word.

God began the process of creation with the command, **Let there be light,** and light came into being, pushing back the primordial darkness. From the context we can discern two reasons God created light first: to limit the primordial darkness, and to begin the flow of time as measured in days. From our knowledge of the world another reason can be added; light was the energy necessary to support the life forms that God was going to create.

God saw that the light was good, thereby making a qualitative judgment about what he had created (also vv. 10, 12, 18, 21, 25, 31). While usually a word carries only one nuance in any given occurrence, "good" in this account is a loaded term. It carries four implications: (a) What came into being functioned precisely as God had purposed. (b) That which had just been created contributed to the well-being of the created order. (c) The new creation had aesthetic qualities—that is, it was pleasing and beautiful—and (d) it had moral force, advancing righteousness on earth (Job 38:12–13).

God went on and **separated the light from the darkness. God called the light "day" and the darkness he called "night."** By naming these elements God defined their function in respect to their essence. God did not eliminate the darkness that was already present; rather he established his authority over it, assigning it a specific role and restricting its influence.

1:6–8 / On the second day God commanded that there be **an expanse . . . to separate** the waters. **God** then **made** (*'asah*) **the expanse.** "Made" usually refers to God's producing something new; "create" *(bara')* is reserved for special creative acts in days five and six. The presence of the word "made" allows for a variety of processes to come into play between God's speaking and the object's coming into existence. God **separated** the massive body of **water** into two parts. One part, stationed below the expanse, fed the seas, rivers, and springs. The other part of the deep was placed above the expanse. **God called the expanse** heavens (**sky,** NIV). The ancients believed that above the solid dome of the heavens was a reservoir housing the rain, hail, and snow. The sun, moon, and stars moved across the surface of this dome, and between this surface and the earth was the sky. The absence of an evaluative statement for the activity on this day suggests that what had been made had been done so in preparation for a higher goal.

1:9–13 / On the third day God carried out two distinct creative acts. First, God ordered the lower water to **be gathered to one place** so that **dry ground** might **appear. God called the dry ground "land,"** and the gathered waters he called **"seas."** As on the first day, God named both the new element and that which already existed. Since the seas sometimes symbolized God's foe or were viewed as the home of frightful sea monsters (v. 21), the picture of God's dominion over the seas bears witness to his sovereignty. Again **God saw** that what had come into being **was good.**

Second, **God said, "Let the land produce vegetation: seed-bearing plants and trees . . . that bear fruit with seed in it."** In this command God bestowed on the land generative power to produce a variety and an abundance of plant life. Possessing this generative power did not make nature a goddess, however. God's command led to the regularity and predictability of nature as well as to the multiplication and adaptation of various kinds of plant life to the various environments on earth. All the plants and the trees are to produce seeds after their kind so that there will be an abundance of plants and trees throughout the earth, providing food for the animals. Again, **God saw** that the vegetation **was good.**

1:14–19 / On the fourth day God brought into existence **lights in the expanse of the sky,** charging them with separating **the day from the night** and with marking **seasons, days and years. God made two great lights—the greater light to govern the day and the lesser light to govern the night** (see Ps. 136:7–9; Jer. 31:35). God clearly defined the extent of the influence that these mighty heavenly bodies have on earthly life. One of their primary tasks is to announce the times, especially the times for holding the feasts that the law requires celebrating at "the appointed time" (e.g., Exod. 23:15; Lev. 23:4). These heavenly bodies were the main gods of various Semitic peoples, and so this description robs them of any divinity. For this reason the author used generic terms ("greater light," "lesser light") rather than names in describing their origin. **God saw** that these heavenly bodies **were good.**

1:20–23 / On the fifth day God filled the spheres ordered on the second day with life by commanding **the water** to **teem** with fish and ordering **birds** to **fly across the expanse of the sky.** These new species were to produce offspring of their own kind. After seeing these new creatures, **God saw** that they were **good.** In place of the usual "it was so" comes a detailed execution of the command: God **created the great creatures of the sea,** the fish, and the birds. The text emphasizes "the great creatures," that is, the serpentine sea monsters, by adding them to the list and putting them first. In the myths of Israel's neighbors, sea monsters often symbolized forces of cosmic evil that opposed the ruling god and order. For example, a Canaanite myth recounts the mighty struggle between Baal, the god of fertility, and Yam, the sea, for kingship.

Scripture depicts three such creatures as God's foes: Rahab, Tannin (the term used here for great sea creatures), and Leviathan. Any of these three may symbolize a powerful enemy of Israel or a cosmic force that opposes God. Rahab symbolizes Egypt (Ps. 87:4; Isa. 30:7) or a dragon-like cosmic foe of Yahweh (Job 26:12; Ps. 89:10; Isa. 51:9). Tannin may be a serpent (Exod. 7:9, 10, 12; Deut. 32:33); a symbol of Pharaoh, perhaps as a crocodile, having superior power (Ezek. 29:3; 32:2); or a symbol of cosmic evil (Job 7:12; Isa. 51:9). Leviathan may be a huge sea creature that sports about in the sea (Ps. 104:26) or a fleeing, twisting serpentine creature that represents the power of evil that Yahweh will defeat in the last days (Isa. 27:1). In Job 41:1–34 it is described in detail; many scholars identify it as a crocodile or a serpentine sea monster. In Psalm 74:13–14 God crushed the heads of both the Tannin (pl.) and Leviathan. It is debated whether these names in this psalm represent Pharaoh and Egypt, whom God defeated at the Red Sea, or cosmic foes that God mastered at creation.

In either case, God is praised as mastering fully whatever foe, earthly or cosmic, opposed Israel or was a threat to the order of creation. Because of the symbolic force of these serpentine sea creatures, this text specifically uses the special term "create" *(bara')* for their origin; this is the first use of this term in the days of creation (cf. v. 1). The use of this verb for the sea monsters' origin refutes any belief that such monsters were co-eternal with God or possessed power that in any way rivaled God's. There is no place in this creation account for cosmic dualism. Then **God blessed** these created life forms, empowering them **to be fruitful, increase,** and **fill** their respective spheres.

1:24–25 / On the sixth day, as on the third day, there were two stages of creation. The animals brought forth on this day occupied the land created on the third day. God began by ordering **the land** to **produce living creatures: livestock,** or large four-footed beasts, **creatures that move along the ground, and wild animals.** This division of animals into domestic and wild is inherent to the created order. In this command God endowed the land *('erets)* with additional generative power. **God saw** that what was made **was good.**

1:26 / Before undertaking the next act of creation God took counsel. This unique reference to God's reflecting in community before making something underscores both the importance and the uniqueness of what God was about to create. That community is either the plurality of the deity or the heavenly council that is witnessed in several texts (1 Kgs. 22:19–22; Job 1:6–12). God considered making humans in God's **image** and **likeness.** Image *(tselem)* and likeness *(demut)* are used in similar ways in the OT. "Image" refers to a copy or a close representation (it is also used infrequently for an idol; Num. 33:52; Ezek. 7:20; 16:17). "Likeness" emphasizes the comparison of one object with another or the correspondence between two objects. Each word tempers the other. The use of two terms for the comparison of humans with God, coupled with God's use of plural pronouns in taking counsel, guards against the belief that humans are divine. Humans, bearing the image of God, therefore are truly like God, but they are not identical to God.

1:27 / The combination of the special term "create" *(bara';* v. 1), its threefold repetition, and the phrase **image of God** conveys that in making humans God reached the goal of creation.

"Create," used elsewhere in the days of creation only with the great creatures of the sea (v. 21), informs us that God was personally involved in the origin of humankind. **Man,** in the statement **God created** man (*'adam*), is a collective standing for all humanity, that is, those God made at the beginning as well as their descendants.

The placement of "the image of God" at the center of a chiastic arrangement stresses its importance, as does the repetition of "the image." There has been an abundance of scholarly discussion about this evocative phrase, for the text does not explicitly define its meaning. Nevertheless, the way "the image of God" functions in this context and in 9:5–6 gives insight into its significance. It conveys here that humans have the highest position in the created order. As God's representatives on earth, humans were invested by God with authority to subdue the earth and rule over the animals (v. 28; see P. Bird, "Male and Female He Created Them," *HTR* 74 [1981], pp. 129–59, esp. pp. 138, 154).

Genesis 9:5–6 states that every person is inviolate by reason of being made in God's image. Besides making murder a heinous crime, this text opposes any type of caste or slavery system. Furthermore, the image carries profound moral implications. Both Testaments teach that whatever one person does to another affects God (e.g., Amos 2:7; 1 John 4:20). A person's manner of interacting with other humans characterizes the way that one relates to God. Moreover, because God made humans in his image, God yearns to redeem those who have disobeyed him by providing the means for them to receive forgiveness and reconciliation.

Male and female he created them. The Hebrew emphasizes the phrase "male and female" by placing it before the verb. This third and final part of the verse contains four important ideas. (a) It ascribes sexuality to God's design for humans. Thus, an essential aspect of human nature is quite different from God's nature. An implication of this is that we need to draw on the outstanding qualities found in each gender to have a full view of God. If we imagine God as predominantly male or female, our picture is partial and distorted. (b) This reference to human sexuality sets the stage for God's blessing humans with fertility and commanding them to populate the earth (v. 28). (c) This phrase establishes the fact that every male and every female is made in God's image. In the essence of being human there is no qualitative difference between male and female. (d) We learn that God made humans as social creatures who discover their identity and destiny in relationships characterized by rapprochement. "Male and female" conveys that the basic reciprocating human relationship is between a man and a woman (see Gen. 2:21–24). Beyond that basic relationship, humans form communities for sustaining and enriching their lives. Living and working together is thus an integral expression of being in the image of God.

Another one of the many important aspects of being human that this section explores is the ability to handle the word, or language. God recognized this ability at the beginning by blessing humans and giving them instructions (vv. 28–30). God can converse with those in his image, and Scripture is a record of those conversations. Moreover, conversation enables humans to have genuine fellowship with God. This is the basis for God's calling of Abraham, in which God established a people who would worship him wholeheartedly. Through conversation people also communicate with each other and thereby gain insight into their own identities. Rich personal interchange brings humans great joy, for it flows out of the innermost being, that is, the aspect of humanity that is in the image of God.

In addition, the ability to handle words raises human acts above biological necessity as it enables a person to conceptualize, plan, evaluate, and anticipate. Being cognizant of what they are doing, humans bear responsibility for their deeds. Skill with words also opens the pursuit of wisdom to humans. Words then become an avenue for humans to exercise their creative instincts.

1:28–31 / God empowered humans with a special blessing in which he commanded them to **be fruitful and increase** in order that they might **fill the earth and subdue** (*kibbesh*) **it.** While the human capability to reproduce is inherent in the human physical constitution, fertility results from God's blessing. This belief differentiated Israel's understanding of fertility from that of its neighbors, who believed that fertility rites practiced at local shrines enabled their lands, flocks, and wives to produce abundantly.

God assigned humans rule over all animals: **the fish of the sea and the birds of the air and . . . every living creature that moves on the ground.** "Rule" (*radah*) means that humans are to promote the well-being of the animals and protect them from danger just as a monarch fosters the welfare of the citizens. "Subdue" (*kibbesh*) is even stronger than "rule"; it means "conquer, subjugate." B. Lohfink demonstrates that this word should be

translated with as little drama as possible; he suggests "take possession of" (*The Theology of the Pentateuch* [Minneapolis: Fortress,
1994], pp. 10–11). Although these commands empower humans
to be masters of the animal kingdom and by extension the earth,
they do not give them the right to abuse or to kill animals wantonly. Nor do they ordain humans to rule imprudently by abusing
the earth so that nature no longer supports the various species.
Such an abuse of authority would be a distortion of God's purpose, which includes working for the benefit of those under
human authority. That God made animals and humans on the
same day, and the fact that they belong to the same classification
of living creatures, attest to their closeness. Consequently, in promoting the welfare of animals, humans advance their own well-
being.

In addition, God gave humans access to **every seed-bearing
plant . . . and every tree that has fruit,** and God assigned to all the
animals **every green plant for food.** This beneficial word on behalf of the animals, given in the context of God's blessing humans,
confirms that God entrusted the care of the animals to humans.

On the sixth day **God saw** that **all that he had made . . . was
very good.** Every part of creation supported all life forms as God
had made them. Everything was beautiful in a setting of complete
harmony. The entire created order honored the human exercise of
moral obedience to God.

2:1–3 / A summary statement tells us that the creation of
the heavens and the earth was **completed.** Since the cosmos was
exactly as God wished and since the world was capable of continuing on its own, **on the seventh day** God **rested.** In resting God
showed that he was neither bound to the creation for support nor
limited in any way by it.

God blessed the seventh day, setting it apart from all other
days by making **it holy.** From the premise that seven units symbolize wholeness or completeness, God's sanctifying the seventh
day certified that the creation was finished and perfect. In doing
this God was expressing divine sovereignty over time. God separated time into ordinary time and holy time, for God did not want
humans to become slaves to endless work. So humans are to rest
one day in every seven in order to praise God and enjoy both the
creation, the result of God's labors, and the results of their own
work. Holy time, therefore, adds meaning to activity done in regular time. Observance of holy time also refreshes the human

spirit, adding a depth of meaning to life. God ties his deliverance of Israel out of Egypt into the observance of the seventh day (Deut. 5:12–15). Thus, on the Sabbath Israel worshiped the God of creation who was also the God of the exodus. In worshiping this great God regularly, humans exercise the spiritual dimension of being in God's image.

2:4a / God's creation of the earth ends with **this is the account of the heavens and the earth when they were created.** This is the first of ten *toledoth* formulas that mark the major divisions of Genesis (see Introduction). *Toledoth* is Hebrew for "generations or genealogy." This formula stands both as a heading to a genealogy (e.g., 5:1) and as an introduction to a narrative having little or no genealogical material (e.g., 37:2). Thus the NIV often renders it "account." This term developed in the direction of family history, for the Hebrews liked to include anecdotal notes in their genealogies. Therefore, other versions sometimes translate *toledoth* as "family history" or "narrative history." In heading a new section it usually names the father of the central figure in that section. Only here does *toledoth* point to the origin of something other than humans. In speaking of the origin of the heavens and the earth it is not implying that the world came into being by natural generation. Rather, it conveys that the heavens and the earth were going to generate a variety of life forms.

Additional Notes §1

1:2 / While many readers understand "earth" to be our planet, the ancients had no concept of a solar system. For them, "earth" was the vast land mass established over the primordial ocean.

The precise meaning of *ruah 'elohim*, "the Spirit of God," is debated. Grammarians have established that *'elohim* is sometimes used as a superlative for the preceding noun; e.g., the phrase "the cedars of God" means "the mighty or majestic cedars." Possibly, then, *'elohim* with *ruah* means "a mighty wind." However, *'elohim* means "God" in thirty other occurrences in this account. A sound exegetical principle is that when the meaning of a term is clearly established in a given text, it has that meaning in each of its occurrences unless a definitive signal indicates otherwise. Since there is no such signal here, it is most likely that *'elohim* here means "God."

In Deut. 32:11, the same word used for "hovering" in Gen. 1:2 (Hb. *r-kh-p*) is used to describe an eagle circling back and forth, ready to swoop under any of its young that grow weary and need to be carried back to the nest on their parent's back. However, in the Ugaritic Tale of Aqhat (Aqht C, 31), the same word is used of the eagle circling about its prey as it prepares to strike. The latter picture seems to fit this text better.

It is interesting to note that the Spirit here is portrayed in the imagery of a large bird of prey, whereas in rabbinic sources before the coming of Jesus and at Jesus' baptism the Spirit is depicted as a dove (Matt. 3:16). The significance of these two very different metaphors for the Spirit is, however, not clear.

1:3 / The presence of light before the creation of the sun is inconceivable from our contemporary understanding of the universe. However, it was possible according to the view of the ancient Hebrews; several OT texts speak of light existing independently of the stars (Job 38:19–20; Isa. 30:26; 60:19–20).

Separation is a major activity in establishing the created order: light from darkness, day from night, upper waters from lower waters, and dry land from water. Separation of the profane from the holy is also a central theme in the law (Lev. 10:10; 11:47) and in the final judgment (Rev. 20:4–6).

1:4 / The term "good" here carries several meanings, including aesthetic and moral; i.e., what God created was beautiful and promoted the moral order.

1:5 / Ancient readers would have taken "day" to be an ordinary day. It is possible that day represents an age, but the text does not readily support that position. A seven-day week of creation anchors the weekly pattern in the created order.

1:10 / Hb. "sea" *(yam)* includes larger bodies of salt water and lakes, e.g., the Sea of Galilee.

1:14–19 / The sun, the moon, and the stars were mighty forces in God's heavenly army. At creation they were members of the heavenly chorus that sang praises glorifying God's work (Job 38:7). God, the director of their course (Isa. 40:26), could marshal them to help defeat Israel's foes (Judg. 5:20). Psalm 121:6 reflects both the fears of the ancient Hebrews that on a long journey the sun or moon might strike them and their faith that God would prevent this from happening.

1:21 / While there is no hint of conflict during God's creating, the OT does witness to such conflict in describing God's defeat of the enemies of Israel. For example, God smashed the great sea creature by defeating the forces that opposed God's people (e.g., Ps. 74:13–14; Isa. 51:9–10). Eschatological texts employ the imagery of opposing creatures to describe God's final defeat of all forces hostile to his rule (e.g., Isa. 27:1).

1:26 / With whom did God enter into counsel? There are many proposals: (a) God took counsel with wisdom (Prov. 8:22–31). But this text does not mention wisdom. (b) "We" is a polite manner of self-expression. But this custom is not attested among the Hebrews (GKC §124gN).

(c) "We" is the plural of majesty (Gen. 11:7; Isa. 6:8). But such usage is not attested for a pronoun in Hb. (Joüon §114eN). (d) "We" was used as an ancient literary device for a person's speaking to himself. But this device is not commonly used in Scripture. (e) The plural reflects the multiplicity within God himself, coinciding with the plural form of *'elohim* in Hb. However, this name of God is used throughout the account as a singular. (f) This "we" reflects the Trinity. The church fathers (e.g., *Barn.* and Justin Martyr) held this view. While the plural pronoun does acquire fuller meaning in light of the coming of Christ, it did not convey to ancient Israel any idea of God's being triune. The following two proposals find the most support in Scripture: (g) God took counsel with his Spirit (so D. Clines, "The Image of God in Man," *TynBul* 19 [1968], p. 68; cf. v. 2). This theory has the advantage of finding the conversation partner in the text. (h) "We" refers to the heavenly council over whom God rules (1 Kgs. 22:19–22; Job 1:6–12; 2:1–7; Ps. 82; it was common for deity to hold councils in Near Eastern myths). Before creating humans, this position argues, God entered into deliberations with this council since their role and destiny would be affected by human behavior. God's words after the first couple ate of the forbidden fruit support this position: they have "become like one of us, knowing good and evil" (3:22).

Is there any connection between the human body and the image of God? The Hebrews viewed each person as a whole, consisting of spirit/breath and body. Since for the Hebrews any separation of the spirit from the body resulted in death, the image of God must include the body. Moreover, there has to be enough correspondence between the human body and the image for God to appear on earth as recognizably human (e.g., the angel of Yahweh, 18:2). Thus the corporeal dimension of human life bears witness in some way to the image of God. This position is crucial for the NT teaching of the incarnation. Genesis 1 emphasizes the theme of separation that is foundational to the ritual purity system; humans are separated from animals by being made in the image of God (this concept rules out bestiality, for example), and the divine creator is very distinct from the created world and its beings. Therefore, Israel denigrated any view that held that a human was a god. It rejected the existence of heroes who were a blend of divinity and humanity (such as Gilgamesh, the legendary ruler of Uruk, who was two-thirds divine). Israel also rejected the view that human rulers were divine or became divine at death. This boundary also means that God is never to be lowered to a human level and so made it difficult for some Jews to accept the NT teaching that God took on human form in Jesus. Thus, the teaching that God created humans in the image of God is essential for the incarnation, for it provides an ontological basis for God's Son clothing himself in human flesh. Thus Jesus is uniquely the image of God (2 Cor. 4:4; Col. 1:15).

Whether the addition of the word "likeness" places more or less distance between God and humans is debated (e.g., H. Preuss, *"damah,"* *TDOT* 3:259, versus Clines, "The Image of God in Man," p. 91).

1:27 / Ancient Near Eastern texts from Egypt and Mesopotamia use the phrase "image of God" to mean an exalted position. Egyptian texts contain many references to the Pharaoh as the image of God.

This accords with their belief that Pharaoh was god incarnate and the son of the god Re. There are also a few references in Mesopotamian texts to a monarch's being in the image of god. This title "the image of god" gave the ruler royal status and defined his role as the god's viceroy on earth. In these two cultures the image of god was primarily limited to the monarch, though in Mesopotamia the phrase referred a few times to a high official. By contrast, Scripture asserts that all humans are in God's image. The biblical account of creation, therefore, has a democratizing force as it assigns a high status to all humans.

The high position of humans in Gen. stands out even more by comparison with the role humans had in the Old Babylonian myth Atrahasis (W. Lambert and A. Millard, *Atra-Hasis: The Babylonian Story of the Flood* [Oxford: Clarendon, 1969]). At the beginning numerous gods had the task of laboring to feed the ruling gods. After forty years of such wearisome toil, these gods grew tired, burned all their tools, and quit working. Enlil, the storm god, decided to deal with their rebellion by killing one god. Enki, the god of wisdom, prepared clay mixed with the dead god's blood and flesh. Then Nintu, mother earth, pinched off fourteen pieces of clay and molded them into seven pairs of humans. After ten months these humans came forth from some kind of a womb (unfortunately the text is broken at this place). The gods then imposed on the humans the toil formerly done by the gods. In this myth humans are the slaves of the gods. But in Gen. all humans, not just the royal line, bear God's image and thus have regal standing.

Some excellent sources on the image of God include J. Barr, "The Image of God in the Book of Genesis—A Study in Terminology," *BJRL* 51 (1968/69), pp. 11–26; Bird, "Male and Female He Created Them"; Clines, "The Image of God in Man," repr. as "Humanity As the Image of God," in *On the Way to the Postmodern: Old Testament Essays, 1967–1998*, vol. 2 (JSOTSup 293; Sheffield: Sheffield Academic Press, 1998), pp. 447–97; G. Jónsson, *The Image of God: Genesis 1:26–28 in a Century of Old Testament Research* (ConBOT 26; Stockholm: Almqvist & Wiksell, 1988); J. F. Kutsko, *Between Heaven and Earth: Divine Presence and Absence in the Book of Ezekiel* (Biblical and Judaic Studies 7; Winona Lake, Ind.: Eisenbrauns, 2000).

1:28 / *Radah* means to rule supremely (1 Kgs. 4:24; 9:23; Isa. 14:2; Ezek. 34:4). Often such rule is implemented by great force (Lev. 26:7; Isa. 14:6), but that does not have to be the case (Ps. 68:28; H.-J. Zobel, "radah," *ThWAT* 7:354–56). The use of *kibbesh* ("subjugate") confirms that this term may connote the exertion of strength in ruling. This concession does not mean, as some people have vociferously argued, that God empowered humans to exploit either the animal or the natural world. The exploitation of nature that has led to the current ecological crisis cannot legitimately be laid at the doorstep of this command. Additional support comes from Lohfink's argument that in this setting *radah* means "care for, manage" (*Theology of the Pentateuch*, p. 12). From another direction we must acknowledge that the primary reason for the ecological crisis of the twenty-first century is human greed, a motivation Scripture soundly denounces. Another possible reason for the use of these strong terms is anticipation of the great effort humans would have to exert in making a living from a harsh world.

2:1–3 / Israel's calendar identified every day by an ordinal number except the seventh day, which was called Sabbath, "rest." This custom was a reaction to the way Israel's neighbors named the days of the week after gods. The term "Sabbath" does not appear here, perhaps because this account looks at the created order before Israel's existence and the giving of the fourth commandment in the Decalogue (Exod. 20:8–11). This text nevertheless provides a foundation in the created order for the observance of the Sabbath.

2:4a / Scholars debate whether the first half of v. 4 belongs with the preceding narrative or with the following one, as the NIV divides the sections. Many contemporary scholars take it as the heading to the next section of Gen. (2:4b–4:26), since all other occurrences of this formula stand at the head of a section. Nevertheless, three factors favor taking this formula with the preceding account. First, it uses "create" *(bara')*, which occurs six times in Gen. 1 but never in Gen. 2:4b–3:24. Second, 2:4a contains the seventh occurrence of *bara'*, which is very significant since the author relishes patterns of seven: the nodal term "good" occurs seven times; the opening sentence has seven Hb. words; creation is divided into seven days; and each of the first three stichoi (or verses of poetry) of the seventh day contains seven words (2:1–2a). The third factor is that heavens and earth with the article occur here in the same order as in 1:1 (also 2:1); thus the two lines form an inclusio. By contrast, these terms in 2:4b occur in inverted order and, more importantly, without the article. Thus the *toledoth* formula here marks the first division of Genesis (1:1–4:26). The reason for its unusual placement is that the author gives priority to the definitive heading (1:1). Since this line contains the seventh occurrence of *bara'*, it is probable that the editor of the first section of Genesis (1:1–4:26) is likely the author of the creation account (1:1–2:4a).

§2 Excursus: Comments on the Creation Account in Relationship to Scientific Views of Origins

A perplexing question facing us is how to read this account in light of scientific theories of origin. Several observations provide some perspective on this question. The length of this account, about a single printed page, greatly limits the information it can provide, and its antiquity means that its viewpoint and its approach will be vastly different from a scientific outlook. It would be impossible for a brief account of creation to address communities of faith over a span of at least thirty centuries and at the same time speak in a way that is compatible with a scientific outlook that is itself ever changing.

One of the major goals of this passage is to counter mythical accounts of origins. In fact, this account contributes to a scientific approach to nature by teaching the unity and coherence of the created order. The teaching that God created the world in wisdom (especially Prov. 8:22–31) encourages the study of nature for gaining knowledge and insight.

This ancient text, therefore, moves beyond mythopoetic thought and toward scientific thinking by denying that the various forces of nature are gods, possessing will, as most of the ancients believed. This text organizes all elements of the created order under one principle—the command of God. In order for science to become a discipline of study, humans had to arrive at the belief that the world is governed by a unifying force. Furthermore, this account represents an attempt, albeit primitive, to organize and classify elements of the cosmos. Since it speaks of God and not a cosmological first principle, it does not immediately lead to a scientific outlook. Such an outlook developed only after those who held this biblical view of creation were influenced by the rediscovery of Greek speculative philosophy.

Although this text does not present a comprehensive description of the order of the cosmos, it cannot be said that it has no regard for cosmology. In addition to its primary goal of establishing key truths about the earth for the proper worship of God, it may also speak about patterns that are in accord with the origin of the solar system. Consequently some of its ideas are compatible with scientific explanations, while others seem far removed. For example, the description of the heavens as a solid dome holding back the heavenly ocean (1:6–8) yields no scientific meaning today, but God's commanding and thereby empowering the earth to produce vegetation and living creatures of various kinds (1:11–12, 24) fits well with the view that species change, adapt, and produce new forms.

Scientists put forth theories about the origin of life, all of which are speculative. Some of these theories are in greater conflict with the account of Genesis 1 than are others. Only as science comes to know more about the actual origin of life on earth will the continuity between this account of creation and scientific theories of origins potentially increase. In the meantime, acknowledging the purposes and the limitations of both scientific knowledge and scriptural truth is necessary for insightful interchange between these two approaches. Ultimately there can be no major conflict between the two approaches, for the world studied by science is the one created by God.

Because of the tension between this biblical account of origin and those of science, biblical theology has focused its exposition on God's saving deeds, shunning references to creation. However, issues such as human equality, including that of male and female, and ecological conservation have rekindled interest in the scriptural teaching on creation. Tremendous advances in scientific knowledge have brought a greater awareness of the limitations of human knowledge, but in reaction the human spirit has sought to assert its spiritual transcendence over the determinism underlying certain scientific approaches. This resurgence centers on the mystic wonder found throughout the world order.

Accompanying this resurgence is a renewed interest in conversations between science and religion. According to W. Brueggemann, two key factors that OT studies may contribute to this discussion are the mystery that transcends the material world and the ethical restraints inherent in the creation process ("The Loss and Recovery of Creation in the Old Testament Theology," *TT* 53 [1996], p. 187). Therefore, it is important to listen again to the biblical account of creation for its contributions to the human spirit and human insight.

§3 The Adventures in the Garden of Eden of the First Humans (Gen. 2:4b–3:24)

This narrative addresses the most troubling question faced by every human: "Why must I die?" In addition it gives a reason for several fundamental features of human experience—wearing clothes, pain in childbirth, toil and sweat in work, growth of thorns and thistles, and the enmity between humans and snakes. Much more importantly, this simple account offers penetrating insight into the human condition before God as well as giving the reason for the deep tensions between husband and wife and between humans and God.

The drama of this narrative is in seven sections, set in a palistrophic (chiastic) pattern.

> A God forms the man and places him in Eden (2:4b–17)
> > B God makes a woman to complement the man (2:18–25)
> > > C The serpent and the woman talk (3:1–5)
> > > > D The couple eats from the tree of the knowledge of good and evil (3:6–8)
> > > C' God interrogates the man and the woman (3:9–13)
> > B' God pronounces punishments (3:14–21)
> A' God expels the couple from the garden (3:22–24)

At the center (D) stands the report of these humans' deciding to disobey God. The interchange among the man, the woman, and the serpent provides dramatic movement, and it captures how motivation to disobey God rises from an inversion of the order of responsibility that God had established.

In act 1 the narrator introduces the characters and defines the crucial props in a topical, not a chronological, order (2:4b–25). Emphasis is on the origin of the man, the woman, and the animals and their relationship to each other. The fact that there is no concern for elements vital to the creation, such as light, seas, heavens, moon, stars, and sea creatures, confirms that this text is not a second creation account parallel to Genesis 1.

2:4b–6 / In a style typical of ancient Near Eastern texts about origins, this account opens with a description of what did not yet exist: before **God made the earth and the heavens—and no shrub . . . had yet appeared** and **no plant . . . had yet sprung up,** since there was neither **rain** nor any human **to work the ground.** Earth stands before the heavens (in contrast to 1:1), preparing the reader for the events that are to take place in the garden of Eden. This wording also implies that humans are necessary for the land to be cultivated. A parenthetical statement reports that beneath the ground **streams** swelled to water the earth's surface. Water symbolizes the potential for the barren earth to support all kinds of life forms, just as the Spirit of God being over the deep held the potential for God to order the chaos into cosmos (1:2).

The primary name for God in this account is LORD God (*yahweh 'elohim*), disclosing that the transcendent God the Creator was also intimately involved with humans as Lord or Yahweh, especially in the events in the garden. This is the only place in Genesis where these two names occur together, and reasons for the repeated use of this double name here elude us.

2:7 / Like a potter, **God formed** (*yatsar*) **man** (*'adam*) **from the dust of the ground** (*'adamah*). There is a wordplay between "man" and "ground." "Ground" represents red soil (from the root *'-d-m*, "red"). Whether it indicates that the man's skin was copper-colored is difficult to determine. Furthermore, *'adam* is particularly hard to translate, for it is used for all humans as well as for the name of the first man. Versions vary widely in rendering *'adam* as Adam or man. The KJV renders it Adam eighteen times out of the thirty-four occurrences, but the NIV translates it Adam only four times (2:20; 3:17, 20, 21), emphasizing the representative role of the first human. Agreeing with this interpretation, this commentary renders *'adam* as "man" until the woman has the name Eve (3:20); then Adam is used. Thereby the representative role of the first man and the first woman is kept in the foreground throughout the narrative.

God then **breathed into** the man's **nostrils the breath of life,** and he **became a living being** (*nepesh khayyah*). The latter phrase classifies humans as members of the animal world (2:19), while "breath" establishes that humans continually and uniquely depend on God for their life force (Job 27:3). Whenever God takes the breath away, that person dies (Ps. 104:29–30).

2:8–9 / **God . . . planted a garden in the east, in Eden; and there he put the man.** The garden was located at the center of the earth, somewhere to the east of the narrator. In the garden God planted **all kinds of trees.** Trees represent the majestic beauty of the garden as well as providing **food,** shade, and shelter for the animals. **In the middle of the garden** God planted **the tree of life** (2:15–17). Nearby was **the tree of the knowledge of good and evil.** In the Hebrew, in contrast to the wording of the NIV, the tree of life was the tree in the middle of the garden.

2:10–14 / A parenthetical paragraph gives information either to anchor the garden of Eden to a definite geography, to place the origin of four great rivers in primeval time, or both. Rising from a huge spring fed by the great deep, the river flowed through Eden and then divided into **four** branches that brought water to the various quarters of the earth.

Two of the rivers are **the Tigris** and **the Euphrates.** The identities of **the Pishon** and **the Gihon** are uncertain, but the Pishon carried water to **Havilah,** a part of southeastern Arabia, rich in **gold** (10:7, 29; 25:18; 1 Sam. 15:7; 1 Chron. 1:9, 23). Other valuable items, possibly **aromatic resin and onyx** (the meaning of the Hebrew terms is unknown), were found there. This fact informs us that God provided an abundance of wealth on the earth.

2:15–17 / The main story resumes with the repetition of words from verse 8. God assigned Adam to **work and take care of** (lit. "keep," *shamar*) the garden. The meaning of *shamar* here is "to take care of" something like a member of the flock (30:31). From the beginning God charged man with responsible work.

In addition, God gave the man two specific commandments, one affirmative and one prohibitive. God generously granted man unlimited access to the fruit of all the trees, including the tree of life, which held the possibility of unending life for humans as long as they ate of its fruit. In the tree God provided the opportunity for patterns of obedience. With the second command God prohibited the man from eating **from the tree of the knowledge of good and evil** under penalty of death (on the significance of this tree, see 3:5). This penalty takes the form found in threats made by kings, in which the king has discretion as to the manner of enforcing the penalty (20:7; 1 Sam. 14:39, 44; 22:16), not the form found in legal texts, in which the king has no such prerogative (G. Wenham, *Genesis 1–15* [WBC 1; Dallas: Word, 1987], p. 67).

Giving these commands conveyed that humans are moral: they could choose either to obey or to disobey God's commands. Obeying God would lead to abundance and the possibility of endless life, but disobeying God would place them under the death penalty.

By giving humans such a prohibition, God was mercifully providing them a tangible symbol of their moral nature. Some people argue, however, that the presence of this tree made it impossible for humans not to sin, given the human proclivity to do what is prohibited. But those who hold this position fail to consider that the first humans did not yet have any inclination of asserting themselves above God. It is difficult for us on this side of Eden to discern how a limit guards freedom rather than serving as a temptation to do what is forbidden. God was protecting human freedom by setting this restriction.

2:18–20a / God perceived that **it** was **not good for the man to be alone.** In striking contrast to the frequent use of "good" in the creation account (1:1–2:4a), God here states that there is something that is not good in regard to the man. This wording grabs our attention as it highlights something that God must provide in order for the man to be fulfilled. This surprising use of "good" communicates how crucial companionship is for humans. The man needed **a helper,** one **suitable for him.** "Suitable" *(negdo)* suggests a person who was significantly different from him so as to contribute distinctively to his life, yet one who was of the same essence and on the same level. "Helper" implies the ability to assist another person. A helper may be inferior or superior, the latter concept substantiated by references to God as the helper of Israel (e.g., Deut. 33:7, 26, 29; Ps. 33:20). By definition, the person needing help admits some type of limitation.

God, the Creator, knew that a man by himself could not experience the full dimensions of human existence. Although the man had to have a complement in order to have offspring, "suitable" suggests that this helping counterpart would also provide enriching companionship. God made humans to find a depth of meaning to life by living together in families.

In the search for this helper God **formed** *(yatsar)* the animals and the birds **out of the ground** (*'adamah;* v. 7). The use of the same verb and the same material as in the formation of the man underscores the bond between humans and animals. Each is a **living creature** *(nepesh khayyah).* The NIV obscures this connection since it has "being" for the man (v. 7) and "creature" for the animals. In addition, the NIV understands that the animals already existed by translating the verb as a past perfect, **had formed.** Usually this type of Hebrew verb describes consecutive action in a narrative. Then the sense is that, after making this assessment about the man, God proceeded to form the animals.

God then **brought** the animals **to the man,** empowering him with the task of naming *(qara')* these new creatures. In so doing, God acknowledged that the man possessed the insight or wisdom necessary for giving each animal a name appropriate to its nature. The man was searching for a true complement while performing this task, but he found none.

2:20b–23 / Since the man found **no suitable helper** among the animals, God set about to make one. Whereas the man's origin is recounted in one verse (v. 7), the origin of the woman is told in three verses, emphasizing God's care in making one who was so important for the man and for the achievement of God's goal in creating. The fact that she is the last of God's creations in this account also conveys her importance.

For this operation **God caused . . . a deep sleep** to fall on the man. God sometimes used such a deep sleep when he communicated directly with a human (15:12). Being asleep, the man did not contribute anything to the woman's structure or character.

In order that the helper might fully correspond to the man, God made her from a part of the man's side rather than of the dust from which he had created both the man and the animals. "Side" is a better rendering for *tsela'* (so NIV margin) than **rib,** for it conveys that God took both bone and flesh for building or constructing *(banah)* the woman. The use of "build" instead of "form" underscores that the woman was made of the same substance and according to the same model as the man. Furthermore, the fact that God made the woman establishes her as a person in her own right. These details teach that no other living creature could ever become woman's rival in serving as man's helper, counterpart, and intimate companion (1:26–27).

On seeing the woman for the first time the man exclaimed ecstatically that she was **bone of** his **bones** and **flesh of** his **flesh,** meaning that she was one with whom he desired to establish a bonding relationship. She truly was the helper, complement, and companion God perceived that the man needed (v. 18). This phraseology certainly conveys that the two were on the same level. The man went on to say she **shall be called "woman"** *('ishah)* since he was **man** *('ish)*. The similarity in the sound of these two Hebrew words underscores that a man may find a true counterpart in a woman and vice versa. It is important to note that "called" *(niqra')* is in the passive and lacks the term *shem*, "name." The man was not naming her but was identifying their commonness in difference (P. Trible, *God and the Rhetoric of Sexuality* [OBT; Philadelphia: Fortress, 1978], pp. 99–100). This is confirmed by the general terms of identification, "man" and "woman"; these terms convey the respective sexuality of each of them. The close bond between them, enriched by their sexual differences, afforded them companionship that overcame loneliness. So together a couple finds fulfillment in life.

2:24 / The narrator's comment here is an aside from the main story, for it speaks about parents, and these first humans had no parents.

In joining with a woman, **a man will leave** his parents. Some interpreters have taken this extraordinary wording as assuming a matriarchal order, but the context does not sustain this view. Consequently, this wording is a shocking rhetorical device that communicates how radically marriage alters a son's authority lines, especially in a patriarchal family. In antiquity parents arranged marriages at significant financial cost, and the groom's parents might easily have thought that they had authority over their son despite the marriage. Therefore the son must leave his parents by breaking the authority line to them and honor his wife as his true counterpart, the central person in his life.

Furthermore, this instruction provides perspective on the commandment to honor one's father and mother (Exod. 20:12; Lev. 19:3). It preempts parents from using the fifth commandment to challenge the supreme place a wife has for their son. This does not mean a son no longer has responsibilities to his parents, but it does mean his wife has a higher standing.

A man also must strive to prevent any dissolution of the relationship by clinging or cleaving (*dabaq*, NIV **be united**) to his wife. Clinging conveys commitment to maintaining the union in loyal love. The Hebrew term does not emphasize the sexual side of the relationship; rather, it describes the closeness and the enduring quality of the bond between people, whether it is among women (Ruth 1:14) or among men (Prov. 18:24; G. Wallis, "*dabaq*," *TDOT* 3:81). In a relationship of mutual trust, a male and a female are free to be open and vulnerable in each other's presence; their commitment to each other provides a secure setting for them to explore their God-given sexuality. The bond between the marriage partners grows as each person contributes significantly to the other's life. Marriage, then, is one community in which a man and a woman can establish the rapprochement that is possible because humans are made in the image of God. The use of "cling" supports this claim, for in Deuteronomy it describes the desired way Israel is to relate to Yahweh, with whom the nation is in covenant (e.g., Deut. 10:20; 11:22; 13:4).

The declaration **they will become one flesh** describes further the unity of a man and a woman. The focus is not on the resulting sexual relationship or the children to be born, though it does not exclude these expressions of their union. Rather, the emphasis is on the spiritual and social unity of the new couple. In becoming one flesh a man and a woman become more closely bonded than their blood kinship (Wenham, *Genesis 1–15*, p. 71). This understanding of the union between a man and a woman is the grounds for the laws of incest (Lev. 18, 20). Because the deepest human relationship is found in marriage, any spouse's abuse or domination of the other denies their mutuality and disrupts the harmony God intended. Divorce, moreover, is a shattering experience.

2:25 / The first human pair were **naked** *('arummim)* and in harmony with each other, all members of the created order, and God. Completely innocent, humans were without **shame.** The use of this symbolism is forceful in light of the strong Israelite aversion to immodesty (cf. Gen. 9:22–23; Exod. 20:26).

3:1–5 / Act 2 of the drama begins with the introduction of a new actor, **the serpent,** one **of the wild animals the LORD God had made** (2:19). The serpent is described as **more crafty** *('arum)* than the other animals. *'Arum* makes a wordplay on "naked" *('arummim)*, which occurs in 2:25, and thus establishes a tie between the two acts.

"Crafty" can describe a positive trait ("prudent, clever, discerning") or a negative trait ("cunning, wily"). When craftiness is used for ill, it leads to masterful manipulation of others (Exod. 21:14; Josh. 9:4; Job 5:12; 15:5; Ps. 83:3). But when it is used for good, this trait enables a person to escape evil and to perform remarkable deeds (Prov. 1:4; 12:23; 13:16; 14:8, 15; 22:3). As the most astute creature, the serpent held the highest position among the animals. Given its description as "more crafty," it is not surprising that this creature, which represents the animals and the forces of nature, could speak.

The serpent initiated conversation with the woman. Her lack of surprise and the depth of the discussion suggest that this was not their first conversation. The serpent would have learned about God's commands from the humans, and the only means the serpent had of influencing their behavior was reason. While the serpent could explore possibilities with humans, it had no means of coercing them to take a certain course. Consequently, whatever decision the humans would make was grounded in their wills, and they bore full culpability for that decision.

At the outset the serpent expressed its astonished disbelief that God would not let the humans eat fruit from the trees in the garden. Its skeptical approach drew the woman into discussion and opened her to considering that God might have acted out of self-serving motives. With this twisted assertion the inquisitor cast a shadow over God's benevolence.

The woman wisely sought to correct the serpent by stating God's two commands. She said that God had permitted them to eat from any tree. But in stating the prohibition she made three small alterations. She first added the restriction that a person **must not touch** the tree **in the middle of the garden,** an addition that made God's command appear more stringent than it was. Next, in restating the permission and the penalty she left out the emphatic tone God had used, thereby softening God's generosity ("you are free to eat" versus "we may eat") and the consequence of violating the command ("you will surely die" versus "you will die"). Finally, in identifying this tree as the one in the middle of the garden, the woman perhaps elevated the importance of this tree above that of the tree of life (2:9). These small but important shifts indicate that the woman had been pondering about how to keep God's command.

The serpent responded cunningly. Using an unusual word order, it cast doubt on whether death was the consequence of eating this fruit. We could translate its opening assertion as either "it is not certain that you will die" or **you will not surely die** (NIV). It is unclear whether the serpent was responding to God's prohibition or to the woman's reformulation of it. In the latter case the serpent would have been denying that touching the tree led to death. Then, if the woman ate of it, the serpent could claim that it had not really misled the woman about *eating* the fruit. By speaking so ambiguously, the serpent kept the woman off guard as it led her to doubt that eating this fruit would bring death.

The serpent then asserted that God had given this restriction in order to prevent humans from becoming like divine beings, **knowing good and evil.** With three potent arguments, the serpent sought to lead the woman and the man to believe that observing the prohibition was foolish. First, God did not intend to put to death anyone who ate of this tree, for like a jealous monarch, God was protecting himself by keeping from them knowledge that would raise their status to that of gods, or heavenly beings. Second, this fruit held the potential for finding self-fulfillment, leading to bold self-assurance in one's own person. Third, eating it would bring them divine, esoteric knowledge. The serpent belittled God as unreasonable in limiting human pleasure and advancement with this prohibition. Rather than making a direct suggestion to disobey God's command, the shrewd serpent indirectly enticed the woman to eat the forbidden fruit. After this exchange the serpent is not heard from again.

What did God not want humans to know? Of the many answers proposed, we will consider three. The first proposal is that the knowledge withheld was about cohabitation. Two details support this position: in the OT "know" may be used euphemistically for sexual intercourse, and eating the fruit made the couple acutely aware of their nakedness. Three facts, however, discount this view: God had instituted marriage for humans to bear offspring; "good" in the OT is never used with sexual overtones; and nakedness usually symbolizes vulnerability, poverty, or shame, not sexual activity (Ezek. 16:7, 22, 39 are exceptions; J. Magonet, "The Themes of Genesis 2–3," in *A Walk in the Garden: Biblical, Iconographical and Literary Images of Eden* [ed. P. Morris and D. Sawyer; JSOTSup 136; Sheffield: JSOT Press, 1992], p. 43).

A second proposal is that if "good and evil" is an example of coupling opposite terms to express a totality, it means "total knowledge." In that light God sought to withhold broad, comprehensive knowledge from humans, but Scripture does not support this view. On the contrary, the sages exhorted youths to get knowledge (Prov. 1:8; 4:7; 5:1–2).

The third proposal is that since "good and evil" often have a moral connotation, the issue at stake was moral knowledge.

"Know" may be interpreted as "to have mastery over." Thus humans were seeking to gain for themselves the prerogative of determining what was good and what was evil.

As humans have learned, gaining the freedom to determine what is good and evil has proven to be a heavy burden, because they must decide continually how they will use everything they have for good and not for evil. This burden is even heavier because the line of demarcation between good and evil is never sharp. This state of affairs explains why so many issues produce strong conflicts in society. When one group advocates a specific position out of concern for the greater good, it arouses resentment in another group at the potential hardship that position will cause the second group. Limited insight clouded by selfish interest leads humans to call good evil and evil good (Isa. 5:20). Whenever society defines an evil as good, a segment of that society suffers oppression.

3:6 / On hearing the serpent's argument, the woman pondered the arguments for and against eating the fruit of this tree. Three strong drives compelled her to eat: physical cravings, aesthetic attraction, and the pride of life or need for self-boasting (1 John 2:16). She perceived that the tree's fruit **was good for food,** stirring within her the desire to taste something new and exotic. And she noticed that the tree was **pleasing to the eye.** The pleasure of having something beautiful tugged at her. She discerned that the tree was **desirable for gaining wisdom** that would give her mastery over her own destiny, that is, the human desire to boast in one's achievements or position. These desires impelled her to take **some** of that fruit **and** eat **it. She also gave some to her husband . . . and he ate it.**

The terse description of this definitive act bypasses many questions that interest readers. What was the discussion between the couple? Did the man seek to dissuade the woman? Did the man encourage her to eat? In the garden the man and the woman were in such agreement that one did what the other did, as the wording "he **was with her**" conveys. In eating, the woman acted in harmony with the man, rather than as an individual set apart from him. This is visible in her use of plural forms in speaking with the serpent, showing that she was speaking for both of them. The serpent likewise used plural forms in addressing the woman. This last fact indicates that the man probably was in hearing range of the conversation between the serpent and the woman. Thus no scene recounts the woman's seeking to influence the man to eat; they were in total accord.

3:7 / The immediate consequences of eating from the tree of knowledge are vividly disclosed. Their act of self-assertion shattered the harmony humans had enjoyed with God, each other, the animals, and the environment.

Instantly becoming aware of their nakedness, the man and woman gathered **fig leaves** and made for themselves makeshift **coverings.** Ironically, the knowledge they acquired did not even give them the skill to make adequate clothing for themselves. Instead of being filled with the pride of achievement and becoming like gods, they were overwhelmed by a deep sense of inadequacy and disturbing self-consciousness.

3:8–13 / When the couple **heard the sound of the LORD God** moving about **in the garden in the cool of the day, they hid . . . among the trees.** Their guilt made them ashamed and fearful of being in God's presence, and the clothing they had made failed to provide them sufficient confidence to meet God. There is further irony here; in striving to become like God they no longer desired to be in God's presence.

Failing to meet the couple in the usual way, the **LORD God called to the man, "Where are you?"** With this simple, open question God was eliciting some explanation for their unusual behavior. Full of guilt, the man answered that being **afraid because** he **was naked,** he had hidden. In seeking to excuse his hiding from God he unwittingly disclosed that he had disobeyed God. Picking up on the man's new awareness, God asked him **who** had **told** him he was **naked.** God went on to ask if he had **eaten from the** restricted **tree.** Before admitting this, the man blamed the woman for having given him some fruit. In an effort to exonerate himself, the man put his relationship with his wife at risk. He even dared to blame God obliquely by identifying the woman as the one whom God had **put with** him in the garden. In striving to become like God the man now mistrusted those closest to him, his counterpart and his Maker.

Without answering the man, God turned to question **the woman** about what had happened. She likewise passed blame, claiming that **the serpent** had **deceived** her. This exchange vividly displays the human traits of making excuses and blaming others instead of acknowledging one's own failure.

3:14–15 / God cursed the serpent and the ground. He did not curse the humans but inflicted pain in their efforts to sustain life, bearing children and producing food. In pronouncing judgment God addressed the parties in inverted order: the serpent, the woman, and the man.

God refused to dignify the serpent by allowing it to account for its involvement in this act of disobedience. Nevertheless, by having encouraged the woman to question God's motivation, the serpent was culpable. God therefore addressed **the serpent,** telling it that it was **cursed** and would **crawl on** its **belly . . . and eat dust.** "Eat dust" is a metaphor for the humiliation of the most exalted animal.

From then on there would be **enmity between** the serpent and **the woman, between** the **offspring** of both. "Offspring" (seed) is singular, connoting all offspring. Serpentine creatures would **strike** at the **heel** of humans, inflicting harm, but the offspring of women would defend themselves by striking a blow, often a fatal one, on the **head** of these creatures. Thus God gave humans the hope of mastering frightful serpents. Metaphorically, this statement meant that humans could rise above natural disasters and forces of evil to fulfill God's commands.

A few late Jewish writers and the church fathers found in this verse a fuller meaning that would one day be realized in the Messiah, when a representative of all humans would strike the serpent, the representative of the forces that oppose God, with a fatal blow. That victory would put an end to the enmity between the serpent and humankind. As Scripture unfolds God's design, it becomes clear that the one to achieve such a major victory is the Messiah (Rom. 16:20), but it would take centuries before any audience would see that meaning in this text.

3:16 / **To the woman** God **said** that he would **greatly increase** her **pains** *('itsabon)* **in childbearing.** In giving birth a woman brings forth new life, thereby finding her highest destiny as man's complement as well as triumphantly challenging death. Furthermore, God informed the woman that from now on stress would exist between her and her **husband.** The woman would have "a **desire**" for her husband, and he in turn would **rule over** her. The use of "rule" intimates that the covenant of marriage (2:23–24) was altered from a reciprocal relationship to one in which a man exercises authority over a woman. In exercising that authority a husband too often inflicts pain on a woman. The woman's "desire," however, makes it hard for her to separate from a man even when she suffers domination or abuse. Alternatively, this "desire" may be interpreted to mean that the woman has a drive to master, even dominate, her husband (S. Foh, "What Is the Woman's Desire?" *WTJ* 37 [1974/75], pp. 376–83). Conflict arises between husband and wife as each party strives to dominate the other.

3:17–19 / God next pronounced punishments against the man for acting as one with the woman in eating the fruit. The man's responsibilities were to obey God and to encourage the woman in obeying God. In the excuses the man put before God there was no hint that he sought to dissuade her from eating this fruit. Thus he failed on two accounts: agreeing with the woman over disobeying God and eating from the tree of knowledge. God declared that **the ground,** the source of life-giving food, was **cursed** because of his act. In contrast to land that is blessed, meaning that it has water and is fertile (Lev. 26:4), land under a curse lacks water, is infertile, and is subject to a variety of plagues (Lev. 26:20). **Thorns and thistles** would grow so thickly that they would rob the soil of moisture and nutrients and choke out the food-bearing plants. Consequently, in working the ground to produce food for life, the man would experience pain (*'itsabon*) from his labor. This term for pain is the same as that for bearing children; similarly in English "labor" is used for work and for bearing children. Thus God did not hold one more blameworthy than the other. The man would now work so hard at producing food that he would **sweat** freely. Affirmatively, God said that **he** would **eat the plants of the field.** God's grace is continually evident, even in judgment.

God placed pain for males and females at the center of the human effort to sustain life. This pain counters the arrogance that motivates humans to build a society apart from God. It also continually reminds humans of their limitations, mortality, and alienation from and dependence on God.

Using an aphorism, God spoke about the inevitable death all humans must face as a consequence of this act of disobedience: **dust you are and to dust you will return.** The certainty of death for all humans is a penalty and not merely a natural process, for God had given humans unlimited access to the tree of life. Is there any connection between this aphorism and the penalty attached to the prohibition against eating from the tree of knowledge? This question arises out of the glaring discrepancy between the penalty and its execution: the penalty for eating from the tree of knowledge implied that if any human ate of its fruit God would straightway set a time for putting to death the guilty, but the first couple lived for hundreds of years after their act of disobedience.

God acted differently from human expectations by displaying mercy in administering this judgment. Nevertheless, God enforced the penalty through a series of steps that eventuate in the inevitable death of every person who lives on earth. First, he pronounced penalties against the man and the woman that altered the character of their earthly life. The pain they experience in the course of sustaining life is the foretaste of death. That foretaste includes feelings of fear, alienation, and mistrust, all of which the first couple experienced after eating the fruit.

Second, God enforced the penalty by expelling Adam and Eve from the garden (vv. 22–24). Wenham likens their expulsion from the garden to the "cut off penalty" attached to several cultic laws (*Genesis 1–15*, p. 74; e.g., Lev. 20:17–18). That penalty deprived a person of access to the tabernacle, God's presence, and community support. In antiquity, whoever was cut off from the support and protection of the community faced a bleak future and mortal danger. Expulsion from the garden was therefore a type of death penalty, underscored here by the loss of access to the tree of life (3:22).

Third, the couple lost access to the abundant supply of food in the garden and had to work the stubborn soil for a seasonal harvest of food that too often was hardly sufficient for the needs of their family. Having to toil in order to live in a harsher environment, the first couple keenly felt the sting of these penalties in daily living. That is, outside the garden the couple continually experienced a foretaste of death.

God's manner of executing this penalty illustrates his character. God acted in mercy, allowing the humans to continue to live. God was true to his word in initiating punishments that led to the eventual execution of the penalty as well as providing a foretaste of death. Thus God carried out the penalty in a sequence of steps: the curses and the punishments, expulsion from the garden, and death itself.

3:20 / **Adam named** (*qara' shem*) the woman **Eve**, that is, "life," for she was to become **the mother of all the living.** By giving her this name Adam asserted that despite the curses pronounced against them the woman would fulfill the destiny of

motherhood for which God had designed her and that he had obligations, such as loving her and protecting her, so that she would
become the mother of all living. Since the woman receives a name
here, this commentary translates *'adam* ("man") by the proper
name Adam when referring to the first man. From this point on
the first couple functioned as two individuals rather than as representatives of all humans.

3:21 / God graciously gave the couple **garments of skin**
to replace the flimsy coverings they had made from fig leaves.
These new garments **clothed them,** providing warmth and protection. God was preparing them for the harsher environment
outside the garden as well as providing them sufficient covering
to be in the divine presence. With this gift God, acting as their
sustainer, expressed his intention to continue to support and fellowship with humans.

3:22–24 / The final scene contrasts sharply with the
opening scene, in which God placed Adam in the garden. Here
God banished the first couple from the garden of Eden to prevent
their eating from **the tree of life** and being able to **live forever**
(2:5–17). Using the plural "us" here for the divine beings, God observed that humans had become like divine beings, **knowing
good and evil.** Outside the garden Adam and Eve settled down **to
work the ground. On the east side of the** garden, that is, at the entrance, God **placed . . . cherubim and a flaming sword** in order to
keep anyone from having access to the tree of life.

Additional Notes §3

2:5 / "Shrub" *(siakh)* refers to bushy plants, ordinarily considered nonedible, and "plant" *('eseb)* to edible vegetation (Wenham, *Genesis
1–15*, p. 58).

2:6 / The precise meaning of *'ed* remains an enigma. It may
refer to a heavy dew, an underground river, or a swell that kept the soil
sufficiently moist for plants to grow.

2:8 / In Ugar. the root for Eden means "delight." References
outside this passage to the garden of Eden occur in Ezek. 36:35 and Joel
2:3. The name Eden occurs alone in the Hb. texts of Gen. 4:16; Isa. 51:3;
Ezek. 31:9, 16, 18 (twice); and Eden as the garden of God in Ezek. 28:13;
31:8–9 (twice). The phrase "garden of Yahweh" occurs in 13:10.

2:9 / The tree of the knowledge of good and evil is mentioned in 2:17; 3:3, 5, 6, 11, 12, and 17 as the tree in the middle of the garden, as the tree, or as "the tree that I commanded you not to eat from." It is never mentioned again in Scripture. The tree of life appears in Prov. 3:18; 11:30; 13:12; 15:4 and in Rev. 2:7; 22:1–2, 14, 19.

2:10–14 / Jerusalem is described in terms of the garden of Eden in Ps. 46:4, and the temple is pictured as having a stream flowing from it (Ezek. 47:1). The etymologies of Pishon as "leaper" *(pwsh)* and Gihon as "burst out" *(gykh)* suggest that the river originated from a mammoth, gushing spring. Some scholars locate Eden in western Iran because Cush in 10:8 refers to the Kassites.

Among the many suggestions for the locations of the Pishon and the Gihon are the Indus and the Nile, but these rivers are not now close to the heads of the Tigris and Euphrates. Another interpretation locates Eden at the place where the four rivers merged, possibly at the head of the Persian Gulf.

The connection of Havilah and Pishon has led to the proposal that Pishon is a river in Arabia or the Persian Gulf.

2:21 / *Tsela'* refers to the side of an object (Exod. 25:12; 27:7) or building (Exod. 26:20) or to a side chamber (1 Kgs. 6:5–6).

3:1 / The serpent's reasoning ability and its hostility toward God outdistance its description as a mere creature of the garden. Nevertheless, this narrative does not address the origin of evil. There is no allusion to any cosmic force being responsible for the disobedience of the humans and no hint of cosmic dualism. As Kidner says, "The chapter speaks not of evil invading, as though it had its own existence, but of creatures rebelling" (*Genesis*, p. 67). Whatever hostility exists against God comes from the creatures God has made, and they bear the full responsibility for disobeying God.

There have been many proposals to identify the serpent further, usually as Satan. The idea of Satan as God's cosmic foe, however, did not develop until much later, sometime in the postexilic era (e.g., 1 Chron. 21:1; Zech. 3:1–2). Furthermore, it is not surprising that in time this serpent became a symbol of Satan, for the behavior of this serpent parallels that of Satan. In any case, the narrator did not connect the serpent and Satan.

3:5 / Whereas NIV reads "like God," it is better to read "like divine beings," for the following Hb. verb is pl. and in 3:22 God used the pl. "us" when he said, "The man has now become like one of us, knowing good and evil."

3:15 / Even though in the MT (Masoretic Text, the received Hb. text of the OT) the two verbs "crush" and "strike" are spelled the same, scholars debate whether or not they come from the same root. Most take both occurrences of the verb from *shup* ("crush, bruise"). The use of the same verb conveys that each opponent will strike the other with similar enmity; the differences will be in the part of the body struck, namely, the head of serpent(s) and the heel of human(s). Some scholars, however, take the second occurrence of the term from another root, *sha'ap* ("crush, trample on"), so NIV. Unfortunately the use of two different words to translate *shup* obscures the intent of the author in using the same spelling both times.

Only by joining this word of deliverance to the promise of salvation through David's line does it have messianic significance (Rom. 16:20; 1 Tim. 2:15; Heb. 2:14; Rev. 12). When this text was composed, such a defined way of fulfilling this hope was beyond the purview of the author.

3:19 / In understanding the penalty of 2:17 some translators render the Hb. literally ("in the day that," NRSV), thus exacerbating the surface discrepancy between the penalty and its execution. It is better to translate the phrase "when," as does the NIV. Another explanation for easing this tension, namely, that "you will die" means "you will become mortal," falls before the fact that the penalty is stated in a definitive legal formulation.

3:20 / Does the one who names another have authority over the one named? There have been opposing answers to this question, both supported with good arguments. Many scholars answer in the affirmative (D. Clines, *What Did Eve Do to Help? and Other Readerly Questions to the Old Testament* [JSOTSup 94; Sheffield: JSOT Press, 1992], pp. 37–39), and others have argued the opposite (P. Trible, "Depatriarchalizing in Biblical Interpretation," *JAAR* 41 [1973], p. 38). The social structure primarily defines the authority that one party has over another, and that structure often invests the one in authority with the right of naming subordinates. It is also possible that one may be given the privilege of naming for other reasons, as when Jacob's wives name their respective children (29:31–30:24). Their authority over the children was secondary to Jacob's and lasted only while the children were growing up.

When God instructed the man to name the animals, man's authority over those animals rested in God's placing him in that role, not in his naming them. Did the man have some authority over the woman in giving her a name? The answer is a modified yes, for in marriage a man forms a close alliance with a woman and takes on certain responsibilities for her welfare. In turn, she owes him loyalty. His authority, though, is limited by his accepting her as a person just like himself.

§4 Excursus: Reflections on the Disobedience of Adam and Eve

With brief, well-defined scenes the narrator has told a story with profound insight into the human dilemma. This account informs humans why death is inevitable. It also teaches us why humans have no one to blame for the hardships of life and for death save themselves. It explains why humans are at odds with the animal world, are estranged from God, and find tensions even in the closest family relationships. Nevertheless, this account leaves us with some major questions.

First, is the account in Genesis 2–3 history? Did this event take place? The account lacks crucial information necessary for it to qualify as a record of a historical event; there is insufficient information about the people involved, the location, or the date. The absence of such essential data tells us that the narrator had a greater purpose. Through symbols, wordplays, and structural design, the narrator addressed the human predicament. The man and the woman (Adam and Eve) represent every man and every woman. These two humans were not individuals acting privately. Their desires, their actions, their responses, and consequently their punishments characterize the experience of all humanity. In the words of J. Walsh, "On a deeper level, every hearer identifies with this 'man and this woman' not finally but personally. The sin depicted is not simply the first sin; it is *all* human sin; it is *my* sin. And I who hear the tale am forced to acknowledge that my sin too has cosmic dimensions; my sin too is an attack on creation and an establishment of moral chaos" ("Genesis 2:4b–3:24: A Synchronic Approach," *JBL* 96 [1977], p. 177). Symbolic language, therefore, allows this account to function as a mirror in which all readers see their own reflections.

The movement of action in Genesis assumes that something took place in the garden with dramatic and long-lasting implications for all of humanity. The following events, especially

Cain's murder of Abel and the increase of violence in society to such an intolerable level that God had to inundate the earth, become explicable and necessary as an outgrowth of the sin of the first humans. For the Apostle Paul the first humans' disobedience is a key element in his theology of redemption (Rom. 5:12–14). Jesus, the second Adam, overcame their failure to provide salvation for all. To classify the dual purposes of this text Wenham uses the terms "protohistorical" and "paradigmatic" (*Genesis 1–15*, p. 91). Protohistorical defines the first act of disobedience as a real event that took place before recorded history, and paradigmatic means that the presentation depicts a typical human pattern.

Another important issue concerns the nature of the relationship God intended for a man and a woman in marriage. Did God place the woman in a subordinate role to the man? The drama shows elements of similarity and dissimilarity in the roles of the genders. Those that are similar enable a man and a woman to become companions, while those that are distinct enable each gender to make a different, vital contribution to their life together.

The text supports both genders having equal standing: the woman was made to correspond to the man; the woman and the man acted in accord in eating the forbidden fruit; and God used the same terms for pain or labor in the respective penalties pronounced on the woman and the man for their disobedience. Some data, however, illustrate the qualities and abilities distinctive to each gender. The man has the task of producing food to support his family. God put the man in the garden to till and keep it (2:15), referred to working the soil (3:17–19), and sent the man from the garden with the task of tilling the ground (3:23). The woman complements the man by bearing children. The nature of her punishment (3:16) and the name Eve, "the mother of all living" (3:20), confirm this role. Her role is crucial, for it guarantees the continuance of the human family on earth (3:16). These differences, rather than elevating one gender over the other, enable each gender to make a true contribution to the other. In living together a man and a woman discover their true humanness. This is the ideal picture.

In disobeying God the first couple jeopardized the ability of a male and a female to establish an ideal union. There are many evidences of the changes from the ideal after they ate the forbidden fruit. Even before God pronounced their punishments, changes in the couple's relationship were evident. They devised makeshift coverings to hide their nakedness from each other. That they no longer completely trusted each other surfaces in their answers to God's inquiries. Each cast blame on the other. This tension is also prominent in God's punishment of the woman (3:16); the wording her "desire" and his "rule" describes the conflict that would arise from each seeking to dominate the other.

For the Christian these punishments affecting the relationship of a woman and a man must be read in light of Christ's work, for Christ came to overcome these curses. Marriage for the believer is to be characterized by love modeled after Christ's self-sacrificing love (Eph. 5:25, 28–30). Such love, acting as an antidote against the drive for one gender to dominate the other, casts out all abuse. Having been redeemed by Christ, both marriage partners can love and honor each other responsibly. Together they build a sound family unit that moves toward the ideal of Genesis 2:21–24. God's goal is for a husband and a wife to have an upbuilding relationship in which they truly become one flesh.

The discord between male and female that took place in Eden has continued into today's gender struggles. Speaking broadly, the gender with political power (male) has sought to impose social structures that promote its dominance, and the so-called inferior or weaker gender has suffered social oppression as a result. This alienation between the genders and the resulting suffering has its roots in human sin. Such discord does not belong to God's ideal design. But Jesus' death reversed the sin of the first couple. He paid the ultimate penalty so that now in Christ no person has higher standing or power by reason of being either male or female (Gal. 3:28). While this truth has begun to be released in society as a powerful ideal, it has a long way to go before it is fully realized.

§5 Cain Slays Abel and Lamech Boasts (Gen. 4:1–26)

The first siblings are unable to live in harmony. Hatred propels Cain to murder his own brother. The tragic, brute power of sin also finds expression in Lamech's boasting song, in which he brazenly gloats over a wanton killing while pronouncing threats against others. These incidents illustrate how Adam and Eve's disobedience unleashed sin as a destructive power in society and brought death into the world.

This chapter has four parts: the births of Cain and Abel (vv. 1–2a), Cain's murder of Abel (vv. 2b–16), Cain's genealogy (vv. 17–24), and the birth of Seth (vv. 25–26). Eve glories in her achievement by naming her first (v. 1) and third sons (v. 25). The reports of Eve's giving birth thus frame the portrait of Cain's family. Reports of the birth of new life surround the hideous stories of hatred and murder, showing that God's grace triumphs over human wickedness.

Two other factors tie together the diverse elements of this chapter: Cain's genealogy and the several occurrences of the number seven, a sacred number that symbolizes completeness or wholeness. The punishment against anybody who kills Cain is set at seven times (v. 15), and Lamech brags of taking vengeance seventy-seven times (v. 24). The genealogy focuses on Lamech, the seventh generation from Adam. Further, in verses 1–17 "Abel" and "brother" occur seven times each, while "Cain" occurs fourteen times (Wenham, *Genesis 1–15*, p. 96).

The dramatic movement of Cain's act of aggression parallels the flow of action in the preceding account of the first humans' eating the forbidden fruit. Humans disobey God (4:8; 3:6), God questions those involved (4:9–10; 3:9–13), God pronounces sentence (4:11–12; 3:14–19), God redefines aspects of the way humans relate to each other (4:15; 3:21), and God banishes the offenders from their original habitations (4:14, 16; 3:23–24). Moreover, the vignettes in chapter 4 disclose consequences that grew out of Adam and Eve's disobedience. Outside the garden death becomes a part of human experience, but in a very different way than anticipated. The first generation experiences death not as a penalty (2:17) but as a malevolent force destroying the innocent (4:8, 14, 15, 23, 25). The first recorded death is inflicted by one brother against another brother. The theme of an older brother's hostility toward a younger brother recurs throughout Genesis: Ishmael's taunting of Isaac (21:9–10), Esau's threatened vengeance against Jacob (27:41–45), and Jacob's sons' plotting to eliminate Joseph (37:20–28). Possibly another death is reported in Lamech's song; then an adult kills a youth.

4:1 / The narrative opens with a triumphant report of the birth of the first human. **Adam lay with** (lit. "knew") . . . **Eve. She** conceived and bore a man. Building on the sound of Hebrew *qanah* ("gain, acquire"), which sometimes means "give birth, produce" (e.g., Exod. 15:16; Ps. 74:2; 78:54; Prov. 8:22), the child was named **Cain** *(qayin)*. Eve proclaimed proudly that she had **brought forth** or acquired *(qaniti)* **a man.** She identified the newborn as "a man" rather than as "a son" or "a child." She made a wordplay based on her having been taken from "a man" *('ish)* and thus called "a woman" *('ishah;* 2:23); now she, a woman, had borne "a man" *('ish)*. She also emphasized that this child was a continuation of humanity. The most likely interpretation of the difficult *'et Yhwh* (NIV "with the help of the LORD") is "together with." Thus Eve, rejoicing in her fertility, claimed to stand alongside Yahweh in her role as the mother of all the living (3:20).

4:2a / Eve bore a second son, named **Abel** *(hebel)*. In contrast to the joy at Cain's birth there is no mention of either Eve's delight at Abel's birth or her naming him (vv. 2, 25, 26). This lack of any reference to her bonding with the newborn, along with the symbolic name Abel, which means "breath, vapor, transitory" (Job 7:16; Eccl. 1:2), foreshadows this child's fate. When *hebel* is used for human life, it captures the sense of worthlessness that daunts human existence, made even more pronounced by its brevity (Ps. 144:4). Being but "a vapor," Abel has no words recorded, and his only action is to bring an offering. His lack of offspring adds to the insignificance of his life.

4:2b–7 / The account of Cain's murdering Abel has four scenes: Cain and Abel present offerings (vv. 2b–5); God warns Cain (vv. 6–7); Cain murders Abel (v. 8); and God punishes Cain

(vv. 9–16). In stark contrast to the relatively lengthy exchanges between Cain and God, a single verse describes the murder. Before the murder God warned Cain about yielding to the dangerous impulse within him. After the murder God questioned Cain and then pronounced punishment on him, but Cain asked for some reprieve and God agreed. The alternation of the names of the two brothers communicates the changing mood: the sequence Cain-Abel-Abel-Cain occurs twice in verses 1–5a; Cain's name occurs by itself twice in verses 5b–7, followed by the pattern of Cain-Abel, which occurs three times in verses 8–9.

The first brothers developed two different professions (v. 2b). Abel became a shepherd, Cain a farmer. This raises the question as to whether the conflict between Cain and Abel is between two brothers or a class conflict between two different ways of life. Nothing in the text supports the latter position. Neither occupation is vaunted nor condemned. If God had favored one of these occupations, it would have been Cain's since he worked the ground, the task God had prescribed for humans (2:5, 15).

After the two brothers began to prosper, each presented an offering *(minkhah)* to God. Their offerings were similar to the first-fruits the Israelites presented to God (Deut. 26:2–4). **Cain brought some of the fruits of the soil, but Abel brought fat portions from some of the firstborn of his flock.** The brothers worshiped God in simplicity, for there is no mention of a shrine, an altar, or a ritual.

Yahweh **looked with favor on Abel and his offering,** but not on Cain's. The text does not state why Yahweh chose Abel's offering over Cain's, nor how the brothers knew that Yahweh favored Abel's offering. The answer to the first question might lie in the nature of the gifts, in the respective dispositions of the brothers, or in the freedom of Yahweh. Those who take the reason to lie in the nature of the gifts posit that a member of the flock made a superior offering over produce from the ground because of the animal's blood. However, if the brothers were offering firstfruits, blood was not of primary importance. The sacrificial legislation (Lev. 1–7) shows that God valued and required offerings of both animals and grain. The term "an offering" *(minkhah)* is used for both presentations; thus the narrator makes no qualitative distinction between the offerings. Therefore, the reason God accepted Abel's offering and not Cain's had nothing to do with the nature of the gifts. Neither did the reason lie arbitrarily in God's freedom, for after the offerings God graciously spoke to Cain about how he could be accepted (v. 7).

One can conclude only that God was responding to a differ-ence in the attitudes of the brothers. The text lauds the high qual-ity of Abel's offering with two phrases, "the firstborn" and "the fat." These terms convey that Abel gave the best to God; he ac-knowledged God's lordship over his flock and the increase of his labor. He also anticipated the later legislation that required the people to bring God the firstlings of the flock (Exod. 13:11–13) and the firstfruits (Exod. 23:16, 19; 34:22, 26). In presenting the first to God, the owner consecrated the entire crop or flock; God then re-leased the rest of the harvest or the offspring of the flock to the owner for his own use. Whereas Abel honored God as Lord with his offering, Cain simply brought an offering. Apparently the firstborn of humans failed to offer the firstfruits of his harvest. An ancient Israelite audience would have quickly noticed this dis-tinction in the two offerings.

How did Yahweh make known his acceptance of Abel's of-fering? The question calls our attention to the fact that the narra-tive is tightly condensed, providing limited details and virtually no time references. Although the text offers no clue, many schol-ars have proposed answers to this question. Medieval Jewish commentators supposed that fire came from heaven and con-sumed Abel's sacrifice. U. Cassuto (*A Commentary on the Book of Genesis,* vol. 1, *From Adam to Noah: A Commentary on Genesis I–VI 8* [trans. I. Abrahams; Jerusalem: Magnes, 1961], p. 207) speculates that after this ceremony Yahweh blessed Abel's flocks but not the ground that Cain worked. This proposal has the merit of the brothers' discovering God's response to their offerings as they continued to labor. If such was the case, there would have been a significant time lapse between the presentation of these offerings and the subsequent murder.

In response to Yahweh's favoring Abel's offering, Cain be-came **very angry,** and his **face** became **downcast.** It is easy to imagine that, having been bested by his younger brother, whom he considered to be less than himself and whose profession he de-spised, Cain was despondent, filled with contempt for Abel. This setback, instead of leading him to contrition, embittered him to-ward his brother. His jealousy had to be dealt with before it led him to do something terribly wrong.

Because Cain harbored such hatred, Yahweh mercifully spoke to him, putting to Cain a double question: **why** was he **angry** and **why** was his **face downcast?** Yahweh alerted Cain that his reaction was too negative. Yahweh did not condemn Cain for his offering. While Cain had erected a small barrier between himself and God, he had not done irreparable damage to that relationship.

Yahweh then challenged Cain by setting before him two alternatives. First, if Cain would do **what** was **right,** would he **not be accepted**? As far as Yahweh was concerned, Cain needed to demonstrate greater devotion in his future offerings. Second, Yahweh alerted him to the danger of not doing what was right, saying that if he did **not do what** was **right, sin** was **crouching at his door.** While "lie or crouch" *(rabats)* usually has a restful connotation (29:21; Ps. 23:2), it also describes the lurking of a wild animal poised to pounce on its prey. "At the door" means that sin was so close that Cain had to deal with it; its desire was for him. "Desire" or "urge" *(teshuqah)* means strong attraction or drive such as a woman feels for a man (3:16). Cain needed to master this sin that impelled him to express his bitter feelings by attacking another. In this warning Yahweh offered Cain the hope that he could control this impulse to commit sin, even though it was strong. Should Cain act wrongfully, it would be because he yielded to the desire of sin, not because God had rejected his offering.

4:8 / Some time later Cain made an appointment with Abel to meet him in a field, a remote place that offered the sense of privacy. In the field Cain spoke with Abel, but the MT records none of that conversation. So various sources, including some of the versions, have supplied a speech. On the basis of the Septuagint (or LXX, the earliest Greek translation of the Hebrew OT, ca. 250 B.C.) the NIV reads, **Let's go out to the field.** Given the outcome, the conversation must have been far from civil. We can imagine that Cain dominated the conversation as he expressed his anger to his brother. **Cain,** yielding to the impulse to sin, **attacked** and **killed** Abel. The Hebrew for "attack" *(qum,* lit. "rise up") makes a play on the description of Cain's "fallen face" and echoes Yahweh's warning about sin's "crouching, lurking." Like an animal Cain sprang against Abel, destroying his prey. Brazenly he walked away, leaving Abel's body lying on the ground.

4:9–10 / Since this first murder took place in the primeval age, Yahweh acted as judge and held Cain accountable (Deut. 21:1). Yahweh asked pointedly, **Where is your brother Abel?** This simple question strikes at the heart of the matter. Cain answered curtly with a lie, **I don't know.** His answer contrasts with Adam's after he ate the forbidden fruit. Adam admitted what he had done, though he cast blame directly on Eve and indirectly on God (3:12). Irritated by Yahweh's question, Cain sought to silence the questioner and remove himself from any responsibility with a sarcastic, rhetorical question, **Am I my brother's keeper?** Despite the question, which anticipates a negative answer, Cain, disgusted at being questioned about his brother, betrayed his disdain for Abel and his disregard of any filial responsibility for his brother. His use of "keeper" is also telling. Animals, not humans, need "keepers" (P. Riemann, "Am I My Brother's Keeper?" *Int* 24 [1970], pp. 482–91). By phrasing the question so sarcastically, Cain coldly rejected the principle that a brother bears responsibility for his brother. Ideally the first line of support in a family comes from the older to the younger; when a younger brother gets into a difficulty that threatens his existence or his property, the older brother acts to deliver him (Lev. 25:25, 47–49). But in the first family, the older brother was so angry at his younger brother that he killed him.

Yahweh refused to entertain Cain's question, making him confront his responsibility for such an appalling deed by asking, **What have you done?** Yahweh then surprised Cain by telling him that there was a witness to his deed. His **brother's blood** was crying **out to** God **from the ground.** It was believed that uncovered human blood cried out for vengeance against the murderer. If no one heard the cry, God was obligated to redress the wrong.

4:11–12 / As judge, Yahweh pronounced Cain's punishment. Yahweh put Cain **under a curse** that drove him **from the ground** that had received his **brother's blood.** This curse was different from the punishments of the first human pair. God made an aspect of Adam and Eve's livelihood harder, but he caused Cain to be alienated from the support of the land, thus consigning him to become **a restless wanderer.** This curse struck at Cain's self-identity; banishment from the soil was almost as harsh as taking his life.

4:13–14 / In contrast to Adam and Eve, who did not speak out against their punishments, Cain exclaimed that his **punishment** was **more than** he could **bear.** He complained bitterly about being driven **from the land,** being **hidden from** God's **presence,** and becoming a **restless wanderer.** He feared that anyone he met might **kill** him. In his complaint Cain showed no remorse for his crime, not even to God. Did Cain request mitigation of his punishment? Not precisely, for the last statement of his lament—"whoever finds me will kill me"—added an outcome fearful to Cain, though not mentioned by Yahweh. Cain requested removal of the continual threat that someone might kill him to avenge Abel's death.

4:15 / Yahweh responded to Cain's complaint, saying definitively, **Not so.** Yahweh put **a mark** or a sign on Cain that would prevent anyone from taking his life (Exod. 12:13). The mark must have been visible so that anyone coming upon Cain would at once be aware of the protection Cain was under. This mark condemned and simultaneously protected Cain; whoever killed Cain would **suffer vengeance seven times over.** That is, the slayer would be judged to the fullest measure.

It is astonishing that Yahweh did not sentence Cain, the first murderer, to death. Instead, seeing value in Cain's life, God graciously let him live. God does not give up quickly even on those who flagrantly violate another's life. God provides them continuing protection.

4:16 / Cain left Yahweh's **presence,** the source of blessing and support. Because his sin alienated him from God, he went to live in a land named **Nod.** This name makes a pun on the verb "to wander" *(nud).* The location of Nod is given as **east of Eden.** Cain was driven farther away from the ideal garden where God had put the first humans, symbolizing that he was further away from fellowship with God.

4:17–22 / The genealogy of Cain includes references to the first human inventions (vv. 17b, 20b, 21, 22) and Lamech's boasting song (vv. 23–24). Humans took up a variety of occupations, including city building, herding, metal working, and playing musical instruments. The creativity of humans led them to invent new patterns for supporting life, artistic works to enhance the human spirit, and technologies for coping with the harsh environment in which they now lived. Recording human achievements in a genealogy demonstrates the vitality in the human spirit blessed by God (C. Westermann, *Genesis 1–11: A Commentary* [trans. J. Scullion; Minneapolis: Augsburg, 1984], p. 61). This creative activity, then, was an expression of humans' being made in God's image and aided humans in carrying out God's commands to fill the earth and to manage it.

Protected by the mark, Cain proceeded to produce offspring. We may surmise that Cain married one of his sisters. Their firstborn was **Enoch,** and Cain built **a city and named it . . . Enoch.**

The building of a city informs us that the population had begun to increase significantly.

Lamech married two women, . . . Adah and . . . Zillah. Thus he introduced polygamy. Lamech had three sons: **Jabal, Jubal,** and **Tubal-Cain,** and they form the seventh generation in the lineage of Cain. These names are built on the Hebrew term *yebul* ("produce") to highlight their talents as progenitors of new occupations (Wenham, *Genesis 1–15,* p. 112). Jabal became **the father of those who live in tents and raise livestock** *(miqneh).* After Abel's death Jabal advanced shepherding. He became the founder of the nomadic way of life and expanded his herds to include large livestock such as cattle and donkeys, as the term *miqneh* indicates, and would have been in a position to engage in trading. Jubal became **the father of all who play the harp and flute,** stringed and wind instruments. There is a play on the sound of his name *(yubal)* and that of "ram's horn" *(yobel).* Jubal might also have been involved in composing music. Tubal-Cain became the lead master craftsman, developing the technology for forging **all kinds of tools out of bronze and iron.** Although working with iron was not common until 1200 B.C., some ancients worked with small amounts of iron found in meteorites.

4:23–24 / Lamech composed a song, presumably to be sung accompanied by instruments that his son Jubal had made. It was a taunt song in which he bragged about a gruesome deed. After exhorting his two wives to **listen** to his song, Lamech boasted about killing **a man for wounding** him. Without restraint he had struck **a young man** for only **injuring** him. If one takes the second line as synonymous to the first, Lamech claimed to have killed one person, not two. One view, based on the verbs being imperfect, holds that Lamech was only boasting about what he would do to anyone who injured him. In any case Lamech displayed contempt for the value of human life.

In contrast to Cain, who sought protection from Yahweh, Lamech shamelessly boasted as he threatened with vengeance anybody who would hold him accountable, up to **seventy-seven times.** This number symbolizes the utmost extent. J. Gabriel ("Die Kainitengenealogie: Gn 4, 17–24," *Bib* 40 [1959], pp. 422–23) posits that Lamech made such an outrageous boast because he had available to him new weapons forged by Tubal-Cain. In arrogance he had no regard for the standard of justice as expressed in the phrase "an eye for an eye, a life for a life" (Exod. 21:24; Lev.

24:19–20). He claimed to be his own law. This song reveals that with the rise of culture the human thirst for violence increases dramatically. The threat to human existence then becomes the abuse of human inventiveness.

4:25 / At this point the narrative returns to Adam and Eve to introduce a new genealogical line of those who worship Yahweh. **Adam lay with** (lit. "knew") Eve **again, and she gave birth to a son.** She **named him Seth.** Eve rejoiced, saying that God had **granted** her a son **in place of Abel.** The verb *shat* ("grant") is a play on the sound of the name Seth, *shet.* This time her rejoicing was more from consolation at the loss of Abel than from triumph (v. 1). **Seth . . . had a son,** whom **he named . . . Enosh,** another Hebrew term for "man" that tends, however, to emphasize human frailty and mortality.

4:26 / Members of Seth's lineage **began to call on the name of** Yahweh (12:8; 13:4; 21:33; 26:25). From the early days of humans' living outside the garden of Eden there was a line who worshiped the one true God. Their devotion was an antidote to the increasing sin in Cain's line. Whereas Cain's line contributed to the arts and crafts, Seth's line developed true worship.

Additional Notes §5

4:1 / The etymology of "Cain" is uncertain. It has often been taken to mean "smith," but Tubal-Cain is credited with being the head of that profession (v. 22). While *qayin* means "lance" (NIV has "spearhead") in 2 Sam. 21:16, it is not the primary Hb. term for "smith." In Judg. 4:11 this term is a gentilic (an adjective formed from a noun to describe a people group) for the tribe of Kenites (Num. 24:22). Consequently, some scholars have proposed a relationship between Cain and that tribe. This claim, however, is hard to substantiate, especially in light of the flood's wiping out all humans. Cassuto (*From Adam to Noah,* pp. 197–98) associates Cain with the Aram. and Arab. terms to mean "one formed, a creature."

The phrase *'et Yhwh* ("with Yahweh") is very difficult. The particle *'et* usually indicates the direct object, in which case Yahweh would be in apposition to Cain, identifying Cain as the son God had promised Eve—even God himself (3:15). Others interpret this grammar to identify Cain as a divine-human creature, but such a view would be anomalous for the monotheistic outlook of Gen. 1–11. Some take *'et* to mean "with the help of" (so NIV), but only here would it have that meaning. The best option, drawing from Akk., interprets *'et* to mean "together with" (Westermann, *Genesis 1–11*, p. 291).

4:3–4 / The narrow meaning of the term *minkhah* is a grain offering (Lev. 2). If that were its usage here, Cain's offering would have been acceptable, especially if it were the grain of the firstfruits (Lev. 2:14; Deut. 26:1–4). But frequently this term refers to offerings in general.

4:7 / This verse is filled with exegetical difficulties. The subject "sin" (fem.) is not in agreement with the verb "crouch, lie" *(rbts)*. Some translators have solved this problem by taking the verb as a substantive. Then "crouching, being on the lurk" stands in apposition to sin: "there is at the door sin, (namely) being on the lurk" (E. van Wolde, "The Story of Cain and Abel: A Narrative Study," *JSOT* 52 [1991], pp. 31–32).

4:13 / *'awon*, rendered "punishment" by NIV, means either "iniquity" or "guilt or punishment" for an iniquity. Since it occurs here after the crime, the best rendering is "punishment." *Nasa'* means "bear," but in certain texts it has the nuance "forgive." Since the latter usage occurs primarily in cultic texts and since Cain gave no evidence of seeking forgiveness, "bear" is the preferred interpretation here (F. Golka, "Cain and Abel: Biblical or Dogmatic Interpretation," *ScrB* 19 [1989], pp. 29–32).

4:15 / The NIV follows the versions in reading "not so." The MT reading, "therefore," is very difficult to understand.

4:17 / The simplest reading of the Hb. text takes Enoch to be the builder. But why would he name a city after himself? It seems better to take Cain as the builder (so NIV); however, he had been condemned to endless wandering. A possible explanation is that after years of wandering Cain built a city in order to cope with that curse. Another possible explanation is that the original name of the city became displaced by Enoch's name. The text would then have read: "Enoch built a city and called it after his son's name, Irad."

4:21 / "Harp" is more precisely identified as a lyre. The term rendered "flute" *('ugab)* has not been identified beyond question. In Arabian history both musical skills and the breeding of flocks are attributed to nomads, who were known for providing minstrels to entertain city dwellers (Westermann, *Genesis 1–11*, p. 331). However, Cain's genealogy does not explicitly state that Jubal lived in tents.

4:22 / It is possible to understand the Hb. to say that Tubal-Cain hammered these metals into tools. Another reading of the Hb. takes him to be an instructor of artisans who made tools. Perhaps he was a bronzesmith and a craftsman of iron. Moreover, archaeologists have discovered in Egypt and Mesopotamia iron objects that date from the third millennium B.C. and that are made from smelted iron (G. Hasel, "Iron," *ISBE* 2:880).

Naamah means "pleasant, graceful, lovely." But if the name comes from the root *n-'-m* ("sing," Syr. and Arab.), she was a "singer" (Gabriel, "Die Kainintengeneaologie," p. 418), a talent that would complement that of her brother.

§6 Excursus: A Note on Culture

Israel's neighbors had myths that attributed most inventions and discoveries to the gods. In Mesopotamian mythology, civilization began among the gods; when humans were finally created, they were placed in a well-ordered society. Some cultures had myths that related how certain gods taught humans the various trades and crafts. In Egypt, Osiris taught the way of farming; in Greece, Prometheus gave humans the skill of making fire.

In other epics there are stories about a god making something superior and giving it to a favored human. Kothar-Hasis, the Canaanite who was a master craftsman and skilled architect, made a special bow for Aqhat, Danel's son; on another occasion he made two clubs for Baal in his battle against Yam (the Sea). After Baal's victory over Yam, Kothar-Hasis built a palace for the victor.

By contrast, the Bible teaches from the outset that work is a central aspect of the responsibilities humans have as God's representatives on earth. God placed the first man in the garden and assigned him the task of tilling and keeping the garden. Outside the garden Cain worked the soil, and Abel tended flocks of sheep and goats (Gen. 4).

In Cain's lineage there are references to several cultural developments. Jabal advanced animal husbandry; Jubal was a musician. By providing an avenue for humans to give expression to their thoughts and feelings, music enhances the quality and depth of human lives. This reference to music anticipates the spectrum of artistic skills that humans come to master.

In another line from Cain, Tubal-Cain discovered the process for making tools out of bronze and iron. The development of metallurgy led to the production of better tools for working the soil and for the construction of larger and stronger buildings. Through these advances in technology societies placed more and more land into food production, thereby promoting an increased population.

Human creativity continued after the flood. Noah learned how to grow vines and make wine. The first vintner gave humans a means for giving their tired spirits rest. Nimrod is credited with the development of hunting (10:9). Early monarchs like Gilgamesh bragged about killing large animals. In the earliest days, though, these heroic leaders hunted primarily to protect their realms from being terrorized by ferocious animals. Hunting did not develop into a sport until much later (Westermann, *Genesis 1–11*, p. 516).

As people began to multiply, they formed cities. The founding of the first city is attributed to Cain or Enoch (4:17). In that Cain was a farmer, as opposed to a nomad, city organization was connected with sedentary life.

New building materials, such as sun-dried bricks, and progress in architectural design enabled humans to build massive structures, such as attested in the account of the Tower of Babel (11:1–9). This episode bears witness to the human drive to gather in cities.

Besides offering security, cities provided people with opportunities to gain wealth, to develop special talents, and to enjoy goods produced in other parts of the earth. As cities grew, great civilizations developed, particularly in Mesopotamia and Egypt. Major cities became the hubs of these civilizations. The strongest cities extended their authority over the surrounding region, forming city-states. This eventually led to the formation of empires. In the Table of Nations, Nimrod is honored as the founder of an empire (10:10–12).

Technological advances also contributed to the building of cities. However, the human flaws of selfishness and greed gave people the potential to use these advances in a way that threatened the very urban centers that fostered the new technology. The human proclivity to adapt their inventions to inflict harm on others might lie behind Lamech's boasting so brazenly about his ability to kill scores of people. History attests a tribe or city-state using a new technology to make better weapons with which one people extended its control over a wider area.

Disaster can also befall a city if its leaders focus the majority of a community's resources on a project designed to become a perpetual monument of that society's greatness. Such projects may place so great a demand on that society's citizens that many become slaves to the project. As a result, human life is devalued. Or humans may become so arrogant about the monuments they

build that God must bring some kind of judgment on that cultural
center, as was the case with the Tower of Babel (11:1–9). Or the citizens of a city may use the urban environment for advancing the
pursuit of pleasure, as was the case in Sodom (13:13; 18:20–21).
Thus cities can develop such a self-sufficient culture that their citizens come to live without regard for either God or high moral
standards. Cities then have the potential of becoming centers
of rebellion against God. In extreme cases like Sodom and Gomorrah, God was moved to judge such centers of wickedness
(18:20–21; 19:24–25).

§7 The Descendants of Seth to Noah (Gen. 5:1–32)

In contrast to the increasing wickedness recounted in Cain's genealogy, the line of those who worshiped God is presented in Seth's genealogy. Ten generations from Adam to Noah span 1,656 years. After the deluge another epoch is identified by the ten generations from Shem, Noah's son, to Abram (11:10–26; also note the ten generations from Perez to David: Ruth 4:18–22; 1 Chron. 2:5, 9–15). Since this list was constructed to include ten generations, "son of" may mean descendant rather than literal son in some cases. The son identified is the most important one, usually the firstborn but not always, as is the case with Seth. The genealogy most likely does not include every generation between Adam and Noah. Thus the exact length of time between the creation and the flood, which was at least several centuries, is impossible to determine. Seth's genealogy ends with Noah, the one truly righteous person whom God found worthy to survive the deluge.

Genealogies are integral to the structure of Genesis. They establish that all humans are united through a common origin. In the primeval era genealogies are linear, moving from generation to generation. In the patriarchal narratives segmented genealogies of two or three generations are more common for the different lines of offspring of a major figure. The genealogies in chapters 5 and 11 end with a segmented entry, and the purpose of these two genealogies is to establish Abraham's lineage back through Noah to Adam. In the second part of Genesis genealogies continue to appear at strategic points, functioning as connectors between characters and events separated by generations. They locate a person or an episode within the context of God's creation and the lineage of the generations. According to Genesis, the earth was populated from one family that multiplied into clans, tribes, and then nations.

5:1–2 / **The written account** renders *seper toledoth*. Only this *toledoth* formula is preceded by the term "book," suggesting that the author took the names that follow from a written record. Or it may refer to the following as a "list" or "document." To stress that the distinctive quality of humans continued after their expulsion from Eden, verses 1a–2 reiterate from the creation account that **God created** humans *('adam)*, both **male and female,** in his **likeness** (1:26–28). All succeeding humans *('adam)* are like the head ancestor Adam *('adam)*. There is a play on Hebrew *'adam,* which occurs three times, once for the first man and twice for all humans of both genders. From the beginning God **blessed** humans, enabling them to produce many offspring.

5:3–5 / Adam fathered **a son** and **named him Seth.** His son was **in his likeness** *(demut)* and **image** *(tselem)*. Thus the image of God passed from parents to their children; each newborn then had intrinsic worth (9:6).

5:6–32 / The construction of Seth's genealogy follows a repeated pattern: person *a* lived *x* years; he became the father of person *b;* after that he lived *y* years and had sons and daughters; altogether person *a* lived *z* years. For example, Adam lived 130 years; then he fathered Seth; altogether he lived 930 years. The total time covered by this genealogy is 1,656 years.

Enoch, the seventh from Adam in Seth's line, was the most godly predeluvian. He **walked with God** (6:9; 17:1; Heb. 11:5), that is, he had intimate fellowship with God. Given the symbolic force of the number seven, his position in the list testifies to the high honor Enoch found with God. When Enoch was 365, about a third of the life span of the other members of this line, **God took him** from earth. That is, he was transported or translated to God's dwelling place without dying. This brief report about Enoch teaches that fellowship with God counters the curse of death.

Lamech . . . named his son **Noah** *(noakh),* for he hoped that his son would **comfort** *(nkhm)* humans burdened by **labor and painful toil** *('itsabon)* as a result of working **the ground** that Yahweh had **cursed** (3:17). This is the first statement in Genesis that humans experienced such agonizing pain and distress that they longed for relief. It also discloses that even those who worshiped God were experiencing God's curse on the ground. Such agony resulted from God's general curse; it was not punishment for specific wrongdoing by members of Seth's line. Lamech's hope for relief was realized when Noah grew the first vineyard and made wine (9:20).

Seth's genealogy concludes with a segmented pattern. Noah's three sons were **Shem, Ham and Japheth.**

Additional Notes §7

5:3–27 / In the Sam. Pent. and LXX some of the ages, for both fathering a child and the length of life, differ. These versions seem to have followed a different numerical scheme (Cassuto, *From Adam to Noah,* pp. 264–65). The time from creation to the flood is 1,307 years in the Sam. Pent. and 2,242 in the LXX.

5:6 / The Sumerian King List, a very ancient document from the third millennium B.C., gives the names of the kings and their cities before and after the flood in Sumer, i.e., southern Mesopotamia, the place where civilization began. Before the flood, each king reigned for an exceedingly long time; e.g., Enmenluanna reigned 43,200 years. In all, eight antediluvian kings reigned for a total of 241,200 years. After the deluge, thirty-nine kings reigned in Sumer for 26,997 years. Thus both Genesis and the Sumerian records witness that after the flood people lived much shorter lives. The Sumerian King List is fundamentally different from the genealogies in Genesis in that it concerns kingship. Genesis, by contrast, is family oriented, concerned with the position of a descendant in the genealogy as a result of God's blessing.

The long life spans of the antediluvians are perplexing. Numerous studies have sought to explain these high numbers, such as Cassuto, *From Adam to Noah,* pp. 252–64, and D. W. Young, "On the Application of Numbers from Babylonian Mathematics to Biblical Life Spans and Epochs," *ZAW* 100 (1988), pp. 331–60, and "The Influence of Babylonian Algebra on Longevity among the Antediluvians," *ZAW* 102 (1990), pp. 321–35. No explanation has won consensus (see Wenham, *Genesis 1–15,* pp. 130–34).

5:6–31 / Many names in Cain's genealogy are similar to those in that of Seth, with Enoch and Lamech being identical. Some scholars have posited that two authors (such as J and P) adapted an ancient genealogy for their distinctive purposes. But others, like Wenham and V. Hamilton (*The Book of Genesis: Chapters 1–17* [NICOT; Grand Rapids: Eerdmans, 1990]), argue that the different spellings of similar sounding names and the different positions of those names in the respective lists demonstrate that the lists originated independently; thus they trace two different lineages.

5:24 / *Laqakh* (lit. "take") may be a technical word for "translate," i.e., to pass directly from the earth to the heavenly realm. Nevertheless, other exegetes interpret the wording "he was no more" to mean a sudden, inexplicable death (e.g., Ps. 39:13; Sarna, *Genesis* [The JPS Torah Commentary; Philadelphia: Jewish Publication Society, 1989], p. 43). But the lack of the phrase "then he died" in this stylized list favors the position that Enoch departed this life in a manner other than death (Wenham, *Genesis 1–15*, p. 128).

5:29 / The wordplay is not on the etymology of Noah but on the similarity in sound of *noakh* ("rest") and *n-kh-m* ("comfort"). The former root occurs in 6:8; 8:4, 9, 20. The latter occurs in 6:6, 7, but with the nuance "regret."

§8 The Increase of Wickedness on Earth (Gen. 6:1–8)

This passage explains why God had to judge the inhabited earth with a deluge (6:9–8:22). It has two distinct sections: a description of the rapid increase in population, when the sons of God married daughters of men (vv. 1–4), and God's response to human violence (vv. 5–8).

The first section reports the population explosion, presumably spurred by the extraordinary marriages between the sons of God and the daughters of men. During that era superheroes are said to have lived in the land. This passage is as enigmatic as it is intriguing. Its brevity, combined with a possible disturbance in the order of the verses, contributes to its obscurity. The first two verses speak of mixed marriages taking place after the population had begun to increase. Verses 3 and 4 present two facts: Yahweh would not let his Spirit continue to contend with humans, and the Nephilim were on the earth at that time. The text does not explicitly connect these facts and the marriages. With so many difficulties no certain interpretation of this passage is possible.

In the second section God decides to execute judgment on every living creature because human society has become completely wicked. The juxtaposition of these two sections suggests that the rapid increase in population has taken place in a way that has compounded wickedness. The worship of the one God, which is attested in Seth's genealogy (4:25–5:32), has been snuffed out save for a single household. The theological principle underlying God's judgment is that gross acts of immorality so pollute nature that the earth can no longer support its inhabitants (Lev. 18:24–28).

6:1–2 / **The sons of God** married **the daughters of men.** The major interpretive issue is the identification of these men and women. Assuming that these verses offer the primary reason for the terrible wickedness in human society (v. 5), a secondary issue is to determine what transgression these marriages caused.

There are three leading proposals for the identification of the sons of God. The first is that they were heavenly beings. Consumed by lust, angels cohabited with human women, thereby transgressing the boundary between the divine and the human realms. The offspring from these unions possessed extraordinary abilities. Lacking moral constraints, they used their abilities to promote wickedness. A second proposal is that the sons of God were the mighty rulers of old. Flaunting their power, they built harems by marrying whomever they wished. Thus, their sin was polygamy, which led to a rapid increase in population. The third possibility is that the sons of God were the men of Seth's line and the daughters of men were the offspring of Cain. These women from the rebellious line of Cain led the Sethites into the pleasures of sin, thereby over time squelching the worship of the one God Yahweh. The scenario of righteous men chasing or marrying beautiful, foreign women and being led into the worship of other gods is a recurring theme in the OT, as in the incident at Baal-Peor (Num. 25:1–2) and the apostasy of Solomon (1 Kgs. 11:1–13).

Tradition favors the first view, and the allusions to it in Jude 6–7 and 2 Peter 2:4–6 support it, but the third view fits the context best by accounting for the loss of true worship on earth among Seth's offspring. Another point in favor of the third position is that God's coming judgment was against all humanity, not against superheroes produced from a blending of divine and human elements. As put forth in the second view, there is not sufficient information for choosing one position over the other. Also making polygamy the grave sin does not find support in the OT.

6:3 / Yahweh **said** that his **Spirit** would **not contend with** humans **forever.** Many sources take the Hebrew word rendered "contend" to mean "abide." With either meaning, God was restraining his life-giving Spirit so that humans would not live longer than **a hundred and twenty years** (2:7; Job 27:3). The context suggests that God limited the length of human life because the offspring of the unions described in verse 2 possessed such extraordinary energy that they lived a very long time and multiplied the doing of evil. One interpretation is that in the future humans would not live to be older than 120. If this is the meaning, it took centuries for that boundary to be put in place. The only major figure in Genesis whose recorded age at death was less than 120 years was Joseph, who died at 110. In another interpretation, God would put an end to the existence of these antediluvians after 120 years. This interpretation is possible given the position of this passage in Genesis. In either case Yahweh was asserting his sovereignty by limiting the life span of these mighty giants.

6:4 / A parenthetical note states that **the Nephilim were on the earth in those days.** The identity of the Nephilim is far from certain. This name occurs in Numbers 13:33 for giants who did vile exploits. But given that the deluge wiped out all humans, it is doubtful that there is any genealogical connection between these two groups called Nephilim. If Nephilim comes from the root *nafal,* it could mean "the fallen ones." Many ancient legends recount how giant warriors or semi-gods lost a major battle and were then imprisoned in the region of the dead. Thus it could refer to those who had fallen from heaven or to great men who at death descended to the grave or hell (Ezek. 32:20–27).

The NIV renders the Hebrew to read that the Nephilim came from the unions of **the sons of God** and **the daughters of men** and that these were **the heroes of old, men of renown.** But the more normal way of reading the Hebrew is that the heroes, but not necessarily the Nephilim, were offspring of these unions. The context suggests that these men were heroes because of their unusual exploits at wrongdoing. It is implied, though, that both the Nephilim and these heroes contributed to the increasing state of wickedness.

6:5–8 / In this second section Yahweh expresses his resolve to wipe out all humans and animals because of the gross wickedness on earth. Although God's goal that humans fill the earth was being realized, his desire that they live together in harmony had been shattered. Humans hurt humans, and people satisfied their own pleasure by oppressing others. These terrible conditions required the Creator to intervene with judgment. The stark contrast between God's coming in both judgment and mercy is amplified by a play on the Hebrew letters *n, kh,* and *m:* "was grieved" *(nkhm),* "wipe out" *(makhah),* Noah *(noakh),* and "found favor" *(hen).*

Yahweh **saw** that **wickedness** in society had reached an intolerable level. This assessment stands in bold contrast to the sixth day of creation, when God saw all that he had made was very good (1:31). Now **every inclination of the thoughts** in the hearts of humans was **only evil all the time.** Inclination means one's orientation or disposition. "Thoughts" is literally "heart," for the

Hebrews took the heart as the center of a person's thinking, feeling, and willing. Also, "thoughts" refers to plans that are about to be acted on, not to imaginations that have little likelihood of ever becoming reality. Because people's hearts were corrupt, they were continually planning and doing baser things. This terrible state of human society **grieved** *(nikhem)* Yahweh, motivating him to take a different course in the way he was relating to humanity. The debased demeanor of those who bore the image of God filled God's **heart . . . with pain** so that God regretted having made humans *(hit'atseb;* 34:7; 1 Sam. 20:34; Isa. 54:6). God's response to human injustice reveals his intimate concern about how those who bear his image think and behave. Furthermore, this wording informs us that in bringing universal judgment on the earth, God did not act out of cold calculation or judge with indifference.

Yahweh declared that he was going to **wipe** out all humans, **animals, and creatures that move along the ground, and birds.** Joining animals with humans in judgment witnesses again to the close connection between these two orders.

A ray of hope shines through this bleak picture in verse 8: **Noah found favor** with Yahweh. This man worshiped Yahweh faithfully and lived righteously (v. 9). Therefore, Yahweh would deliver him and his family from the coming judgment.

Additional Notes §8

6:1–4 / It is possible that at one time v. 4 followed v. 2; then v. 2 would describe the offspring of the extraordinary unions recounted in v. 4. Another difficulty in interpreting this passage is that the precise meaning of three key terms is unknown: *yadon* (v. 3; NIV "contend"), *beshaggam* (v. 3; NIV "for"), and *nefilim* (v. 4; NIV "Nephilim").

Late in the Second Temple period (ca. 200 B.C.) apocalyptic writers became so fascinated with this narrative that they composed intricate stories of how a host of angels rebelled against God, fell from their high position, and spread evil on earth. According to these writers, the rebellion of the ancients resulted from their entering into unnatural unions with human women (e.g., *1 En.* 6–11).

6:2 / The daughters are described as good *(tobot).* Most often "good" is translated "beautiful," the usual understanding for the attraction of the sons of God. However, it may mean that they were morally good, especially since this is the dominant meaning of the word in the primeval account (e.g., 1:31; 2:9; E. van Wolde, *Words Become Worlds: Se-*

mantic Studies of Genesis 1–11[Biblical Interpretation Series 6; Leiden: E. J. Brill, 1994], pp. 73–74). In that case it may support the position that the daughters were from Seth's line, the line that worshiped Yahweh (4:26); only his genealogy customarily mentions the birth of daughters. So for van Wolde vv. 1–3 do not recount some sin; rather they give the reason that God placed a limit on the life span of the children from this union. For her the issue in this narrative is immortality, not immorality.

6:3 / Suggestions for the meaning of *yadon* include "be humbled, humiliated" (based on Arab. *dun*) and "be strong, powerful" (based on Akk. *dananu*). Most translators follow the LXX and Vg. rendering "remain," but the basis for this meaning is unknown.

6:6 / "Grieve" *(nkhm)* is very difficult to translate, especially when God is the subject. One of its meanings is to take a different course of action as a result of one's compassion being either warmed (Hos. 11:8–9) or grieved (here). Translating it "grieve" captures the emotion behind the action but fails to convey the person's strong resolve to take a different course of action. Often *nkhm* is translated "repent" or "relent." However, when God is the subject "repent" is a poor Eng. translation, for repent carries the idea of remorse for wrongdoing. The sense of "relent" or "change the mind" fails to capture the deep emotions that compel God to take a different course. Thus no Eng. equivalent proves satisfactory.

God's relenting usually means that out of mercy he foregoes intended punishment (e.g., Exod. 32:12, 14; Amos 7:3, 6). Only twice in the OT does "relenting" describe God's turning from favor to punishment (here and God's rejection of Saul in 1 Sam. 15:11).

There is a linguistic tie between v. 6 and 5:29. Lamech named his son Noah that he might comfort *(nkhm)* people from their labor *(ma'aseh)* and painful toil *('itsabon)*. Here God was grieved *(nkhm)* that he had made *('asah)* humans, and he was filled with pain *(hit'atseb;* Cassuto, *From Adam to Noah,* p. 303).

§9 The Great Deluge (Gen. 6:9–8:22)

Because violence has increased to an intolerable level (6:1–8), God enters as judge. The Creator produces a great flood whose waters inundate the dry ground, wiping out all animal life. God thereby uncreates the earth by returning it to a chaotic condition similar to that described in 1:2. In mercy God delivers Noah, his family, and representatives of all the animals in order that they may populate a renewed earth. Afterward God declares that human life will never again be wiped out by a flood.

Frequent references to time with two distinct numbering systems structure this account. One system is based on the day, month, and year of Noah's age, and a second defines a period in the number of days between stages:

Dates *(month, day, year)*		*Verse*
2-17-600	Waters begin	7:11
7-17-600	Ark rests on Ararat	8:4
10-1-600	Tops of mountains appear	8:5
1-1-601	Waters dry up	8:13
2-27-601	Noah leaves ark	8:14–15

Days	
7 days for the flood to begin	7:4
7 days for loading the ark	7:10
40 days of rain	7:12
40 days of deluge	7:17
150 days of floodwaters	7:24
150 days for floodwaters to recede	8:3
40 days before sending out raven	8:6–7
7 days later sending out a dove	8:10
7 days later sending out a dove	8:12

The second system gives the number of days leading to the deluge, for the deluge, and for disembarking. The forty days of rain and the forty days of the deluge refer to the same period and seem to be included in the 150 days of floodwaters. If this is correct, this numbering system has the flood lasting 361 days, or 368 days if the first dove was sent out seven days after the raven. According to the system of dates, the deluge lasted around 370 days, assuming months of thirty days. If the months lasted 29.5 days, the duration of the flood was a solar year of 365 days. Thus the numbers are very close. Since the numbers of days have symbolic value and are set in a palistrophic pattern, the two numbering systems mesh quite well.

Using repetition and numerous words for totality, the author conveys that all the dry land inhabited by humans was inundated. Forty-four times "all" modifies a word pertaining to the deluge. In 7:18–24 there is a concentration of categorical terms. These verses say four times that the waters swelled (i.e., "triumphed"; *gabar,* 7:18, 19, 20, 24; NIV has "rose," and "flooded" in 7:24). Many words are modified by "all": the entire heavens (v. 19), all the high mountains (v. 19), all the creatures (*basar;* v. 21), all humankind (v. 21), every living thing (*yequm,* v. 23), everything that had the breath of life (v. 22), and all on dry ground (v. 22, NIV blends these last two phrases). The statements that "only" Noah survived (v. 23) and that "the waters covered the mountains to a depth of more than twenty feet" (v. 20) add to this emphasis.

This account contains nine units arranged in a palistrophic (chiastic) pattern (A, B, C, D, E, D′, C′, B′, A′):

A Noah's righteous character in a violent culture (6:9–12)
    B God instructs Noah to build an ark (6:13–22) and the remnant enters the ark (7:1–10)
        C The start of the deluge (7:11–16)
            D The waters rise (7:17–24)
                E God remembers Noah (8:1a)
            D′ The waters recede (8:1b–5)
        C′ The waters dry up (8:6–14)
    B′ God instructs Noah to leave the ark (8:15–19)
A′ Noah sacrifices (8:20–22)

God's remembrance of Noah stands at the center (8:1a) of this arrangement. This pattern also augments the theme of the ebb and flow of the waters (Wenham, *Genesis 1–15,* p. 157).

6:9–10 / Noah's *toledoth* heads the account of the cataclysmic flood. Verse 9 identifies him as **a righteous man** *(tsaddiq),*

blameless *(tamim)* **among the people.** "Righteous" describes a person who faithfully observes God's laws and avoids wrong-doing; "blameless" depicts a person of integrity who zealously seeks to please God in everything. Like Enoch before him (5:22), Noah **walked** in close fellowship **with God. He had three sons: Shem, Ham and Japheth** (5:32).

6:11–12 / During Noah's time **the earth** had become ut-terly **corrupt and was full of violence** (6:5). Such wickedness pol-luted the earth (Lev. 18:24–28). There is a wordplay on "corrupt" *(shakhat)* in verses 11–13. Since the earth was corrupt (vv. 11, 12), made corrupt by humans sinning (v. 12), God would destroy (lit. "cause corruption," v. 13) both the humans and the earth. The repetition of this root stresses that God was acting justly in bring-ing judgment.

6:13–22 / **God** informed **Noah** of the imminent deluge and instructed him to build **an ark** *(tebah)* in order that he and his household might survive. The text does not mention the time it took Noah to build the ark. God spoke to Noah three times (see also 7:1; 8:15), but no verbal reply from Noah is recorded. Instead, Noah demonstrated that he was truly righteous by faith-fully carrying out God's instructions (6:22; 7:5, 9, 16). God in-structed Noah to **make an ark of cypress wood,** having **rooms,** and to **coat it with pitch.** It was to have three decks, **a roof,** and **a door in the side.** It measured 450 feet long, seventy-five feet wide, and forty-five feet high with a displacement of about forty-three thousand tons. Given that the Hebrew term *tebah* ("ark") occurs only here and in reference to the basket in which baby Moses was placed (Exod. 2:3, 5), it describes a vessel capable of floating in order to deliver its occupant(s) from danger. Strictly speaking the ark was not a boat, for it lacked both a means of power and a steering mechanism. Consequently, the course it took and its ability to deliver its occupants were completely under God's direction.

God told Noah that he was **going to bring floodwaters** *(mabbul)* **on the earth to destroy all life** in which there was **breath** (v. 17). However, God promised to **establish** his **covenant,** a for-mal agreement that defines a variety of relationships, **with** Noah. God spoke of it as "my covenant," because he was committing to it unilaterally. "Establish" *(qum)* usually occurs with a covenant that is already in existence (9:9, 11, 17; 17:7, 19, 21). This covenant, then, was either the one God had made with humans at creation (implied by humans' being made in the image of God, 1:28), or God was anticipating the covenant he would establish after the deluge (9:8–17).

Noah was to **enter** the ark with his **sons,** his **wife,** and his **sons' wives.** Also he was **to bring into the ark two of all living creatures, male and female,** including **every kind of bird,** beast, and **creature that moves along the ground.** The account does not mention fish; these inhabitants of the waters would survive the flood. God also instructed Noah to put on board an abundant supply of **food.** Obediently **Noah did everything just as God commanded.**

7:1–10 / **Seven days** before the deluge was to begin, Yahweh commanded **Noah** to enter **the ark** with his **whole family.** This time God directed him to take **seven** pairs of every **clean animal** and every **bird** and **two of every kind of unclean animal.** These instructions about clean animals supplement the earlier ones God gave (6:19–20) and explain how Noah could make sacrifices after the deluge without depleting any species. Prior to the Sinaitic law, animals were most likely classified as clean and unclean in regard to which ones could be sacrificed, not according to which were edible (Sarna, *Genesis,* p. 54). Noah had seven days to load the ark before God would **send rain . . . for forty days and forty nights.** Doing as Yahweh **commanded, Noah,** his family, and the **animals . . . entered the ark.**

7:11–24 / **On the seventeenth day of the second month** of Noah's **six hundredth year,** God produced a cataclysmic flood by letting **all the springs of the great deep burst forth, and** opening **the floodgates of the heavens.** God hereby reversed the steps taken on the second and third days of creation, when he divided the primordial water into two main bodies and set them securely in place, one beneath the earth and one above the heavenly dome (1:6–10). Once released, these waters inundated the inhabited earth. After the occupants had **entered the ark,** Yahweh **shut** the door. This statement is theologically crucial, for it informs us that God, the sovereign Judge, took sole responsibility for those who were not permitted to board the ark.

The waters continued to rise **for forty days.** Four references to the death of the animals, with differing verbs, stress that outside the ark no life that breathed survived. As the waters bore the ark away, the occupants were safe from the turbulence.

8:1–5 / **God remembered Noah** and all the occupants of the ark. This short, powerful statement is underscored by its position at the center of the palistrophic pattern of this account. "Remember" (cf. 19:29; 30:22) means that God was entering the scene to reverse the destructive forces of water in order to reclaim the earth for habitation. This simple but powerful sentence stands at the center of the account as it marks God's putting a stop to the forces of destruction and initiating the restoration of the earth. God **sent a wind over the earth, and the waters receded. The springs of the deep and the floodgates of the heavens** were **closed.** Just as the Spirit manifest as wind controlled the chaotic waters prior to creation (1:2), so God again employed the wind to drive the waters back to their reservoirs, where they would be securely held. By **the seventeenth day of the seventh month** the waters had receded sufficiently for **the ark** to come **to rest on the mountains of Ararat.**

8:6–13 / **After forty days Noah opened the window.** In order to discover how far the waters had receded, he **sent out a raven.** Possibly it went out from the ark several times; then one time it did not return. Since it was a feeder on carrion, it must have eventually found abundant food. Presumably seven days later, Noah **sent out a dove,** a gentler bird that prefers lowlands and whose food sources would require land that had been dry for a while. This bird would let him know if **the water had receded** from the valleys. The dove **returned. Seven days** later he released **the dove.** This time it **returned** with **a freshly plucked olive leaf,** informing Noah that plant life was growing and the earth could again sustain the animals that were on board. **Seven days** later Noah **sent the dove out again.** When **it did not return,** Noah knew that **the waters had** fully **receded** so that the animals might safely leave the ark. He took **the covering from the ark and saw** for himself that **the ground was dry.**

8:14–19 / Nevertheless, Noah waited patiently for God's orders before leaving the ark. Those orders came on **the twenty-seventh day of the second month.** God charged all those leaving the ark to **be fruitful and increase** on earth. This command reiterated the one God had given humans at creation (1:28), indicating that God's purpose for the population of the earth remained the same.

8:20–21 / As his first act on dry ground **Noah built an altar to** Yahweh. He took **some of all the clean animals and clean birds,** slaughtered them, and offered **burnt offerings.** He presented these animals as praise offerings, lauding God for deliverance from the terrors of the deluge. In contrast to other gods of the ancient Near East, Yahweh was not dependent on sacrifices for sustenance; God's acceptance of a sacrifice is therefore noted by God's smelling a pleasant aroma. Smell is a powerful sense, being crucial to enjoying and discerning different tastes in foods and being a great stimulator of the memory. The smoke of this sacrifice stirred God's compassion, moving him to be favorably disposed to humanity.

God then declared that he **never again** would **curse the ground** by a deluge because of humans, **even though every inclination of** the human **heart is evil from childhood.** Westermann (*Genesis 1–11*, p. 456) points out that "curse" *(qillel)* in this form and in this context has a broad meaning ("treat disdainfully"). It says that the deluge had not changed human nature. This statement underscores God's mercy toward humans in the continuation of human life on earth, and it alerts humans not to expect that societies from then on would be free from wickedness. Thus God had caused the deluge to punish intolerable violence on earth, not to transform human nature (6:5).

Nevertheless, despite the human inclination toward evil, God promised that **never again** would he **destroy all living creatures.** In other judgment accounts in Genesis, such as the Tower of Babel (11:1–9) and Sodom and Gomorrah (ch. 19), God judged selectively, not universally. From now on God would hold communities accountable in a manner that would prevent the entire earth from becoming corrupted by human wickedness. Furthermore, God's mercy, not anger, would set the tone for divine-human relationships. Since humans would continue to do wicked deeds, God did not want them to fear extinction.

8:22 / From now on the movement of the seasons would be dependable, despite the crises humans face. The seasons—**seedtime and harvest, cold and heat, summer and winter**—along with **day and night,** mark the flow of time. This assures humans that life on earth continues uninterrupted, while at the same time letting them know that as individuals they are getting older.

Additional Notes §9

The relationship of this account to the Babylonian flood accounts, the literary character of this account, and the extent of the deluge need some comment. First, numerous flood accounts from throughout the world have survived. The biblical account has most in common with those from Mesopotamia, namely, Ziusudra, Atrahasis, and tablet eleven of the Gilgamesh Epic. The similarity of the biblical account to the Babylonian accounts suggests either that the biblical author adapted a Babylonian account or that both accounts go back to a common source. A. Heidel argued persuasively for the latter position (*The Gilgamesh Epic and Old Testament Parallels* [Chicago: University of Chicago Press, 1949], pp. 260–67).

Two major characteristics set the biblical account apart from the Babylonian accounts: the sovereignty of God and moral principle. Unlike the Babylonian gods, who cowered in fear before the rising waters (Gilgamesh Epic 11:113–26), the one God was not threatened by the waters (Ps. 29:10). When Utnapishtim, the Babylonian Noah, offered a sacrifice after the flood, the gods crowded about the ascending smoke as flies (11:160–61). Apparently they were very hungry, since the catastrophe had prevented humans from providing them food. God, however, accepted Noah's sacrifice just like any other offering of praise.

Furthermore, God judged righteously in Genesis, punishing the wicked and rescuing the righteous. God forewarned Noah, giving him instructions to deliver his household and the animals from the flood. But Enlil, the god of the storm, brought on the flood irrationally (11:168), making no distinction between the characters of those who were destroyed and those who survived the flood (11:179–88). Ea, the Babylonian god of wisdom, however, devised a scheme to alert Utnapishtim, a resident of Shurippak, about the coming destruction. Ea did so indirectly, by speaking to the reed hut where Utnapishtim lived (11:20–31) so that some humans might survive. Ea took this devious means in order to avoid Enlil's wrath, threatened against any of the gods who would forewarn any human of the coming deluge (11:170–73). No reason is given for Ea's favoring Utnapishtim.

After building a boat in seven days, Utnapishtim took on board a variety of skilled workers, seemingly with no regard for their character (11:84–85). Utnapishtim, however, duped the people of his city by telling them that he had to leave their city because Enlil had turned hostile to him, while Enlil was going to make them prosper (11:39–47). Just before the deluge Utnapishtim made a great feast with rivers of liquor so that the citizens would not be alarmed by the rising waters (11:70–74). After the flood Enlil granted Utnapishtim and his wife eternal life, but they had to live at the mouth of the rivers, which was far removed from society (11:189–95). By contrast, God delivered only Noah and his household because of Noah's righteous character. Nothing is reported in the biblical account of how Noah responded to his neighbors (but see 2 Pet. 2:5). God displayed his mercy after the deluge by establishing a unilateral covenant of peace with all humans, not just Noah. In fact, Noah continued to live like the other primeval peoples until his death.

A second problem is the literary issue of how to explain the repetitions that mark this account. Those repetitions include two names for God, Yahweh and Elohim; a flood of forty days (7:4, 12, 17a) and a deluge of 150 days (7:24; 8:3); the command to take on board a pair of all animals (6:19–20) in contrast to the command to preserve seven pairs of clean animals (7:2–3); and the twofold command to enter the ark (6:18b–20 and 7:1–3), along with the double report of taking occupants on board (7:7–9 and 13–16a). Throughout the twentieth century, scholars attributed these repetitions to an editor who wove together two flood stories that had circulated independently in the collections of the Yahwist (J) and of the priestly source (P). The segments they assigned to the respective sources are as follows: J (Yahwist): 6:5–8; 7:1–5, 7–8, 10, 12, 16b, 17, 22–23; 8:2b, 3a, 6–12, 13b, 20–22; and P: 6:9–22; 7:6, 9, 11, 13–16a, 18–21, 24; 8:1–2a, 3b–5, 13a, 14–19.

Several studies have reevaluated this literary analysis and discovered that the final form of this account of the deluge was composed as a whole (e.g., B. Anderson, "From Analysis to Synthesis: The Interpretation of Genesis 1–11," *JBL* 97 [1978], pp. 23–39). Its palistrophic construction is as a story that moves in stages toward and away from a center, with the respective stages echoing each other. The time spans also follow such a pattern: 7, 7, 40, 40, 150, 150, 40, 7, and 7 days. G. Wenham discovers other examples of this pattern in smaller segments of the account ("The Coherence of the Flood Narrative," *VT* 28 [1978], pp. 337–42). This intricate, unified structure requires a final author who used the repetition for emphasis.

A third perplexing issue is whether this account reports a universal or a local flood. It is important to stress that the cosmology of the OT allowed for a universal flood. At creation God divided the sea into two parts and then formed the mountains (1:6–10). In ancient thought God could reverse the steps of creation at will, causing the mountains to sink and the seas to rise (Ps. 104:5–9). Furthermore, the view of chaos-cosmos is tied into that of God's blessing and cursing. Thus in judgment God moves the earth toward chaos (see on 1:2), but in blessing he brings the forces of cosmic order to flourish. Second, we know from the great number of flood accounts that the tradition of a great flood was widespread. This evidence, however, is offset by the fact that several peoples in a variety of locations lack a flood account, including two of ancient Israel's closest neighbors, Egypt and Ugarit. Another difficulty is the lack of geological evidence of a global flood after humans occupied the earth.

The local flood view is not necessarily the opposite of a global view. Since, from the biblical author's perspective, the deluge covered the known land mass, the flood is spoken of in categorical terms. But for that author the earth was a landmass surrounded by water, not a giant sphere. Consequently the categorical language does not require a global flood. Thus, the acceptance of a deluge of reduced dimensions squarely faces the lack of geological evidence that a common flood covered the entire Levant. Future geological studies might close the gap between the written record and human knowledge. In the meantime this text teaches soundly that all humans are morally accountable to God.

6:14 / The precise meaning of *goper,* translated either "cypress" or "cedar wood," has been lost. "Rooms" is *qinnim* (lit. "nests"), but others prefer to read *qanim* ("reeds"), for both Moses' ark and the ark in the Babylonian account were made from reeds.

6:17 / *Mabbul* ("floodwaters") is used for this deluge. The precise meaning is debated. It may mean "destruction," or it may refer to the part of the great body of water confined above the expanse (1:7). The only other occurrence of this term is Ps. 29:10: "The LORD sits enthroned over the flood."

8:4 / The ark came to rest somewhere in the mountain range of Ararat, in Urartu in the area of Lake Van, not necessarily on the highest peak, Mount Massia, which is about seventeen thousand feet in elevation. Over the centuries this mountain has often been identified as Mount Ararat.

§10 God's Blessing on Noah and His Offspring (Gen. 9:1–17)

After the great deluge God gives to Noah and his sons the same blessing he gave to humans at their creation (1:28), empowering them to prosper and to replenish the earth. Further, we learn that humans continue to bear the image of God; each person possesses intrinsic value. Yet God introduces three drastic changes. First, God grants humans permission to eat meat. Second, dread of humans henceforth characterizes the way animals respond to humans. Third, God also establishes a covenant with Noah and his offspring, guaranteeing never again to destroy the earth by a flood. This covenant gives humans confidence to build communities without fearing another catastrophe of total devastation.

Two speeches from God provide the structure for this section: God blesses Noah and his children (vv. 1–7), and God makes a covenant with all humans (vv. 8–17). The first speech, framed by the command that humans are to be fruitful, multiply, and fill the earth, emphasizes God's design for humans (vv. 1, 7).

9:1–7 / God defined the future relationship of humans to the earth and to himself in four definitive statements. First, **God blessed** them, commanding them to **be fruitful and increase in number and fill the earth.** Next, humans had mastery over the animals. Now all animals would have **fear and dread** before humans. The character of human relationship to animals shifted from one of commonality to one of apprehensive distance. Then, in addition to the diet of **green plants,** God granted humans permission to eat **everything that lives and moves.** To this provision God attached a strong prohibition: humans **must not eat meat that has its lifeblood still in it.** This principle became a central premise of the food laws in the Sinaitic covenant (e.g., Lev. 3:17; 17:10–14). Finally, God categorically prohibited the shedding of human blood, backing up this law by affirming that he would **surely demand an accounting** for any human blood shed, whether by animals (Exod. 21:28–32) or by humans. The threefold repetition of "I will demand an accounting" (*'edrosh*) underscores God's determination. Since every human bears **the image of God,** "murder is direct and unbridled revolt against God" (Westermann, *Genesis 1–11,* p. 468). God therefore declared that a murderer is subject to capital punishment. This penalty is based on the principle of *lex talionis* and is warranted by the fact that the murderer has violated God's image.

9:8–17 / In this second speech God solemnly bound himself by a covenant never again to wipe out the inhabitants of the earth by a deluge. This covenant was unilateral; that is, no conditions were laid on humans for keeping it in force. This was an **everlasting covenant** (v. 16) **for all generations to come** (v. 12).

The repetition of several pivotal terms communicates God's goal. In the Hebrew the key term "covenant" *(berit)* occurs seven times (three times with **establish,** *heqim,* vv. 9, 11, 17, two times with **remember,** *zakar,* vv. 15, 16, one time with **making,** *natan,* v. 12, and one time in the phrase "the sign of the covenant," v. 13; NIV, however, reads "covenant" eight times by inserting this word in its second occurrence in v. 12). The repetition of **every living creature** *(kol nepesh khayyah,* four times) and **all life** *(kol basar,* five times) stresses that God's covenant is with all humans. This covenant also concerns God's relationship to **the earth** *('erets),* which he mentions seven times (in the MT; the NIV has this only six times). As a **sign** and guarantee of this covenant God placed **a rainbow** *(qeshet,* three times) **in the clouds** *(be'anan,* three times). The interweaving of these pivotal terms evokes the image of a beautiful tapestry of God's desire that all humans have confidence in divine mercy as they populate the earth. Moreover, in this way God fulfills the promise made to Noah before the deluge (6:18).

Whenever he sees the rainbow, God **will remember** (keep in force) this **covenant.** It is implied also that the rainbow reminds humans of God's promise. Throughout the OT various signs and symbols characterize the relationship between God and humans. These symbols inspire humans to worship God wholeheartedly and gratefully.

Additional Notes §10

9:1–7 / The rabbis find here God's law for Gentiles and refer to it as the Noachide covenant. Joining the principles of this passage with their understanding of God's commands to Adam, the rabbis identify seven universal commandments: against idolatry, against blasphemy, against shedding of blood, against unchastity, against theft, against cutting off a live animal's limb, and for civil courts. Accordingly Gentiles do God's will by keeping these commandments.

9:6 / It is possible that the second line is better translated "for a human shall his blood be shed" instead of "by a human." This human, then, is the victim, not the executioner (J. Lust, " 'For Man Shall His Blood Be Shed': Gen. 9:6 in Hebrew and Greek," in *Tradition of the Text* [ed. G. Norton and S. Pisano; OBO 109; Freiburt, Switzerland: Universitäts-verlag, 1991], pp. 91–102).

9:13 / Hb. *qeshet* means both "bow" and "rainbow." The bow is an important symbol in Near Eastern myths. In Hb. poetry it sometimes stands for God's aggression (e.g., Ps. 7:12–13; Lam. 2:4; 3:12; Hab. 3:9). Hanging up the bow symbolizes God's commitment to act peacefully toward humans. But since the best rendering of this term is "rainbow," any allusion to a myth of God's defeating the turbulent waters with his deadly bow is discounted.

§11 Noah Curses Canaan and Blesses Shem and Japheth (Gen. 9:18–29)

In a style characteristic of Genesis, the account of Noah closes with his genealogy. Attached to this genealogy are Noah's contribution to culture, the report of a troubling incident, and Noah's blessings and curses.

9:18–19 / The three sons of **Noah, Shem, Ham and Japheth,** are identified as those who left **the ark.** These sons of Noah were the heads of the peoples who populated the earth. Only one grandson, **Canaan,** is mentioned because of his place in what follows.

9:20–23 / After the deluge **Noah,** like Adam, worked **the soil.** He developed viniculture, which places him on the same plane as the other predeluvian innovators (4:20–22). From the harvest of his vineyard he made **wine,** a highly prized drink. The ancients had little variety in drinks, and this new product brought joy and relaxation to humans ("wine . . . gladdens the heart," Ps. 104:15). This achievement is in accord with Noah's name, which means "rest." This also confirms that after the deluge God continued to bless the ground for the benefit of humans.

On one occasion Noah drank so much wine that **he became drunk.** Drunkenness leaves one vulnerable to acting shamefully or becoming the object of a shameful act (Prov. 23:20–21, 29–35), as happened to Noah. That night Noah entered his tent and took off his clothes, possibly to have relations with his wife. That he was in the privacy of his tent indicates that he was still acting with some discretion.

Ham saw his father's nakedness. The ordinary reading of this text finds that Ham's only offense is that he saw his father's nakedness. Interpreters have sought, however, to discover in these words a more scandalous action, such as Ham's sodomizing Noah or even castrating him. On the basis that the idiom "to uncover a man's nakedness" is a euphemism for having intercourse (e.g., Lev. 18:6–17), another proposal has Ham committing incest with his mother. In that case Canaan might have been born from the result of that illicit union. This reconstruction has the advantage of accounting for Noah's curse on Canaan, Ham's youngest son. However, it fails because of the way "saw" and "uncover" are used in this text and because the remedy was "covering" Noah. In that society the offense of seeing a parent's nakedness brought shame and dishonor on the parent. Suffering such an indignity was a severe affront, especially to a person of high standing like Noah.

Ham increased his transgression by reporting the incident to **his two brothers;** this is particularly true if he bragged about what he had seen. In antiquity shaming a parent was a serious offense, as evidenced by the death penalty for striking or cursing a parent (Exod. 21:15, 17).

On learning what Ham had seen, **Shem and Japheth** acted honorably. Taking discreet steps that make carrying out their mission very awkward, they **covered their father's nakedness** in such a way that they **would not see** him. They seek to remove the cause of their father's shame without adding to it.

9:24–27 / **When Noah awoke,** he came to know **what his youngest son** Ham **had done.** The text does not state how he found out. In a response typical of a patriarch, he **cursed . . . Canaan** and **blessed** his other two sons, Shem and Japheth. These blessings and curses are important, for the ancients believed that they influenced the destiny of their offspring down through the centuries. Canaan was to become **the lowest of slaves . . . to his brothers.** This curse meant that Canaan's descendants would be defeated in battle by peoples from Shem and Japheth. Why Noah directed his wrath at Canaan is far from clear; all suggestions are at best conjectures. A. P. Ross ("The Curse of Canaan," *BSac* 137 [1980], p. 233) postulates that Noah perceived the same traits in Canaan that had motivated Ham to commit such an offense.

It is preferable, however, to interpret these as blessings and curses on the nations or peoples descending from the sons rather than on them as individuals. Canaan is referred to here because of the key role his people would play in redemptive history. Israel had a long, hard struggle against the Canaanites in order that Israel might fully occupy the promised land. The Canaanites also caused Israel several setbacks, especially in influencing the nation with their illicit sexual practices. Thus Ham's treatment of his father represented the immoral practices of the Canaanites (15:16; Lev. 18:24–30; 20:23). In this light the curse may be viewed as a prophetic oracle rather than as a direct curse on Noah's grandson (Ross).

Noah blessed his other two sons, Shem and Japheth. Uniquely he blessed Yahweh through Shem rather than blessing Shem directly. Noah stated to each son that **Canaan** would **be his slave.** In addition, Noah said, **May Japheth live in the tents of Shem.** This blessing means either that Japheth would have strong, peaceful relations with the people of Shem or that, increasing in strength, Japheth would infringe on Shem's territory. Another view is that this unique formulation points to Israel, the people of God, coming through the line of Shem and bringing blessing to the peoples descending from Japheth.

Comparing the response of Noah's sons to the transgression of Ham with the reactions of Adam's sons to murder yields valuable insight. Cain showed no remorse for having killed his brother, and Lamech boasted of his willingness to commit multiple murders (4:9, 23–24). Although Ham bragged about what he had seen, two of Noah's three sons, including the oldest, acted redemptively by seeking to remove their father's shame, a hopeful sign that brother with brother would protect members of the family and would help each other deal with troubling situations.

9:28–29 / Noah's family history states that he lived **350 years** after the deluge. Thus he saw the beginning of the new order of civilization. In all Noah lived **950 years.** This family history underscores the fact that in contrast to his Babylonian counterpart, Atrahasis, who received eternal life after surviving the deluge, Noah lived a normal life and died as did other humans.

Additional Notes §11

9:25 / It is very troubling that Ham's youngest son is cursed because of his father's actions. Scholars have proposed several solutions, but none has been found compelling. An old rabbinic interpretation holds that Noah could not curse Ham, who had been blessed, so he cursed his son. A few think that the text originally read "cursed be the father of Canaan" (R. Saadia Gaon) or that Ham's name accidentally was displaced by Canaan's. Others argue that since Ham was Noah's youngest son—the order in v. 18 not being according to age—Noah in retaliation cursed Ham's youngest son. Another view postulates that Canaan was cursed for participating in the sin with his father (Ber. Rab. 36:7). The fact is that only one grandson of Noah was cursed, in contrast to the recent judgment of the deluge. Though this is troubling to contemporary readers, it indicates that although the offense against Noah was serious, it was a single occurrence. If Noah had cursed Ham, many more peoples would have been affected. In the context of Scripture, it is best to understand the curse as on the Canaanites for their immoral practices (so U. Cassuto, *A Commentary on the Book of Genesis,* vol. 2, *From Noah to Abraham: A Commentary on Genesis VI 9–XI 32* [trans. I. Abrahams; Jerusalem: Magnes, 1964], pp. 154–55). This view understands Noah's sons to characterize the nations that descended from them.

This curse has played an important role in race relations. Slave traders and owners in the seventeenth and eighteenth centuries A.D. in particular used it as a defense for their cruel trafficking in humans, even to the point of claiming that they were carrying out God's will in their slave trading. Their faulty identification of Canaanites with Africans and the obscurity of the curse show how they twisted a text for justification of their brutal deeds. Furthermore, these slavers were very wrong in a second sense: in his redemptive death Christ freed all humans from the curses found in the old covenant.

9:28 / The phrase "after the flood" is taken by Cassuto (*From Noah to Abraham,* p. 171) to mean the flood of forty days (7:17); otherwise, if it meant after the ark landed on Mount Ararat, Noah would have been 951 when he died.

§12 The Table of Nations (Gen. 10:1–32)

The Table of Nations presents a geographic picture of the nations as they occupied the earth at the end of the primeval age. The peoples, all descended from Noah, were divided into three major groups according to their lineage from each of Noah's sons. The geography in this table covers parts of Asia, Europe, and Africa, from the Iranian plateau in the east to the Mediterranean coastlands in the west, from the Black Sea in the north to Somalia in Africa. The locus is Canaan, the future land of Israel.

The names in this table include personal names (Japheth and Nimrod), gentilics for tribal groups (Hamite and Amorite), place names (Kittim and Sidon), countries (Egypt), and professions (Canaanites, or traders). The bonds connecting the subgroups vary. Some have a common ancestry, while others are united by a treaty. In antiquity, parties to a treaty referred to each other in terms of family relationships, as father, son, and brother. Two other elements connecting peoples are cultural influence, such as Egypt and Babylon, and geographical proximity, such as the descendants of Japheth. Language is not a criterion for any of the groupings in this table.

B. Oded proposes that the three divisions correspond to different sociopolitical organizations that grew out of the distinctive cultural contributions of the peoples in each division ("The Table of Nations [Genesis 10]—A Socio-Cultural Approach," *ZAW* 98 [1986], pp. 14–31). Among the sons of Japheth many were famous for seafaring skills. Shem was the head of those who lived as nomads or enclosed nomads, a line to which Abraham would belong through Eber. Ham was the head of those who developed urban civilization based on the economics of farming and industry. The flowering of civilization and the building of city-states took place in Mesopotamia and Egypt.

This table mentions only one hero, Nimrod. Two reasons might account for this anomalous inclusion. His story parallels that of the cultural heroes of Genesis 4, and he plays a key role as the founder of the first empire.

This text teaches that all peoples and tribes are interrelated. No tribe exists independently of the others; nor is one inherently superior. This teaching stands in marked contrast to the ideology found among other peoples of the ancient Near East. Many people had a story in which their god founded them first; afterward the gods founded the other nations. Such a story elevated that people far above the other peoples on earth. This table shows God's desire that there be a multitude of nations as a result of his blessing Noah and his sons (9:1, 7). Later God would elect one nation from Shem's line. That election, however, is the means by which God's blessing would reach all tribes and peoples. Whatever God achieves for and through his people has merit for all the peoples, since God's people are an integral part of the fabric of all nations.

Reference to Noah's sons frames the table (vv. 1, 32). The three lists of peoples coming from these sons occur in inverted order to their names in verse 1: the sons of Japheth (vv. 2–5), the sons of Ham (vv. 6–20), and the sons of Shem (vv. 21–31). The list moves from the offspring of Japheth, with whom Israel had little contact, to the offspring of Ham, some being Israel's neighbors, and then to Shem, the line of Israel's ancestors. The genealogical depth varies from three generations for Japheth to six for Shem.

Seventy symbolizes that a group is whole and complete (e.g., seventy of Jacob's descendants went down to Egypt [46:27; Deut. 32:8]). While there are seventy-one names in this table, most think that the list proper consists of seventy names, given the importance of the number seventy in Hebraic thought. One way to gain this ideal number is by not counting Nimrod, who is a person, not a tribe (Cassuto, *From Noah to Abraham*, p. 177). Another option is not to count the Philistines, for they are identified in relationship to geography, not by lineage as the other members of the list (Wenham, *Genesis 1–15*, p. 213). The symbolic force of this number conveys that all nations and tribes are interconnected, including those not named.

10:1 / Verses 1 and 32 frame the Table of Nations. They affirm that all the peoples, tribes, and nations descended from Noah's three sons **after the flood.**

10:2–5 / **The sons of Japheth** are essentially Indo-European peoples who populated the vast area from India across Asia Minor into southern Europe. Settling along the seacoast and on numerous islands of the Mediterranean, many of them became highly skilled sailors. The distance of these nations from Israel explains the brief coverage given to Japheth's sons.

10:6–20 / **The sons of Ham** are the peoples of northeastern Africa and Palestine: **Cush** (Ethiopia), **Mizraim** (Egypt), **Put** (possibly Somalia or Libya), and **Canaan.** Hamilton (*Genesis: Chapters 1–17*, p. 336) postulates that Canaan is placed here because the Canaanites were city dwellers like others among the sons of Ham.

Nimrod (vv. 8–12), the son of Cush, was a legendary hero (Mic. 5:6). Several proposals have been put forth for his identity, from historical figures like Naram Sin, grandson of Sargon I of Akkad, who ruled for fifty years in the second half of the third millennium B.C., to legendary figures like Gilgamesh. **A mighty hunter,** Nimrod was typical of ancient Mesopotamian and Egyptian kings who prided themselves on their hunting feats. The text states twice that Nimrod achieved fame as a hunter "**before** Yahweh." This phrase elevates Nimrod's achievement to a superior level. It also shows that Yahweh was involved in the course of the development of the nations.

Nimrod established a kingdom in southern Mesopotamia. **Babylon** served as a capital for great kingdoms that included northern Mesopotamia in the eighteenth century B.C. and the sixth century B.C. **Erech** is the Sumerian city Uruk. According to Mesopotamian tradition, it was the second seat of kingship after the flood, and Gilgamesh was ruler of this city. **Akkad** succeeded Uruk as the center of kingship. There Sargon I set up a Semitic dynasty in the twenty-fourth century B.C. **Calneh, in Shinar** (Babylon), remains unidentified.

Nimrod also founded cities in **Assyria** (Asshur); this statement indicates that centers of power in Babylon extended their influence into Assyria. Thus Nimrod is honored as the first empire builder. **Calah,** present-day Nimrud, is located close to where the Upper Zab empties into the Tigris. It served as capital of Assyria in the ninth century. **Nineveh,** often serving as the capital of Assyria, was on the Tigris.

The peoples listed in verses 13–14 are connected with Egypt.

Verses 15–18a list some of Canaan's city-states and tribal groups. **Sidon** was the key Phoenician port city during the second millennium B.C.; it represents all of Phoenicia. In Genesis, **Hittites** refers to the inhabitants of the hill country of Canaan, not to the citizens of the famous empire in Anatolia, although some scholars hold that the former were survivors of that empire. **Jebusites** occupied the hill country in the Cisjordan, the land area west of the Jordan river. In David's time their center was Jerusalem (Josh. 15:63; 2 Sam. 5:6). **Amorites** lived across a wide area of the Levant during the first part of the second millennium B.C. In Akkadian texts they particularly occupy Syria and Lebanon (14:7; 48:22). By the end of the third millennium the Amorites had moved into many of the centers of population in Mesopotamia (Ezek. 16:3, 45), and by the end of the second millennium B.C. they had become assimilated with the other inhabitants of Canaan (there are references to them in Josh. 2:10; 3:10; 9:1; A. H. Sayce and J. A. Soggin, "Amorites," *ISBE* 1:113–14; 14:7). The identity of the **Girgashites,** one of the tribes that occupied Canaan, is unknown (15:21; Deut. 7:1; Josh. 3:10; 24:11). **Hivites,** whose settlements were from Shechem north through Lebanon, are sometimes identified with the Horites; more precise information is unavailable. **Hamathites** were the citizens of Hamath, an important city on the Orontes, over 130 miles north of Damascus (Num. 13:21; 1 Kgs. 8:65).

Since **Canaan** (vv. 18b–19) became the land of promise, its boundaries are given (Num. 34:2–12). The western boundary went from **Sidon** in the northwest to **Gerar** in the southwest, a site about fifteen miles west and north of Beersheba (20:1). The eastern boundary went through the Arabah, as indicated by the names **Sodom, Gomorrah, Admah and Zeboiim,** which are cities located at the southern end of the Dead Sea (ch. 14). The most northeastern point was **Lasha,** possibly Laish (Dan), but its identification is uncertain.

10:21–31 / The line of **Shem** stands last, for from it came the people God elected. The relationship of Japheth to Shem in v. 21 may be read in one of two ways: his **older brother was Japheth** (NIV, LXX, Rashi [a medieval Jewish commentary]) or "the oldest brother of Japheth" (RSV and most scholars). Three arguments favor the latter reading: Shem comes first in all the lists of Noah's sons (5:32; 6:10; 7:13; 9:18; 10:1); the Hebrews come from this line; and the need to mention this fact here arises from the fact that Shem's descendants stand last in this table, otherwise the addition of this detail is superfluous.

Shem had five sons. His youngest son, **Aram,** the ancestor of the Arameans (or Syrians), had four sons. The genealogy of

Shem's middle son, **Arphaxad,** is given for two generations to **Eber,** for Abraham belonged to his line.

Eber had two sons, **Peleg** and **Joktan.** Scholars are divided on explaining the connection between Eber and Hebrew; possibly Hebrew is the gentilic form of Eber (see additional note on 14:13). In Peleg's time the **earth was divided;** this statement is a play on the meaning of his name, "divide." The event that is referred to is uncertain; it might be a reference to the Tower of Babel (11:1–9). Peleg's genealogy is given in 11:18–26. **Joktan** had thirteen sons. Their territory ranged from **Mesha toward Sephar.** The location of Mesha is uncertain; many take it to be in northern Arabia. As for Sephar, two sites have the name Zafar: the Himyarite capital near Sana in present-day Yemen, and a site on the coast close to Shihr in the Hadramaut (G. Oller, "Sephar," *ABD* 5:1089). Another possibility is to take this term as a noun meaning "borderland"; the line then reads "from Mesha, as far as the border, namely, the hill country of the east."

Verse 31 is a summary statement regarding **the sons of Shem.**

10:32 / See comments on 10:1.

Additional Notes §12

10:2 / **Gomer** may be identified with the Cimmerians, who eventually settled in Cappadocia (Ezek. 38:6). **Magog,** coupled with Gog in Ezek. 38:2 (cf. Ezek. 39:1), was probably located in Asia Minor. **Madai** is the father of the Medes. They lived between the upper Tigris and the Caspian Sea, possibly as early as the latter part of the second millennium. They became famous for their great empire in the middle of the seventh century B.C. (Isa. 13:17; 21:2). Cyrus incorporated them into the Persian Empire. **Javan** identifies the Ionian Greeks, settlers on the western coast of Asia Minor (Ezek. 27:13). **Tubal** is connected with Tabal, a site south of the Halys River and west of Togarmah (Ezek. 27:13; 32:26; D. Baker, "Tubal," *ABD* 6:670). **Meshech,** the Mushki, occupied central and eastern Anatolia. **Tiras** may be connected with the Tyrrhenians, later known as the Etruscans; they settled in Italy after being forced out of Phrygia in central Asia Minor.

10:3 / **Ashkenaz** is usually identified with the Ashkuza or Ish-kuza, the Scythians in Herodotus. They lived in the area of the Black and Caspian Seas (eighth–seventh centuries B.C.; R. Hess, "Ashkenaz," *ABD* 1:490). **Riphath** has not been identified. **Togarmah** refers to a people in the area between the upper Halys and the upper Euphrates, the land of the Hittites (Ezek. 27:14; 38:6).

10:4 / **Elishah,** also spelled Alashiya, was either part or all of Cyprus (Ezek. 27:7) or a city on Crete, since Kittim is identified with Cyprus. Westermann (*Genesis 1–11*, p. 507) takes the two names for different parts of Cyprus. **Tarshish** is usually located in the western Mediterranean (1 Kgs. 10:22 margin; Jonah 1:3). One suggestion is Tartessus in southwestern Spain, but most scholars think that this city is too far west. If **Kittim** is the same as Kition, it is a city on the southeastern coast of Cyprus, present-day Larnaka; by extension it came to refer to the whole island (Num. 24:24; Jer. 2:10; Ezek. 27:6). Dodanim is better read **Rodanim** (LXX, NIV), i.e., for the island of Rhodes. Dodanim may refer to the people of Danuna, located north of Tyre (Wenham, *Genesis 1–15*, p. 219).

10:6 / **Put** is in Africa, but its precise location is unknown (Jer. 46:9; Ezek. 38:5). The strongest arguments favor Libya (LXX and Vg.), but another possibility is Somalia.

10:7 / **The sons of Cush** are located in Africa or Arabia. **Seba** is either along the Ethiopian coast or a place in present-day Suakin (W. Müller, "Seba," *ABD* 5:1064). **Havilah** is the tribal federation of Haulan, a group with many branches. This particular branch may be located in the west of Sa'da. It is probably a different site than Havilah in 2:11 (W. Müller, "Havilah," *ABD* 3:81). Havilah is also mentioned in v. 29; the double reference may represent the converging of two lines (D. Block, "Table of Nations," *ISBE* 4:710). Some identify **Sabtah** as the capital of Hadramaut (W. Müller, "Sabtah," *ABD* 5:861–62). **Sabtecah** is unknown. **Raamah** was possibly Ragmatum, the capital in the Oasis of Nagran, which is in present-day southwestern Saudi Arabia (W. Müller, "Raamah," *ABD* 5:597). **Sheba** was a famous trading center in southwestern Arabia, flourishing in the first half of the first millennium B.C. (25:3; 1 Kgs. 10:1–2; Isa. 60:6). Its inhabitants were the Sabeans. There is also Sheba, a son of Joktan, in Shem's line (v. 28). The two names have been explained as the convergence of Hamite and Semitic groups in South Arabia. **Dedan** was a tribe in northwestern Arabia, close to Edom. It was also the name of Khuraybah, a town in the Hijaz (25:3; Ezek. 27:20; 38:13; D. Graf, "Dedan," *ABD* 2:121–22). On the basis of an inscription Wenham locates it at Al-Alula, southwest of Tema (*Genesis 1–15*, p. 222; Gen. 25:3; 1 Chron. 1:32).

10:8 / It is an enigma that a Cushite is ruling among peoples of Mesopotamia. Some scholars therefore identify Nimrod as a great Egyptian ruler; proposals include Pharaoh Amenhotep III, who also had the name Nimmuri (fourteenth century B.C.). On one hunting expedition this pharaoh claimed to capture 102 lions. Since Nimrod is tied to Mesopotamia, Cush is more likely the city Kish, which in Mesopotamian tradition was the center of kingship after the flood. Another view links Cush with the Kassite rulers in Babylon in the second half of the second millennium B.C. Or Nimrod may have been a god, possibly Ninurta, the war god and the god of the hunt.

10:11–12 / **Rehoboth Ir,** which means "city squares," may have been an area in Nineveh or another name for that great city (J. Davila, "Rehoboth-Ir," *ABD* 5:664). **Resen,** said to be between Nineveh and Calah, remains unidentified.

10:13–14 / **Ludites** are generally presumed to be settlers in North Africa, since they are named with African peoples in Jer. 46:9 and Ezek. 30:5 and with peoples in Asia Minor in Isa. 66:19. **Anamites** are unknown. **Lehabites** may be an alternate spelling for the Libyans. According to G. Rendsburg ("Gen 10:13–14: An Authentic Hebrew Tradition Concerning the Origin of the Philistines," *JNSL* 13 [1987], pp. 89–96), the following three names are inhabitants of different areas of Egypt: **Pathrusites** in Upper Egypt, **Naphtuhites** in Middle Egypt, and **Casluhites** in Lower Egypt. The text states that **the Philistines** came from the Casluhites, but they migrated from Crete, not Egypt. A possible solution is that some of these Egyptians migrated to Crete and later became part of the wave of Sea Peoples that included the Philistines (R. Hess, "Casluhim," *ABD* 1:877–78). During this migration the Sea Peoples attempted to settle in the Nile delta, but they were driven back. Some of them then settled on the coast of southwestern Canaan (Amos 9:7; Jer. 47:4). **Caphtorites** were the inhabitants of Crete.

10:17–18 / These verses list peoples associated with the Phoenicians. **Arkites** could be the citizens of Irqata (1 Chron. 1:15). **Sinites** may be the people of Siyannu, a city-state south of Ugarit. **Arvadites** are the citizens of Arvad, a northern Phoenician city built on an island, two miles from the coast (1 Chron. 1:16; Ezek. 27:8, 11). **Zemarites** remain unidentified; they are found in lists of the early inhabitants of Canaan. **Hamathites** are the citizens of Hamath on the Orontes.

10:22 / **Elam** was an important state to the east of Mesopotamia in the Iranian plateau (14:1), a continual rival to the peoples in Mesopotamia. That region was the source of several natural resources and was on the trade routes to the east and the north. **Asshur,** an important city on the Tigris, gave its name to the Assyrians, founders of a great empire in northern Mesopotamia. This city served as their capital from the fourteenth to the ninth centuries B.C. **Arphaxad** is unidentified (11:10). The identification of **Lud** is far from certain.

10:23 / **Uz** may be a site in the area of Syria (Job 1:1, but many locate the Uz of Job in Edom). **Hul, Gether and Meshech** (or Mash, MT) may be other Syrian cities.

10:24 / The location of **Shelah,** a member of Jesus' lineage according to Luke 3:35, is unknown (11:12–15; 46:12; Num. 26:20; 1 Chron. 2:3).

10:26–29 / This list contains names of various Arab clans and tribes. **Almodad** may have been a tribe in the area of Qataban, an ancient kingdom located in southern Yemen with Timna as its capital (W. Müller, "Almodad," *ABD* 1:160). **Sheleph** may be the name of a district in Yemen or the tribe as-Salif or as-Sulaf in the area of Ibb. **Hazar-**

maveth refers to a tribe living in the Wadi Hadramaut in South Arabia. Jerah may refer to another people of that area. Hadoram may be the Yemenite *Dauran,* who occupied the upper area of the Wadi Dahr, about ten miles northwest of Sanaa. Uzal has been explained as an earlier name for Sana, capital of Yemen, but the Sabean inscriptions do not support this identification. W. Müller ("Uzal," *ABD* 6:775) points out that two other places in Yemen have the name Azal, a region in ar-Radama and a region of the Banu 'Ammar, northeast of Ibb. If Diklah comes from Aram. *diqlah* ("date palm"), it was an oasis with date groves, possibly in the area of Sirwah. Obal and Abimael are not known. Sheba (see v. 7) may refer to the Sabeans, a Semitic people of the southwestern Arabian Peninsula (25:3). Ophir, a place famous for gold (1 Kgs. 9:28; Job 22:24), may have been on the Arabian coast. Jobab may be Juhaibab, a town near Mecca, or possibly the name of a Sabean tribe in ancient Sumay in the center of Yemen (W. Müller, "Jobab," *ABD* 3:81).

§13 The Dispersion of Humans for Their Building at Babel (Gen. 11:1–9)

The preceding Table of Nations describes the unity among all peoples on earth, while this narrative gives the reason for the diversity, discord, and distrust that exist among the various clans, tribes, and nations. In this narrative the people take counsel and begin to build a tower (vv. 1–4); God in response takes counsel and puts an end to their building (vv. 5–8); and the episode is memorialized by naming that place Babel, that is, Babylon (v. 9). This famous city symbolizes commerce, human achievement, and the pursuit of pleasure. It is also known for its ziggurat, named Etemenanki, a temple with a terraced tower of three to seven successively receding stories. Mesopotamians thought that the earth met heaven at the top of the tower.

The author makes skillful use of alliteration and wordplays (see Cassuto, *From Noah to Abraham*, pp. 232–36). The consonants *l*, *b*, and *n* are stressed; in verse 3 there are five *l*s, four *b*s, and five *n*s. The inversion of the letters of a key word in the first section creates a subtle play in the second section: *nilbenah*, "let us make bricks," in verse 3 is echoed in *nabelah*, "let us confuse" in verse 7. There is a play on three other terms: "fame" or "name" (*shem*, vv. 4, 9 [not represented in NIV]), "place" (*sham*; vv. 2, 7, 8 [not represented in NIV]), and "heaven" (*shamayim*, v. 4). And there is a pun on the name Babel and "confuse" *(balal)*. These sounds build toward the naming of the city Babel (v. 9; Wenham, *Genesis 1–15*, p. 234) and forcefully tie the story with every mention of that name. The alliteration heightens the tension between the design of these city dwellers and God's judgment of their actions. Such precise use of terms allows a great event to be told in a few sentences as well as making the story memorable.

11:1–4 / The events these verses record took place over a long span of time, possibly decades. A majority of the population, who presumably spoke a common language, migrated eastward

into a broad **plain in Shinar,** southern Mesopotamia. Having
lived as nomads, the people decided that life would be better if
they **settled** down. Over time they discovered how to make bricks
in large quantities. Inspired by this discovery, they took counsel
and decided that they would **build . . . a city** and **a tower** to reach
to the heavens. It is possible that the tower they envisioned was a
ziggurat. The people undertook this mammoth project because
they wanted to make a name for themselves, for they were
searching for some type of immortality. That humans find a sense
of immortality in erecting monumental buildings is seen even in
ancient times.

The survival of great monuments attests that these buildings do leave an enduring heritage. Several ancient rulers are still
famous for a major building; for example, Ur-Nammu for the ziggurat of Ur, Gudea for Eninnu, a temple in Lagash, and Djoser for
the Great Pyramid. Furthermore, such monuments, which survive through the ages, offer a sense of eternity.

The people also wanted to avoid being scattered over the
earth by establishing their own power base without any regard
for God. A city enables a mass of people to live together in a small
area, and it offers an environment far less dominated by the vicis-
situdes of nature.

The aspirations of these settlers in Shinar are characteristic
of the human search for utopia, but all humans in that region
would have had to submit to a common system. Oppression
would have become intolerable as no exceptions to the common
laws and rule would have been allowed. Those in leadership
would be lords, and those at the bottom would be enslaved
to the system. As W. Brueggemann says, "The narrative then is a
protest against every effort at oneness derived from human self-
sufficiency and autonomy" (*Genesis* [Interpretation; Atlanta: John
Knox, 1982], p. 100).

11:5–8   /   Concerned about what was happening in Shinar, Yahweh **came down** to inspect **the city** and **the tower.** This
bold anthropomorphic language has a dual purpose. Since God
was about to execute judgment with profound consequences for
humanity, the author makes it clear that God acted sagaciously
and judiciously (cf. 18:16–21). Also, a strong note of sarcasm is lev-
eled against these great plans. Whereas the builders aimed for
heaven, their work was so minuscule that God had to come down
to earth in order to see it.

Aware that humans who spoke a common language had the potential for accomplishing whatever they planned, God foresaw that their course would lead to an intolerably oppressive society. God also saw that this plan opposed his intention that the people multiply and disperse over the earth (1:28; 9:1). To put an end to such potential wickedness God judged their effort by confusing **their language so** that **they** would **not understand each other.** Different languages separate peoples. Groups who are unable to communicate with each other tend to fear and despise those they call foreigners. The twofold loss of workers and of collective knowledge brought the building activity to a halt. No longer able to communicate with each other, these peoples became **scattered . . . over** the face of **the earth.** This story accounts for the multiple dialects and languages spoken throughout the earth.

11:9 / That place received the name **Babel because** Yahweh **confused** *(balal)* **the language of the whole world.** The name Babel *(babel)* is a play on the cacophony of numerous languages.

Additional Notes §13

11:1 / Since Scripture holds that all humans descended from a common ancestor, it is necessary to account for the origin of numerous languages. However, present-day study of languages has not been able to support the position that all languages come from a common source. Hamilton *(Genesis: Chapters 1–17*, p. 350) answers this difficulty with a different interpretation of "one language" in this text. He supposes that the inhabitants of Shinar spoke a *lingua franca*. This view also addresses the conflict between the way this account is usually understood and the references to local languages in the Table of Nations (10:5, 20, 31). However, there is no signal in the text to require taking chs. 10 and 11 as reports of events in chronological order. It is possible that the narrator wanted to present the general picture of the dispersion of peoples in the Table of Nations before recounting a major cause, but not the only cause, for this dispersion. Moreover, this order permits the description of the dispersion of the nations as God's plan without the added sense that the dispersion was caused by a divine judgment, which would be the primary reading if the narrative of Babel stood before the Table of Nations.

11:3 / These construction methods are typical of Mesopotamia. The lack of stones prodded people to make buildings out of dried bricks. They used bitumen as mortar, but peoples west of there did not.

11:4 / "With its head in heavens" is a Semitic expression for something very tall (e.g., Deut. 1:28; 9:1); this is supported by a line in the Babylonian Creation Epic that reads, "they raised the head of Esagila (the name of the temple) toward heaven" (Westermann, *Genesis 1–11*, p. 547).

11:6 / Two rare roots, *z-m-m* ("purpose, devise") and *b-ts-r* ("be impossible") occur together only here and in Job 42:2. Job employs these terms to laud God's ability to do exactly as he plans. Here they describe the hubris of humans in thinking that like God they can achieve anything they plan.

11:7 / The shift to first person plural cohortatives indicates that God took counsel with the heavenly court (1:26). The fact that God's activity mirrors that of the city dwellers (v. 4), both cohortatives being preceded by *habah* ("come"), supports this interpretation.

§14 The Descendants of Shem to Abraham (Gen. 11:10–26)

11:10–26 / This linear genealogy opens with a *toledoth* formula and recounts the lineage of Noah's son Shem. Following the Table of Nations (ch. 10), this genealogy focuses on the line that leads from Noah to Abraham, through whom God would build his own people. The list consists of nine persons as it points to a tenth person (Westermann, *Genesis 1–11*, p. 560) and probably does not include every ancestor from Shem to Terah. The list establishes that the era from Noah's leaving the ark to the call of Abraham was 365 years. The pattern is person *a* was *x* years old when he fathered person *b*; person *a* lived *y* years and fathered sons and daughters. For example, Shem was one hundred years old when he fathered Arphaxad; afterward he lived five hundred years and had other sons and daughters.

Besides Shem, who became a father at one hundred, the age for giving birth was around thirty; this age is closer to human experience than are the ages for giving birth recorded in Genesis 5. Furthermore, the life span of these people diminishes rapidly from six hundred years for Shem to 433 years for Shelah to 205 years for Terah. These numbers witness to the transition from the primeval age to the early historical period. Most of the names are Aramean. The names of Terah's three sons, in a concluding segmented genealogy, correspond to place names in upper Mesopotamia in the region of Haran, the setting for a large part of the patriarchal narratives.

Additional Notes §14

11:10–26 / The Sam. Pent. and LXX have different ages for the time of fathering and for the life span. The reasons for these differences are far from clear.

11:26 / This Haran is spelled differently than the place Haran (12:4)—the former with *h* and the latter with *kh*.

§15 God Calls Abram (Gen. 11:27–12:9)

This section begins the Abraham narrative (11:27–25:18), which details Abraham's life from the time he receives God's call to the time of his death. (See the Introduction for a survey of the Abraham narrative as a unit.) The Abraham narrative opens with a travelog and the family history, or *toledoth*, of Terah, which begins here, and continues through 25:18. Members of this family set out from their home in Ur of the Chaldeans to go to Canaan (11:31). They stop at Haran, where they decide to settle. Later God commands Abram to go on to Canaan, and Abram obeys. Once there, he moves through the land, making three stops for indefinite periods: at Shechem (12:6), between Bethel and Ai (12:8), and in the Negev (12:9). At the center of this account is Yahweh's call of Abram and the wonderful promises Yahweh makes to Abram. These promises, God's program for establishing his kingdom on earth, are the key both to Genesis and to the Pentateuch. Further, they continue to be fulfilled in the lineage of the children of Abraham and in those who follow Christ, who came to make these promises available to all who believe in him.

These verses divide naturally into two sections, Abram's lineage (11:27–32) and Abram's call (12:1–9). This second section contains a unit about God's commands and promises to Abram (vv. 1–3) and another unit about Abram's journey to Canaan (vv. 4–9). The word "go" ties these two parts together; God commands Abram to "go" (12:1), and in obedience he "went" (12:4).

11:27–28 / **This is the account** *(toledoth)* **of Terah.** Even though Terah plays no role in the following episodes, the narrator of Genesis traditionally introduces a major section with the genealogy of the main character, beginning with that person's father. This account also contains essential information for understanding what follows. The mention of the death of **Haran**, Lot's father, prepares the reader to understand why Abram takes Lot under his care (12:4).

11:29–30 / **Abram's wife was Sarai.** In Hebrew her name means "princess," and in Akkadian it means "queen," the name of the moon god's consort. None of her lineage is given, but in 20:12 we learn that she is Abram's half-sister, born to Terah by a different mother than Abram's. **Nahor** married his niece **Milcah,** another Akkadian term for "queen" and the title of Ishtar, the moon god's daughter. These names indicate that this family came from a culture that worshiped the moon god (Josh. 24:2, 15). The note that **Sarai was barren** will be a major factor in Abram's journey of faith.

11:31–32 / **Terah,** along with members of his immediate family, **set out from Ur of the Chaldeans** for **Canaan.** Abram, Lot, and Sarai accompanied him. It is not stated whether Nahor and Milcah went along at this time or later; they did come to Haran, as 22:20–24 and 24:10 indicate. When these travelers arrived at **Haran,** an important trading center in upper Mesopotamia located on the Balikh River, which flows into the Euphrates, they decided to settle. At Haran, a center for the Amorites, and Ur, the chief god was the moon god (Akk. *Sin*). At this point the text reports that Terah **died** there at the age of **205.** A comparison of the dates in the following narratives indicates that he died only two years before Sarah did (23:1). The narrator records his death here since he has no role in the following stories.

Although the text does not state why Terah left Ur, God prompted his movement. Two facts support this idea. First, his initial destination was Canaan. Second, the description of Abram's departure from Haran and arrival in Canaan (12:5) is expressed in the same way as Terah's leaving Ur. What Terah began and failed to complete, Abram accomplished. An early credo also traces Israel's origin to Abram's leaving Ur (Josh. 24:2–13). In the early church Stephen also interpreted Abram's move from Ur to Haran in this way (Acts 7:2–5). Having accompanied Terah from Ur, Abram possessed a framework for understanding the directions God was about to give him.

12:1 / Yahweh addressed **Abram,** ordering him **to leave** his **country,** his **people, and** his **father's household.** The text offers no description of the manner of Yahweh's appearing, no superfluous detail to detract from the definiteness of this call. In Hebrew a play on sounds in the command "leave" *(lek leka)* underscores its urgency (cf. 22:2). God identified precisely what Abram was to leave by using three terms that move from the general to the specific; the threefold repetition stresses that Abram had to separate completely from his family. "Country" is the region around Haran. "People" is the larger ethnic group to which Abram belonged. "His father's household" was his extended family, identified in the preceding genealogy of Terah. People in the Western world who prize the freedom of moving freely from place to place fail to realize how demanding this call was for Abram. A father's house was the basis of a person's identity, livelihood, and security; most ancients never wanted to leave the solidarity of the family. For Abram, however, God's command demanded that he shift his orientation and security from his lineage and his homeland to God and his promises.

Why did God demand that Abram leave Haran in order to become the bearer of these promises? The answer probably lies in the cultural practices of that day. If Abram had begun to worship only one God in Haran, he would have placed his life in jeopardy. For example, his new devotion would have led to his absence from various celebrations such as the great new year's festival at which the destinies for the coming year were set. The community would have frowned at his absence on such important occasions. Should they have tolerated Abram's presence, the citizens would have immediately considered that the gods were angry at them if disaster struck Haran. They would have blamed Abram, and at best they would have banished him. Consequently, for Abram to follow God with singleness of purpose, he needed to leave Haran and wander about in a land under no sovereignty but God's.

12:2–3 / God supported the call with two sets of three promises each. In the first set, God expressed a commitment to Abram. The first promise was that God would **make** him **into a great nation.** The term "nation" (*goy*) for Abram's offspring indicates that his lineage would become so numerous that one day they would become a nation counted among those listed in the Table of Nations (ch. 10; cf. ch. 17). This promise addressed the future far beyond Abram's life. In accepting this promise Abram placed the destiny of his descendants above his own welfare. At this time God did not identify the land where Abram's offspring would develop into a nation. Only after Abram had arrived in the land of promise did God make a specific promise about land (v. 7). God's second promise was to **bless** Abram. Blessing, which corresponds to the English word "success," encompasses the well-being of a person or a people: good health, long life, numerous offspring, fertile fields and flocks, harmony within the clan, and freedom from oppression. Emphasis falls on this word "blessing," which occurs five times. By its nature a blessing is a process that takes considerable time for its realization. Thus in calling Abram God was looking far into the future. The third promise is that God would **make** his **name great.** In this promise God addressed the human search for recognition and respect and thus provided the proper way to fame, in bold contrast to the misguided search for fame that inspired the building of the tower of Babel (11:4). The noblest reputation comes from a life directed by God for the good of others.

Between these two sets of promises, Yahweh exhorted Abram to "become **a blessing**" (NIV renders the line "you will be a blessing"). That is, Abram was to let this blessing work in him and his family in order that he might become the agent through whom God might bless others.

God then gave the second set of three promises. The first two are a complementary pair, showing how God would affect other nations through Abram and how God would protect Abram among the nations (27:29; Num. 24:9). God would **bless those who** blessed him. Any person or people who sought or promoted Abram's welfare would be blessed. Conversely, **whoever cursed** Abram God would **curse.** One cursed Abram or his seed by hindering him, inflicting harm on him, or undermining his reputation.

Then God stated the highest goal for Abram's calling. **All peoples on earth will be blessed through** him. The verb may be better translated "find or obtain blessing." God's primary way of working among the nations is through Abram's seed. Thus, to experience God's blessing, the various peoples must interact with Abram's offspring. Having selected one family, God in a sense shows favoritism, but his design is not parochial. God was and is working through one family for the benefit of all families. Through Abram's seed he is achieving his goal in creating the earth, namely, people worshiping only him. That this program is just rests in God's wise sovereignty.

The centrality of these promises is evident in the way they function as a uniting link throughout Genesis. The promise of numerous descendants occurs many times: 13:16; 15:5; 17:5–6; 22:16–17; 26:4; 28:14; 35:11. Their number will be as great as the dust (13:16; 28:14), the stars (15:5; 22:17; 26:4), and the sand on the seashore (22:17). Twice God specifically promises that Sarai will bear a son (17:16; 18:10). The promise that the nations will find blessing through Abram's seed appears in 22:18; 26:4; 28:14; Acts 3:25; Gal. 3:8 (cf. 27:29). At other times these promises are a part of the flow of the narrative (24:7; 48:3-4). In addition, God directly tells Isaac (26:3-4) and Jacob (28:13-14; 35:11-12) that they are heirs of the promises given to Abram. The promise of land, first given in 12:7, is repeated in 13:14-15, 17; 15:18-21; 17:8; 26:3-4; 28:13-14; 35:12.

12:4-6 / Abram acted immediately on God's word. At the age of **seventy-five** he left Haran with **his wife Sarai** and **his nephew Lot.** We may assume that he invited other relatives to accompany him, but only Lot, whom Abram had reared after his father's death, accepted. Abram also took along their **possessions** and **the people,** presumably servants, **they had acquired in Haran.** The band set out for Canaan. There is no information about their journey, but they most likely took the main highway to Damascus, then traveled through the Huleh Valley to the Sea of Galilee. Once in Canaan, Abram left the main highway, the Via Maris, across the lush Jezreel Valley, possibly because this road went through a more heavily settled region. Instead he went through the sparsely settled hill country, where there was plenty of open land for his flocks to graze.

Arriving **at Shechem,** a strategic site in the heart of Canaan, Abram stayed a while at **the great tree of Moreh.** This tree was either a terebinth or an oak. The name Moreh, meaning "teacher, diviner," indicates that this place might have been famous for receiving oracles.

A parenthetic note states that **the Canaanites were in the land.** Abram's descendants would have to deal with them before they occupied the land.

12:7 / After Abram had pitched his tent in Canaan, Yahweh **appeared to** him in recognition of his obedience in leaving Haran for Canaan. The initiative for this divine appearance rests solely with Yahweh; God did not appear because Abram was in the vicinity of a sacred tree. As in verse 1, there is no mention of any phenomena accompanying Yahweh's appearance, for the focus is on the new promise: **to your offspring** (seed) **I will give this land.** "To your seed" stands at the head of the sentence for emphasis, making it clear that this promise is to be realized by Abram's descendants. This is the first time God included the gift of the land as a part of the promises. The land was necessary for Abram's descendants to develop into a great nation (v. 2).

In joyful response to God's confirming word, Abram **built an altar** to Yahweh, **who had appeared to him.** His action indicates that he did not go to an existing shrine or temple but erected a new altar to the God who had called him at Haran. Probably he built the altar by piling up either dirt or stones (Exod. 20:24–25). Building an altar implies that Abram offered up some kind of sacrifice, but the text says nothing about either the type of sacrifice or the ritual. Since Abram was worshiping God spontaneously in a new land, the thrust of this report is Abram's devotion to God.

12:8–9 / Abram continued his journey, moving eastward through the hill country, pitching **his tent** next at a place identified as **Bethel on the west and Ai on the east.** "Pitching" suggests that he camped there for a period of time. Again he **built an altar to** Yahweh **and called on the name of** Yahweh. He continued to honor God for guiding and protecting his company in their journey. This place, where Jacob is to have a dream when he flees from Esau (ch. 28), does not have a name here. Giving a name is an honor that will become Jacob's. Afterward Abram continued to travel through Canaan, moving **toward the Negev.** The Negev, the region south of the hill country, is an expansive, high steppe with little rainfall. Whenever the rainfall is normal or better, sufficient grass grows to provide good grazing for flocks in the spring. Abram had traversed the land of promise from north to south, marking out the land that God was promising his seed.

Additional Notes §15

11:28 / Ur was an important city-state in southern Mesopotamia for several centuries; it was the leading center from around 2100 to 2000 B.C. The phrase "of the Chaldeans" was probably added in the retelling of these patriarchal stories to identify Ur for later generations, for the Chaldeans are not mentioned in Akkadian texts until after the ninth century B.C. (de Vaux, *Early History of Israel,* pp. 187–88). Because of the great distance between Ur and Haran, about five hundred miles, various scholars have proposed different sites in northern Mesopotamia for this Ur. An identification that goes back to the nineteenth century is Urfa, present-day Edessa, a town some twenty miles northwest of Haran. The journey from there to Haran would have been a normal trip for people of that day. A city to the north of Haran overcomes another difficulty, namely, that Haran was not on the main highway from Ur to Canaan. Also, it helps deal with the problem that if Abram came from southern

Mesopotamia his journey was in the opposite direction of the Amorite migration at the end of the third millennium B.C. This alternative view has not won wide acceptance. At present the information from that time is too scarce to decide conclusively which site is the most likely home of Abram.

11:31 / In Akk. Haran means "route, journey, caravan." Haran was an important trading center where Amorite tribes lived at the beginning of the second millennium B.C., and its culture was a blend of Amorite and Hurrian elements (Y. Kobayashi, "Haran," *ABD* 3:58). There is no connection between this town and the name of Terah's son, for in Hb. the two names are spelled differently.

12:2 / Usually in the OT Israel is "the people" *('am)* or "the children of Israel" *(bene yisra'el)*, and *goy* refers to the other nations. That "nation" occurs here is significant; it conveys that the number of Abram's descendants will increase enough to be organized into a nation numbered among the other nations (ch. 10).

12:3 / There are two different words for curse in v. 3b. Such a variation is unusual, for the Hebrews like to repeat terms for assonance and emphasis. The first verb, *qll,* has a wider usage, meaning "disdain, treat with contempt, curse," but the second term, *'rr,* is stronger and more focused, and it denotes God's release of a harmful force such as a plague to punish those who obstruct the way of or mistreat any of Abram's descendants. The strength of the term with God shows God's resolve to protect Abram and his seed from all opposition. This latter word dominates curse formulas such as those found in Deut. 27:15–26.

The best way to render the verb "bless" at the end of v. 3 is debated. It stands in the Niphal, thus having either a middle or a passive sense. Which sense is preferable? The versions, including Vg. and Tg., along with Eng. translations, have favored the passive. But some scholars advocate a reflexive meaning, "bless themselves," drawing support from restatements of this promise with the Hitpael (22:18; 26:4). Others have argued for a middle sense, i.e., "find or obtain a blessing." This latter position captures the need of the nations to actively be involved in promoting Abram's seed as the way to participate in his blessing.

12:6 / The precise identification of the tree meant by Hb. *'elon* is debated. While many consider it a terebinth, a deciduous tree, a few identify it as an oak, either the Tabor oak or the evergreen oak (M. Zohary, *Plants of the Bible* [Cambridge: Cambridge University Press, 1982], pp. 108–11). The fact that the Hb. terms for these two trees are so similar adds to the confusion. Curiously, accounts about Shechem mention a tree several times (35:4; Josh. 24:25–26; Judg. 9:6, 37).

12:7 / "Seed" (often translated "descendant") is a motif that runs through the Abraham narratives; it is placed in parentheses throughout this commentary so that readers may know when it stands in the Hb. text (13:15, 16; 17:7, 8, 9, 10, 12, 19; 22:17, 18; 24:7; 26:3; 28:13).

§16 Abram's Perilous Encounter in Egypt (Gen. 12:10–20)

On reaching the southern region of the land of promise, Abram faces two dangers that cast a heavy shadow over the promises God has made. A severe famine strikes Canaan, causing Abram to leave the land of promise for Egypt. Then, in Egypt Sarai is taken to Pharaoh's harem. Only God's intervention delivers Abram and Sarai from Pharaoh's power so that they may return to Canaan together.

12:10–13 / Up to this point Abram had journeyed from Haran through Canaan apparently without incident. Now, at the southern boundary of the land of promise, he discovered first-hand that this land has a major drawback. It is a land periodically subject to famine, since its rainfall is sporadic. During such a crisis many of the inhabitants had to migrate in order to keep themselves and their flocks alive. Therefore, as did occupants of Canaan before him, Abram **went down to Egypt** to find food. Until the Aswan Dam was built, Egypt, which never has significant rainfall, received its water from the annual flooding of the Nile. That flooding made Egypt lush, for the waters soaked the soil, depositing rich new silt. After the Nile receded, the inundated land produced bumper crops. The height of the Nile varied from year to year, depending on the amount of rainfall central Africa received. Whenever the Nile did not rise very high, Egypt faced a famine. Such occasions were rare, however, and they did not correspond to the rainfall in Canaan.

On approaching Egypt, Abram became apprehensive about the way the Egyptians might receive them, fearing that they might **kill** him in order to take Sarai, **a** very **beautiful woman.** Given Sarai's age, it is possible that the Egyptians favored a mature mother figure with an attractive countenance. Abram, therefore, devised a shrewd scheme. He asked Sarai to identify herself as his **sister.** Possibly Abram anticipated that if anyone desired to marry Sarai, that person would have to negotiate with him. In that case he could forestall the suitor until the famine lifted; then he could return to Canaan with his wife. This scenario draws on the important role a brother played in a sister's marriage in the patriarchal age, as is evident in Laban's role in permitting Rebekah to become Isaac's bride (24:29–60) and Jacob's sons' obstructing their sister's marriage to Shechem (34:13–17, 25–29). Abram's immediate apprehensions clouded his memory of God's protection and blessing, causing him to jeopardize God's promise of a great nation through his offspring from Sarai.

Abram's passing his wife off as his sister troubles us as it has troubled students of the Bible throughout the centuries. Why did the great patriarch offer information in a way that was sure to deceive others? If she was his sister, even a half-sister, why was he in a marriage defined as incestuous in the law (Lev. 18:9, 11)? In answer to this last problem, God had not revealed to Abram the standards of the covenant. Moreover, Abram's failures, including this one, remind us that Abram was a real person, not a perfect, ideal character such as is found in heroic tales. At times he displayed great courage and acted in bold faith; at other times he succumbed to fear and acted in a weak, self-serving manner. While his failures warn us against stumbling, his journey informs us that a great feat of faith, such as Abram's leaving Haran for an unknown destination, does not guarantee that the doer will face every difficult situation with such great faith. There is an ebb and flow in a person's relationship with God. The crucial issue for one who falters while walking with God is the response to that failure. If a person shows genuine remorse for the wrong done, then that person continues walking with God.

12:14–16 / In Egypt Sarai's beauty enamored the people, as Abram had feared. Some **officials** brought **Pharaoh** a glowing report of her beauty. To Abram's surprise Pharaoh had Sarai brought to the **palace** so that she might become a member of his harem—without consulting Abram. Pharaoh then **treated Abram,** her brother, **well.** There is an ironic play on "well." Abram encouraged Sarai to identify herself as his sister so that he might be treated well (v. 13), i.e., allowing him to feed his family and flocks during the famine in Canaan. He did not have in mind the way Pharaoh treated him *well* **for her sake** by sending him gifts of **sheep, cattle, male and female donkeys, menservants, maidservants, and camels.** The large number and diversity of animals indicate that Pharaoh viewed Abram as nobility. These gifts may also be viewed as an elaborate dowry for Sarai. P. Reis ("Take My Wife, Please: On the Utility of the Wife/Sister Motif," *Judaism* 41 [1992], pp. 307–8) argues that Abram acted shrewdly in designing a plan whereby he might become rich by receiving a dowry for his own wife. This view is suggestive, but Abram never appears that cunning or that greedy. Further, it is significant that Pharaoh sent these gifts after he had taken Sarai. This fact, along with the great value of these gifts, suggests that he indirectly conceded that he had not followed proper protocol. He had failed to negotiate with Abram for the privilege of taking his sister into his harem. These gifts demonstrated that Pharaoh knew that Sarai was under Abram's protection. Pharaoh could have moved more slowly, winning Abram's confidence and then seeking his permission to marry his sister.

12:17–20 / Since the promise of abundant seed through Sarai was in jeopardy, Yahweh entered the scene to rescue Sarai and to protect Abram. He **inflicted serious diseases on Pharaoh and his household.** The Hebrew term rendered "diseases" can be translated "plagues." This affliction alerted Pharaoh that a powerful deity was cursing him because of Sarai's presence in his household. Since Pharaoh himself was considered to be a god, he would respond with deference to Abram and Sarai only if he believed that the source of the plagues was a mighty god. From another perspective, as monarch, he should have sought to protect these visitors to his land instead of being enamored with Sarai's beauty.

Pharaoh responded by summoning **Abram** to the palace. Outraged at being thwarted and desiring to save face, he challenged Abram with three questions in rapid succession. He asked **what** Abram had **done** to him and blamed Abram for what had taken place. He next asked **why** Abram had not told him outright that this woman was his **wife.** Finally he inquired as to **why** Abram had identified her as his **sister** with the result that he had taken her **to be** his **wife.** With the third question Pharaoh passed blame for the serious ailments in his household from himself to Abram.

Apparently without giving Abram any opportunity to offer a defense, Pharaoh ordered Abram to **take** his wife and **go.** Abram realized that Pharaoh had some basis for condemning him and that, being an absolute monarch, he acted with a degree of mercy in letting both of them leave Egypt with all these gifts.

To end this infuriating situation Pharaoh ordered **his men** to escort **Abram** and his wife with their possessions out of Egypt. Aware that God was watching over Abram, Pharaoh wanted to guarantee their safe passage and to make sure that they left Egypt.

God was directing Abram's experiences so that they would parallel the destiny of his offspring. Furthermore, these experiences in Egypt prepared Abram to understand the prophetic word about the destiny of his seed that God would give him during the covenant ceremony (15:13–16). Like Abram, his descendants would journey to Egypt because of a heavy famine in Canaan. Over time their welcome would fade, and Pharaoh would take control of them for his own purpose. In order to deliver Abram's descendants from this bondage, God would again smite a pharaoh with plagues, and that pharaoh would expel the Israelites. His guard would drive them out of Egypt, and Israel likewise would depart with many goods taken from the Egyptians (Exod. 12:35–36).

It has concerned interpreters that this basic plot occurs two more times in Genesis, once with Abram (ch. 20) and once with Isaac (26:6–11). These latter two incidents took place in Gerar; both times the king's name was Abimelech, though presumably they were different persons. Many scholars postulate that a single story has been adapted for three different settings. Others explain the repetition as a result of the same story's being preserved in different sources; this incident and the one involving Isaac are assigned to the Yahwist (J), and the one with Abimelech to the Elohist (E). That explanation does not account for the presence of all three in the final edition of Genesis. Why would all of them be included?

A few scholars have sought to interpret each account according to its distinctive characteristics (e.g., S. Niditch, *Underdogs and Tricksters: A Prelude to Biblical Folklore* [New Voices in Biblical Studies; San Francisco: Harper & Row, 1987], pp. 23–69; M. Biddle, "The 'Endangered Ancestress' and Blessing for the Nations," *JBL* 109 [1990], pp. 599–611). They point out that major details in the three accounts differ.

Biddle demonstrates that each of these stories expresses how God directed the promise of curse and blessing made to Abram (12:2–3). Because Pharaoh violated Sarai, God overrode the disastrous consequences of Abram's stratagem by cursing Pharaoh's house and removing the curse only when Pharaoh restored Sarai to Abram. Since Pharaoh expelled them from Egypt, there is no report of God's blessing Egypt. In chapter 20 God placed a curse on Abimelech's household because Abimelech had taken Sarah into his house. Then in a dream God instructed Abimelech to return Sarah and to have Abraham, a prophet, pray for him. When Abraham interceded for Abimelech and his people, the curse was removed. Several months later Abimelech discerned that God was blessing Abraham (21:22–32), so he made a covenant with Abraham in order to share in God's blessing on Abraham. In chapter 26, Isaac took up residence in Gerar ruled by Abimelech and he too, out of fear, identified Rebekah as his sister. Before taking Isaac's wife into his household, Abimelech discovered that Rebekah was Isaac's wife. He then granted them protection and the right to dwell in Gerar, and God blessed Isaac. But the increase in Isaac's flocks led Abimelech to ask him to leave Gerar, because there was not enough water for his own people and for Isaac. But later, coming to recognize that God was with Isaac, Abimelech went and made a covenant with him in order to participate in the blessing. In each of these accounts the patriarch was the means of curse or blessing.

Additional Notes §16

12:15 / "Pharaoh" means literally "the great house," i.e., the palace. By metonymy it became the title for Egypt's ruler. In the Pentateuch the Egyptian ruler always has this title, never his throne name, which makes it hard to coordinate these events with those in Egyptian history.

12:16 / Male donkeys were draft animals, and female donkeys were preferred for riding. The mention of camels in Genesis remains an enigma. Because the thousands of texts from the second millennium B.C. make only a few references to camels, many scholars view these references in Genesis as anachronisms. But excavations in a variety of places, including the Wadi Arabah, have uncovered camel bones in levels of the second half of the second millennium B.C. In more distant places like East Iran, camel bones dating back to 2700 B.C. have been found (J. Zarins, "Camel," *ABD* 1:827). Thus, some very ancient peoples did possess camels. At the earliest stages they seem to have been prized more for milk and food than for transportation. Solid evidence for their use as pack animals and for riding does not emerge until 1500 B.C. This is in accord with the fact that in accounts of the patriarchs where one might expect camels to be used, as when Jacob's sons traveled to Egypt for grain (42:26–27), donkeys are mentioned.

12:19 / When Abram used this tactic a second time with Abimelech of Gerar, he explained that he had not directly lied, for Sarai was his half-sister by another wife of his father (20:12).

§17 Abram and Lot Separate (Gen. 13:1–18)

This account unfolds in the four scenes of Abram's return to Canaan (vv. 1–4), the separation of Abram and Lot (vv. 5–13), God's renewal of the promise of land and offspring to Abram (vv. 14–17), and Abram's settling near Mamre (v. 18).

13:1–4 / **Abram went up from Egypt** with Sarai and Lot to the area south of Canaan called **the Negev.** Abram **had become very wealthy in livestock and in silver and gold.** Leaving the Negev, Abram traveled north through the hill country, eventually arriving at the place **between Bethel and Ai** where he had earlier pitched his tent and **built an altar.** This time Abram **called on** Yahweh's **name.** There is no report that Abram performed an act of worship outside the promised land. In Egypt and Mesopotamia the established cults probably would have prevented him from performing such activity in the open. But in the land of promise, which was not under the control of a strong central government, Abram was free to worship the one true God at a variety of places. The narrator's interest is in reporting Abram's worship of Yahweh in the land of promise.

13:5–7 / **Lot** also **had** a large number of **flocks, herds, and tents.** The increase was so great that **the land could** no longer **support** both Abram and Lot. There is no mention of the size of their camps; however, in the next account Abram was able to muster 318 men born in his household, indicating that a large number of people were moving about with him. As a result of the increase in their flocks, tension between Lot's herders and Abram's had escalated to open **quarreling.** Although there had not yet been any outright clashes, both men knew that conflict would soon break out. Because **the Canaanites and Perizzites** dwelt **in the land at that time,** Abram and Lot had to take their presence into account.

13:8–13 / Recognizing the potential danger of the situation, Abram went to Lot to make sure that there was no **quarreling between** them or their herdsmen since they were **brothers,** or relatives. Abram desired to resolve the mounting tension informally. Their conversation leads us to imagine that Abram took Lot to a lookout in order that they could see the lands both to the west, toward the Mediterranean, and to the east—the deep rift Arabah, which included the majestic Dead Sea. Abram suggested to Lot that they part ways as he offered him the choice of whatever region he wanted for his herds. Abram promised to move in the other direction. Abram displayed compassion, confidence, and insight as he placed his nephew's wishes above his own position and ambition. His leadership on this occasion strongly contrasts with his timidity before Pharaoh.

Looking out, **Lot** was greatly impressed by the rich Jordan Valley, being so fertile that it was comparable to **the garden of** Yahweh, that is, Eden, and to **the land of Egypt.** This deep rift valley lies some twelve hundred feet below sea level. Thus its climate is warm all year, with temperatures ranging from the pleasant eighties in winter to well over a hundred degrees Fahrenheit in summer. It receives virtually no rainfall. During the cold winters that buffet the Canaanite hills, this region offers pleasant relief. At the north side of the Dead Sea, springs, channeled for irrigation, permit the growing of lush crops year-round. Therefore, farming in that region approximates the kind of farming done in Egypt, a desert made fertile by the Nile. **Zoar** was a small village, probably at the southern end of the Jordan Plain on the eastern side (19:22–23). This plain was very fertile before the destruction of Sodom and Gomorrah. Lot **parted company** from Abram as he journeyed east. Leaving the land of promise, he no longer participated directly in Abram's call.

This account is unusual. The reader expects that Lot would have followed the ancient custom of bargaining with Abram before settling on the terms of the separation. Both men were prone to negotiate, as seen in Abram's dealing with the leaders of Hebron to buy the Cave of Machpelah (23:3–16) and in Lot's arguing for concessions from the messengers who came to deliver him from Sodom (19:17–22). Moreover, one would expect Lot to defer to Abram, his uncle, and let him make the first choice. Contrary to these expectations, Lot took the opportunity to separate from Abram and quickly chose the area in the Arabah. His experiences in Egypt might have awakened in him a desire to live in a lush, affluent urban environment. Some traits of his personality, evidenced in his decision to refrain from showing more honor to his uncle, cast a shadow over his character and prepare the reader for the troubles Lot is to face. The narrator points ahead to Lot's fate by mentioning Zoar, the city to which Lot flees in escaping from the conflagration of Sodom (19:18–23).

A summary statement records the separation: **Abram lived in the land of Canaan, while Lot lived among the cities of the plain and pitched his tents near Sodom.** This wording suggests that after Lot had lived for a time in the plain of Jordan, he moved his tents closer to Sodom. He was attracted perhaps by the exciting culture of this great town where the people **were wicked and** sinned **greatly.** The unusual use of two terms for the people as sinners, plus the adverb, captures the extent of the wickedness in Sodom. They had developed a culture that was fundamentally contrary to the ways of justice.

The contrasting destinies of Abram and Lot provide additional evidence why Abram had to leave Haran and move about in order to serve Yahweh wholeheartedly. Living in a sparsely settled land outside the urban centers, Abram could worship Yahweh and at the same time gain a reputation as a noble sheik. Lot, by contrast, ended up in Sodom and sought to become a citizen of that wicked city. In order to be accepted by the citizenry, he had to place his principles at risk. In spite of Abram's faithfulness to his nephew and his great efforts to help him, Lot came to a tragic end. By contrast, Abram grew stronger and wealthier.

13:14–17 / After Lot departed, Yahweh spoke to Abram. Again there is no detail about the manner of Yahweh's appearance. At pivotal times Yahweh guided Abram by speaking to him in a special way. Usually several years elapsed between these encounters. On this occasion Yahweh came to affirm Abram with a special assurance in recognition of the gracious way he had treated Lot. By letting Lot choose the most fertile area of that region, Abram had avoided covetousness; he did not grasp after the land of promise at the risk of alienating his nephew.

Yahweh commanded Abram **to lift up** his **eyes.** This command serves as the counterpart to Lot's looking up and choosing the most fertile place (v. 10). We may assume that Abram was standing on a rise where he could look out over the landscape for miles in all directions: **north** toward Shechem and **south** toward Jerusalem, **east** toward the Jordan Valley, and **west** toward the

Plain of Sharon. Yahweh promised to **give** him **and his offspring** (seed) **all the land** he saw. This time Yahweh underscored the promise by saying it was **forever** (17:8; 48:4; Lev. 25:23–34; Num. 36:5–9). Next, Yahweh promised to **make** his **offspring** (seed) **like the dust of the earth.** With this hyperbole Yahweh stressed the vast potential inherent in his promise. The terms "forever" and "beyond numbering" enhanced the original promises God had given Abram in Haran (12:2–3) by asserting that the potential number of his offspring was without limit.

Yahweh next commanded Abram to **walk through the length and breadth of the land,** explaining why Abram journeyed throughout the land rather than settling down, especially in the initial years in Canaan. By moving throughout the land, he was laying claim to all of the land.

13:18 / After this word from Yahweh, Abram **moved his tents and went to live near the great trees of Mamre,** which were in the vicinity of **Hebron.** These lush oaks, which grow to a height of twenty to twenty-five feet, offer shade in a hot, windy climate. In recognition of Yahweh's lordship and his trust in the promises, Abram **built an altar to** Yahweh.

Abram's kind dealings with Lot reveal that Yahweh had rightly chosen him as the vessel of his promise. Though he stumbled from time to time, Abram continued to serve God faithfully and rise above each failure. God honored him with enhanced promises and blessed him richly.

Additional Notes §17

13:7 / "Canaanites" is a general designation for the inhabitants of Canaan, the name for the land between the Mediterranean and the great rift valley, from Lebanon to the northern Sinai. It included peoples of a variety of ethnic origins.

The Perizzites appear in twenty-one out of twenty-seven lists identifying the various groups that occupied Canaan. They are usually mentioned with the Canaanites. They do not appear to be Semites; some scholars believe them to be a subgroup of the Hurrians and others to be members of the Amorites (G. Hugenberger, "Perizzites," *ISBE* 3:771).

13:10 / Sodom was located on the western side of the Dead Sea, toward the south.

13:18 / Mamre, where Abram dwelt for a considerable time, may be present-day Ramat el-Khalil, just less than two miles north of Hebron (cf. 18:1; 23:17, 19; 25:9; 35:27). It is west of the Cave of Machpelah, where the patriarchs were interred (23:17–20). Isaac also lived here (35:27). In addition, an Amorite has this name in 14:13, 24.

These trees are usually called "oaks" rather than "great trees" (NIV), though some Eng. translations read "the oak" based on the LXX and Syr. Cf. 12:6.

§18 Abram Rescues Lot from Captivity (Gen. 14:1–24)

This episode reveals Abram as a strong military commander. Employing shrewd battle tactics, Abram defeats a coalition of four kings from the East who have taken his nephew Lot captive. On his triumphant return Melchizedek, priest-king of Salem, comes out to meet him and blesses him. Abram in turn gives him a tithe of the spoil.

This episode describes Kedorlaomer's campaign against the cities around the Dead Sea (vv. 1–12), Abram's defeat of these marauding troops (vv. 13–16), and Abram's meeting the king of Sodom and the priest-king Melchizedek (vv. 17–24).

14:1–7 / Four kings from the East, **Amraphel king of Shinar, Arioch king of Ellasar, Kedorlaomer king of Elam, and Tidal king of Goiim,** had asserted their influence over five city-states in the area of the Dead Sea for twelve years. Kedorlaomer was the leader. The five local kings were **Bera king of Sodom, Birsha king of Gomorrah, Shinab king of Admah, Shemeber king of Zeboiim, and the king of Bela,** otherwise known as **Zoar** (19:22). These city-states had not been incorporated into an empire, for that type of rule had not yet been developed. Instead, the kings of the East had subjugated these cities in a military campaign and continued to exercise enough control over them to exact annual tribute. Tired of paying tribute, these local kings **rebelled in the thirteenth year.** Petty kings often rebelled when a powerful overlord was facing problems at home or was having to deal with uprisings in another area of his rule. Kedorlaomer did not respond to the rebellion for a year, which indicates that some serious political or military issue held him back from immediately dealing with the rebellion in the west.

In the fourteenth year Kedorlaomer and his allies marched westward to put down the rebellion. His troops would not have been numerous; they probably were highly trained soldiers, skilled at handling small city-states. The narrative recounts the itinerary of this force through the Transjordan. There they traveled down the King's Highway, the north-south route through the plateau of Transjordan (Num. 20:17). Along the way they **defeated** several peoples, including **the Rephaites in Ashteroth Karnaim, the Zuzites in Ham, the Emites in Shaveh Kiriathaim and the Horites in the hill country of Seir** (i.e., Edom, 25:30). Either these tribes had also rebelled or the kings from the East were extending their influence. At **El-Paran,** possibly Elat, they turned northwest, going to **En Misphat** ("the spring of justice"), which is identified as **Kadesh,** that is, Kadesh-barnea. In this area and to the north of it **they conquered the whole territory of the Amalekites.** Moving northward to **Hazazon Tamar,** they defeated **the Amorites.** These troops were traveling slowly toward the Dead Sea to punish the rebels. By going around that territory they intensified the anxiety and fear of the peoples in those city-states as they heard reports of the devastation being done.

14:8–12 / The four kings in league with Sodom **marched out and** engaged Kedorlaomer and his allies **in the Valley of Siddim,** or the Valley of Salt, which is the area around the Dead (Salt) Sea. The warrior kings quickly routed the five local kings. Some of the routed troops sought to escape (see additional note) by lowering themselves into **tar pits** that lined the valley, while others ran to the hills. During the confusion, Kedorlaomer's forces plundered **Sodom and Gomorrah** without opposition. Taking large amounts of spoil and some captives, including Lot, these kings started back to their homeland by traveling north toward Damascus.

14:13–16 / An escapee ran and **reported** what had happened **to Abram the Hebrew.** This epithet identified Abram with a larger ethnic group; it was a name understood in wider circles. At that time **Abram was living near the great trees of Mamre** (13:18). **When Abram heard** what had happened to Lot, he sought assistance from three allies: **Mamre the Amorite, . . . Eshcol and Aner.** The text is somewhat difficult to understand, but verse 24 makes it clear that Abram's allies numbered three. He also **called out the 318 trained men born in his household.** These forces quickly assembled and started out in pursuit of Kedorlaomer. This incident reveals how seriously Abram took his role as Lot's uncle. Since he was Lot's only close kinsman in Canaan, Abram acted like a kinsman-redeemer (*go'el;* Lev. 25:25–28, 47–53).

Rescuing the next of kin was an institution in Israel whereby one's closest kin took the responsibility to rescue a family member who had fallen into deep trouble without any means of escape (including being taken captive, being sold into servitude to pay a debt, and having to lease out family property because of debt). In the case of a person's being taken captive, the kinsman secured his or her release by paying ransom or forcefully rescuing him. Abram took the latter approach.

One night Abram and his men came upon the forces from the East camped at **Dan,** at the base of Mount Hermon. Taking advantage of the darkness and the element of surprise, Abram immediately divided his troops into two companies. They attacked and **routed** their enemies, **pursuing them as far as Hobab,** a town **north of Damascus.** The enemy fled so quickly that they left the spoil they had taken. As a result Abram was able to recover **all the goods,** along with **Lot and his possessions, the women,** and other captives.

14:17 / As **Abram returned** triumphantly, **the king of Sodom came out to meet him in the Valley of Shaveh,** identified as **the King's Valley.** This valley was possibly where the Valley of Hinnom joins the Kidron Valley. This location would account for the presence of Melchizedek (v. 18), who presumably had accompanied the king of Sodom. The text also suggests that Abram was returning to Mamre by a route that bypassed the cities of the plain; thus the king of Sodom had to ascend the steep Judean hills to meet Abram. That king's coming so far with empty hands is evidence that he was displeased with Abram. He thought that Abram wanted to keep the spoils for himself. Moreover, the narrator downplays the importance of the king of Sodom by not mentioning his name.

14:18–20 / At this point **Melchizedek, king of Salem** and **priest of God Most High,** suddenly appeared. This king and priest was committed to promoting righteousness in his realm, as attested by the meaning of his name, "my King (i.e., God) is righteous." Since Salem means "peace" in Hebrew, tradition has identified Salem with Jerusalem; for example, in Psalm 76:2 the temple mount is called Salem. This priest-king, prompted by God, greatly honored Abram in coming out to meet him. **Melchizedek brought** along **bread and wine,** the basic provisions, to graciously provide Abram and his retainers refreshment on their long journey back from battle. Melchizedek's strategic role in this account shows us that God was working with and through other people while he was directing Abram's course. The text does not explain how God led these special people.

Melchizedek **blessed Abram by God Most High, Creator of heaven and earth.** The term translated "Creator" is usually rendered "possessor, owner"; this latter meaning fits this context well. Abram had taken numerous spoils from his raid, but, as will be seen shortly, he renounced any personal claim to these goods, relying solely on God as his source of wealth. Melchizedek applauded Abram's stance on this by acclaiming God Most High as the owner, not only of all this property but also of all creation. Melchizedek then **blessed God Most High** for having **delivered** Abram's **enemies** into his control. This priest-king attested that Abram had won this decisive military clash because God had empowered him.

Honoring God for empowering him to win this victory, Abram paid **a tenth of everything** to Melchizedek, the priest-king, thereby recognizing God as the primary owner of these goods.

While tradition has not preserved any other information about Melchizedek, his service as Abram's priest has immortalized him as the model of a priestly messiah. He became the symbolic figure for a royal priesthood from David's line that was superior to Aaron's (Ps. 110:4). The writer of the book of Hebrews, building on this psalm, interprets the priestly ministry of Jesus as a continuation of Melchizedek's line, not Aaron's (Heb. 5:5–10; 6:20; 7:1–22; Melchizedek also appears in extracanonical literature).

14:21–24 / The narrative returns to **the king of Sodom,** whose demeanor toward Abram sharply contrasted with that of Melchizedek. Bluntly he asked Abram to return his **people** while conceding to him **the goods,** indicating his apprehension that Abram was going to keep the citizens of Sodom in his service. In making this offer the king of Sodom followed the customs of war: a general who rescued a city kept the goods recovered but had no claim on the city itself. But Abram refused the king's offer, revealing that before undertaking the campaign to recover Lot and the goods of Sodom he had **taken an oath** that he would **accept nothing, not even a thread or the thong of a sandal** from all the spoil. He had solemnized his oath by lifting up his hand to Yahweh, identified with **God Most High, Creator of heaven and earth.** Abram did not want any earthly king to be able to claim that he had **made Abram rich.** He then restated that he would take nothing save what his own **men** had **eaten.** In this Abram followed protocol in a military effort; the party on whose behalf a military action was taken was obligated to pay for the necessary provisions. Abram also protected **the share** belonging to the three members of the coalition.

In denying any claim to the property he had recovered, Abram gave strong evidence of his complete trust in God for his wealth. Abram's devotion to God was one of the reasons Melchizedek came out to bless Abram. He extolled Abram before God, and his blessing confirmed that Abram need not fear want since he served this great God with such firm and unselfish devotion. This God had protected Abram in his travels from Haran, in his sojourn in Egypt, and now in battle with a coalition of mighty kings. In return, Abram's refusal to keep the spoils for himself stands in bold contrast to Lot's attraction to the pleasures and wealth Sodom offered (ch. 19).

Additional Notes §18

This account attracts great interest, for only in this story does Abram engage with key figures from other Near Eastern countries. Names of kings from Elam and place names from Syria to Sinai open the possibility of locating Abram in a specific time frame. Unfortunately, connections between the names, places, and events related here and the information found in ancient documents from the Near East remain elusive. Nevertheless, the abundance of proper names, along with a distinctive vocabulary and style, indicate that this account had an origin different from that of the other stories about Abram. The double names for various places—an archaic name and a current name—indicate that the story has been adapted for a later audience in its retelling.

14:1 / The identity of these ancient kings continues to baffle scholars. In the past some identified Amraphel with Hammurabi, the great king of Babylon in the seventeenth century B.C., but lack of supporting evidence plus linguistic obstacles to the equation of these two names have led scholars to abandon that position. Arioch is a Hurrian name found in several Mesopotamian texts, most of which are prior to the second millennium B.C. The identification of Ellasar is still questioned. Tidal may be Tudhalia, a Hittite royal name. The title "king of nations" is unusual. It may mean that Tidal was the head of marauding tribes. These names suggest that this was a coalition of diverse ethnic groups: Elamite, Amorite, Hurrian, and Hittite. Elam was a powerful state in the first part of the second millennium B.C.

14:2 / Admah and Zeboiim, two cities near Sodom, are mentioned together in 10:19; Deut. 29:23; and Hos. 11:8.

14:5 / The Rephaites lived in the area of Bashan, the region east and north of the Jordan. In Deut. 2:20–21; 3:11 they were reported to be giants. Ashteroth and Karnaim are two neighboring cities. The former Tell 'Ashtarah was capital of Bashan. Karnaim, lit. "twin peaks," was about two miles north of Ashteroth. At times it served as the capital of this region in place of Ashteroth. The Zuzites may be related to the Zamzummim mentioned in Deut. 2:20. Ham was on the King's Highway, a few miles east of Bethshean. Emites were another group of giants who inhabited the area later known as Moab (Deut. 2:10–11); their name may mean "frightful." Shaveh Kiriathaim has not been identified.

14:6 / Horites were pastoralists who inhabited the mountains of Seir located in the Transjordan going north from the Gulf of Aqaba.

14:7 / The name En Misphat suggests that it was a place where pastoralists came to resolve disputes.

The Amalekites were nomadic pastoralists who lived in the northern Sinai and Negev (36:11–12, 15–16). Israel confronted these peoples in the wilderness journey (Exod. 17:8, 14; Num. 13:29). The Amorites are one of the peoples living in the hill country (15:16); in some texts this name represents all the inhabitants of Canaan.

Several sites have been proposed for Hazazon Tamar. One is En Gedi, a well-known spring on the west side of the Dead Sea (2 Chron. 20:2). Other scholars connect it with Wadi Hazaza, a few miles north of En Gedi. Given that these troops were moving northward from Kadesh-barnea toward the Dead Sea, the best identification is Tamar, some twenty miles to the south-southwest of the Dead Sea at 'Ain Hush (M. Astour, "Hazazon-Tamar," *ABD* 3:86).

14:10 / Y. Muffs ("Abraham the Noble Warrior: Patriarchal Politics and Laws of War in Ancient Israel," *JJS* 33 [1982], p. 81, n. 1), drawing on Ibn Ezra, shows that Hb. *napal* ("fall") may mean "lower" oneself voluntarily (e.g., 24:64). He goes on to argue that it may have the overtone of "flee." This understanding of "fall" keeps the balance: some of the fleeing troops hid in tar pits, and others fled to the hills.

14:13 / The name "Hebrew" appears only some thirty times in Scripture. Its occurrences come in three clusters: the story of Joseph, the events of the exodus, and the era of conflict with the Philistines (1 Sam.). This name is used for Israelites primarily in relationship to foreigners (e.g., 40:15; 43:32; Exod. 1:15). Either a non-Israelite identifies one of Abram's seed in distinction from his own racial stock with this name (39:14, 17; 41:12; Exod. 1:16; 2:6), or an Israelite uses it to identify himself to a foreigner (40:15; Exod. 2:11, 13; Jonah 1:9). The name was probably known throughout the Near East and identified the Israelites as part of a larger group of peoples; thus this broader term meant something to those who were unfamiliar with the small band of Israelites.

Eshkol, which in Hb. means "a cluster of grapes," is the name of a wadi in the vicinity of Hebron.

14:15 / This is the only occurrence of Hobah in the Bible.

14:18 / God's name here is *'el 'elyon*. El is the common north-west Semitic term for God; *'elyon* is an abstract meaning "the exalted one." This compound title lauds God as the Supreme One. The name God Most High occurs elsewhere only in Ps. 78:35. Most High may be used alone (Num. 24:16; Deut. 32:8; Isa. 14:14; but in Num. 24:16 and Ps. 73:11 it stands parallel to El).

In the Karatepe inscription, El is the god of earth while Baal is the god of heaven. Thus identifying El Elyon as the God of heaven and earth is a singular statement, indicating that Melchizedek's view of God transcended that of his neighbors. Even though Melchizedek came from Canaanite culture, in God's merciful providence Melchizedek had come to realize that there is one supreme God.

Abram used this name after the name Yahweh (v. 22). In the OT, Yahweh Most High occurs three times (Ps. 7:17; 47:2; 97:9), and Yahweh is parallel with Most High in seven instances (Ps. 9:1–2; 18:13 = 2 Sam. 22:14; Ps. 21:7; 83:18; 91:9; 92:1; see Sarna, *Genesis*, p. 381).

§19 God's Covenant with Abram (Gen. 15:1–21)

In this account God appears twice to Abram, each time giving him special promises. The text gives no indication of the length of time between these appearances, although it must have been at least a day. In the first appearance God gives Abram an object lesson at night (v. 5), and in the next there is mention of the sun setting (v. 12).

On both occasions Abram receives God's word like a prophet. In the first he has a vision in which he receives two words, both introduced by a prophetic formula (vv. 1, 4–5). In the second God causes a deep sleep to fall on Abram and then tells him about his descendants' future (vv. 12–16). The structures of these accounts stand in tandem: God speaks to Abram a word of encouragement (vv. 1, 7); Abram responds by expressing an agonizing concern (vv. 2–3, 8); God replies to that concern (vv. 4–5, 9); and a statement recounting what has taken place concludes each report (vv. 6, 18–21). Recurring terms in Hebrew further unite both sections. "Descendants (seed)," the key term, occurs in verses 3, 5, 13, and 18 and connects God's promises: the multiplication of Abram's seed (v. 5) and their inheritance of the land (vv. 18–21). Without land, offspring scatter and loss of identity threatens them; without occupants, land becomes overrun. Two other key terms are "inherit" (vv. 4 [twice], 7, 8) and "bring out" (vv. 5, 7). The fulcrum between the two sections is verse 6, in which the narrator defines the nature of Abram's standing with God. Abram's faith becomes the basis for God's covenant with him.

15:1 / Sometime after Abram had rescued Lot, **the word of** Yahweh **came** to him **in a vision.** The formula "the word of Yahweh came," though unique in Genesis, appears frequently in the writings of the prophets. God gave Abram a word of confidence, **Do not be afraid,** and backed it by identifying himself as

Abram's **shield.** A shield symbolizes protection during conflict
(Ps. 3:3; 84:11), and "shield" *(magen)* establishes a connection with
Melchizedek's blessing the Most High for "delivering" *(miggen;*
14:20) Abram's enemies into his power.

Next God promised Abram a **very great reward;** the NIV,
however, renders the line so that God is Abram's reward. However, the context of the preceding battle favors the former reading. "Reward or pay" refers to the pay soldiers receive from the
spoil (Ezek. 29:19), but Abram had refused to take any of the spoil
from his defeat of the kings of the East (14:23–24). Therefore, in
making this assertion, God sanctioned Abram's generosity in paying a tithe to Melchizedek and giving back the spoils to the cities
of the plain. Yahweh promised to be his protector and to make
sure that Abram was well paid.

15:2–3 / After addressing God very formally, **O Sovereign LORD** (Yahweh), Abram made a bitter complaint cast in the
form of a sarcastic question: **what** could God **give** him since he
was **childless?** Using a rare, harsh word for "childless" *('ariri),*
he expressed his hopelessness at ever having children by Sarai.
Abram made his question more caustic by setting God's new
promise of reward against the nonfulfillment of the earlier promise of making him a great nation (12:2). He pointed out that this
new promise possessed little value if he could not pass on the reward to his own seed. Abram was voicing his deep disappointment at God for not having fulfilled the promise of an heir even
though he had obeyed God in leaving his home at Haran.

Abram focused his complaint by pointing out that his only
heir was **Eliezer of Damascus.** This statement appears to reflect
an ancient custom whereby a childless couple adopted a son in
order to have someone to care for them in their old age, ensure
that they would receive a proper burial, and attend the family
grave. The adopted son became their major heir. Adoption contracts contained a clause that stated if a natural son was born,
he became the principal heir. Thus Abram had either adopted
Eliezer or anticipated having to do so in order that he might have
an heir. He reiterated his complaint, lamenting that God had not
given him "seed," which NIV renders **children** (15:3).

15:4–5 / The same prophetic formula from verse 1 heads
God's response. God addressed Abram's concern by saying unequivocally, **This man** [Eliezer] **will not be your heir.** Abram's
worries were groundless, since a son was going to come from his

own body. To impress on Abram the vastness of the promise, God **took him outside** his tent and ordered him **to look up at the heavens and count the stars**—as though that were possible. Then God proclaimed that his seed would become like the stars in number (22:17; 26:4; 37:9). Little did Abram realize that he was to have multitudes of descendants by natural birth complemented by additional multitudes joined to his lineage by faith. God thus answered Abram's complaint, not with arguments backed by irrefutable logic but by reaffirming his promise and adding a powerful visual sign.

15:6 / The narrator defines Abram's relationship to God: **Abram believed** Yahweh, and Yahweh **credited it to him as righteousness.** "Believe in" means "put trust in, rely on." Here it means that Abram put his full trust in God. In expressing his complaint to God Abram demonstrated that trust. Instead of letting his bitter frustration at God's apparent failure to keep his promise fester inside him, he voiced his distress when God came to him. Thus he preempted it from eroding his faith in God and in the promise of a son.

As a result, God credited Abram's faith as righteousness. The term "righteousness" is variously interpreted. Many Jewish scholars understand it as reward or merit, an interpretation that accords with God's promise of wages (v. 1). But since God had already promised Abram rewards, something more is meant by this statement. Other scholars take righteousness in the moral sense of keeping the law, since righteousness is often used with that meaning (e.g., Ezek. 18:5), but law was not an issue in Abram's relationship with God. G. von Rad understands it as describing a right relationship (*Genesis: A Commentary* [trans. J. Marks; rev. ed.; OTL; Philadelphia: Westminster, 1972], p. 185). The verb "credit," however, moves the term "righteousness" away from a relational meaning. "Credit" implies some type of official action; that is, God declared Abram's belief to be the basis for his having full standing in God's presence. That means no accusation made against one whom God declared to be righteous would stand in the heavenly court. In this radical reorientation of the divine-human relationship, God declared that Abram had this privileged position on the basis of his faith, not on the basis of righteous deeds or acts of devotion.

Abram thereby becomes the model of all who worship Yahweh by faith. The audacity of his believing stands out against the bleakness of his situation. Furthermore, Abram's complaints show that a person of faith at times feels keen disappointment and frustration. Nevertheless, such a person is not afraid to express that feeling to God. On hearing God's answer, Abram had to decide whether to continue to exercise faith or not. Now as then, God often demands that one maintain faith in the face of improbable circumstances in which belief appears ridiculous. Such was Abram's experience. If he had told one of his Canaanite neighbors about God's promise, his words would have sounded incredible. Nevertheless, God wanted him to believe the promise despite the physical improbabilities of its being fulfilled. Although God reaffirmed and strengthened the promise through the symbol of the vast starry heavens, God made no commitment to fulfilling it in the near future. God thus called on Abram to continue to exercise faith. In the words of Brueggemann, "Those who believe the promise and hope against barrenness nevertheless must live with the barrenness" (*Genesis,* p. 140).

Paul draws on this verse to undergird his teaching that a person is justified solely by faith (Rom. 4:3–4, 9, 22–25; Gal. 3:6–9). He argues that because no human can do sufficient works of righteousness to be just before God, a person can be declared just or innocent only on the basis of faith in God. Everyone who is justified by faith has peace with God (Rom. 5:1).

15:7 / God's goal in appearing to Abram a second time was to solidify the bond between himself and Abram by entering into a covenant. This section includes Yahweh's self-introduction (v. 7), Abram's question (v. 8), Yahweh's instruction (v. 9), Abram's execution of the instructions (vv. 10–11), Yahweh's revelatory word about Israel's bondage in Egypt (vv. 12–16), Yahweh's sealing the sacrifice (v. 17), and Yahweh's declaration of the boundaries of the promised land (vv. 18–21). Here God gives two significant words in regard to the future of Abram's seed, one concerning Israel's future bondage (vv. 13–14) and one describing the boundaries of the promised land (vv. 18–21).

Yahweh made a covenant with Abram, just as Yahweh would enter into covenant with Abram's seed at Sinai (Exod. 19–24). Covenants were common in the Near East for defining various kinds of long-term relationships, such as between individuals (e.g., the agreement between Laban and Jacob in Gen. 31), between city-states, between a city-state and an empire, and between empires. Through this agreement the parties regulated specific aspects of their relationship, such as boundaries and privileges. Each party pledged to adhere to the obligations and to promote the relationship. The most common elements of an ancient covenant included identification of the parties, a recounting of the mutual history, stipulations, gods serving as witnesses, blessings and curses, deposit in a significant place such as in the footstool of a major deity, public reading of the covenant, and a ratification ceremony. Since it was virtually impossible to enforce a covenant, blessings and curses served to encourage compliance. Should one of the parties violate the covenant, it was expected that the gods would activate the particular curse regarding that violation. More specifically, M. Weinfeld ("The Covenant of Grant in the Old Testament and in the Ancient Near East," *JAOS* 90 [1970], pp. 184–203) argues that the details of this account fit closest to a land grant made by a king to a servant, usually in perpetuity.

The covenants found in the OT are similar to those from the ancient Near East, but there are some variations. Since the text reports the covenant ceremony rather than giving details of the covenant, it provides only the information necessary for understanding the character of this agreement between Yahweh and Abram. It includes the identification of the initiator, a brief statement of God's history with Abram, blessing in terms of the gift of land, and a description of the ratifying ceremony. The text implies the other elements that belong to a covenant. Significantly, God laid no stipulations on Abram.

At the beginning of verse 7 is God's self-introduction, containing the first two components of a covenant. Yahweh initiated the covenant. Then a relative clause recounts the history, stating that Yahweh had **brought** Abram **out of Ur of the Chaldeans.** This wording parallels God's self-introduction to the Decalogue: "I am Yahweh your God, who brought you out of Egypt" (Exod. 20:2). This parallel is intentional as it interprets Abram's journey from Ur to Canaan as a foreshadowing of Israel's journey from Egypt to Canaan. Both had to leave a locale in which they had lived a long time. Both had to take a long journey before reaching the land of promise. Just as the children of Israel were delivered from bondage, Abram, by a journey from Ur, was delivered from a culture burdened by the worship of many gods.

In his self-introduction Yahweh also stated that he delivered Abram **to give** him **this land** as a possession. God's promise that Abram was to become a great nation (12:2) thus has two key elements: numerous offspring and land. In this particular encounter God focused on the issue of land. Later, in the covenant renewal ceremony (ch. 17), God would focus on the issue of an heir. On this occasion God dealt with the land issue because Abram had journeyed throughout the land as Yahweh had instructed him (13:17). Having separated from his uncle, Lot was no longer a factor in determining the owner of this land. God could now define more specifically his promises to Abram. Given that the occupation of the promised land by Abram's seed lay far in the future, God provided the covenant as a promissory note to guarantee their claim to the land.

15:8–10 / Abram responded with a question: **how** could he **know** that he was going to possess this land? Although his question was pointed, it was free from the caustic tone he had used in the preceding exchange (vv. 2–3). Abram asked for some guarantee that what Yahweh had said would take place. Yahweh answered by instructing him to **bring** several animals, namely, **a heifer, a goat and a ram, each three years old, along with a dove and a young pigeon.** The context implies that these animals were to be the sacrifice for the covenant ceremony. Since this was the initial covenant that God entered into with the seed of Israel, the variety of animals represents the offerings that are to be acceptable in the official worship of Yahweh.

Abram **brought** all the animals, **cut them in two,** except for the birds, **and arranged the halves** so that they faced each other. Birds, being small, usually were not split for sacrifice (Lev. 1:14–17).

15:11 / While Abram waited for God to accept the sacrifice, **birds of prey came down** to consume **the carcasses.** These birds represent hostile forces opposed to the making of this covenant. Perhaps they are symbolic of the enemies Israel will face in occupying Canaan. Wenham (*Genesis 1–15*, p. 332) postulates that the birds symbolize Egypt, the nation God would defeat in delivering his people from bondage. Whatever these birds symbolize, their threat to this sacrifice was real. Abram responded by driving them off. It is instructive to realize that Yahweh left to Abram the task of warding off the forces that sought to destroy the sacrifice.

15:12–15 / At dusk, **a deep sleep** came over Abram, and **a thick and dreadful darkness came** down around him. In Hebrew both the sleep and the darkness "fell on" *(napal 'al)* Abram, although NIV translates it with two different verbs. The use of "fall" communicates that Yahweh caused Abram's sleep, not that Abram dozed. In Scripture, God sometimes induces a deep sleep on one with whom he wishes to communicate in a special way (2:21). God is thus ominously present in the thick, dreadful darkness.

On this momentous occasion Yahweh outlined for Abram the course of events his seed would meet before taking possession of the promised land. Abram was able to understand what Yahweh was foretelling because of his recent experience in Egypt (12:10–20). That experience served as a pattern for the events God was talking about. His **descendants** would become **strangers,** resident aliens, **in a** foreign **country.** There **they** would **be enslaved and mistreated** for **four hundred years.** Four hundred years symbolizes an epoch. In verse 16 the span is four generations, based on taking a generation as a period of a hundred years. At the start of the new epoch God would **punish** or judge **the nation** that had enslaved them. Abram's seed would then **come out** of bondage **with great possessions.**

God next promised Abram that he would go to his **fathers in peace and be buried at a good old age.** "Old age" is literally "having silvery white hair" (25:8). In that culture, white hair was associated with wisdom, nobility, and authority. Abram would live a long, prosperous life free from major conflict with his neighbors. Going to his fathers implies some kind of afterlife.

15:16 / Abram's descendants would have to wait such a long time before taking possession of the land because **the sin of the Amorites** had **not yet reached its full measure.** Here the Amorites represent all the tribes who occupied Canaan (vv. 19–21). This statement is crucial, for it establishes the moral basis for giving to God's people land occupied by others. Scripture teaches that acts of sin pollute the land. Sexual immorality is particularly polluting (Lev. 18:24–28). When people persist in sinning, the pollution mounts up, making the land so sick that in time the land vomits out its inhabitants. God usually accomplishes this by empowering a nation to be an instrument of judgment to drive out the sinful occupants. In this case Israel was to be God's rod of punishment against the Amorites. God did not show partiality in using this method of punishment, for centuries later he used the cruel Assyrian army as the rod of punishment against Israel for their continual violation of the covenant (Isa. 10:5–19).

15:17 / At dark **a smoking firepot with a blazing torch appeared and passed between the pieces.** This fire represents Yahweh, passing between the pieces of the sacrifice to seal the covenant. In the ancient ritual of making a covenant the parties passed together between the pieces of the sacrifice to formalize the covenant. God's passing between the pieces alone means that he was making a unilateral, unconditional covenant. Many scholars believe that this rite meant that the parties submitted themselves to the same fate as these animals should they fail to keep the covenant (e.g., Jer. 34:18). That interpretation faces difficulties in that God is the party who passed between the pieces. D. Petersen ("Covenant Ritual: A Traditio-Historical Perspective," *BR* 22 [1977], pp. 7–18) traces the history of this practice and finds that the idea of putting oneself under a curse by passing between the pieces did not arise until the first millennium B.C. In the earlier period this rite was to create a new relationship.

15:18–21 / A summary statement provides clarity and emphasis. Through this covenant God is obligated **to give this land to** Abram's **descendants** ("seed"). He then defined the boundaries of the land to be **from the river of Egypt to the ... Euphrates.** In other texts the southern boundary was the Wadi of Egypt, or the Wadi el Arish (Num. 34:5), a natural boundary in Sinai between Egypt and Canaan. In this text the river of Egypt could be this wadi or possibly the easternmost branch of the Nile. The northern boundary was the Euphrates as it dips down into Syria.

Additional Notes §19

15:1 / In Genesis God gave this word of salvation, "do not be afraid," to Hagar (21:17), Isaac (26:24), and Jacob (46:3). It is also the word of salvation that God spoke to the Israelites caught between the advancing Egyptian army and the waters of the sea (Exod. 14:13).

15:2 / De Vaux (*Early History of Israel*, p. 249) interprets this text a little differently. Abram was stating his testament: Eliezer, a prized servant. Should he die without children, Eliezer would become a free man and his principal heir.

The phrase *ben meshek* is variously interpreted. If *meshek* is the former name of Damascus, the phrase means "of Damascus" (Tg., Vg., and NIV). Other sources render it "the one in charge of my house."

15:6 / This well-known verse is difficult to interpret. The verb translated "credit" *(khshb)* means to consider a person to be in a specific position or status or to have certain rights (Job 19:11; 33:10). It also means to credit one's due to one's account (Lev. 7:18; 17:4; Num. 18:27; 2 Sam. 19:19; Ps. 32:2, 106:31; Prov. 27:14). In Ps. 106:31, the high priest Phinehas, acting zealously for God, stayed a plague; afterward his zeal was accounted to him as righteousness.

"Believe in" *(he'emin b)* occurs infrequently in the OT. Its usage here and in Exod. 14:31—the conclusion to the narrative about Israel's passage through the sea—indicates that believing was an important dynamic in Israel's relationship with God (Ps. 106:12). In other instances this phrase occurs with a negative particle in reference to Israel's display of unbelief (e.g., Num. 14:11; 20:12; Ps. 78:22, 32; 106:24).

Another issue is that the subject of the verb "credit" is not clear in the Hb. Traditionally it has been taken as God, but in the ordinary flow of the sentence one assumes that the antecedent is Abram. According to that reading, Abram accepted God's promises as evidence that God was acting justly toward him. The traditional reading with God as the subject has the advantage of fitting best with the flow of ideas. Support comes from the fact that the noun "righteousness" is used only for human activity in the Pentateuch (Wenham, *Genesis 1–15*, p. 330).

15:9 / S. Talmon (" '400 Jahre' oder 'vier Generation' [Gen 15,13–15]: Geschichtliche Zeitangabe oder literarische Motive?" in *Die Hebräische Bibel und ihre zweifache Nachgeschichte* [festschrift for R. Rendtorff; ed. E. Blum et al.; Neukirchen-Vluyn: Neukirchener, 1990], p. 23) argues that the phrase *tor wegozal* ("a dove and a pigeon") is a hendiadys in which the second term describes the bird as "young," just as "three years old" describes the age of the animals.

15:12 / The time of Egyptian bondage was to be around 400 years (also Acts 7:6). According to Exod. 12:40–41, Israel was in Egypt for 430 years (for the symbolic use of 430 see Ezek. 4:5, 6). Numerically 400 does not equal 430, but in both texts the respective number symbolizes an epoch. At one stage the symbolic nuance of the numbers must have differed, but that nuance disappeared over time. Verse 16 sets the length of Israel's stay in Egypt at four generations. On the surface there appears to be a wide disparity between 400 years and four generations in that a generation is usually considered to be twenty to twenty-five years. Talmon (" '400 Jahre' oder 'vier Generation,' " p. 20) found a tradition in Egyptian literature that takes a generation to be a hundred years (Isa. 65:20). The genealogy of Moses attests that there were four generations: Levi-Kohath-Amram-Moses (Exod. 6:16–20; Num. 3:17–19; 26:57–59). Another way to understand generation *(dor)* is "lifetime" (Hamilton, *Genesis: Chapters 1–17*, p. 436).

The symbol for an epoch is significant, teaching that God works with his people differently from epoch to epoch. For the ancients this was a way of understanding periods of history similar to the contemporary idea of dividing human history into eras such as the Renaissance, the modern era, and the postmodern era. Thus the biblical author is dealing with general time frames, not exact dates.

15:16 / Amorites is the name given for the occupants of the hill country (10:16).

15:19–21 / There are several lists of the peoples of the land (e.g., Exod. 3:8, 17; 13:5; Deut. 7:1; Josh. 3:10). The number of groups in the lists varies from ten to three. The first three names and the Rephaites do not appear in any of the other lists. Kenites are usually located in the Negev (Num. 24:21; 1 Sam. 27:10), but according to Judg. 4:11–17 they lived to the north of the Negev. Kenizzites lived in the southeastern Negev and had ties to the Edomites (36:4, 11). Kenaz, grandson of Esau, may have been the father of this group (J. Kuntz, "Kenaz," *ABD* 4:17). Kadmonites, a name occurring only here, means "easterners"; they may be associated with "sons of the East" (29:1; S. Reed, "Kadmonites," *ABD* 4:4). For Hittites see 23:10; for Perizzites and Canaanites see 13:7; for Rephaites see 14:5; for Girgashites and Jebusites see 10:16.

§20 The Birth of Ishmael (Gen. 16:1–16)

In this account Sarai gives Hagar to Abram (vv. 1–6); the angel of Yahweh instructs and blesses Hagar (vv. 7–12); and Hagar responds and gives birth to Ishmael (vv. 13–16). The setting alternates in the pattern of A:B:A': Abram's house (first and third scenes) and the desert (second scene).

16:1–2 / **Sarai, Abram's** principal **wife,** remained without children despite God's reiterated promise of seed to Abram (ch. 15). Like most wives of prominent persons in ancient times, Sarai had a **maidservant, Hagar, an Egyptian.** The contrast between the two women is striking. Sarai was from the consummate lineage, free, brittle, aging, and barren. Hagar was a foreigner, a slave, resilient, young, and fertile (P. Trible, "The Other Woman: A Literary and Theological Study of the Hagar Narratives," in *Understanding the Word* [ed. J. Butler, E. Conrad, and B. Ollenburger; JSOTSup 37; Sheffield: JSOT Press, 1985], p. 222).

To cope with the shame of being childless, Sarai devised a plan by which Abram might have a blood heir (15:2) and she might **build** her own **family.** She suggested **to Abram** that he **sleep with** Hagar and have a son by her. In presenting the subject to Abram, Sarai revealed the depth of her distress by casting blame for her barrenness on Yahweh. The ancients believed that God's blessing in bestowing fertility was necessary for conception to take place. In asking Abram to take this course Sarai was in effect telling him that he needed to act since God had not acted.

In the ancient Near East barrenness was a disgrace for a wife. People addressed this problem in many ways. For example, marriage contracts from Mesopotamia had a clause that obligated an infertile wife to provide her husband a surrogate so that he might have a family. In responding to the great social pressure on her to deal with her barrenness, Sarai might have been following this custom. She formulated her plan by using wording similar to that of Abram when he asked her to tell the Egyptians that she was his sister (12:11–13). She subtly pressured Abram to repay her something for having followed his plan to her own dishonor (Reis, "Take My Wife, Please," p. 311).

Abram **agreed to** his wife's plan; the text reads literally, "he obeyed Sarai's voice." G. Wenham (*Genesis 16–50* [WBC 2; Dallas: Word, 1994], p. 7) points out that this is the same phrase employed when Adam obeyed Eve (3:17); possibly the narrator is reprimanding Abram for his lack of leadership. Just as Abram's scheme to protect himself by calling Sarai his sister was severely flawed, so too Sarai's plan would bring great aggravation.

16:3–4a / Having lived **in Canaan** for **ten years,** Sarai **took her Egyptian maidservant Hagar and gave her to** Abram as a **wife.** The term "wife" indicates that in becoming Sarai's surrogate, Hagar received elevated status in the household. The authority over her passed from Sarai to Abram. Sarai initiated this arrangement, which was rooted in Sarai's longing for a family, not in sensuality. Abram **slept with Hagar, and she conceived.**

16:4b–6 / Hagar's new position and her pregnancy boosted her self-image so much that she began to gloat in Sarai's presence. Unable to tolerate Hagar's haughty attitude, Sarai took her complaint to Abram. She was so upset that she directly accused him of having caused **the wrong** she was **suffering.** The word "wrong" (*khamas*), often translated "violence," is the word used to describe the reason for the flood (6:11, 13). When one under attack cries "Violence!" the hearer is obligated to come to that person's defense (Job 19:7). With this word Sarai obligated Abram, the head of the house, to restore her position by correcting the cause of her distress (von Rad, *Genesis,* p. 192). She added that Hagar now despised her. In order to make sure that Abram did something, Sarai concluded her complaint with a prayer that Yahweh **judge between** her and Abram. Reis ("Take My Wife, Please," p. 311) interprets this short prayer as Sarai's seeking to persuade Abram on the basis that her request is not nearly as morally repugnant as his request that she identify herself as his sister.

Abram acquiesced to Sarai again, stating that her **servant** was under her authority. This was a legal pronouncement by which he returned Hagar to her former status as a maidservant under Sarai's authority. He specifically empowered Sarai **to do with her** as she thought **best.** In the OT this expression often describes a concession to a request to which one is opposed (Judg. 19:24; 1 Sam. 1:23; 3:18; 14:36, 40). Sarai did not control her jealousy. She

mistreated Hagar so badly that **she fled.** "Mistreat" *('innah)* is for
harsh, cruel treatment; this word describes the terrible conditions
of slavery that the Israelites suffered in Egypt (15:13; Exod. 1:12).

16:7–12 / **The angel of** Yahweh **found Hagar near a
spring in the desert,** namely, **the spring beside the road to Shur.**
Shur was a site in the Negev on the way to Egypt; its location indicates that Hagar was fleeing toward her homeland. Assuming
that Abram was living near Mamre (13:18), she had traveled a
long distance. Addressing Hagar as **servant of Sarai,** the angel
asked **where** she had **come from and where** she was **going.** She
responded that she was **running away from** her **mistress Sarai.**
Her answer indicates that she had been so distraught that she had
fled without any specific destination in mind.

The identity of "the angel of Yahweh" is a mystery. This
angel is a heavenly servant, one of a kind, who appeared on earth
to do God's bidding. At times this angel appears to be identified
with God. The translation "messenger" suits this account better
because Hagar first took this angel to be a human. By speaking directly to her the messenger affirmed Hagar, raising her self-esteem.
Then he gave her a divine word in three speeches (vv. 9–12).

The angel first instructed Hagar to return to her **mistress**
and **submit to her.** "Submit" intimates that she would continue to
face mistreatment at Sarai's hands. The messenger then encouraged her to endure any abuse with the wonderful promise that he
would **increase** her **descendants** (seed) beyond number. Hagar is
the only woman in Genesis who received such a promise directly
from God. Next the messenger blessed her with the promise that
she would bear **a son.** Given the large number of pregnancies that
did not come to full term and the number of deaths at childbirth
in ancient times, this promise of bearing a healthy boy was an assuring word to Hagar. The messenger then spoke about the character of the child. Hagar was to **name** the child **Ishmael,** meaning
"God has heard," for indeed Yahweh had **heard of** her **misery.**
Ishmael's character would be comparable to that of **a wild donkey**
or an onager. The onager, a sturdy animal of the desert, is impossible to domesticate. In exchange for its fierce love of freedom, it
has to endure the sparse food supply of the desert (Job 39:5–8).
Ishmael was to have such a love of freedom that he would gladly
live in the harsh land of the desert. His offspring would develop
into an independent tribal federation away from the centers of

civilization and enter into fierce conflict with those who traveled through the desert, even with those related to them.

16:13–14 / In a surprising move unparalleled in Scripture, Hagar, a woman, gave a **name to** God: "You are **the God who sees me**" *('el ro'i)*. With this name she praised God for having come to her rescue and for giving her a promise of hope. Although Hagar was only a handmaid, God treated her as a person who needed protection and encouragement. God also blessed a person who had faithfully served Abram (12:3).

As was customary in ancient times, the place where Hagar encountered the angel of Yahweh was given a name, **Beer Lahai Roi,** that recalled the divine appearance. It was located **between Kadesh** and **Bered** (24:62; 25:11). Sarna (*Genesis,* p. 122) translates the name Beer Lahai Roi as "the well belonging to the clan of Roi," while Hamilton (*Genesis: Chapters 1–17,* p. 457) renders it "the well belonging to the Living One who sees me."

16:15–16 / Obeying the messenger's instructions, Hagar returned to Abram's household. There she bore **Abram a son.** Abram gave him **the name Ishmael.** His naming the child meant he received the boy as his own with all the privileges that attended such a position. His action also indicated that he had heard and accepted Hagar's report of the special visitation of the messenger of Yahweh. For the time being Abram accepted this son as the fulfillment of God's special promise. At Ishmael's birth Abram was **eighty-six years old.**

Additional Notes §20

16:2 / Several laws found in texts from the ancient Near East regulate a childless marriage (de Vaux, *Early History of Israel,* pp. 244–45). A marriage contract found at Kültepe, a city of Asia Minor, from the nineteenth century B.C. contains the stipulation that if a wife does not have children two years after the wedding, she has to provide a slave for her husband. That slave is to be sold after delivering the desired child. A text from Egypt recounts that a childless couple took a slave who bore three children to the family (A. Gardiner, "Adoption Extraordinary," *JEA* 26 [1940], pp. 23–29). The laws regulating the lines of authority over such children and their inheritance rights varied. In many cases the head wife, rather than the natural mother, had the authority. In the Code of

Hammurabi a son's inheritance was guaranteed only if the father recognized him (§§171, 172).

16:6 / According to a law in the Code of Hammurabi (§146), a maid who bore a child for her lord and then elevated herself before the head wife was punished by being lowered to the status of a slave.

16:7 / The angel of Yahweh was a special messenger from God. The term "the angel of Yahweh" occurs fifty-eight times in the OT (e.g., Judg. 13:3), and "the angel of God" occurs eleven times. In places this angel appears to be identified with God, as here, where Hagar called him God (v. 13; 21:17; 22:11 with v. 12; 31:11 with v. 13; Judg. 6:12 with v. 14). In other places a clear distinction is made between God and this messenger. On the occasion of the Lord's appearance to Abram, "three men" visit (18:2, 16, 22). After the period of the judges there are scarcely any reports of God's appearing in this manner. As Hamilton says, the messenger is more of a representation of God than a representative of God (*Genesis: Chapters 1–17*, p. 451). For von Rad, "he is God himself in human form" (*Genesis*, p. 193).

16:12 / There are no records of any conflict between the descendants of Ishmael and the children of Israel (Sarna, *Genesis*, p. 122). David's administrators included Obil the Ishmaelite and Jaziz the Hagrite (1 Chron. 27:30–31), and his sister married an Ishmaelite (1 Chron. 2:13–17).

16:14 / Kadesh-barnea, located in northeastern Sinai, is where Israel camped for years after leaving Egypt. Scripture does not mention Bered again.

§21 The Covenant of Circumcision (Gen. 17:1–27)

A year before the birth of the promised son, Yahweh strengthens the relationship with Abram by renewing their covenant. Covenant is central to this narrative: "my covenant" occurs nine times (vv. 2, 4, 7, 9, 10, 13, 14, 19, 21) and "covenant" four times (vv. 7, 11, 13, 19). The use of the word "everlasting" captures God's firm resolution to establish a people through Abram. That word occurs three times with covenant (vv. 7, 13, 19) and once with possession (v. 8).

Here God defines his relationship with Abram specifically. God exhorts Abram to conduct himself with integrity. God changes the names of Abram and Sarai. God prescribes circumcision. God announces that Sarah will bear a son within a year. Finally, God tells Abraham to name his son Isaac. The sign of circumcision and the birth of the promised son go hand in hand, for Isaac, the first heir of the covenant, will be the first seed of Abraham to be circumcised on the eighth day, as commanded.

Many critics have claimed that this account merely echoes the earlier covenant ceremony of chapter 15. However, God's augmentation of the covenant with new elements assumes a preexisting covenant. An elaborate sacrifice sealed the initial covenant (15:9–11, 17), but there is no reference to a sacrifice here. Rather, God emphasizes his purpose for having a covenant with Abram. Although both the earlier account and this one speak of land and offspring, the focus here is on offspring, whereas in the initial covenant it was on land. On that occasion Abram asked God a question that greatly troubled him (15:8), but this time he bows low in humble submission to God. Nevertheless, while God is speaking, Abram breaks out laughing at the incredulous nature of the promise God makes. He even offers God an alternative way to meet the promise (vv. 17–18). Therefore, these two reports of the covenant between God and Abram are better considered as distinct and sequential, carefully integrated into the framework of Genesis.

Two changes that take place on this occasion function as a divide in the Abraham cycle. First, God changes Abram's and Sarai's names, and from here on Genesis always uses their new names. Second, God establishes the regulation of circumcision for every male on the eighth day.

This narrative consists of two sections: the strengthening of the covenant (vv. 1–22) and Abraham's compliance with God's instructions by circumcising all the members of his household (vv. 23–27). The first section includes three units, each dominated by a speech from Yahweh. An introduction and a conclusion frame this section (vv. 1a, 22). "And God said to Abr(ah)am (him)" (vv. 1b, 9, 15) introduces each speech. The first and third units consist of an exchange between Yahweh and Abram in this pattern: God gives a speech, Abram makes a response, and God defines more closely his intention. By contrast, the middle unit consists of a speech from God alone (vv. 9–14).

17:1–2 / **When Abram was ninety-nine years old,** thirteen years after the events in chapter 16, Yahweh **appeared to him,** identified as **God Almighty.** Tradition claims that this was the primary name by which the patriarchs knew God (Exod. 6:3). God reaffirmed that Abram's family would greatly increase (12:2; 15:5). To this promise God added the injunction: **walk before me and be blameless.** Abram was therefore to conduct himself as always being in God's presence and was to be blameless *(tamim)*. When used with animals (Lev. 1:3, 10) *tamim* means "without blemish." Morally it means to keep one's commitment to God with integrity. The standard is pure devotion toward God, not moral perfection (16:9; Job 1:1, 8 [*tam*]). In contrast to the initial covenant in which God had acted unilaterally (15:7–21), this time God exhorted Abram to keep the covenant by living by the highest moral standards (Wenham, *Genesis 16–50,* p. 20).

After this ethical exhortation God informed Abram that he wished to **confirm** *(natan)* the **covenant between** them. The nuance of *natan* (lit. "give") as "confirm" is clarified by the use of "establish *(heqim)* a covenant" in verses 7, 19, and 21. These two verbs indicate that God is strengthening an earlier covenant by defining its terms more precisely. At the outset God reaffirmed the promise of numerous offspring, the focus of the original covenant (12:2; 15:5).

17:3–8 / Awed by God's appearance and moved by his words, **Abram fell facedown,** prostrating himself before God.

God continued to speak, stating that the covenant with Abram meant that he was to become **the father of many nations.** "Nations" is key, occurring three times in verses 4–6. Thus Abram was to be the father of nations other than Israel. Genesis carries this theme through, particularly in the genealogies of Abraham's children by Keturah (25:1–4), Ishmael (25:12–18), and Esau (ch. 36). To give a visible sign of his commitment to his servant, God changed his name from **Abram** ("exalted father") to **Abraham** ("father of a multitude" or "father of multitudes"). In that culture a change in name meant a change in either one's character or one's destiny. God defined the purpose of the name change, declaring that he would **make** Abraham **very fruitful** with the result that **nations** and **kings** would **come from** him. The terms "greatly increase" and "be fruitful" echo God's command to Adam (1:28), which God reaffirmed to Noah (8:17; 9:1, 7; Wenham, *Genesis 16–50*, pp. 21–22). The connection between these blessings indicates that God empowered Abraham to fulfill the divine purpose begun in creating Adam and delivering Noah.

God assured Abraham that this covenant was **an everlasting covenant,** continuing in force **between** himself and Abraham's **descendants** (seed) **for the generations to come.** God promised to be Abraham's **God and the God of** his **descendants** (seed). In order that this seed might become a nation, they needed a land. Thus God promised to give them **the whole land of Canaan,** where Abraham was living as **an alien, . . . as an everlasting possession.**

After making these great promises, God declared again that he was to **be their God.** God's purpose in entering into this covenant, then, was to have a people who worshiped only him. This affirmation lays the basis for the expectation that Abraham's seed was never to recognize any other deity. God sets himself apart from the other gods of the Near East. Pagan gods were identified with a place, but this God was identified with a people. Thus God was known as "God of the fathers," that is, the God of Abraham, Isaac, and Jacob. This meant that his people would introduce this God to other peoples on earth.

The promise of the land as an everlasting possession was deep in the consciousness of Jewish people. However, as later stipulated in the law, their occupation of the land was conditional on their obedience to God's laws (e.g., Lev. 26:27–39). Whenever Israel stubbornly persisted in disobeying God's laws, God would expel it from the land as the severest punishment. Nevertheless, should his people become scattered far from the promised land, God promised to restore them to the land upon their repentance (e.g., Lev. 26:40–45). During the exile, this promise of the land as an eternal possession, combined with the possibility for restoration expressed in the law and prophets, kept alive the people's hope of returning to Canaan.

17:9–14 / In a second speech God established a new requirement for the covenant in the context of a charge that Abraham and his seed **keep** this **covenant** throughout **the generations** (Exod. 19:5). God commanded that **every male** of Abraham's seed **be circumcised** and that every newborn **male . . . be circumcised** on the eighth day, thus becoming a member of the covenant from birth. This command also applied to all Abraham's servants, whether **born in** his **household** or **bought** from a foreigner. Servants held by Israelites were thus considered members of the people Israel. Thus there was to be no distinction between bond and free as being full-fledged members of the covenant. For emphasis, God stated that this **covenant in** their **flesh** was **to be an everlasting covenant.** While other ancient peoples also practiced circumcision, often as a puberty rite, the Israelite distinctive was circumcising each newborn male on the eighth day as a sign of the child's becoming a member of the covenant.

Circumcision was **the sign of the covenant** (v. 11). It symbolized the close bond between God and one of Abraham's seed. The presence of this sign on the male members signified that members of Abraham's seed had life more as the consequence of divine blessing than by natural generation.

Was circumcision primarily a sign to remind God of the promises to Abraham as the rainbow reminds him of the destruction caused by the flood? Or was it a sign for the people to remind them of the covenant relationship as the Sabbath reminded the people of their deliverance from Egyptian bondage (Deut. 5:15)? It is possible to see that this sign functioned in both directions. As the sign of the covenant it was a reminder that God was to relate to the one circumcised as a member of this covenant and to bless him with numerous children. That the sign was for God is borne out by the unilateral character of this covenant (ch. 15). Circumcision also functioned as a sign for all Israelites. It identified them as members together in covenant with God. In this regard it had moral force, reminding the Israelites that God gave the rite of circumcision with the exhortation to keep the covenant and that

God had enjoined Abraham to conduct himself with integrity as being always in his presence. Honorable sexual behavior enhances one's fertility and leads to the fulfillment of the promise of numerous seed. This sign alerted a member of the covenant never to use the organ bearing this mark in a promiscuous manner (cf. the laws of incest and illicit sexual relations in Lev. 18 and 20).

Breaking this commandment carried a heavy penalty. **Any male who** was **not circumcised** was to **be cut off from his people** because he had **broken** the **covenant.** The precise meaning of being "cut off" has not been established. Possibly it meant that a person lost privilege to the benefits of the covenant. After Israel's cult became operational, this penalty most likely excluded a person from worshiping at the central shrine.

17:15–16 / In the third speech, God announced to Abraham that his wife's name was being changed from **Sarai** to **Sarah.** Since this change was only a dialectic variation, the nuance remains obscure. Nevertheless, in changing her name God changed her destiny from that of a barren woman to the mother of Israel. God promised to **bless her** so that she would **give** Abraham **a son.** God's blessing would make her **the mother of nations,** and **kings of peoples** would **come from her** (vv. 15–16). For emphasis, Sarah's name occurs three times in this brief speech.

17:17–18 / On hearing God's words that Sarah was soon to bear a son, Abraham was so flabbergasted, given his and his wife's advanced age, that he **fell facedown** and broke out laughing. His response revealed that his hope of having a son by Sarah had been extinguished. Reference to his spontaneous display of incredulity establishes that Abraham did nothing to earn the gift of a son. The birth of Isaac was solely a gift of God's grace. Neither Sarah nor Abraham could do anything in themselves to bear this child. At a later time Sarah, too, would laugh at God's announcement that she was soon to bear a son (18:12–15).

Skeptical that God's promise would be realized, Abraham put to God an alternative. He asked that **Ishmael might live under** his **blessing.** That is, Ishmael should become the official heir of this covenant. Abraham spoke as though he wanted to protect God from the embarrassment of failing to keep his word.

17:19–20 / God rejected Abraham's proposal and affirmed that **Sarah** was going to **bear a son.** To make the promise more tangible, God told Abraham to name the boy **Isaac,** meaning "he laughs." God thus made an ironic play on Abraham's response and his son's name. Every time he heard his son's name, Abraham would be reminded of the miraculous birth. God promised to **establish** God's **covenant with** Isaac **as an everlasting covenant,** passing down through **his descendants** (seed).

Acknowledging Abraham's concern **for Ishmael,** God promised to **bless him** by making **him fruitful** and **greatly** increasing **his numbers.** Ishmael was to become **the father of twelve rulers** (25:13–16). These tribes would also become **a great nation,** and this took place a generation earlier than it did in Isaac's seed. Now it becomes clear why the angel of Yahweh instructed Hagar to return to Abraham's house, even though she had to endure mistreatment (16:9); it was in order that Ishmael might become the recipient of these promises. God's instructions to her do not indicate that God approves any person's abuse of another; but given human nature God does lead people to live in oppressive situations for a period of time in order to accomplish a higher purpose. After a time, though, God released Hagar from living in Abraham's household (21:8–21).

17:21–22 / After making these promises about Ishmael, for clarity and emphasis he reiterates that he would **establish** his **covenant with Isaac, "whom Sarah will bear to you by this time next year."** For the first time, God gave a specific date for the birth of the promised son. Within a year Abraham would know whether or not God had fulfilled his promise.

This interchange between God and Abraham displays the character of faith. One way faith is expressed is in a definite course of action, such as when Abraham left Haran in immediate response to God's call. Another way faith is expressed is by trusting God's promises over long spans of time despite ever-changing circumstances, including those that cast a heavy shadow over the promises. Even the greatest followers of God experience a mixture of faith and doubt when time passes with no concrete evidence that God's promise is going to be fulfilled. Faith hopes against the evidence, but at times it wilts before the reality of unrelenting circumstances. The inexorable ways of nature wear faith down. Doubt, engendered by the impossibility of the situation, has a tendency to increase while waiting for God to act. While God remains silent, a person is apt to follow a course that is a threat to faith. Often at such a juncture God seeks to nurture the one whose faith is languishing. As is the case here with Abraham,

God offers encouragement to continue believing, regardless of the nature of the obstacles. Now that it seemed impossible to Abraham and Sarah that the promise of an heir would be fulfilled, God asked them to believe for one more year. Abraham accepted that challenge.

17:23–27 / Excited at what God had told him, Abraham carried out God's instruction regarding circumcision **that very day.** His swift obedience demonstrates that his faith had been revitalized. Abraham circumcised **Ishmael,** who was thirteen, **and all those born in his household** and the servants he had **bought. Abraham was** also **circumcised,** being **ninety-nine years old.** The episode ends with a reiterating statement that **every male in Abraham's household . . . was circumcised with him** to stress the completeness of Abraham's obedience to God.

Additional Notes §21

17:1 / The name El Shaddai occurs six times in Gen. (28:3; 35:11; 43:14; 48:3; 49:25) and thirty-one times in Job. The other references are scattered throughout the OT (Ps. 68:14; 91:1; Ezek. 10:5). The etymology and the meaning of this term have not been settled. Frequently it has been translated Almighty, dating back to the LXX. It comes from *shadad* ("overpower, destroy"; see Isa. 13:6 for a paronomasia between this root and this divine name). Early Jewish sources, however, understood the name as composed of *sh* ("which") and *day* ("sufficient"), i.e., "he who is sufficient." The Albright school proposes that it comes from Akk. *shadu* ("mountain", i.e., "El of the mountain"; that is, "the cosmic mountain"; Cross, *Canaanite Myth and Hebrew Epic*, pp. 54–56).

17:4 / There are specific parallels between God's covenant with Abraham and his covenant with Noah (9:8–17). Both are identified as eternal covenants (9:16; 17:7, 13, 19); both are to continue through succeeding generations (9:9, 12; 17:7, 9); and both have a sign, i.e., the rainbow (9:12–16) and circumcision (17:11) respectively.

17:10 / In the ancient Near East several tribal groups practiced circumcision, including the Moabites, Amorites, Edomites, and Egyptians. But other tribes, such as the Philistines, the Hivites, and a variety of peoples from Mesopotamia, did not circumcise.

That only males bore the sign of the covenant on their bodies should not be interpreted as evidence that God considered female members of the covenant to be inferior. Rather, it is to be understood in light of the orientation of the OT to social units instead of to individuals. Circumcision signified that an entire family was in covenant with God.

In Scripture, circumcision also functions as a symbol of righteousness. This symbolic force coincides with God's exhorting Abraham to be blameless in the same context as his commanding him to practice circumcision. Those who obey God have their hearts circumcised (Lev. 26:41; Deut. 10:16; 30:6; Jer. 4:4), while those who are stubbornly disobedient have uncircumcised hearts (Jer. 9:25–26; Ezek. 44:7; Wenham, *Genesis 16–50,* p. 24). Those whose hearts are impervious to God's word may be radically changed by the removal of its hard foreskin. This divine operation makes the heart tender and pliable so that it becomes pure and holy, loving to do what God commands.

17:25 / Nations descended from Ishmael continue to circumcise their children at the age of thirteen, as a rite of passage from childhood to adulthood.

§22 *Abraham Entertains Three Messengers from Heaven (Gen. 18:1–33)*

It is important to interpret this account in tandem with the story of the destruction of Sodom. Abraham's position with God contrasts with the fate of his nephew Lot. Abraham is about to realize God's promise for an heir through Sarah. Conversely, Lot's dream of becoming a citizen of Sodom is about to be shattered. Having separated from Abraham to pursue wealth and pleasure, Lot will lose all his possessions. By contrast, Abraham is increasing in wealth and reputation because of God's blessing in his life.

This chapter consists of two major sections. In the first, three visitors come to Abraham and Sarah (vv. 1–15). Abraham welcomes them and is the key actor to begin with (vv. 1–8), and then the focus shifts to Sarah as she hears the promise of Isaac's birth (vv. 9–15). In the second major section (vv. 16–33) Yahweh ponders how much to tell Abraham about the fate of Sodom (vv. 16–22a), then Abraham pleads for Sodom's deliverance (vv. 22b–32), and finally Yahweh departs (v. 33).

18:1 / The narrator identifies what is about to take place as an appearance of Yahweh to Abraham in order that the reader might understand what is happening before Abraham does. This divine visit took place while Abraham **was sitting at the entrance to his tent,** pitched **near the great trees of Mamre** (13:18). He was seeking relief from **the heat of the day.**

18:2–5 / Abraham **looked up** and was surprised to see **three men standing nearby.** They had stationed themselves at some distance from his tent, as was customary, waiting to see how they might be received. His guests are identified as men, for that is how Abraham first perceived them. His failure to notice their approach is an indication that they were heavenly messengers. Abraham, however, became aware of their true identity only gradually. Excitedly he ran **to meet them.** On reaching them he

bowed low to the ground in deference. His bowing and addressing the leader as **my lord** show that he took these visitors to be nobility. While such an address was proper protocol, the narrative
allows Abraham to be more correct than he realized at first. He
welcomed them warmly, offering to bring them **a little water** to
wash their **feet** so that they could **rest under this tree.** He went on
to offer to **get** them **something to eat,** saying that after being **re-
freshed** they could **go on** their **way.** The strangers accepted his
invitation. Abraham anticipated that, in the custom of ancient
hospitality, his guests would enter into conversation before they
continued on their journey.

18:6–8 / Although he offered them some bread (NIV renders *lekhem* [lit. "bread"] "something to eat" in v. 5; however, *pat,*
"piece, morsel," standing before *lekhem,* favors the literal meaning
"bread"), Abraham hastened to prepare a feast. He instructed
Sarah to **bake bread** from **fine flour,** the kind of bread served on
very special occasions. Next he **ran to the herd and selected a
choice, tender calf** (Judg. 6:19; 13:15), a gesture that showed his
high regard for these visitors. After Sarah and the servant had
prepared the food, he set before his visitors **curds** (a rich yogurt
made from milk fat), **milk,** and tender veal. **While they ate,** Abraham **stood** beside a tree, ready to attend to their needs. That he
did not eat with the guests further indicates that Abraham considered them superior to himself.

18:9–10 / After the meal, the messengers began to converse by asking the whereabouts of **Sarah.** Following patriarchal
custom, Abraham's wife was nearby but unseen. In that culture
women were not present in the company of male visitors. The fact
that they knew her name and wished to address her—for in that
culture strangers did not address another's wife—revealed conclusively that these men were not ordinary travelers. Abraham informed them that she was **in the tent.** Following proper etiquette,
the lead guest delivered the message for Sarah by speaking to
Abraham. Identified now as Yahweh, the messenger said that
about this time next year Sarah would **have a son.** The specific
terms of this promise reinforced the one God had recently given
Abraham (17:21). The time was approximate, and the mention of
returning in a year did not mean that this messenger was to return in person. The promise, however, meant that God would
have to perform a miracle. Listening attentively from her place in
the tent, Sarah heard the message.

18:11 / The narrator adds a comment to remind the audience of how difficult it would be for Abraham and Sarah to experience the fulfillment of this promise, given their advanced age. Three phrases stress their age: **already old, well advanced in years, and . . . past the age of childbearing.** Since Sarah no longer had a monthly period, it was impossible for her to conceive naturally. Her only hope was for God to intervene. God had delayed giving a son in order that Abraham and his descendants might know conclusively that the birth of Isaac was not a happenstance but a divine gift of grace. Isaac was a son of promise, just as the people of Israel were to become the people of promise.

18:12–14 / On hearing these words, Sarah was so dumbfounded at the absurdity of what was said that she **laughed to herself.** She asked herself how she, who was **worn out** and whose **master** was **old,** could have the **pleasure** of giving birth. Sarah's laughter corresponds to Abraham's laughter regarding the same promise (17:17). The narrative highlights their laughter to underscore the stupendous nature of God's promise. To counter her unbelief and to reinforce his message, Yahweh reaffirmed that through his intervention Sarah was to bear **a son at the appointed time.**

Continuing to speak to Sarah through Abraham, Yahweh asked him **why Sarah** had laughed. Yahweh pressed the issue, addressing the note of unbelief in her laughter by asking if there was **anything too hard for** Yahweh to perform. This is the great question that daunts people of faith. Can God enter into an impossible situation and bring redemption? Yes, for God refuses to be bound by convention, natural cycles, and any other obstacle in achieving his purpose. As Creator, God can do the impossible, entering the natural order with a new surge of creative energy. In doing so God does not shatter or alter the created order. As its architect God is able to enter that order to bring about something new that will then become an integral part of the natural order. Even in a miracle God makes primary use of the natural order to achieve his purpose. The miracle on this occasion was that God enabled a woman who no longer had a monthly period to conceive. The rest of the circumstances leading to the birth of Isaac took place naturally. Abraham impregnated Sarah; she conceived and then carried the baby to full term.

18:15 / Having received a rebuke from the stranger, **Sarah was afraid.** Her response indicates that both she and Abraham were becoming fully aware that they were speaking with

messengers from the heavenly realm. Sarah then hid her embarrassment by denying that she had laughed. Because she had spoken an untruth that emanated from disbelief, the messenger held
her accountable by saying politely but firmly that she **did laugh.**
The narrator highlights this exchange because the child's name
was to be Isaac, "laughter" (17:19). Even though Abraham had already been told what was to take place (ch. 17), God honored
Sarah by informing her that she was to become the matriarch in
the fulfillment of God's original promise to Abraham. God valued
Sarah's person as much as Abraham's, working through both in
order to achieve the promises. This was evident earlier in God's
giving each of them a new name. In God's eyes they were equally
essential in order for him to bring blessing to the earth. We need to
keep the honor and role of the matriarch before us in our understanding of how the kingdom of God advances on earth.

18:16–17 / This is the beginning of the second major
section of this chapter (vv. 16–33). Having accomplished their
primary purpose in visiting Abraham and Sarah, the three messengers set out on their journey. The reference to their looking
down toward Sodom introduces the subject of this section. Continuing to be hospitable, Abraham **walked along with them** for a
while **to see them on their way.** Yahweh then spoke. Whether he
spoke to himself or to the messengers is not clear. Yahweh wondered if he should inform Abraham about the nature of his next
mission. Yahweh wanted to honor Abraham's deep love for Lot
but also anticipated that Abraham would oppose the intended
judgment against Sodom.

18:18–19 / Before speaking to Abraham about his mission, Yahweh restated his promise of blessing Abraham. The implication is that Yahweh was speaking in such a way that Abraham
could overhear. Abraham was **surely** to **become a great and powerful nation.** The addition of "powerful" enhances the original
promise (12:2). Yahweh then reiterated that **all nations on earth**
would receive blessing **through him.** Yahweh was thinking about
speaking with Abraham concerning the possibility of punishing
Sodom and Gomorrah, especially since, in the great promises to
Abraham, Abraham was the means of blessing and curse for the
other nations (12:3). By sharing his plan with Abraham, God was
implementing the dimension of the promise that the nations
would find blessing through Abraham. Furthermore, this approach reveals that God wants his people to be engaged with him

in interceding for the peoples, especially those under threat of judgment. Yahweh continued by describing Abraham as the one he had **chosen,** literally "known." "Know" here carries the sense of selecting a person in order to develop a close personal relationship. Having chosen Abraham, God charged him with the responsibility of directing **his children and his household after him to keep the way of** Yahweh. That is, they are to do **what** was **right and just.** When they are obedient to God, God may work through them dynamically to achieve what he had **promised** Abraham. This point is stressed, because it is the spiritual/moral basis that enabled Abraham to intercede for the deliverance of Sodom. It was also on the basis of Abraham's right relationship with God that Yahweh guaranteed to deliver Lot from the coming conflagration of these cities (19:29). Furthermore, in this account Abraham, a doer of righteousness, stands in sharp relief to the doers of wickedness in Sodom.

18:20–21 / In light of Abraham's position through the covenant, Yahweh decided to discuss with Abraham his plans for Sodom and Gomorrah. In doing this Yahweh put on display Abraham's role as the bearer of the promises in relationship to other peoples. Yahweh described for Abraham the depraved morality in Sodom and Gomorrah with two phrases: "great outcry" and "grievous sin." **The outcry** rising from these two cities was so loud that it had **reached** him in heaven. An "outcry" in Scripture generally comes from the oppression suffered by the weak or disenfranchised. It obligates anyone within hearing to come to the rescue (e.g., Jer. 20:8; Job 19:7; Hab. 1:2). If no one responds, God becomes the last hope of help. Being singular, "outcry" here stands for all the cries of the oppressed blended into one horrific noise. In response, God was going to Sodom to investigate the cause to see if the volume of the cry matched the reality of the oppression. If the wickedness was as great as the outcry, he would have to wipe out these cities. God's disposition in this account indicates that judgment is never light or quick, but occurs only after careful deliberation and after being convinced of the character of the people or place to be judged.

18:22–26 / At this point two of the messengers continued on to Sodom, while **Abraham remained standing before** Yahweh. Yahweh waited for Abraham to speak. Abraham did not accept Yahweh's words. With humble boldness, he **approached** his Lord and pleaded for Sodom. Abraham is allowed the privilege of trying to dissuade Yahweh from the planned course of action. Yahweh expects humans to be concerned for the welfare of others. Those who are righteous thus have the opportunity of interceding for the wicked, even for those about to be punished for their wickedness. Yahweh longs for those who will risk their own standing with him by pleading for those who are hurting, displaced, or under threat of punishment. To be effectual, such prayer must flow out of genuine concern and pure motives. Furthermore, God demonstrated an openness to be moved by intercessory prayer. God works with humans to achieve his design.

Abraham began forcefully with a rhetorical question appealing to God's justice: Would God **sweep away the righteous with the wicked?** The premise of this question is that those who live righteously generate moral value that acts as a preservative for a corrupt society threatened by judgment. Abraham asked Yahweh if the city would be spared if there were **fifty righteous** in it. His premise was that it would be uncharacteristic of God's just nature **to kill the righteous with the wicked.** The intensity of his concern led him to utter twice during his intercession, **Far be it from you.** He concluded his pleading for Sodom with a moving rhetorical question grounded in the nature of God: **will not the Judge of all the earth do right** (e.g., Ps. 96:10; 97:1–2)? Petition gains power by appealing to God's essential nature and to the fundamental way he rules. Yahweh accepted Abraham's petition, agreeing to spare the entire city for **fifty righteous.**

18:27–32 / That Abraham continued to pray indicates that Sodom lacked fifty righteous citizens. Showing deference to his Lord, Abraham confessed that he was **nothing but dust and ashes** (Job 30:19; 42:6). An intercessor confronts God boldly and forthrightly, not arrogantly. The basis of petition is God's mercy and commitment to justice, not the intercessor's own righteousness. Abraham persevered by asking Yahweh to spare the city for forty-five righteous persons. Yahweh agreed, saying that he would **not destroy** the city if **forty-five** were found. Abraham continued to intercede, slowly lowering the number of righteous, from **forty,** to **thirty,** to **twenty.** Each time God agreed, and each time Abraham continued to pray. Pleading with his Lord **not** to **be angry** with him and seeking permission to **speak** one more time, he asked that the city be spared for **ten.** Again Yahweh agreed.

18:33 / At this point, the narrator reports that Yahweh **finished speaking with Abraham.** Yahweh's posture must have told Abraham that the dialogue was over. Yahweh then **left, and Abraham returned home.**

The continual recounting of the number of righteous underscores the fact that the moral climate in Sodom and Gomorrah had decayed so badly that there were virtually no righteous left in those cities. There were no moral grounds for God to preserve them from destruction. In chapter 19 the reader learns that the heavenly messengers invited six people to flee based on their relationship to Lot, but only three of them accepted and so escaped the terrible destruction. Yahweh was not willing to spare the city for so few righteous. Just as he had provided deliverance for Noah and his family from the deluge, he would remove the righteous from the city so that only the wicked died in the terrible judgment.

Additional Notes §22

18:1 / The narrative opens with the report that Yahweh appeared to Abraham. Then, in v. 2, three men stood before Abraham. Was Yahweh one of the three? That is possible since in the second story two of the men went on to Sodom while Yahweh stayed behind to speak with Abraham (v. 22). However, von Rad (*Genesis*, pp. 204–5) proposes that Yahweh appeared in the three messengers, thus accounting for the fact that when Yahweh spoke it was in the singular (vv. 10, 13). He admits that this is a peculiarly unique report of God's appearing in the OT. Another possibility is that Yahweh is identified with the angel of Yahweh.

18:3 / According to the MT, Abraham said, "my lords" (*'adonay*). In the postexilic era Jews used the plural form of this term in lieu of pronouncing the divine name Yhwh. The singular verb, however, favors the reading *'adoni*. Accepting the slight change in the vowels of the MT form, many translate the MT as "my Lord," i.e., for the angel of Yahweh. But Abraham had not yet realized that these men were messengers from heaven. Therefore, it is possible that he addressed all of them by speaking to the leader using the singular *'adoni* ("my lord"). If the MT form is kept, it is better to translate it "my lords."

18:6 / Since this bread was made without yeast, the time for baking it was short. The dough was cooked over a rounded tin on an open fire.

18:20–21 / Yahweh's concern for these two cities gives evidence of his universal rule. Though Yahweh works through one family to reach all nations, he is concerned with and involved in the affairs of all peoples, cities, and nations. Nevertheless, one wonders why Yahweh needed to investigate the situation in Sodom and Gomorrah. In reading Scripture we need to be careful not to let our perspective obscure our understanding of how God interacts with humans. The principle conveyed is that God, being just, wanted to make sure that the situation corresponded to what he was hearing. God does not execute punishment on the basis of hearsay, but investigates a matter meticulously to ensure a just judgment.

18:22 / The ancient scribes considered the original reading— "Yahweh stood before Abraham"—to be too anthropomorphic, so they corrected the passage to read "Abraham stood before Yahweh." Such changes are very rare and are technically called *Tiqqune sopherim*, i.e., "emendations of the scribes."

18:23–25 / Abraham's statements seem ridiculous in the sense that God knows them to be true. Nevertheless, intercessory prayer gains its power by affirming the basic premises by which God rules. In stating these principles one adds intensity, argument, and power to intercession. Since God has equipped humans with moral insight, they have spiritual power in pleading for that which is right (M. Roshwald, "A Dialogue between Man and God," *SJT* 42 [1989], p. 149). Furthermore, by petitioning on the basis of central theological truths, intercessors ingrain these premises in their own thinking, purifying their own motives. Self-purification adds power to the intercession.

§23 The Rescue of Lot from the Destruction of Sodom (Gen. 19:1–38)

God finds it necessary to execute judgment again, and as was the case in the deluge, God rescues those who are righteous. The great difference in these two accounts of judgment is that this time God punishes only a small region where wickedness had increased intolerably, rather than the entire inhabited land.

The narrator tells about Lot's fleeing Sodom (vv. 1–29) and the children of Lot's daughters (vv. 30–38). In the first section there are five scenes, in which Lot extends hospitality to the two messengers (vv. 1–11), Lot prepares to flee Sodom (vv. 12–15), Lot's family flees (vv. 16–23), the cities of the plain are destroyed (vv. 23–26), and Abraham learns about the fate of Sodom and Gomorrah (vv. 27–29).

19:1–2 / Two of the three messengers from heaven who had visited Abraham (ch. 18) journeyed on to Sodom, arriving at **evening.** Given the distance, either they hastened their journey by drawing on their heavenly powers, or they arrived the second evening after leaving Abraham. On entering the city they found **Lot sitting in the gateway.** One of the gates of a walled city served as the main access. A large open area inside that gate was the hub of city life. Throughout the day citizens assembled in the square to buy and sell and conduct a variety of transactions. In the early evening the leading citizens of the town gathered there to visit and deliberate on matters of concern.

After separating from Abraham, Lot had pitched his tent near Sodom (13:12). Strongly attracted by the pleasures of urban life, he eventually moved into the city itself (14:12). Now he was sitting among the leading citizens, apparently aspiring to become a citizen of Sodom. He had pledged his daughters to local men rather than making sure they would marry from the line of Haran, as Abraham would do for Isaac. Lot's ambition to join the people of Sodom had caused him to compromise his values. Little did Lot realize that his ambition had placed him in mortal danger.

When Lot **saw** the messengers enter the city, he rose **to meet them and bowed** low before them. He invited them to **spend the night** at his **house.** It was out of the ordinary for Lot, a resident alien, to offer hospitality to recently arrived strangers, for this was the prerogative of citizens. Likely he had deferred meeting the strangers for a reasonable span of time in order to permit any citizen to welcome them. As he watched these men, being aware of the attitudes in Sodom toward strangers, Lot felt compelled to offer them hospitality for their own safety. Caught between his desire for acceptance by the citizens of Sodom and his deep concern for the well-being of these travelers, Lot acted righteously by placing the welfare of these strangers above his own ambitions.

Politely the messengers declined Lot's invitation, saying that they intended to **spend the night in** the town **square,** a wide area not far from the gate, where travelers were permitted to lodge for the night. Sojourners often lingered in such an area so they might be invited to a home (Judg. 19:15). It is possible that these messengers wished to spend the night in the square in order to observe the behavior of the citizens of Sodom.

The messengers' hesitation in accepting Lot's invitation provided another opportunity for any citizen to offer hospitality. But none did so. This lack of hospitality was a definitive symptom of the city's perverted values. Lot's compassion stood in marked contrast to the callous attitude of Sodom's citizens.

19:3 / Lot pressed the strangers to come to his house. This indicates how apprehensive he was about their safety should they spend the night in the square. The messengers yielded and went with Lot to his house. **He prepared a meal for them.** In contrast to the sumptuous feast Abraham had prepared for these travelers, only unleavened bread is mentioned here. Perhaps the cost of living was so high in this great city that Lot was not able to be as generous as Abraham had been, or perhaps Lot was not as inclined to treat strangers that generously.

19:4–5 / That evening an incident served to inform these travelers of the kind of behavior that was taking place in Sodom. **All the men from every part of the city of Sodom—both young and old—surrounded** Lot's **house.** The emphasis on "all" indicates that the entire male population of Sodom was in accord with what was about to take place. Having taken offense at Lot's offer of hospitality when he was only a resident alien, these men had come to embarrass Lot and to satisfy their lust at the expense of these strangers. Brazenly they ordered Lot to **bring . . . out** the visitors that they might satisfy their sexual desires. These men had no regard for the weak or for strangers. This incident was symptomatic of the gross depravity that had overtaken Sodom; other texts depict Sodom as full of all kinds of acts of oppression and violence (Jer. 23:14; Ezek. 16:49).

19:6–8 / Displaying great courage, **Lot went outside** to face the crowd, shutting **the door** behind him to protect his guests from harm. He addressed the men of Sodom as **friends,** literally "brothers," showing that he identified himself with them. He pleaded with them not to **do this wicked thing.** Beside himself as to how to divert the aggression of this unruly crowd, Lot offered them his **two** virgin **daughters** to satisfy their lust. That his daughters were betrothed and still virgins offers further testimony to the fact that Lot lived by a higher moral standard than did the citizens of Sodom. Faced with a great moral dilemma, Lot placed the protection of his guests above the honor of his daughters; the code of hospitality motivated him to think first of these guests. Unfortunately, Lot was willing to concede the integrity of his own daughters. He viewed his daughters as a means of his own advancement, as is evident in his pledging them to citizens of Sodom. Thus he had moved far from the standard God desired. What other course Lot could have taken is a matter for conjecture.

19:9 / The men of Sodom yelled at Lot, **"Get out of our way,"** ridiculing him by referring to him as **fellow,** literally "the one," the outsider. They went on to taunt him, deriding him, **an alien,** for acting as their **judge.** They then threatened to **treat** him **worse than** they intended to treat the visitors. In showing hospitality to these visitors Lot had so incensed the citizens that they considered him an offensive person who had to be removed from their city. All of Lot's efforts at becoming a citizen of Sodom were coming undone. Nevertheless, because he placed the honor of these strangers above his own ambitions, Lot showed that there was still some fear of God in him, at least in contrast to the wicked inhabitants of Sodom. The crowd became more aggressive, moving **forward to break down the door** of his house.

19:10–11 / Sensing the danger Lot was facing, the visitors drew on their heavenly powers to rescue him. They grabbed him, **pulled** him **into the house and shut the door.** To gain more time they smote the crowd **with blindness so that they could not find the door.** This blindness may have been caused by a very bright flash of light (2 Kgs. 6:18).

19:12–14 / The visitors ordered Lot to **get . . . out** of Sodom with his family, for they were **going to destroy** Sodom because of **the** great **outcry.** The aggression of the Sodomites against these strangers had provided them proof that the outcry rising from Sodom to God was genuine (18:20–21).

Lot responded by going **to his** future **sons-in-law** and warning them of Yahweh's intent **to destroy the city.** They thought he was **joking.** At the critical moment Lot's words of warning made no impact on them, suggesting that in their presence Lot had behaved like the citizens of Sodom rather than as one who had accompanied Abraham from Haran. Now, despite the imminent danger they faced, he appeared to them as a mocking fool. Their response bears additional witness to the moral decay of this city.

19:15 / As **dawn** was about to break, the messengers **urged Lot** to hurry and leave with his **wife and . . . two daughters** lest he be caught in the conflagration. Given the frightful events of the evening and the concern the visitors had extended to him, Lot should have responded quickly to their warning. But he delayed, reluctant to leave the town that held such a fatal attraction for him.

19:16–17 / As Lot lingered, the messengers **grasped his hand and the hands of his wife and of his two daughters and led them safely out of the city.** The forceful deliverance of Lot's family displayed Yahweh's mercy toward Abraham. Outside the city, one of the messengers ordered Lot to **flee,** not to **look back,** nor even to **stop anywhere in the plain.** To escape unharmed they had to stay focused on their destination.

19:18–22 / Lot objected. His craving for the life of the city again asserted itself. Expressing his gratitude for the **favor** and the **kindness** they had **shown in sparing** his **life,** he asked for a concession. Pointing out that he could not reach **the mountains** before the **disaster** overtook him, he asked to flee to a nearby **town** named Zoar. Twice he mentioned that this town was **small,** implying that it could not be as wicked as Sodom. There is a play on "small" and the name of Zoar, meaning "small" (14:8). Conceding his request and assuring him that they would **not overthrow** that **town,** they strongly enjoined Lot to **flee there quickly.**

19:23–25 / **Lot reached Zoar as the sun** was coming up. Meanwhile, Yahweh **rained down burning sulfur on Sodom and Gomorrah.** On this day of judgment **those cities and the entire plain** were overthrown, and all **vegetation** destroyed. This region, which had been as lush as Egypt (13:10), was turned into a desolate, moon-like landscape. The devastation was so astounding that Sodom and Gomorrah have become the ultimate symbol of destruction (e.g., Amos 4:11). **Overthrew** suggests the possibility that an earthquake contributed to the destruction.

19:26 / The furious noise of the destruction, along with her longing for the exciting life of Sodom, compelled Lot's wife to look back and see what was happening. Because she disobeyed the specific orders of the messengers, she was overcome by the intense heat of the conflagration and is reported to have been turned into **a pillar of salt.**

19:27–28 / The narrative shifts back to Abraham. **Early the next morning** he went out **to the place where** he had interceded for Sodom and **looked down** on the cities of the plain. **He saw dense smoke rising from the land.** Although he had no idea of Lot's safety, he was most likely confident of the angel of Yahweh's promise that Lot would be rescued.

19:29 / The narrator provides a theological interpretation for Lot's rescue. God had made sure that Lot escaped the destruction of Sodom and Gomorrah because **he remembered Abraham** (8:1). God showed mercy to Lot on the basis of Abraham's faithfulness and his intercession for Sodom. Abraham, therefore, was the reason for Lot's deliverance (12:2–3).

19:30–38 / In fleeing to the east, rather than to the west to rejoin Abraham and seek help in rebuilding his family's life, Lot's behavior led to a situation that was to result in conflict for the children of Abraham. Out of this situation came the Moabites and the Ammonites. These two nations, which were to be a thorn in Israel's side for a large part of its history, were related to Israel through Lot, Abraham's nephew (Deut. 2:9, 19; 23:3; Ps. 83:6). Lot also confirmed in going to the east that he chose to leave the ideals by which Abraham lived.

19:30–31 / With his dreams of becoming a citizen of Sodom shattered and with the loss of his wealth (13:5–6), Lot suffered great trauma. He **left Zoar** and with his two daughters went to live **in a cave** in the mountains of Moab.

Lot's inability to cope with his losses greatly distressed his daughters. They were in their prime childbearing years and had no idea how long they would live as refugees in a cave. The elder complained that **there** was **no man around.** In desperation, she concocted a scheme by which both of them might become pregnant by their father. After getting him drunk with **wine,** at night one of them would go to him and become impregnated. Their father's willingness to compromise their honor to protect strangers (v. 8) must have diminished their respect for him. His behavior showed them how one could use a person, even a close relative, to achieve a selfish goal. Consequently, on two successive nights, each daughter in turn carried out this scheme. Both times Lot was so drunk that he was unaware of what was taking place. And **both . . . daughters became pregnant.** The text does not tell us when and how they informed their father of what had taken place. **The older daughter** bore **a son** and called his name **Moab,** that is, "from the father." He became **the father of the Moabites. The younger daughter** bore **a son** and **named him Ben-Ammi,** that is, "son of my kinsman," who became **the father of the Ammonites.**

This narrative does not make a moral judgment against Lot's daughters; rather it pictures the tragic way Lot lived out the rest of his life. This sad scene shows the consequences of Lot's longing to settle in such a wicked city, and it accounts for the origin of two peoples who lived in proximity to Israel. It also explains why the patriarchs never arranged marriages with Lot's descendants.

This scene completes the story of Lot, who had left from Haran with Abraham (12:4). In the Abraham cycle Lot serves as a foil against which Abraham's faith and obedience shine more brightly. Having lost his ability to act clearly on his faith, Lot faded into ignominy.

Additional Note §23

19:24–25 / Sarna postulates that a fire storm resulted from a great earthquake in the Syrian-African Rift, the great rift that reaches from Syria in Palestine to Lake Nyasa in East Africa (*Genesis*, p. 138). The earth opened up, releasing gases and fumes. During the earthquake, lightning struck and ignited these gases, setting on fire the bitumen and sulfur in that region. To date no external witness or archaeological data identify the location of these cities.

§24 *Abraham before Abimelech of Gerar (Gen. 20:1–18)*

Abraham settles for a brief time in Gerar, a city-state in the Negev to the west of Beersheba, ruled by a Philistine king, where he again identifies Sarah as his sister. The local king, Abimelech, takes her into his harem. The rabbis speculate on the legendary beauty of Sarah in her old age, believing it to be a result of God's blessing on the great matriarch of Israel. More likely, though, Abimelech may have been seeking an alliance through marriage with the people whom he took Abraham to represent. This time God protects not only Abraham and Sarah but also the king. The drama takes place in six scenes: Abimelech takes Sarah (vv. 1–2); God warns Abimelech (vv. 3–7); Abimelech holds a meeting with his officials (v. 8); Abimelech confronts Abraham (vv. 9–13); Abimelech rights matters with Abraham (vv. 14–16); and Abraham prays for Abimelech (vv. 17–18).

The drama unfolds by the interchange of action (vv. 2, 8, 14, 17–18) and dialogue (vv. 3–7, 9–13, 15–16). The point of reversal comes at verse 8: Abimelech holds a special meeting and informs his officials of the difficult situation they face in that Sarah, a married woman, is a part of the royal harem. Dialogue occurs before and after the meeting. Preceding it, God holds Abimelech accountable for having taken Sarah (vv. 3–7); afterward Abimelech holds Abraham accountable for having deceived him about Sarah (vv. 9–13).

The narrator assumes the reader's knowledge of the similar incident with Pharaoh (12:10–20), for striking differences carry important nuances. Whereas Abraham went to Egypt because of famine in Canaan, he chooses to settle in Gerar. God cursed Pharaoh's house for his having approached Sarah; this time God warns Abimelech in a dream before he touches Sarah. In compensation for the wrong done, both rulers gave Abraham gifts. Whereas Pharaoh appeared to give the gifts as a dowry, Abimelech compensates Abraham for the damages he has incurred. Afterward Pharaoh expelled Abraham, but Abimelech invites him to remain in his land. Abimelech handled this awkward situation much more honorably than did Pharaoh.

20:1 / Abraham departed from an unidentified place, presumably Mamre (18:1), and went south through the land of promise to **the Negev** (12:9). Although the text gives no reason for this move, by traveling through the land of promise Abraham laid claim to it for his seed. For a short time he **lived between Kadesh,** an oasis, and **Shur,** an Egyptian fortress (25:18). Turning north, **he stayed in Gerar,** a city under the rule of Abimelech, a Philistine (10:14; 21:32).

20:2–5 / In Gerar, Abraham again feared for his life on account of Sarah (12:11–16). Ancient monarchs had the reputation of expanding their harems at the expense of a foreigner's wife (2 Sam. 11, David and Bathsheba). Resorting to the stratagem he had used in Egypt, Abraham introduced Sarah as his **sister.** Presumably having heard rave reports about Sarah, who had recently arrived in his capital with her brother, Abimelech sent officers to bring Sarah to the palace. After Sarah arrived at the king's household, she possibly had to remain in special quarters as she underwent a variety of rituals preparing her to join the harem (see Esth. 2:12–13 for an extreme example).

God came to Abimelech in a dream one night and warned him that he was under threat of death for having **taken . . . a married woman** into his household. The text explicitly states that **Abimelech had not** yet **gone near** Sarah. God spoke directly to a Gentile king, demonstrating that though he was working primarily through Abraham, God was not silent to the rest of humanity. Moreover, it appears that God honored Abimelech for his efforts to promote a high standard in his realm. Thus God intervened to prevent him from violating his own integrity. In response to God's warning, Abimelech vigorously defended his integrity to God. Appealing to God's justice, he asked if God would **destroy an innocent nation.** He referred to the "nation" instead of to himself, because as king he knew that whatever would happen to him would happen to his people. With this rhetorical question he sought to dissuade God from inflicting harm on his people for something he was intending to do with no malice aforethought. He also stressed that Abraham had told him that **she** was his **sister** and that Sarah had confirmed Abraham's words. He brought his self-defense to a climax by asserting that he had acted **with a clear conscience,** literally "in integrity of heart," **and clean hands.** Shrewdly Abimelech ignored his failure to negotiate with Abraham in order that Sarah might become his wife (v. 16).

20:6–7 / God acknowledged that Abimelech had acted out of pure motives, adding that for this reason he had intervened to restrain him **from sinning against** God. When one person violates another, the sin is not only against the other person but also against God (26:10; 39:9b). God's statement that he had not allowed Abimelech to touch Sarah bears great theological force. According to Israel's theology, no ruler, especially one who has dealings with God's people, has any power except what God grants. Since Abimelech had acted with proper motivation, God intervened to prevent him from committing a great sin that would bring harm on his people. This portrait shows one way God justly interacts with foreign rulers in their dealings with his people.

God then gave Abimelech specific instructions for resolving the untoward situation. He told him to **return** Sarah to Abraham, whom he identified as **a prophet.** In that role Abraham would **pray** that Abimelech might **live.** Should Abimelech fail to return Sarah, however, God would place him and his family under the death penalty. God often requires those who have inflicted harm on others to follow a difficult path in order to achieve reconciliation. In some cases he lays a hard requirement even on those who have suffered, such as praying for the restoration of the ones who have troubled them (Job 42:8). Such a demand humbles both parties. This instruction to Abimelech that he submit to the one who had caused this awkward situation tested the sincerity of his claim of having acted innocently. Furthermore, God was preempting any desire in Abimelech to seek retaliation, overt or covert, against Abraham.

20:8 / Not wasting any time in carrying out God's directives, Abimelech wisely **summoned all his officials** and informed them of the matter. What they heard made them so **afraid** that they were ready to do exactly as Abimelech ordered to avert God's punishment. This is the pivotal verse, and "fear" is the key term. The whole problem began because Abraham feared for his life. Now the entire house of Abimelech was highly motivated to resolve the crisis—out of fear.

20:9–10 / **Abimelech called Abraham in** and straightaway Abimelech confronted him with two rhetorical questions and a direct accusation. First, he alerted Abraham that he knew about his scheme by asking **what** he had **done to** them. Then, in polite deference, he asked Abraham how he might have **wronged** *(khata')* him to make him bring **such great guilt** *(khata'ah)* upon him **and** his **kingdom.** *Khata'ah* means both "sin" and "guilt" caused by sin; this great sin made the whole population culpable. Abimelech was graciously offering Abraham an opportunity to lodge any complaint against the king or the citizens. This was an open opportunity for him to clear himself. Then Abimelech directly accused Abraham of doing **things . . . that should not be done.** He had violated the standard of behavior among peoples.

Apparently Abraham stood by silently, for Abimelech's next words have another introduction. To prod Abraham into responding, Abimelech asked why he had done this. With this final question Abimelech displayed his desire that all living under his rule would act justly.

20:11–13 / Abraham responded with a threefold defense. First, he was apprehensive that since there was **no fear of God in this place,** he would be killed for his **wife.** Lack of the fear of God in a society means that the people act without high regard for human rights, especially for the weak and foreigners. But Abimelech proved to be one who was willing to listen to God. So Abraham had misjudged the character of this ruler. Next, Abraham claimed on technical grounds that he had not lied, because Sarah was his **sister** through a common **father.** Since the intent of a statement bears greater moral weight than its factual accuracy, Abraham's self-defense was very weak. Finally, Abraham made an amazing confession, saying that on leaving Haran the two of them had made a pact that wherever they went Sarah could **show** her **love** for him by identifying him as her **brother.** With this disclosure he betrayed the depth of his apprehension about the safety of Sarah and himself on leaving Haran for such a distant land. This confession provides some explanation for his employing this scheme twice. Thus Abraham did not rely totally on God for their safety while journeying in strange territory.

20:14–16 / Out of fear from God's warning, Abimelech did not press Abraham further on his miscalculation. The king was also aware that he had inflicted damages on Abraham by having taken his wife into his household without having completely followed proper protocol in this matter. That is, he had not waited long enough for the sojourners to become settled, and he had not made sufficient inquiry into Sarah's identity. Nor had he sought Abraham's permission to take Sarah into his household. Accordingly, he compensated Abraham with **sheep and cattle and male and female slaves.** What is more important, **he returned Sarah** to Abraham as God had instructed. Then he graciously extended an invitation to Abraham to **live** anywhere in his territory.

Abimelech informed Sarah that he was **giving a thousand shekels of silver** to her **brother.** His use of "your brother," the very words that had caused this situation, served as a barb to impress on her that Abraham bore blame for what had taken place. Von Rad (*Genesis,* p. 229), however, believes that Abimelech used "your brother" on legal grounds in order to avoid increasing Abraham's embarrassment. In either case, this large sum was **to cover the offense** that she had suffered. Abimelech then declared that Sarah was **completely vindicated.** His goal was to restore the honor of Abraham and Sarah as well as his own.

20:17–18 / After Abimelech had taken these steps to address the wrong he had done, Abraham obeyed God by praying for him. God heard Abraham's prayer and **healed Abimelech, his wife and his slave girls** from the curse of infertility. Only at this point does the reader learn that God had inflicted a curse of infertility on Abimelech's household **because of . . . Sarah.**

Additional Notes §24

This episode in Abraham's life functions as a model by which the people Israel could understand their national experience with the Philistines. Like Abraham, Israel was going to face peril from the Philistines. As with Abraham, God would intervene, bring hardship on the Philistines, and direct events so that his people would prevail. Specifically, there are parallels between this account and the Philistines' capturing the ark of the covenant (1 Sam. 4–6; Reis, "Take My Wife, Please," pp. 313–14). As Abimelech had taken Abraham's beloved wife, the Philistines captured the ark. God then inflicted them with a curse that caused great discomfort, just as he had inflicted the members of Abimelech's household with infertility. As God had warned Abimelech in the night, he humiliated the Philistine god Dagon in the night by causing him to fall prostrate before the ark of the covenant. And, parallel to Abimelech's gifts to Abraham, the Philistines gave the Israelites an offering with the return of the ark.

20:9 / The phrase "a great sin" for adultery has been found in marriage contracts from Ugarit and Egypt (J. Van Seters, *Abraham in History and Tradition* [New Haven, Conn.: Yale University Press, 1975], p. 76). This crime was a capital offense; since it was considered an offense against the husband, he could mitigate the extent of the punishment.

20:12 / In some societies marrying a half-sister is not considered a consanguineous marriage. For the greatest patriarch to have entered into such a marriage defined in the law as incestuous (Lev. 18:9, 11; 20:17; Deut. 27:22) indicates that he lived according to different marital customs than those Israel observed.

§25 The Birth of Isaac and the Expulsion of Ishmael (Gen. 21:1–21)

Sarah bears the child of promise. In light of this couple's waiting twenty-five years for God's promise to be fulfilled, it is amazing how matter-of-fact is the report of Isaac's birth. Directly following this happy, triumphal account comes the report of an ugly incident in which Sarah demands that Hagar and Ishmael be expelled from the household. The latter incident receives more coverage because it relates the drastic rearrangement the birth of the son of promise causes in Abraham's household.

The two episodes in this section are the birth of Isaac (vv. 1–7) and the expulsion of Hagar and Ishmael from Abraham's house (vv. 8–20). A play on the name Isaac binds the two accounts. In the first account Sarah laughs because of the gift of Isaac ("laughter"). In the second, Ishmael makes fun of (i.e., causes people to laugh at) Isaac.

21:1 / This verse is a heading to the notice of Isaac's birth. Out of grace and despite Sarah's disbelief (18:12), God fulfilled the promise of a child to Abraham and Sarah. Behind the NIV "be gracious" is Hebrew *paqad* ("visit," 1 Sam. 2:21). This term conveys that God directed the course of nature for a specific outcome (50:24–25; Exod. 3:16; 4:31).

21:2–7 / When Abraham was a hundred years old, **Sarah became pregnant and bore a son to Abraham . . . at the very time God had promised** (18:14). Her fertility parallels the restoration of fertility to the women of Abimelech's house after Abraham prayed (20:17–18). In obedience to God, **Abraham** named his **son Isaac,** meaning "laughter" (17:19). The text adds that this was the son Sarah bore him in order to identify Isaac unequivocally as the son of promise. Keeping the covenant, **Abraham circumcised** Isaac on the eighth day, **as God** had **commanded** (17:10, 12).

Sarah also rejoiced at the laughter **God** had **brought** into her life by this astonishing birth. It turned her earlier laughter of disbelief, which masked her deep anguish (18:12, 15), into joyful laughter. She was glad that those who heard of her triumph in having a child at such an old age would laugh with her. Full of excitement, Sarah composed poetic lines celebrating her triumph in nursing children and bearing Abraham **a son** when he was **old.** She who had laughed in disbelief at the angel's announcement that she would bear a son (18:12–15) now laughs in joyful glee for her son named "laughter."

21:8 / Delighted at finally having a son by Sarah and desirous of cherishing the stages of his son's growth, **Abraham held a great feast** when Isaac **was weaned.** Although weaning took place at different ages, Isaac must have been older than three (1 Sam. 1:22, 24; 2 Macc. 7:27).

21:9–10 / At this feast Sarah became extremely jealous when she saw Hagar's **son . . . mocking.** "Mocking" or "sporting" *(metsakheq)* is from the same root as Isaac's name. Possibly Ishmael was showing his prowess in order to draw the attention of the guests away from Isaac. It is likely, though, that he was making fun of Isaac by abusing his name. It is also important to note that the narrator mocks Ishmael by never using his name in this account. Whatever Ishmael was doing maddened Sarah. Perhaps his behavior made her apprehensive that he might do something, even a violent act, to take Isaac's place. In no way did Sarah want Ishmael to receive any praise, position, or affirmation that was greater than Isaac's, and in no way would she tolerate Ishmael's acting in a way that would put down Isaac. Therefore, she pleaded with Abraham to banish Hagar, **that slave woman, and her son.** This language reflects the increasing distance between the two women (Trible, "The Other Woman," p. 232). Sarah's determination to expel Hagar shows that her confidence as a matriarch had increased with Isaac's birth. To persuade Abraham she used an argument that concerned him intimately by saying that she did not want Hagar's son to **share in the inheritance with** her **son Isaac.**

21:11 / Sarah's words struck Abraham hard, for he considered Hagar's son **his son**—not on the same plane as Isaac but nonetheless his son. Before the birth of Isaac he had treated Ishmael as his rightful heir. Even though Ishmael lost that position with the birth of Isaac, Abraham's love for him had not diminished. But there was little Abraham could do to counter Sarah's demands, especially since she had risked herself by identifying herself to Abimelech as Abram's sister in order to save his life (Reis, "Take My Wife, Please," pp. 311–12).

21:12–13 / While pondering Sarah's demand, Abraham received guidance from God, **Do not be so distressed about the boy and your maidservant.** The reference to Ishmael as "the boy" distanced him from Abraham (Trible, "The Other Woman," p. 232). God instructed Abraham to do as Sarah had asked, for he had appointed **Isaac** as his true **offspring** (seed). God unequivocally identified Isaac as the heir of the great Abrahamic promises. In addition, God promised to **make** Hagar's **son into a nation,** for he was Abraham's **offspring** (seed).

21:14–21 / **Early the next morning** Abraham acted on Sarah's demand in light of God's instructions. Compassionately he **took some food and a skin of water and gave them to Hagar.** Then, entrusting the boy to her, Abraham **sent** them **off.** Hagar **wandered** about **in the desert of Beersheba,** apparently lacking direction. After **the water in the skin** had been consumed, **she put the boy under** a bush for some protection from the burning sun. She then went a little way—as far as one could shoot an arrow—**and sat down.** In agony, fearful that her son would soon die from lack of water, she thought, "Do not let me look on the child's dying." Her words were a desperate prayer. Her only hope for either of them to survive was through God's intervention. **She began to sob** in the deepest anguish. Ishmael, too, was crying.

God heard the boy crying. Then **the angel of God called to Hagar from heaven, . . .** "**Do not be afraid; God has heard the boy crying**" (16:7–8). The angel gave her a word of deliverance, a word of hope to overcome her deep fear (15:1). The angel instructed her to **lift the boy up and take him by the hand,** for God was going **to make him into a great nation.** God remembered and reasserted his earlier promise to Hagar of numerous descendants (16:10).

Then God opened her eyes so that Hagar **saw a well of water** nearby. She took **the skin** and **filled** it **with water.** Likely she dampened a cloth, wiped the boy's face, and **gave** him some to **drink.** Growing up in the steppe, Ishmael became a skilled **archer** with God watching over him. Eventually he settled **in the Desert of Paran,** and **his mother** arranged his marriage with an Egyptian woman.

Additional Note §25

21:21 / Paran is the desert or wilderness between Canaan and Sinai. Israel passed through this region on their journey from Egypt to the promised land (Num. 12:16).

§26 The Treaty between Abraham and Abimelech (Gen. 21:22–34)

The report of Abimelech's entering into covenant with Abraham is presented so tersely that it is hard to understand fully the transaction that takes place between them. The outer frame (vv. 22–24, 27, 31) describes the making of the covenant. In the heart of the story Abraham lodges a formal complaint against Abimelech's servants for seizing a well he had dug (vv. 25–26, 28–30). Pressing his claim, Abraham achieves a pretrial settlement. Both men swear that Abraham had dug the well, and then they seal the covenant. In God's providence Abraham regains access to an important well in a way that increases his reputation.

It is possible that two distinct episodes have been woven together. It is also possible that Abimelech's initiation of a covenant provides Abraham the opportunity to settle successfully a standing grievance. The recurrence of the number seven is evidence that the present narrative is a single account. Abraham gives seven ewes; Beersheba is the well of "seven"; the names of Abraham and Abimelech occur seven times (Sarna, *Genesis*, p. 148).

21:22 / Abimelech, the local Philistine chieftain, noticed Abraham's increasing prosperity. To protect his own family, flocks, and access to the wells of the desert, and also to participate in Abraham's blessing, he desired to establish peaceful relations with Abraham. Abraham is pictured as a sheik or local king on par with Abimelech. **At that time** ties this account into the Abrahamic cycle. **Abimelech and Phicol the commander of his forces** (ch. 20) went from Gerar to Beersheba to speak with Abraham. Abimelech opened the conversation with a high compliment about how **God** was **with** Abraham **in everything** he did. Because Abraham was prospering as God had promised (12:2), Abimelech wanted to make a covenant with him (12:3).

21:23–24 / This covenant was to protect their **children** and **descendants** and to guarantee nonaggression between them. Abimelech appealed to Abraham on two bases. Abraham, being **an alien,** needed such a pact to strengthen his position in that region. Abimelech had shown him **kindness** *(hesed).* He claimed that the way he had acted in resolving the situation with Sarah was evidence that he would act loyally and kindly in a covenant relationship. He petitioned Abraham to take an oath that he would not **deal falsely with** him and his descendants. "Falsely" alludes to the way Abraham had deceived him about Sarah (ch. 20). An oath has meaning in direct proportion to how firmly people believe in God, for God has the oversight to enforce the oath justly. Since these parties believed in the God who had spoken to each of them, this oath had the highest possible meaning. Abraham swore as Abimelech requested.

21:25–26 / Taking advantage of Abimelech's friendly demeanor, **Abraham** presented a formal complaint about **a well seized** by his **servants.** Abraham asserted his claim to this well and tested Abimelech's purpose for entering into a covenant relationship. Abimelech defended himself from any wrongdoing in this matter by stating his ignorance about this deed. Since Abraham had not informed him, there had been no opportunity for him to correct this matter. Indirectly, he conceded the well to Abraham.

21:27–34 / Abraham accepted Abimelech's answer, for he **brought sheep and cattle and gave them to Abimelech.** Abraham's provision of the animals indicated that he accepted Abimelech's proposal that they enter into covenant. The two men slaughtered the animals and solemnized the covenant as was customary in ancient times.

Abraham surprised Abimelech by giving him **seven ewe lambs,** most likely as a payment for settling the dispute about the well. He realized that Abimelech would be much more willing to recognize his claim to the well on receiving some compensation for the loss of a watering place. **Abimelech asked Abraham** why he had **set apart** the ewes. Abraham answered that Abimelech was to **accept** them **as a witness** that he had truly **dug this well.** Afterward, Abraham named that place **Beersheba,** meaning both "the well of seven" and "the well of the oath." In Hebrew, seven is such an important number that it is used for the verb to "swear."

The giving of seven ewe lambs empowered the oath. Then the **two men swore an oath,** sealing the covenant between them.

Abimelech and Phicol . . . returned home **to the land of the Philistines. Abraham** responded by planting **a tamarisk tree in Beersheba.** This deed corresponded to his building an altar at other sites (e.g., 12:7), for **he called upon the name of** Yahweh, **the Eternal God.** Since it takes many seasons for a tree to mature, Abraham's action indicated that he planned to stay in that region. The covenant gave Abraham the sense of security that he could live there undisturbed by the local population. **Abraham stayed** there **for a long time.**

Additional Notes §26

21:32 / Reference to the Philistines presents a problem in that the well-known Philistines did not settle in Canaan until the twelfth century B.C. K. Kitchen (*Peoples of Old Testament Times* [ed. D. Wiseman; Oxford: Clarendon, 1973], pp. 56–57) proposes that this name was used for people who had come from the Aegean area and had settled along the southern coast of Canaan but whose specific name had become lost. Or it may be a case of using a familiar name for a people who were indirectly related to the later, famous inhabitants of this region. If the name Phicol has its origin in Anatolia, this fact supports a connection between these Philistines and the Aegean. These Philistines, however, had a very different politicocultural orientation from the later Philistines. They were governed by a king, not a council of lords from the five lead cities. Since our information is limited, it is important not to prejudge the use of the term Philistines as an anachronism (Millard, "Methods of Studying the Patriarchal Texts," in *Essays on the Patriarchal Narratives,* p. 44).

21:33 / A tamarisk grows to thirty feet, even without much water. Bedouins plant them for shade and so that their flocks may nibble on the soft branches.

It is known that the Canaanites used trees and poles in worship. Since such worship was tied to fertility rites, the law later castigated the use of sacred trees in worship of Yahweh (Deut. 16:21).

§27 The Binding of Isaac (Gen. 22:1–19)

In an episode repulsive to a contemporary audience, God commands Abraham to offer up his son Isaac as a whole burnt offering. How could the God who created life and blessed humans with fertility require his faithful servant to offer up his only, beloved, son as a sacrifice? How could God ask Abraham to give up the son of promise for whom he had waited so long? On the other hand, how could Abraham obey God's command without energetically entreating for Isaac's life as he had done for Sodom and Gomorrah (18:23–32)? These are hard questions, and the text only hints at answers. The text's reticence at becoming engaged with these kinds of questions belongs to the artistic design of the narrative, which is to keep in focus the central issue of Abraham's wholehearted obedience to God in regard to his firstborn.

The two key figures are Abraham and Isaac. Abraham is the dominant character; his name occurs sixteen times. Isaac, although he speaks only once (v. 7), is mentioned nineteen times: by name six times (vv. 2, 3, 6, 7 [twice], 9), as "the only one" three times (vv. 2, 12, 16), and as "son" ten times (vv. 2, 3, 6, 7, 8, 9, 10, 12, 13, 16). The repeated references to Isaac keep before the reader the agonizing pain that the test caused Abraham. "Burnt offering" (*'olah*) is a central term, occurring six times (vv. 2, 3, 6, 7, 8, 13). The nodal term "see" (*r'h*) marks turning points in the action. Abraham *saw* the place for the sacrifice (v. 4); God will provide (*see*) a lamb (v. 8); Abraham *saw* a ram (v. 13); Yahweh provides (lit. "sees," v. 14a); and Yahweh *appears* ("makes himself seen," v. 14b).

The drama has two foci: preparations for the offering of Isaac (vv. 1–10) and the outcome of Abraham's complete obedience in this matter (vv. 11–19). Both of these begin with a voice from heaven calling Abraham by name (vv. 1, 11). Within these major divisions are eight sections: a prologue (v. 1a), God's command about sacrificing Isaac (vv. 1b–2), the journey to Mount Moriah (vv. 3–4), conversation between Abraham and the servants (vv. 5–6), dialogue between Abraham and Isaac (vv. 7–8),

the binding of Isaac (vv. 9–11), promises made by the angel of
Yahweh (vv. 12–18), and an epilogue (v. 19). Scenes alternate between speaking (sections 2, 4, 5, 7) and action (3, 6).

22:1 / **Some time later,** God put Abraham to the supreme test. To prepare the reader to hear this disturbing account,
the narrator departs from the usual oblique style of the patriarchal narratives by stating at the outset the purpose of what was
about to take place: **God** was going to test **Abraham.** God, however, never gave Abraham a hint that this was only a test.

That God needs to test a person might seem incomprehen-
sible in light of the belief in God's full knowledge, but God is involved with those who fear him—leading, guiding, and testing
them. There are many references in the OT to God's testing Israel (Exod. 15:22–26; 16:4; 20:18–20; Deut. 8:12–16; 13:1–3; Judg.
2:21–22; 3:1–4). God's test of Hezekiah is another reference to
an individual being examined (2 Chron. 32:31). God examines
people not only to discover their true character but also to develop in them certain desirable qualities.

On this occasion God called Abraham, speaking his name a
single time. This style contrasts with the times God repeated a
name to get a person's attention (e.g., v. 11; Exod. 3:4, the call of
Moses; 1 Sam. 3:10, the call of Samuel). The ease with which God
got Abraham's attention attests that he was in close fellowship
with God. Responsively Abraham **replied: "Here I am,"** indicating that he was ready to do whatever God asked.

22:2 / With three crisp imperatives God gave Abraham a
threefold order: **take your son** Isaac, **go to the region of Moriah,**
and **sacrifice him there.** The first command, **take,** stands in a polite form. God then made it clear to Abraham that he was to take
Isaac by using three terms with narrowing focus: **your son, your
only son, Isaac.** In Hebrew a threefold repetition has superlative
force (1:27; 12:1). God made the command as strong as possible by
using the threefold pattern and by casting the middle command,
"go," in the same form as when he had ordered Abram to leave his
father's household (*lek-leka;* 12:1). The phrase "whom you love"
further underscores Abraham's relationship to his son. God made
sure that Abraham understood that he could fulfill this command
only with Isaac, not with Eliezer (possibly an adopted son, 15:2),
or with Ishmael, his son by Hagar. God told him to **go to the region of Moriah,** and that there he would point out the exact place
for the sacrifice. The third command defined the crux of the test.

God ordered Abraham to **sacrifice** Isaac **as a burnt offering.** This order sealed Isaac's fate, for a burnt offering was consumed by fire (Lev. 1). Because God addressed Abraham as he had when he commanded him to leave Haran (12:1–3), Abraham quickly grasped the decisiveness in God's command. On this occasion there was no room for debating with God.

22:3 / **Early the next morning Abraham** prepared to do as God had commanded. The heaviness of Abraham's heart at God's orders is communicated not by word but by the inverted way he went about preparing for the trip. Doing the last task first, Abraham **saddled his donkey.** Then he instructed two servants and Isaac to get ready for a trip. The author intentionally inverted the order of these persons by mentioning the servants before Isaac, the beloved son, to signal further the stress Abraham felt. His troubled thoughts at offering up his beloved son chafed against his inclination to obey God. Next Abraham **cut . . . wood for the burnt offering.** This detail indicates Abraham's anticipation that the region to which he was going had little wood. By not delegating this chore to his servants, Abraham sought to identify with the sacrifice of Isaac through expending his own effort in preparing for the sacrifice. Such details tie this remarkable episode to reality, attesting that Abraham was not merely having a bad dream and that this is not a made-up story. Abraham's resolve overcame his resistance as **he set out for the place God had told him about.**

22:4–5 / **On the third day Abraham looked up and saw the place in the distance.** We can imagine that their pace had been quite deliberate as Abraham cherished the brief time he had left with Isaac. Apparently he did so in silence; the silence conveys the sobriety of his feelings as he carried out God's command. Having arrived in the vicinity of the designated place, Abraham needed to give instructions. Wanting to make the sacrifice in private, he instructed **his servants** to **stay** there while Isaac and he went ahead and worshiped. Abraham used an imprecise term for worship so that the servants would not surmise what he intended to do. He concluded with the assertion, **We will come back to you.** This statement was designed to belie any suspicion that they might have had of what he was about to do with Isaac. Abraham spoke definitively by using intense Hebrew verbal forms (cohortatives): we will go, we will worship, we will return. He was thereby expressing both his resolve to obey God and his hope for Isaac's survival.

22:6–8 / Acting with even greater deliberation to slow down their arrival at the place of sacrifice, Abraham left the donkey laden with supplies with the servants and continued the journey on foot. He **took the wood for the burnt offering and placed it on his son Isaac.** He was identifying his son with the offering. Abraham himself took the lethal materials, that is, **the fire,** possibly some kind of fire stick, and **the knife.** This mention of Abraham's picking up the knife heightens the terror of the story and signals that his resolve to obey God was intact. The brief clause **the two of them went on together,** stated twice in verses 6b and 8b, underscores the bond between Abraham and Isaac at this ominous moment.

Perplexed about the lack of a lamb for the sacrifice, **Isaac** caught his father's attention. Abraham alertly responded, "Here I am, **my son.**" This simple answer, the same in Hebrew as his response to God's call (v. 1), shows Abraham's sensitivity to Isaac's every move. The similarity of these responses is unfortunately lost in NIV's rendering, "Yes, my son." Observing that there was **fire** and **wood** but no animal, **Isaac** asked where **the lamb** was **for the burnt offering.** Although he asked this innocently, it cut to the quick of Abraham's resolve to obey God. Confronted with the reality of what was about to take place, **Abraham answered** with hopeful words: "**God himself will provide the lamb for the burnt offering.**" The verb "provide" is literally "see." With this assertion, was Abraham refusing to face what was about to take place, or was he venturing a statement of great faith? This assertion, along with the one made to his servants about returning, suggests Abraham had a hope deep within himself that God would not let him kill the child of promise. The writer of Hebrews read the text in this way (11:17–19).

Isaac accepted the explanation, but, we can conjecture, with skeptical apprehension. **The two of them** proceeded on their journey **together.** Just as Abraham was being obedient to God, Isaac was being obedient to his father.

22:9 / On reaching **the place God had told him about,** Abraham **built an altar** as he had often done while traveling through Canaan. This altar, however, he built in solemn obedience. He **arranged the wood.** Then he **bound his son Isaac and laid him on the altar, on top of the wood.** The rapid sequence of verbs—built, arranged, bound, laid—communicates that Abraham went about his work systematically and deliberately. The wording also suggests that little or no conversation took place between the two of them. Since Isaac was at least in his early twenties and Abraham was more than one hundred years old, Isaac was strong enough to have withstood his father. Therefore, he must have let himself be bound and placed on the altar.

22:10–14 / Abraham **reached out his hand and took the knife to slay his son.** The activity of preparing the sacrifice is slowed by detailing the ominous steps leading to the slaughter: sending out the hand, taking the knife out of its sheath, and, by implication, raising it to slay. The word "slay" focuses on the impending death of the victim. At the moment Abraham was about to inflict the fatal blow, a voice from heaven cried out, stopping him. Since Abraham's resolve to obey God was beyond question, **the angel of** Yahweh **called out to him from heaven, "Abraham! Abraham!"** The double calling of Abraham's name in contrast to the single mention of his name at the opening of the narrative conveys the angel's urgency in getting Abraham's attention. Abraham responded in the way he did to God's first call: **Here I am.** "From heaven" is mentioned because sometimes the angel of Yahweh walked about on earth (chs. 18–19). Abraham was ready to hear any word from heaven, especially a word of release for his son.

The angel ordered Abraham **not** to **lay a hand on** the lad. He was **not** to **do anything to him. Now** the angel knew that Abraham feared **God** totally, since he had not held back his **son,** his **only son,** from God. His commitment to God had been put to the ultimate test and proven genuine.

Abraham lifted up his eyes. **In a thicket he saw a ram caught by its horns.** The motif of seeing underscores Abraham's relief at seeing an animal for making the sacrifice. Abraham **took the ram and sacrificed it as a burnt offering instead of his son.** The provision of this ram enabled Abraham to worship God with a burnt offering as he had intended in coming to the region of Moriah. One can only imagine their exuberant joy as the two of them watched this ram ascend to God as a sweet-smelling aroma. It was possibly the greatest praise offering of all time. The use of the same three verbs here as in God's ordering Abraham to sacrifice Isaac—go, take, and sacrifice (v. 2)—attests that Abraham accomplished what he had set out to do (J. Ska, "Gn 22,1–19: Essai sur les niveaux de lecture," *Bib* 69 [1988], p. 336). This report of the sacrifice is brief compared with the report about putting Isaac on the altar because the focus of this narrative falls on Abraham's binding of Isaac, the act of supreme obedience.

To commemorate this momentous occasion Abraham named that place Yahweh Yireh, "Yahweh sees (or provides)." Through this name he expressed his conviction that God meets every need of the one who trusts in him. This name led to a proverbial expression: **On the mountain of** Yahweh **it will be provided.**

22:15–18 / **The angel of** Yahweh **called to Abraham from heaven a second time.** Since there was neither a command to be given (v. 1) nor an urgent situation (v. 11), the angel did not call Abraham by name. The angel affirmed the promises God had originally made to Abraham, strengthening them in four ways. First, Yahweh swore to them by himself (see Exod. 32:13, "your own self"). This is the highest oath. Because of the oath Yahweh, in being true to himself, could do nothing other than fulfill what he had said. Second, this oath is highlighted by the introduction "**declares** Yahweh," a phrase that frequently heads God's word to a prophet but occurs only here in Genesis (e.g., Num. 14:28; 24:3, 4, 15, 16; Isa. 1:24; Jer. 1:8). The text restates the reason for God's strong assurances: **because** Abraham had **not withheld** his **son.** Third, God affirmed that he would bless Abraham unconditionally. The strength of the Hebrew expression is translated by **surely,** both with "bless" and "increase" or **make numerous.** This is the only time God stated the blessing so strongly. Fourth, with two similes God promised Abraham that he would "make" his **descendants** (seed) as "numerous" **as the stars in the sky and as the sand on the seashore.** This is the only time that the number of his descendants is compared with sand. In addition, his **descendants** (seed) would **take possession** of the gate **of their enemies.** "Gate" symbolizes a city's defensive strength. Abraham's descendants would gain control of even their enemies' strongholds. Furthermore, **all nations on earth** would find blessing **through** Abraham's **offspring** (seed). The assurance and the abundance of these promises had been strengthened by reason of Abraham's obedience. While the promises were initiated solely by God's grace, God allowed Abraham to participate in enhancing their scope by his full obedience.

22:19 / The account of Abraham's testing ends abruptly with a detail that anchors it to real life: **Abraham returned to his servants.** They gathered up all the goods and **set off together for Beersheba.** The group who had come to Mount Moriah on a solemn mission returned to Beersheba in joy. There Abraham continued to live.

Additional Notes §27

22:2 / In the Hb. "whom you love" is attached to "your only son." Given the number of terms here for Isaac, it is hard to capture the Hb. wording and emphasis in the Eng. translation.

The location of the land of Moriah is unknown. The versions render Moriah by a variety of terms, e.g., "up-country" (LXX) and "worship" (Tg.). Later tradition identified Mount Moriah with the Temple mount (2 Chron. 3:1). See also the phrase "mount of Yahweh" in v. 14b for the temple area (Ps. 24:3; Isa. 2:3; R. Moberly, "The Earliest Commentary on the Akedah," *VT* 38 [1988], p. 307). The text offers no clues as to the location of Mount Moriah save the three-day journey. The author of Chronicles may have understood Mount Moriah and the Temple mount as possessing the same sacred identity in God's purpose and that this identification was more important than their geographical identity. Thus Abraham's sacrifice of the ram in place of Isaac inaugurated in principle sacrifice on Mount Moriah, where the altar of the temple stood. This interconnectedness endows the altar in the temple with the spiritual achievements of Abraham's obedience.

22:3 / The narrator allows the reader to sense the response of the characters through subtle changes and notations. "Deeds executed by the biblical hero may proficiently reflect his thoughts and feelings," according to Y. Mazor ("Genesis 22: The Ideological Rhetoric and the Psychological Composition," *Bib* 67 [1986], p. 84). He adds, "An example of the Bible's indirect means of psychological characterization is inlaid in the compositional stratum of the biblical text and may be entitled the expressive order of presentation." About Abraham's chopping wood last, Mazor says, "Since Abraham suspends this emotionally-loaded act to the very end, he displays his natural intuitive recoil from his shocking obligation to his Lord and demonstrates the pestering psychological struggle within his bisected consciousness" (p. 85).

22:12 / The Heb. term *na'ar* means "a boy, a youth, or a young adult," who, being unmarried, is still under parental authority; it is also used for "a servant" under the authority of a master as in vv. 3, 5, 19. Thus, the NIV's "boy" is not the best translation.

22:13 / God's provision of a ram (*'ayil*), not a lamb (*seh*), as Isaac had asked about, establishes a link with the ram being one of the animals slaughtered in making the covenant (15:9–10; S. Walters, "Wood, Sand and Stars: Structure and Theology in Gn 22:1–19," *TJT* 3 [1986], p. 309). In a few passages a ram functions as a synecdoche for the whole sacrificial system (1 Sam. 15:22; Mic. 6:7). Therefore, Abraham's sacrifice of a ram on Mount Moriah foreshadowed the entire sacrificial system (Walters, "Wood, Sand and Stars," pp. 309–11).

22:16 / This oath by God is mentioned again in 24:7; 26:3; 50:24.

§28 Excursus: Reflections on the Broader Implications of the Sacrifice of Isaac

Since this narrative is at the heart of the biblical message, it is important to reflect on its teaching. It clearly and unequivocally teaches that Yahweh, the only God, never accepts human sacrifice. If God did not accept the sacrifice of Isaac, the first child of promise, surely no other sacrifice of a child would be acceptable to him. Given the popularity of child sacrifice in some cultures close to Israel, this was a vital truth for Israel to learn (cf. Lev. 18:21; 20:2–5). Amid all the possibilities medicine makes available to humans in this age, we need to hear this truth afresh.

Referred to by the Jewish community as the Akedah, from the Hebrew term "bind," this account has had great impact on Jewish imagination. Its influence is found in their liturgy and in their writings (Sarna, *Genesis*, pp. 393–94; R. Daly, "The Soteriological Significance of the Sacrifice of Isaac," *CBQ* 39 [1977], pp. 50–93). In the service for the New Year one prayer asks God to be mindful of how Abraham suppressed his compassion by binding his son to the altar in wholehearted obedience; in the same way God is asked to let his compassion exceed his anger as he recalls Abraham's obedience with compassion. Further, the reading from the Torah on the second day of the New Year is the Akedah. The Targum to the Song of Songs, read at Passover, states that God did not execute his wrath against Israel for making the golden calf because he remembered to their advantage the binding of Isaac (*Tg. Cant.* 1:13; Daly, "Soteriological Significance," p. 53). Also, several texts from the Second Temple period refer to this account. The Akedah has in addition provided great inspiration to the Jews during the numerous cruel persecutions they have faced throughout the centuries. That they drew courage and determination from this story is already attested in 4 Maccabees (e.g., 13:12; 16:18–20).

In the NT the Akedah played an important role for understanding God's work in Christ. Explicit references to it are found in Hebrews 11:17–19 and James 2:21–23. The wording of Romans 8:32 ("he who did not spare his own Son, but gave him up for us all—how will he not also, along with him, graciously give us all things?") echoes Abraham's willingness to offer his son to God (Daly, "Soteriological Significance," p. 67). Daly finds other allusions to the Akedah in Romans 4:16–25; John 3:16; Mark 1:11; 9:7; and 1 Corinthians 15:4 ("Soteriological Significance," pp. 65–74).

The tie between the command for Abraham to offer up Isaac and God's offering his own Son on the cross provides insight into why God tested Abraham in this manner. It informs us that God was just in making this request of Abraham, for God asked him to do what God would do in offering up his own Son at Calvary. God displayed justice also in providing a substitute for Isaac. In the case of the death of his obedient Son Jesus, God proved committed to justice by raising him from the dead. Therefore, Abraham's obedience in the Akedah prepared the way for God to bring his kingdom to all nations through the obedience of his Son unto death. Being the firstborn of the dead (1 Cor. 15:20, 23; Col. 1:18), Jesus empowered the promises to Abraham to extend to all the families of the earth (Rev. 1:5) and guaranteed that all who believe in him will participate in the final resurrection.

The broader canonical context provides additional insight into God's commanding Abraham to offer up Isaac. For Abraham, Isaac was the firstborn son, a specific fulfillment of the promises God gave him at the outset of his journey with God (12:1–3). This point is crucial. Paramount to God's lordship over all earthly life is his absolute claim on every firstborn. The law required Israel to present all the firstborn of animals and the firstfruits to God (Exod. 13:2; 23:16, 19; 34:26; Deut. 26:1–11). By giving the first to God, the people recognized God's ownership of all their produce and herds. After the presentation of the first, God released the rest of the harvest and the herds for the people to use as they wished. The firstborn children also had to be redeemed (Exod. 13:13). In ancient Israel the Levites, being dedicated to the service of God, took the place of all the firstborn Israelites (Num. 3:12–13, 40–48). This principle of the firstborn underlies God's command for Abraham to sacrifice Isaac. Because Isaac was the firstborn of the promised seed, God's claim on him was total. Since Abraham willingly offered the promised seed to God in faith (Heb. 11:17–19), God identifies Abraham's seed as his people for as long as there is life on earth. In addition, this consecration of Isaac, the firstborn among nations in God's economy, dedicates all peoples to God. Jesus' saying on the seed illuminates this principle of offering the first: "Unless a kernel of wheat falls to the ground and dies, it remains only a single seed. But if it dies, it produces many seeds" (John 12:24). Therefore, Isaac, the first seed, figuratively died in being bound to the altar. Consequently, out of his death God was able to multiply Abraham's seed, empowering it to become as numerous as the stars of the sky.

§29 The Genealogy of Nahor (Gen. 22:20–24)

22:20–24 / After the events on Mount Moriah, **Abraham** learned about the children born to his **brother Nahor.** This genealogy identifies Nahor's eight sons by his primary wife, **Milcah,** and his four sons by a **concubine** named **Reumah,** continuing the list found in 11:27–32. The genealogy's location here provides background information for the course of Isaac's life. Isaac's future bride, **Rebekah,** was introduced to Abraham in this genealogy.

Nahor's sons became the twelve Aramean tribes, corresponding to the twelve tribes of Israel (49:28) and the twelve tribes of Ishmael (25:12–16). The narrator saw God's hand at work in constructing tribal organizations of twelve linked by a common ancestry. Only a little is known about some of these names. **Nahor** is also the name of a key city on the Upper Euphrates in the Balikh Valley, where these tribes were located. Two other names are also place names: **Uz** in Edom (10:23; 36:28; possibly Job 1:1) and **Buz** in the region of Edom or northern Arabia (Jer. 25:23). It is possible that **Kesed** was the ancestor of the Chaldeans, that **Hazo** was connected with the Hazu region in northern Arabia, and that **Reumah** became a tribal league in the central Syrian region (Sarna, *Genesis,* pp. 155–56). There is an important city named **Tebah** in southern Syria. **Tahash** may refer to a locality between Damascus and the Orontes River. **Maacah** is also the name of a small state in northern Transjordan. There is no further information on the other names.

§30 Abraham Purchases the Cave of Machpelah (Gen. 23:1–20)

In the preceding episode Abraham reached the pinnacle of his journey with God by proving his complete obedience to God even in regard to his beloved son (ch. 22). Before his death he faces two more basic issues: the burial of Sarah and finding a wife for Isaac. In this chapter, Abraham deals with the first of these.

This account consists of the report of Sarah's death (vv. 1–2), the negotiations for the purchase of a lot (vv. 3–16), and Abraham's taking ownership of the Cave of Machpelah (vv. 17–20). The terms "give" *(natan)* and "hear" *(shama')* dominate the account. Frequently, one party in the negotiations opens a presentation by asking the other party to listen (vv. 6, 8, 11, 13, 15). This term also signals the completion of the negotiations: "Abraham heard Ephron" (v. 16). Instead of using the terms "buy" and "sell" for a major transaction, the ancients preferred the more indirect, polite term "give." Abraham uses it four times (vv. 4, 9, 13) and Ephron three times (v. 11). Another pivotal term is "property for a burial site" *('akhuzzat-qeber;* vv. 4, 9, 20), for this plot became Abraham's in perpetuity. This account also carries great interest because it is an ancient report of a real estate transaction in Canaan.

23:1–2 / At the age of 127 **Sarah died** near **Hebron,** a city located in the Judean hills about twenty miles south of Jerusalem. It was formerly known as **Kiriath Arba.** This obituary highly esteems Sarah, the matriarch of Israel. Abraham lamented her death by weeping aloud, tearing his garments, putting on sackcloth, cutting his beard, and fasting. Even though he was full of grief, he had to find a place to inter her.

23:3–4 / Abraham went to the Hittite leaders of Hebron to gain permission to bury Sarah on one of their plots of land. In the ancient manner of negotiating courteously and indirectly, for which the Near East is famous, Abraham sought clear title to a burial plot. His determination to secure this land bears witness to the depth of his conviction that God's promises to him were sure (Sarna, *Genesis,* p. 156). The negotiations moved through three rounds. In the first the citizens of Hebron agreed that Abraham could have access to a field to bury his wife. Then they agreed that he could have the field with the Cave of Machpelah in it. In the third round Ephron willingly sold that field for a set price. The indirectness and the slow movement of the negotiations lend the account a dramatic flavor.

At that time **the Hittites** lived in Hebron. The identity of these people is unclear, as is also their connection to the well-known Hittites of Anatolia. Their Semitic names suggest that they were a different ethnic group from the well-known Hittites. Yet in the Table of Nations, Heth (NIV Hittites) is a descendant of Canaan (10:15). Abraham went to Hebron, which was close to the oaks of Mamre, and spoke with the elders at the city gates.

Before the citizens of Hebron, Abraham identified himself as **an alien and a stranger,** thereby conceding that he had no inherent right to buy real estate from them. He acknowledged that he was at their mercy in his request that they **sell** him **some property for a burial site.** While the NIV reads "sell," Abraham uses the general term "give." The NIV's rendering is correct in that Abraham used the term to mean more than "give," but it obscures his indirect, polite approach. With great courtesy Abraham provided the Hittites latitude for formulating a reply. His use of "property" (*'akhuzzah*) indicated that his goal was lasting ownership, for this Hebrew term identifies a plot with inheritance rights.

23:5–6 / **The Hittites** likewise answered **Abraham** with great respect, by addressing him as **a mighty prince among** them. "Mighty prince" is literally "prince of God." Beyond being a noble title, it conveys that the Hittites recognized God's blessing on Abraham. God's initial promises to Abraham (12:2–3) were operative, elevating his stature to a level recognized by the inhabitants of the land. The Hittites signaled also that they were open to dealing with him by using the pronoun **us.** They responded first with a general offer of **the choicest of** their **tombs for burying** his deceased. Skillfully, they spoke to his major concern while at the same time avoiding his request to acquire his own property. They did not yet indicate whether they would permit Abraham to take full ownership of the land.

23:7–9 / Abraham stood up. Since negotiations were usually conducted while sitting, his standing indicated his eagerness to persuade the Hittites to let him acquire a piece of property that he could call his own. After showing deference by bowing **down before** them, Abraham sought to establish common ground by restating their willingness **to let** him **bury** his **dead** in order. Then he became more direct, asking that they act as intermediaries in speaking to **Ephron son of Zohar** about "giving" him **the cave of Machpelah,** located at **the end of his field,** for a burial place. The formal identification of Ephron as son of Zohar shows his high rank in the community, for seldom is the patronym of a non-Israelite given in Scripture (Sarna, *Genesis,* p. 158). Abraham offered to pay **the full price.** He reinforced his goal by repeating the term "property" with "burial site" (v. 4), but NIV does not render the term for property.

Politely, according to ancient custom, Abraham did not address Ephron directly. Rather, he entreated those assembled at the gate to take his offer to the owner of the field. He addressed Ephron indirectly, however, for Ephron was present in the assembly. Abraham's approach allowed the person directly involved with his request an opportunity to make a reply through a third party. Furthermore, it was the custom in the Near East to have an intermediary negotiate one's position, particularly in buying land and in arranging marriages.

23:10–11 / **Ephron** had been **sitting among his people** at the gate of the city. Willing to entertain Abraham's offer, he responded **in the hearing of all the Hittites.** Politely addressing Abraham as **my lord,** he made an offer to sell him some land in three definite statements all headed by **I give.** Ephron was willing to "give" **the field** and **the cave** in the field and to complete the transaction **in the presence of** his **people,** thereby making the transaction official. Ephron's use of the verb "give" carried two possibilities. He may have been offering Abraham access to the cave for burying Sarah while refusing to sell it (v. 4). Or he may have been letting Abraham know that he was prepared to sell the cave, but only if Abraham bought the entire field. As the negotiations developed, it became clear that Ephron took this opportunity to sell more than Abraham had intended to buy. His reasons are unknown. A possible explanation is that he wanted to free himself from civil obligations, such as taxes, that went along with owning land and that were relieved only by selling the entire plot.

23:12–13 / **Again Abraham bowed** in deference **before the people.** He pressed **Ephron** to accept cash for the field. Abraham agreed to buy **the field,** not just the cave, for whatever **price** Ephron would set. Shrewdly and politely he did not name a price. He strengthened his offer with an appeal that it be **accepted.**

23:14–15 / **Ephron** accepted and set the price at **four hundred shekels of silver**—about ten pounds. Without knowledge of land values in that time, it is impossible to determine how expensive the field was. The text has noted several times that Abraham was wealthy, so the price was not a heavy burden for him. In fact, he had received a thousand shekels from Abimelech of Gerar (20:16). Ephron played down the price by saying that the amount should not stand between the two of them. His expression means that, in his opinion, paying such an amount will not be a hardship on Abraham. Then, with a command, he told Abraham to **bury** his deceased.

23:16 / **Abraham** quickly put an end to the bargaining by agreeing **to Ephron's terms.** He then **weighed out** the exact amount of silver to purchase the field. Since there were no standard weights in those days, the weight must be identified along with the price. The weights used on this occasion were those **current among the merchants.**

23:17–20 / A summary of Abraham's purchase of Ephron's field confirms that this is a binding, legal sale. Abraham received the deed to **the field, the cave,** and **all the trees within** its **borders.** For the record it is stated that the transaction and the payment took place **in the presence of all the Hittites who had come to the gate of the city.** Should any dispute arise, numerous witnesses could testify to the conditions of the transaction. Abraham then **buried his wife Sarah in the cave in the field of Machpelah.** This step sealed the purchase because Abraham used the property for the purpose he had said. A family burial plot highly honored Sarah as the great matriarch of the chosen people.

This account carries great religious significance. The Cave of Machpelah became the burial place for the patriarchs Abraham (25:9), Isaac (35:27–29; 49:31), and Jacob (49:29–30; 50:13), as well as for their wives, except Rachel. Today Jews, Muslims, and Christians come to worship and pay their respect to these great patriarchs and matriarchs. From time to time control of this cave has

been hotly contested. Continued conflict at this important shrine
has led the authorities to impose limited access to the cave.

Additional Notes §30

23:3 / It is possible that a group of Hittites from Anatolia had
migrated to Canaan and established their own settlement. The presence
of Hittites in Canaan is attested in other sources. Hittite jugs found at
Megiddo date to ca. 1650 B.C. At other sites Hittite hieroglyphics and jewelry have been found in Late Bronze Age levels (1600–1700 B.C.; Sarna,
Genesis, p. 396; also see Hamilton, *The Book of Genesis: Chapters 18–50*
[NICOT; Grand Rapids: Eerdmans, 1995], pp. 27–28).

23:14–15 / Such an agreement settled in the hearing of the city
elders guaranteed Abraham that he had acquired inalienable property,
i.e., property classified as "a hereditary estate" (R. Westbrook, "Purchase
of the Cave of Machpelah," in *Property and the Family in Biblical Law*
[JSOTSup 113; Sheffield: JSOT Press, 1991], pp. 32–34). Westbrook claims
that the Hittites participated with Ephron in the sale as is evidenced in
Akkadian land contracts found at Ugarit.

23:16 / Since coins had not yet been minted, merchants carried
small, collapsible scales for weighing commodities against weights. Since
there was no bureau of standards, weights varied; for this reason the
shekel in this transaction is identified as that used by merchants.

23:17 / Trees are frequently mentioned in ancient property
contracts. It is possible that they were specified in order for the new
owner to have full right to them, similar to deeds in the U.S.A. that treat
mineral rights as separate from land ownership.

§31 Finding a Wife for Isaac (Gen. 24:1–67)

Abraham's last major responsibility in light of God's promises is to find a wife for Isaac. Otherwise the promise of numerous offspring will perish for lack of an heir. The text does not address why Abraham waited so long to fulfill this responsibility. Abraham commissions his most trusted senior servant to travel to Haran to find a wife for his son. In order to preserve the integrity of his offspring, this wife must come from the line of Terah. The servant is confident that he will succeed because God will direct his path, and the servant justifies Abraham's trust in him, for he continually seeks God's direction throughout his search. An honorable servant who acts reliably and trusts God explicitly brings great honor to his master (Prov. 13:17b).

Three characters dominate this narrative. The lead character is the anonymous servant. The reader becomes acquainted with him through his speeches, which are very long by the standards of Genesis. He is a thoughtful, obedient servant who makes sure of the exact requirements of an assigned task (v. 5) and seeks to carry them out both expeditiously and diplomatically. This servant relies heavily on God's direction, praying before each major decision and then praising God openly for his guidance. A master of words, he skillfully and politely directs conversations to the outcome he desires. This servant acts deliberately in hastening the outcome, yet he displays restrained patience.

The second main character is Rebekah. She is a generous, energetic woman whose beauty is complemented by a gracious, hospitable manner. With self-confidence she makes important decisions quickly and then acts on them with resolve. She treats Abraham's servant, a stranger, with compassion, warmth, and discernment.

Isaac, the third character, is almost invisible. Usually he is referred to as the son of his mother. This anonymity is in keeping with his role in other narratives.

The titles used here are suggestive. Abraham's servant is called "the servant" *(ha'ebed)* thirteen times and "the man" *(ha'ish)* nine times. Laban calls him "blessed of Yahweh" *(beruk yhwh;* v. 31), corresponding to the characterization of Abraham at the beginning of this narrative (v. 1). The way the servant refers to Isaac is important. In praying to God he calls Isaac "your servant" (v. 14). In the final scene he calls Isaac "my master" (v. 65), signaling that leadership has shifted from Abraham to Isaac, not only for the servant, but also in the unfolding history of God's people.

This beautiful story witnesses to the reciprocity between the servant's trust in God and God's directing the flow of events. Not only does the servant find an ideal bride for Isaac, but remarkably she is willing to leave her father's house for the long journey to Canaan to marry a man she has never met. In so ordering circumstances God shows loyalty and faithfulness to Abraham (vv. 12, 14, 27, 49).

A note of urgency runs through this narrative, even though several extended speeches slow the pace. The decisive actions of the characters pick up this pace. After arriving in Haran, the servant pauses to pray; Rebekah appears before he finishes his prayer. As soon as she fills her water jar, the servant runs to meet her. Quickly she lowers her water jar in order to give him a drink. After entering Bethuel's house, the servant, even before eating, puts forth his request that Rebekah become the bride of his master's son. The next day the servant forthrightly rejects the family's request that Rebekah remain at home for a few days before starting on the long journey to Canaan. Then Rebekah agrees to depart immediately. This sense of urgency contrasts sharply with Abraham's slowness in taking on the task of finding a wife for Isaac.

In the narrative's four scenes Abraham commissions his servant (vv. 1–9); the servant meets Rebekah (vv. 10–31); the servant negotiates for Rebekah to become Isaac's bride (vv. 32–60); and Rebekah marries Isaac (vv. 61–67).

24:1–4 / Abraham had grown very **old.** This description, along with the extent of the responsibilities given to the head servant, indicates that Abraham was close to death. Yahweh **had blessed** all areas of Abraham's life, particularly with the birth of Isaac and in giving him great wealth. Now that he needed to fulfill a special obligation, Abraham summoned his most trusted servant. To make sure that the servant would faithfully carry out his instructions, Abraham made him take a solemn oath by placing his **hand under** his **thigh,** the area that symbolized his virile strength. He was **to swear** by Yahweh, **the God of heaven and the God of earth,** that he would not take **a wife** for Isaac **from . . . the Canaanites.** His assignment was to take a long journey to the place of Abraham's **relatives** and **get a wife for Isaac** there.

24:5–9 / Before taking the oath, the servant sought to clarify the precise extent of his obligation. He **asked** what he should do if **the woman** he found was **unwilling to come back with** him. In such a case should he **take** Isaac **back to the country** from which Abraham had come? Abraham strongly rejected that suggestion; he knew God's promises (12:1–3) were to be fulfilled in Canaan, and thus he would not allow the possible repatriation of his own son. Affirming his confidence in Yahweh, **the God of heaven, who** had **brought** him **out of** his **father's household** and had sworn to give **this land** to his own seed, Abraham assured his servant that God would **send his angel before** him so that he would indeed find **a wife** for Isaac there. Abraham was certain that God would lead his servant to the woman whose heart God had prepared to come to Canaan and become his son's wife. However, he eased the servant's responsibility by asserting that **if the woman** was **unwilling to come back with** him to Canaan, he would **be released from this oath. The servant** then **put his hand under** Abraham's **thigh and swore an oath** to carry out this commission.

24:10–14 / Immediately **the servant** prepared for the journey by loading **ten camels,** a considerable number especially in that day, with provisions and numerous gifts for the potential bride and her family. Taking along several servants, who are mentioned only later (vv. 32, 54, 59), he **set out for Aram Naharaim,** the area in upper Syria where the Habor and Euphrates Rivers converge. His specific destination was Haran, where Abraham's brother **Nahor** lived.

The narrative then skips to the evening of the servant's arrival in the vicinity of Haran. **Near the well outside the town** the servant made **the camels kneel down,** aware that a well was an excellent place for meeting the local people, especially the young, for they had the chore of watering the flocks. With his mission foremost in his mind, he began to pray earnestly that Yahweh, **God of** his **master Abraham,** might **give** him **success** that very day and **show kindness to . . . Abraham.** "Kindness" *(hesed)*

means loyalty, especially covenant loyalty. The servant was asking God to act in remembrance of the covenant with Abraham,
since the purpose of that covenant required that Isaac have a wife.
Because it was the time of day when **the daughters of the towns-
people** were **coming out to draw water,** he asked Yahweh to direct him to the girl whom he had **chosen for . . . Isaac.** He
formulated the request in such a way that he would have a sign
identifying the right girl: when he asked one of them for **a drink,**
she not only would give him a drink but also would **water** his
camels. Such an extraordinary response to a stranger would tell
him that this girl had a wonderful spirit of hospitality. His prayer
shows that in those days people prayed directly to God, sensing
no need for a priest, and that they expected God to answer specifically in the flow of daily events.

24:15–27 / Even **before he had finished praying,** the servant saw **Rebekah** approaching the well **with her jar on her shoulder.** The author introduces her in such a way that the reader becomes aware of God's direction before the servant does. **She was
the daughter of Bethuel son of Milcah, . . . the wife of Abraham's
brother Nahor.** Her lineage identifies her as an appropriate bridal
candidate for Isaac. Furthermore, she was **very beautiful** and **a virgin.** Rebekah **went down to the spring, filled her jar,** ascended, and
started back to the town. The well must have been low with steps
leading down to its entrance. The servant, not wanting her to get far
away, ran toward her. Reaching her, he asked for a drink from her
jar. She **quickly lowered the jar to her hands and gave him a drink.**
She offered **to draw water for** the **camels** until they were full. Given
that a camel requires at least twenty-five gallons of water after a
journey, according to Sarna (*Genesis*, p. 164), Rebekah was obligat-
ing herself to descend the steps to the well and fill her water jar
many times. Her concern for the camels and the servant's welfare
confirmed Yahweh's word to the servant.

As Rebekah undertook the arduous task of watering the
camels, the servant looked on in astonishment, restraining his excitement as he sought to discern if this truly was the woman
Yahweh had chosen. **When the camels had finished drinking,**
the servant gave her **a gold nose ring . . . and two gold bracelets.**
His generosity demonstrates his conviction that this woman was
indeed the one Yahweh had appointed for Isaac.

Next the servant **asked** her identity and if **there** was **room
in** her **father's house** for lodging for **the night.** She identified her-

self, adding that there was **plenty of straw and fodder** and there was **room** for him **to spend the night.** Before such a gracious display of hospitality and grateful for God's leading, the servant **bowed down and worshiped** Yahweh, uttering words of praise. He declared that Yahweh had shown his master **kindness** *(hesed)* **and faithfulness** *('emet)* by guiding him **to the house of** his **master's relatives.**

24:28–32 / Full of excitement, Rebekah **ran** back to **her mother's household** and told them of her meeting at the well. The fact that the text emphasizes that she went to her mother's household may be a clue that Bethuel had more than one wife. Furthermore, it was most likely that Rebekah needed agreement from her household to confirm the invitation. When **Laban,** her **brother,** heard her story, he ran to **the spring** to meet this visitor. Curiously, the narrative repeats this fact (vv. 29, 30). The second report emphasizes that on seeing **the nose ring, and the bracelets on his sister's arms,** Laban **went out to** the servant and **found him** with **the camels near the spring.** It captures Laban's attraction to the servant's display of wealth. Greeting the servant warmly, he said, "**Come, you who are blessed by** Yahweh." He went on to inform the servant that he had **prepared the house** for him and **a place for the camels.** The servant gladly followed him **to the house.** The camels were unsaddled and fed. **Water** was brought for the servant and **his men to wash their feet.**

24:33–41 / **Food was set before** the servant, but he declined to eat until he had spoken to his host about the reason for his visit. After identifying himself as **Abraham's servant,** he spoke at length about his master in preparation for presenting his request, namely, that Rebekah be given to Isaac as his bride. He mentioned how Yahweh had **blessed** Abraham **abundantly.** As a result his master had **become wealthy,** having large flocks, **silver and gold,** numerous servants, and **camels and donkeys.** Next he related that **Sarah** had **borne a son in her old age,** a further witness to God's blessing on Abraham. This detail also informed Laban and his mother that Isaac was not too old for Rebekah. The servant emphasized that Isaac was the sole heir of Abraham's wealth. This vivid picture of his master's wealth was a strong incentive for them to agree to the request he was about to make.

Next, as a way of stating the purpose of his visit, the servant recounted the instructions Abraham had given him about finding Isaac **a wife.** Since Abraham had stipulated that the bride must come from his own **father's family,** not from **the Canaanites,** the servant had traveled to Haran. He recounted how Abraham had told him that the **angel** of Yahweh would go with him and make his mission **a success.** The servant stressed his own and Abraham's conviction that God indeed had directed his path to their house to persuade Rebekah's family. He included the provision that if the woman did not wish to return to Canaan he would be free from the oath. He did this in order to avoid the appearance of being overbearing when he put forth the request for their daughter and sister to become Isaac's wife. The servant was making it clear that there could be no compromise on the issue of Rebekah's traveling to Canaan should she agree to become Isaac's bride.

24:42–48 / The servant went on to recount the events of the day so that his audience might see for themselves how God had led him to Rebekah. In this retelling he adapted the story for the best effect on his audience. In his account of giving Rebekah the jewelry he made a significant change by reversing the actual order to maintain a sense of propriety. That is, he related that he had asked her identity before presenting the gift. Then he had praised Yahweh for leading him. The inclusion of this note about praising God underscores his conviction that God had appointed Rebekah as Isaac's bride.

24:49 / The servant then asked if they would **show kindness and faithfulness to** his **master.** Obliquely he was asking them to decide whether or not Rebekah was to become Isaac's wife. He presented this request in such a polite manner that it was difficult for them to refuse it; a refusal would make them feel as if they were going against the directions of God.

24:50–58 / Both **Laban and Bethuel answered** him. The sudden appearance of Bethuel, Rebekah's father, is surprising. Perhaps because of Bethuel's age or because of a polygamous marriage, her brother and mother were foremost in carrying on a conversation about Rebekah's betrothal. Nevertheless, the inclusion of this detail suggests that custom required the father's consent for a daughter to marry. The narrator communicates that Laban remained the leading spokesman by placing his name before his father's. The two men acknowledged that the servant's request for Rebekah was from Yahweh. Not wanting to resist God, both her father and her brother agreed to the transaction. They declared formally that Rebekah was free to go with the servant and **become the wife of** his **master's son, as** Yahweh had **directed.** This does not mean that they believed in Yahweh as the one and only God, but that they recognized that divine providence was operative in the sequence of encounters that had led to the request that Rebekah marry Isaac.

Overjoyed at their consent, **Abraham's servant . . . bowed down to the ground** in worship of Yahweh. Earlier the servant had earnestly asked for Yahweh's guidance in his mission; now that success had been achieved he immediately expressed his gratitude to Yahweh by praising him before his hosts. Afterward he rose and gave Rebekah **gold and silver jewelry** and elegant **clothing. He** also **gave costly gifts to her brother and to her mother.** With a warm sense of accomplishment the servant and the men who accompanied him sat down and **ate.**

The next morning the servant tested the agreement that Rebekah should become Isaac's bride. Possibly either she or her parents or her brother might feel differently and no longer be willing for her to go to Canaan. The servant therefore skillfully brought up the subject in order to learn their resolve. Speaking as though he was at their service, the servant asked them to **send** him back to his **master.** This was a very polite way of asking them to get Rebekah ready to go with him. Laban and **her mother** hesitated, requesting that Rebekah be allowed to **remain** with them for a while, at least **ten days,** before leaving. But the servant demurred, asking not to be detained since Yahweh had **granted success to** his **journey.** He realized that should Rebekah's departure be delayed, a pattern of delays might be established that could threaten his taking her to Canaan (e.g., Judg. 19:5–10).

Laban and his mother proposed that the matter be settled by calling **Rebekah** and letting her decide. They must have assumed that Rebekah would not want to depart immediately. But when they **asked** her, she agreed to leave at once. As Abraham had responded to God's call (12:4), so too Rebekah agreed to leave home in response to God's leading. This is confirmed by the sevenfold occurrence of "go" (*halak*), the very word God used when he commanded Abraham that he go from his land (12:1; Sarna, *Genesis,* p. 161).

24:59–61 / The family **sent . . . Rebekah on her way . . . with Abraham's servant and his men.** Her nurse, Deborah, accompanied her (35:8). Before her departure the family pronounced a twofold blessing on Rebekah. She was to be fruitful, bearing many children, and her **offspring** (seed) was to **possess the gates of their enemies** (22:17). This blessing is similar to Noah's blessing on his sons Shem and Japheth (9:26–27). Future events would produce an amazing twist to this blessing. Decades later her son Jacob would end up in conflict with her brother Laban and prevail; the one being blessed proved to be superior to the one who pronounced the blessing. Then **Rebekah and her maids got ready and mounted their camels and went** with Abraham's servant **back** to Canaan.

24:62–65 / In Canaan, **Isaac** was now living near **Beer Lahai Roi . . . in the Negev** (16:14). No reason is given for his change of residence. Furthermore, the lack of any reference to Abraham in this final scene leads to the likelihood that he had died (so Wenham, *Genesis 16–50*, p. 151). Isaac **went out to the field one evening to meditate, and as he looked up, he saw** a train of **camels approaching.** At the same time **Rebekah looked up and saw Isaac.** Quickly **she got down from her camel and asked the servant** the identity of the man walking toward them. He replied that it was his **master** Isaac. Rebekah's haste in dismounting indicates that she suspected that the man was Isaac. On learning of his identity she put on her **veil,** symbolizing that she was his bride (Sarna, *Genesis*, p. 170).

24:66–67 / **The servant told Isaac all** that had happened. **Isaac** then took Rebekah **into the tent of his mother.** Thereby he made her **his wife** and the matriarch of the family. His love for Rebekah brought him comfort **after his mother's death.**

Additional Notes §31

24:2 / Most commentators say that the servant swore by Abraham's genitals. It is true that *yarek* ("thigh, loin") represents male virility (46:26; Exod. 1:5) and that Abraham was having his servant swear by his strength and virility. But just as *yarek* is a euphemism for genitals, it is likely that the servant put his hand under Abraham's thigh rather than directly on the genitals, given the reserve of that culture.

24:10 / Aram Naharaim, occurring only here in Genesis, refers to the land in northern Mesopotamia, especially the land between the Euphrates and the Balikh Rivers.

24:32 / While the fact that other servants accompanied Abraham's servant is not reported until this place, an ancient audience would be aware that a servant would not take such a long journey with ten camels alone.

24:50 / The role taken by Laban, the bride's brother, in agreeing to the marriage is attested in the Old and Neo-Babylonian period (Selman, "Comparative Customs," p. 138).

24:55 / The length of time requested for Rebekah to remain at home is lit. "days or ten." Many take "days" to mean a year; if that is correct, "ten" may mean a month. In any case, the family appears to be leaving the exact length of time open.

24:62 / It is curious that the servant returned directly to Isaac and not to Abraham. Even more curious is the lack of mention of Abraham after the servant returned, save for his genealogy and obituary. Although Abraham's precise location is not given in this narrative, the earlier accounts would place it in the vicinity of Hebron (ch. 23), some distance from Beer Lahai Roi. Thus either Isaac had separated from his father, or, his father having died, he moved here. Therefore, the servant was returning to Isaac, his new master. Although the chronologies in Genesis seem to indicate that Abraham lived thirty-five years after Isaac's marriage, the dates may be more symbolic than actual, thus making it difficult to establish a precise chronology.

§32 Abraham's Death (Gen. 25:1–11)

Just as the narrative of Abraham begins with a genealogical list (11:27–31), so a genealogy closes his story. This text lists the names of the children born to Abraham's concubine (vv. 1–4), describes the distribution of Abraham's heritage (vv. 5–6), and gives Abraham's obituary (vv. 7–11).

25:1–4 / **Abraham** had married **another** woman named **Keturah.** Since traditions like this one have been preserved without a chronological reference, there is no indication in the text as to when Abraham married Keturah. The location of this report in the narrative gives the impression that this marriage took place after Sarah's death. However, in light of Abraham's age at Sarah's death and the fact that Keturah bore him six children, this marriage must have paralleled his marriage to Sarah for a number of years. Not only was polygamy not frowned on in those days, but Abraham's having more than one wife contributes to his portrait as a king. Keturah is not mentioned earlier because the narrator did not wish to interrupt the drama about Abraham's great struggle to receive the son of promise through Sarah and also because she, being a concubine, had a lower status than Hagar (1 Chron. 1:32). Abraham's treatment of her children coincides with that assessment, even though the text identifies Keturah as a wife. Her children were outside the promise God had given Abraham (12:2–3), for their mother was not from the Terahite patrilineage. The children of this union developed into tribal groups that became numbered with the Arab tribes.

25:5–6 / In accord with ancient custom, Abraham assigned his inheritance before his death. He gave **everything he owned to Isaac,** while **he gave gifts to the sons of his concubines.** According to a law in the Code of Hammurabi (§171), if sons of a concubine had not been acknowledged by their father to be on the level of his children by his primary wife during his life, they had no claim on the inheritance. Abraham then **sent** these children **away . . . to the land of the east** to make sure that they would not interfere with Isaac's claim to any of the promised heritage.

25:7–10 / The obituary reports that **Abraham lived a hundred and seventy-five years.** Abraham died with a strong sense that he had pleased God. His living such a long time and dying in peace witness to God's blessing on his life. The phrase **gathered to his people** refers to the idea that the deceased became numbered with his departed ancestors. This language, which occurs only ten times and only in the Pentateuch, hints at a belief in some type of life after death. **Isaac and Ishmael** overlooked their differences as together they attended to burying their father **in the cave of Machpelah,** located **in the field of Ephron** (ch. 23; also 35:29). **Abraham was buried** there **with Sarah, his** principal **wife.**

25:11 / **After Abraham's death** Yahweh fully acknowledged **Isaac** as heir of the promises to Abraham by blessing him. At that time Isaac **lived near Beer Lahai Roi** (24:62), the well in the Negev named by Hagar (16:14). This statement about Isaac prepares for the episodes concerning him (ch. 26).

Additional Notes §32

25:1 / Keturah comes from *qetoret* ("incense"), which suggests that her tribe was engaged in incense trade (E. Knauf, "Keturah," *ABD* 4:31).

25:2 / Not all these names have been identified. Zimran may be the ancestor of an Arabian tribe Zimri (Jer. 25:25). Midian is a tribe known for raids into Canaan during the era of the judges (Judg. 6–8). Traveling merchants identified as Midianites took Joseph to Egypt (37:28, 36); other sources describe them as traders in frankincense (Isa. 60:6). Their territory was along the eastern shore of the Gulf of Aqabah. The Midianites consisted of five tribes as reported here. Sarna (*Genesis,* p. 172) equates Ishbak with a Syrian tribe named Iasbuq. Shuah may refer to a country on the middle Euphrates near where the Habur River empties into it. Jokshan and Medan remain unidentified.

25:3 / Sheba and Dedan occur together as the sons of Raamah in 10:7, but it is better to take them as different peoples. Uncharacteristically for genealogical lists, Dedan's three descendants occur as gentilics in the plural. Asshurites, not the forerunners of the Assyrian Empire, might be connected with a people named Asshur mentioned in Num. 24:22, 24 and Ps. 83:8.

25:4 / Midian, Keturah's fourth son, had five sons. An Ephah is mentioned in Isa. 60:6. No information about these children is preserved.

25:5–6 / The practice of the oldest son's receiving a larger share of the family inheritance is well attested in the ancient Near East (43:33; 49:3–4).

25:6 / Hb. *qedem* is translated "east"; possibly it is in the area east to southeast of the Dead Sea (Hamilton, *Genesis: Chapters 18–50*, p. 167).

§33 Ishmael's Lineage and Death (Gen. 25:12–18)

Since Abraham had great affection for Ishmael and since he played a major role in two different episodes, the tradition includes his lineage and obituary. As elsewhere in Genesis, the genealogy of the nonelect occurs before that of the elect (chs. 4, 36).

25:12–16 / Ishmael's genealogy *(toledoth)* is given. His sons numbered twelve like Nahor's (22:20–24), Esau's (36:9–14; cf. commentary on that text), and Jacob's (35:22b–26). Twelve represents a complete tribal unit; thus all of these groups were blessed by God in reaching this fullness. The tribes of Ishmael, headed by princes, lived in unfortified villages.

25:17–18 / **Ishmael lived a hundred and thirty-seven years.** The number of his sons and a long life testify to God's blessing him as the angel of Yahweh had promised Hagar (16:10–12). **His descendants** roamed in the vast area from **Havilah** (2:11; 10:7), possibly located in Arabia, to **Shur** in northern Sinai (16:7; 20:1). They, however, **lived in hostility toward all their brothers;** that is, they were in conflict even with those of similar lineage, as the angel of Yahweh had told Hagar (16:12).

Additional Notes §33

25:13–14 / Nebaioth and Kedar are referred to in Isa. 60:7. Esau married the sister of Nebaioth (25:13; 36:3). Kedar, the most powerful of these tribes, shepherded flocks east of Israel (Jer. 2:10). Dumah was north of Tema and served as the main religious center of the Qedarites (1 Chron. 1:30; Isa. 21:11). The name Massa appears in 1 Chron. 1:30, and possibly in Prov. 30:1; 31:1. Tema is an important oasis in the Arabian desert (Job 6:19; Isa. 21:14; Jer. 25:23–24). Naphish lived in the northern Transjordan (1 Chron. 5:19). Kedemah may be another way of referring to the "people of the East" (E. Knauf, "Ishmaelites," *ABD* 3:513–20, esp. pp. 514–15).

25:16 / Ishmael's sons became tribes. They were organized into settlements *(khatserim)*. This term is used in the Mari texts for unwalled villages of pastoral nomads (Sarna, *Genesis,* p. 176). "Camp" suggests tents set up in an orderly fashion and protected by a stone wall (Num. 31:10). The term for tribe relates to an Akk. term for a large tribal unit.

§34 The Birth and Early Rivalry of Esau and Jacob (Gen. 25:19–34)

The next patriarchal narrative, that of Jacob (25:19–36:43), extends from Jacob's birth to Esau's lineage. (See the Introduction for an overview of the Jacob narrative as a whole and its relationship to the Joseph story.) Three incidents set the stage for the drama of Jacob's life: the struggle of Jacob and Esau in the womb and at birth (vv. 19–26), a brief portrait of the two boys (vv. 27–28), and Jacob's stealing the birthright from Esau (vv. 29–34).

25:19–20 / The birth of Isaac's children is introduced as **the account** *(toledoth)* **of Abraham's son Isaac.** Typically the genealogy *(toledoth)* of the former leader heads material about the next generation (11:27–32). This *toledoth* parallels the one before Ishmael's genealogy (25:12). It includes Abraham because he received God's blessing, while Laban is mentioned because of the significant role he would have in Jacob's life.

25:21 / Like Sarah, Rebekah had difficulty becoming pregnant. **Isaac prayed** to Yahweh, the God of Abraham, for a child. The term here for prayer *('atar)* emphasizes its fervency. Yahweh **answered his prayer,** and **Rebekah became pregnant.** Isaac is the only patriarch who was monogamous.

25:22 / In Rebekah's womb **the babies jostled each other.** "Jostle" *(hitratsats)* is a strong term, meaning "crushing each other." The fierce struggling of these fetuses caused Rebekah agony, both physical and emotional. In exasperation she asked herself **why** this was **happening to** her. The wording of the Hebrew, which is an unintelligible utterance cast as a question, conveys her anguish. Being troubled, Rebekah went to make special inquiry of Yahweh. This language means that she traveled to either a prophet, a priest, or a special shrine where she might receive a word from God (e.g., 2 Kgs. 8:7–15). It is possible that she sought

God directly by going to Beer Lahai Roi (v. 11), where Hagar had
heard from the messenger of Yahweh (16:7–14).

25:23 / Yahweh answered, telling Rebekah that she was
carrying twins who would become **two nations.** However, **the
older** would **serve the younger,** and one of the peoples would **be
stronger.** Her experience coincides with two motifs in the patriarchal narratives. All the primary wives of the heirs of God's
promise—Sarah, Rebekah, and Rachel—experienced barrenness
until God intervened. Also, God at times chose a younger child
to carry out his purpose: Jacob over Esau and Joseph over his
brothers. In directing human experiences in these ways God expressed his sovereignty, thereby countering human presumption
and arrogance.

25:24–26 / Rebekah's **time** to deliver arrived, and she
gave birth to **twin boys.** The boy who came out first was **red**
(*'admoni*), though the Hebrew term refers to a more tawny color.
He was covered with so much hair that he was **like a hairy garment, so they named him Esau.** The full meaning of the wordplay
between Esau (*'esaw*) and "hair" (*se'ar*), as well as the meaning of
Esau, is no longer known. His reddish complexion, however, corresponds to the name of the land where he settled, namely, Edom
(*'edom*), which comes from the same Hebrew root. The second
twin came out of the womb **with his hand grasping Esau's heel**
(*'aqeb*). This so struck the fancy of his parents that they **named** him
Jacob (*ya'aqob*), "one who grabs a heel, a finagler." His behavior at
birth symbolized the strife between him and Esau throughout
their childhood. At this time **Isaac was sixty years old.**

25:27–28 / **The boys grew** quickly. Possessing a love for
the outdoors and the ability to handle himself in the open country, **Esau became a skillful hunter.** Jacob, however, being **quiet,**
preferred to dwell in **tents.** He was a shepherd. Each parent gravi-
tated toward the boy closer to his or her own interests. Isaac **loved
Esau,** for he brought Isaac the **wild game** that he relished, while
Rebekah loved Jacob, who was her companion at chores.

25:29–31 / The narrator presents an episode at the center of the twins' rivalry. It probably took place toward the end of
their teens. The results of this incident profoundly affected their
destinies.

As was his custom, **Jacob was** at home **cooking some stew.**
On this day **Esau** returned **famished** from hunting. Apparently

he had searched long and hard for game but had found none. When he arrived at the tent, he found the smell of food cooking too much for him. He pleaded with **Jacob** to give him some **red stew** (*'adom*) right away. A wordplay establishes a connection between Esau's desiring this reddish-brown stew and his getting the nickname Edom, "reddish brown," which is also the name of his future homeland.

Jacob, seeing an opportunity to take advantage of Esau, responded by proposing that Esau **sell** him his **birthright** in exchange for some stew. The birthright gave one the rights of first position in the family. The firstborn received a larger portion of the inheritance; according to Deuteronomy 21:17, the firstborn received a double share. Jacob, the master manipulator, perceived that Esau was too exhausted to value something as abstract as a birthright over tangible food at that moment. The skill with which Jacob handled the opportunity suggests that he had been pondering for some time how he might get the birthright.

25:32–33 / Esau was so fatigued that the stew's aroma clouded his judgment. He made himself further vulnerable to Jacob's proposal by uttering that he was **about to die.** He reasons out loud as to **what good the birthright** would be to him given how hungry he felt. His self-questioning led him to accept Jacob's proposal. To seal the transaction Jacob ordered Esau to take an oath.

25:34 / Delighted with the prize he had just secured, **Jacob** gladly gave **Esau some bread and some lentil stew.** Esau **ate and drank, and then got up and left.** This string of four verbs in succession, unusual in Hebrew, communicates that he ate the food quickly and left immediately. Filling his stomach for a brief time was more important to Esau than keeping the birthright that lasted through the generations. The narrator adds a condemning statement: **Esau despised his birthright.** "Despise" (*bazah*) means "treat as worthless."

The fame of this story is in inverse proportion to its length. By selling his birthright so cheaply, Esau became the epitome of folly. He symbolizes those who place satisfying the feelings of the moment above valuing issues that matter over time (Heb. 12:15–16).

Additional Notes §34

25:20 /   Paddan Aram, which may mean "road of Aram," is possibly another name for Haran. It is also possible to take *paddan* as "field"; then it was another name for Aram Naharaim (24:10).

25:26 /   Scholars have proposed different ways of understanding the name Jacob. The theophoric element may be suppressed; its full form is then "Jacob-El," i.e., "may El protect him" (Deut. 33:28). Another suggestion is that it is a denominative of the Hb. *'qb* ("heel"), meaning "strike the heel" (LXX). Yet another view is that it means "finagle," based on the Arab. root meaning "follow at the heel or footsteps" to "take the place of another by deception" (W. D. Whitt, "The Jacob Traditions in Hosea and Their Relation to Genesis," *ZAW* 103 [1991], pp. 28–29). This interpretation is supported by 27:36.

25:30 /   The range of colors a given term conveys varies from culture to culture. Since cooked lentils are yellowish brown in color, the Hb. term *'adom* includes this color in its range of meaning, in contrast to Eng. "red" (Hamilton, *Genesis: Chapters 18–50*, p. 186). In cultures of the eastern Mediterranean the color red or reddish brown was used to depict heroic individuals; people painted themselves with these tones for ceremonies (C. Gordon, *The Common Background of Greek and Hebrew Civilizations* [New York: Norton, 1965], pp. 230–31).

Located to the southeast of Canaan, Edom's southern border was the Gulf of Elat, and its northern border was Nahal Zered, about one hundred miles to the north.

§35 Isaac Settles in the Negev (Gen. 26:1–35)

Genesis preserves only a few of the traditions about Isaac. The episodes in which Isaac is the main actor cluster primarily in this chapter, which opens by identifying him as the true heir of the promises to Abraham (vv. 3–5). These accounts picture Isaac as following in the footsteps of Abraham. Both face famine in the land (26:1–6 // 12:10); during the famine both go to live in a foreign setting and identify their wives as sisters for self-protection (26:7–11 // 12:10–20); both identify their wives as their sisters in Gerar, ruled by an Abimelech (26:7–11 // 20:1–18); both dig wells and face opposition from the Philistines (26:12–25 // 21:25–26, 28–30); both make a treaty with an Abimelech, king of Gerar (26:26–31 // 21:22–32); and both name a well Beersheba (26:32–33 // 21:31). At Beersheba Isaac builds an altar and calls on the name of Yahweh; building altars characterized Abraham's journey through Canaan (e.g., 12:7–8). Casting Isaac's experiences to be like Abraham's elevates him in the tradition that is dominated by his father and his son Jacob.

Although these accounts of Isaac appear to interrupt the Jacob cycle begun in chapter 25, Fishbane points out that the material concerning Isaac functions as an interlude to divert the pace in the Jacob cycle, similar to the story of Judah (ch. 38) inserted between episodes in the story of Joseph (*Text and Texture*, pp. 46–48).

The three sections in this chapter recount Isaac's dealings in Gerar (vv. 1–17), his living at Beersheba (vv. 18–33), and Esau's marriages (vv. 34–35).

26:1–6 / In three scenes we read about Isaac's journey to Gerar (vv. 1–6), the conflict with Abimelech over Rebekah (vv. 7–11), and Isaac's increase in wealth (vv. 12–17).

Like Abraham, Isaac faced a severe **famine in the land** of promise (12:10). Usually inhabitants of Canaan sought relief in Egypt. This time, however, Yahweh **appeared to Isaac** and told him not to **go down to Egypt** but to **live in the land** that Yahweh would indicate to him. Only a divine word would have led Isaac to settle in Gerar, a city of the Negev, since that area receives very limited rainfall. How this city had escaped the famine is not reported. Abimelech, identified as king of the Philistines, ruled Gerar. When Abraham visited this city, the ruler's name was Abimelech (ch. 20), but given the number of years that had elapsed since that visit, this ruler had to be another person with the same name. Possibly Abimelech was a dynastic name.

In the epiphany Yahweh blessed Isaac with six great promises. God promised to **be with** him, giving him his power and protection (28:15; 31:3; 46:4). God promised to **bless** him (12:2; 22:17; 26:24; 27:7). God would **give** him and his **descendants** (seed) . . . **all these lands** to **confirm the oath** he had sworn to **Abraham** (17:8; 22:17). "Oath," which is used only here and in 22:16–18 for the Abrahamic promises, specifically recalls the promises Abraham had received after placing Isaac on the altar. These words, then, were packed with meaning for Isaac. "All these lands" refers to the diverse geographic areas of Canaan, including the area around Gerar, that were occupied by a variety of ethnic groups. Yahweh reasserted that he was going to make Isaac's **descendants** (seed) **as numerous as the stars in the sky** (15:5). God was going to **give them all these lands.** And **all nations on earth** would find blessing **through** his **offspring** (seed). This last promise ties directly to Yahweh's original promise to Abraham as the seal that Isaac was the true heir of the Abrahamic promises (12:2–3). Yahweh concluded by asserting that he was giving these promises to Isaac **because Abraham** had **obeyed** him **and kept** his **requirements.** Four terms, **requirements, commands, decrees,** and **laws,** describe Abraham's wholehearted obedience to God's call.

26:7 / Soon after Isaac took up residence in Gerar, **the men of that place asked him about** Rebekah, seeking to find out her marital status. Fearful, Isaac replied that **she** was his **sister.** Like his father, he concealed his relationship to his wife in apprehension that **the men of** that **place might kill** him **on account of Rebekah, because she** was **beautiful.**

26:8–11 / Before anything happened to Rebekah, **Abimelech** became aware of her true relationship to Isaac. One day he **looked** out of **a window** in his palace and **saw Isaac caressing Rebekah.** Since in ancient society men and women kept themselves distant from one another in public, Abimelech immediately understood that Rebekah was Isaac's wife. Filled with anger at having been lied to and at the potential danger that his community faced because of Isaac's deception, he **summoned Isaac** to his palace. On this occasion God used Isaac's love for Rebekah—shown through his caresses—as the means of protecting her from harm and also of protecting Abimelech from placing his people under God's anger (20:17–18).

When Isaac arrived, Abimelech came to the point, stating that Rebekah was really his **wife.** He then challenged Isaac to account for deceiving him about their true relationship. Isaac responded lamely that he feared that he **might lose** his **life on account of her.** Abimelech retorted sharply, charging that in seeking to protect himself he had placed a whole community in danger. Since ancient people considered the community a unit, the wrongdoing of one person affected the community. If any man of Gerar had **slept with** Rebekah, **guilt** *('asham)* would have fallen on the community, even though that person would have acted believing that Rebekah was not married (20:9). "Guilt" means that the people of Gerar would have come under divine punishment for the wrong done to Rebekah. Deeply shamed, Isaac offered no response. Abimelech reassured Isaac by placing Rebekah under the protection of the crown with an official declaration that anyone who molested **this man or his wife** would **surely be put to death.**

This is the third account of a patriarch passing off his wife as his sister in order to protect himself from a foreign king (12:10–20; see the discussion there on the integrity of each account; 20:1–18). Each of these stories is paradigmatic for the destiny of Israel as a nation. Since both Abraham (ch. 20) and Isaac had a similar experience with a king of Gerar named Abimelech, their experiences foreshadowed Israel's long, agonizing conflict with the Philistines in their effort to gain control of the promised land.

26:12–15 / Confident of his welcome in Gerar, **Isaac planted crops.** This is the first mention of a patriarch farming, and Yahweh **blessed** his efforts with a bountiful harvest. Such success bore witness to the fertility of the promised land. Isaac gradually grew wealthier, increasing in **flocks, herds,** and **servants.** His success, however, aroused the Philistines' envy. They began to be concerned that the increase of Isaac's flocks endangered their access to the scarce water supply of that region. Furthermore, they feared that he might take over land they desired. To curtail Isaac's success they **stopped up all the wells his father's**

servants had dug. This report indicates that Isaac's shepherds grazed his flocks over a large area. Even though these wells were crucial to his increasing flocks, Isaac did not retaliate. Throughout these episodes Isaac never acts aggressively toward the Philistines.

26:16 / The Philistines stepped up their rancorous acts. Fearful that these skirmishes were about to break into open fighting, Abimelech summoned Isaac and ordered him to **move away** from Gerar. He pointed out that the increase in Isaac's power made it unlikely that he could continue to live peacefully among them.

26:17–18 / In this section Isaac, like his father Abraham, makes Beersheba his base. The action unfolds in four scenes: conflict between the Philistines and Isaac's servants over wells dug (vv. 17–22), Isaac's return to Beersheba (vv. 23–25), the covenant between Isaac and Abimelech (vv. 26–31), and the discovery of a new well at Beersheba (vv. 32–33).

Having been expelled from the city of Gerar, Isaac **moved** and set up camp **in the Valley of Gerar.** There he **reopened the wells that had been dug** in Abraham's day but later **stopped up** by **the Philistines.** The action of the Philistines reveals that they no longer honored the covenant between Abraham and Abimelech (21:22–31). Isaac called the wells by **the same names his father had given them,** thereby reclaiming for himself these valued sources of water.

26:19–22 / **Isaac's servants** next dug for water **in the valley** of Gerar. They found **fresh water,** but when **the herdsmen of Gerar** heard the good news, they came to claim the well. So Isaac **named the well Esek,** meaning "quarrel." His servants then dug **another well,** leading to another quarrel with the herdsmen of Gerar. This new well he **named Sitnah,** "hostility." Detesting the continued conflict, Isaac **moved** on further and dug **another well.** Having moved far enough away from Gerar, this time he received no opposition. Jubilant at the absence of conflict, Isaac **named** the well **Rehoboth,** "open space or room." In Hebraic thought an open space represents prosperity or salvation (e.g., Isa. 54:2–3). Isaac praised Yahweh for providing enough **room** for both peoples to live peaceably. Then he expressed his expectation that he would **flourish in the land** as God had promised. These incidents concerning the wells reveal Isaac's sensitivity to the needs of the herdsmen of Gerar even as his own needs expanded. He conducted himself prudently, never letting the contention escalate into fighting.

26:23–25 / Isaac then settled in **Beersheba,** having discovered sufficient sources of water to allow him to shepherd his flocks from that location. There he prospered as had Abraham. Since Isaac had overcome these obstacles with the people of Gerar, Yahweh again **appeared to him,** identifying himself as **the God of** his **father Abraham.** Yahweh then spoke to him the same word of assurance that he had given Abraham: **Do not be afraid** (15:1), undergirding this word with the promise of his presence (v. 3). God reiterated the promise to **bless** him and **increase the number of** his **descendants** (seed) because of the promises made to Abraham, God's **servant.** Yahweh affirmed Isaac for moving away from Gerar in order to put an end to the conflict with the local herdsmen and assured him that no force, human or natural, would be able to deprive him of these blessings. Like Abraham, Isaac responded to God's visitation by building **an altar** (cf. 12:7–8; 13:4, 18) **and** calling **on the name of** Yahweh. Trusting in God's promises, **he pitched his tent** there. Then **his servants dug a well.**

26:26–29 / Since Isaac had settled in Beersheba and since his stature was increasing, Abimelech came to realize that it would be beneficial to make a pact with Isaac. Taking along two high-ranking officials, **Ahuzzath his personal adviser and Phicol the commander of his forces,** Abimelech visited Isaac. Isaac, however, disgusted at Abimelech's earlier treatment, confronted him about the reason for his visit, pointing out how he had acted with hostility toward him, especially in ordering him to leave Gerar.

At once Abimelech sought to mollify Isaac by conceding that he had become aware of Isaac's success as a result of Yahweh's being **with** him. Abimelech's awareness motivated him to propose that there be **a sworn agreement between** them, **a treaty** or a covenant that would continue with their children. He was concerned that Isaac, who was growing stronger, might someday **harm** his people either by usurping some of their grazing areas or by an outright display of force. At last Abimelech treated Isaac as an equal. He reminded Isaac that when he had lived in Gerar they did not **molest** him but had **treated** him **well.** When they **sent** him **away,** they did so peacefully. Abimelech was thus motivated to seek an agreement with Isaac in order to participate in God's blessing on Isaac. Abimelech's advocating this treaty is an early example of God's fulfilling the promise that the nations would find blessing in Abraham's seed (12:3).

26:30–31 / Isaac responded favorably to Abimelech's proposal, not by words, but by actions. He prepared **a feast** for the visitors from Gerar. Not having welcomed Abimelech with a meal upon his arrival meant that Isaac had received him as an unwelcome guest (contrast 18:1–8). His display of hospitality informs us that he had changed his attitude toward the king of Gerar. Abimelech and his company spend the night with Isaac. **Early the next morning** they take **an oath** to seal the accord. Then **Isaac sent them** away **in peace.**

26:32–33 / **Isaac's servants** came to him and reported that they **had dug** another well and had **found water.** This new discovery confirmed that God continued to bless Isaac, affirming him for entering into covenant with Abimelech. Isaac **called** that well **Shibah,** which means both "seven" and "oath." From then on that **town** was called **Beersheba,** the name Abraham had given it earlier (21:31). Isaac's experience again parallels Abraham's. In this sequence of episodes Isaac perseveres, displays high moral integrity, and is so blessed by Yahweh that even his enemy comes to recognize God's blessing on his life.

26:34–35 / The narrative goes on to preserve a fragment from the traditions about Esau. This brief report provides information important for understanding some events that were soon to take place in Isaac's household. At the age of **forty Esau married** two **Hittite** women, **Judith daughter of Beeri** and **Basemath daughter of Elon.** Did Esau marry outside the line of Terah in defiance or out of convenience? The latter seems more likely, given the way he handled his birthright. He was inclined to take the path of least resistance when it came to fulfilling his needs. Since none of Terah's family lived nearby, Esau took wives from a local tribal group. One wonders why Isaac did not give Esau more direction regarding the great importance of patrilineal marriages for inheritance rights. With regard to carrying on the lineage of the chosen seed there is a strong contrast between Isaac and Abraham. Whereas Abraham was careful to secure for Isaac a bride from Terah's lineage, Isaac failed to find wives for his sons until Rebekah pressed him to send Jacob to her brother's house in Haran. However, Rebekah brought this issue up only as a pretext to protect her favorite son from Esau's seething anger (27:46–28:4).

Thus God used circumstance in order that Jacob might have a bride from the right line; Jacob was not carefully guided in this important matter by either of his parents. This account closes by showing how Isaac's passivity worked to Esau's harm and to the **grief** of **Isaac and Rebekah.**

Additional Notes §35

26:8 / "Caressing" comes from the same Hb. root, *ts-kh-q*, as Isaac's name. This wordplay establishes a bold irony. In acting true to his identity Isaac, unawares, disclosed his deception.

26:11 / The terms "touch" *(ng')* and "guilt" *('shm)* are integrally related in texts that deal with the sanctuary. By touching sancta a person commits a breach of faith against God and becomes guilty. In this light the patriarch and his wife are considered holy to God. Anyone who touches them incurs great guilt for having violated sancta. Thus this account of the endangered ancestress, i.e., a threat to the life or fertility of a matriarch, has the deepest theological explanation.

The experience of Israel as a nation that parallels Isaac's experience is harder to identify. Reis ("Take My Wife, Please," pp. 313–15) shows parallels between this story and the conflict between Michal and David when David brought the ark into Jerusalem. In both episodes "making merry" is key. Because Isaac "made merry" with Rebekah, Abimelech came to realize that she was his wife. Because David "made merry" before the ark of the covenant, Michal became so jealous that a rift separated her and David. After the difficulties were resolved, God blessed both Isaac and David with success over their foes.

26:26 / Although this commander, Phicol, had the same name as the one Abraham had met (21:22), it must have been a different person. According to J. Safren ("Ahuzzath and the Pact of Beer-sheba," *ZAW* 101 [1989], pp. 190–98), Ahuzzath was the supervisor of pastorates. The Mari tablets indicate that such an officer had guards to enforce his orders.

26:34 / Different traditions of Esau's marriages have been preserved in 28:9 and 36:2–3. No certain way of reconciling them has been found.

§36 Jacob Steals Esau's Blessing (Gen. 27:1–28:9)

This suspense-filled narrative portrays a family torn between the conflicting wills of a father and a mother. An indulgent father favors a rugged, athletic, unpretentious older son while a brilliant, domineering mother manipulates matters to the advantage of her younger son, who loves to take care of the animals and do chores around the tent. "Son" is a controlling word in this narrative, being employed by each parent to emphasize his or her respective love for and favoritism to one son. Isaac calls Esau "my son" (vv. 18, 20, 21 [twice], 24, 25, 26, 27, though mistakenly for Jacob in these verses, 37); Esau is "his [i.e., Isaac's] son" (vv. 1, 5, 20). Rebekah calls Jacob "my son" (vv. 8, 13, 43), and he is "her son" in verse 17 (I. Willi-Plein, "Genesis 27 als Rebekka-geschichte," *ThZ* 45 [1989], pp. 326–27). Neither son is ever spoken of as "our son." Another key term is "bless" (*brk*; vv. 4, 7, 10, 12, 19, 23, 25, 27 [twice], 30, 31, 33 [twice], 34, 35, 36 [twice], 38 [twice], 41).

The drama unfolds as Isaac gives Esau instructions in preparation for blessing him (27:1–4); Rebekah prepares Jacob to come before Isaac to receive the blessing (27:5–17); Isaac blesses Jacob (27:18–29); Isaac learns of the deception and blesses Esau (27:30– 40); Rebekah devises a plan to save Jacob from Esau's wrath (27:41–28:5); and Esau marries an Ishmaelite woman (28:6–9). There are only two actors in each scene. In the first four scenes the actors rotate in this pattern: Isaac-Esau, Rebekah-Jacob, Isaac-Jacob, and Isaac-Esau. The fifth act, in which the conflict is resolved, has three scenes and the actors are Rebekah-Jacob, Rebekah-Isaac, and Isaac-Jacob. Because of the deep rift in the family Esau never meets with Jacob or Rebekah.

The narrative is full of pathos as each parent seeks to fulfill deep longings in regard to the favorite son. Isaac wants nothing more than to empower Esau with his blessing, while Rebekah is determined to have Jacob blessed by Isaac, thus fulfilling the divine words of promise given her during her troubled pregnancy (25:23). Each son obediently carries out his parent's instructions. The key figure is Rebekah, whose plans direct the drama.

In hearing this story we should not classify the characters as good versus bad. All the characters have both admirable and deplorable traits. Esau is cast as genuine, simple, and accepting. Carefree, he does not protect himself from unforeseen obstacles. Thus he receives sympathy for his naive vulnerability. Jacob, dominated by his mother, is cautious and cunning. Rebekah is a perceptive, domineering mother who looks out for her favorite son. The deceit of Rebekah and Jacob hardens the audience toward them; the sense is that they deserve the pain they get for their conniving. The sympathies of the audience gravitate toward Isaac, a weak, aging figure whose fatherly desire to honor a loved son is thwarted. The outcomes of this act of deception are harsh. Esau weeps bitterly for the lost blessing. Jacob has to spend twenty years in exile, where he must deal with a clever father-in-law. Rebekah loses the companionship of her favorite son and never sees him again. Little is known of Isaac's sorrow. Nevertheless, through these humans with their strengths and frailties, God works out the plan of building his own people.

27:1–4 / In a detail key to the plot we learn that Isaac's eyesight had become very dim, awakening him to his mortality. Isaac realized that he needed to perform his patriarchal duty of blessing his firstborn son. Such blessings were crucial, for they guided the destiny of ancient tribes. This was even truer for the patriarchs as heirs of the great Abrahamic promises. They believed that God empowered the blessing by directing nature to produce bountifully and by making those who were blessed strong and able to withstand any foe. The blessing thus bonded together the patriarchs and God. It also instilled confidence, encouraging the one blessed to walk with God as his forefathers had done before him. The son who received the Abrahamic blessing became the next leader. The fact that Isaac lived many years after this episode suggests that fear of death motivated him more than imminence of his dying.

Isaac summoned his elder son and instructed him to take his **quiver and bow** and **go out to the open country to hunt some wild game** in order that he might prepare for Isaac the **tasty food** he liked. Then they would share a festive meal, and Isaac would **give** his son his **blessing**. Receiving his father's request with a glad heart, **Esau left** at once to go hunting. **Rebekah** overheard the conversation.

What blessing did Isaac intend to give Esau? As this episode unfolds, there are three distinct blessings: a general blessing by a parent to a child (27:39–40), the special blessing by the patriarch to a son whom he had selected as the leader (27:27b–29), and the special promises of God to Abraham (28:3–4; 12:2–3). A comparison of these blessings indicates that Isaac intended to pronounce a special blessing on Esau, one grounded in his son's love of nature. Thus it appears that Isaac realized that the spiritual blessing God had given Abraham belonged to Jacob. Two facts confirm this position: when Isaac thought he was blessing Esau, he made no reference to the Abrahamic promises, and he blessed Jacob with the Abrahamic promises just before his departure for Haran. These facts explain why Isaac wanted to bless Esau without Jacob's being present. His departure from protocol (49:1; 50:24–25), coupled with his neglecting to guide Esau in the selection of a proper wife, indicates that Isaac had not given his sons spiritual leadership. His failures in these important matters provide an explanation for the reversal he was to experience in regard to his blessing for Esau.

27:5–13 / After overhearing Isaac's directions to Esau, Rebekah implemented a scheme to secure the patriarchal blessing for Jacob. She informed him about Isaac's conversation with Esau and then exhorted him to obey her directions so that he might seize opportunity. It is instructive to compare the differing approaches of these two parents with their children. Isaac spoke to Esau (27:5), but Rebekah commanded Jacob to **do what** she told him. This wording indicates that Rebekah dominated Jacob, whereas Isaac and Esau had a more reciprocal relationship. According to her plan Rebekah would **prepare some tasty food** that Isaac liked from **two choice young goats,** and Jacob would take this food to his father and receive the patriarchal blessing.

Jacob raised an obvious obstacle to carrying out this plan; his **brother Esau** was **a hairy man,** while he had **smooth skin.** When Isaac touched him, he would detect the deception and consider his younger son a trickster. "Trickster" captures how dishonorable Rebekah's plan was. A later law condemned everyone who took advantage of another's physical limitation for personal advantage (Lev. 19:14; Deut. 27:18). Jacob was aware that if Isaac discovered his disguise, he would curse rather than bless him.

While sympathetic to his mother's scheme, Jacob feared the consequences should it fail. Rebekah addressed his fears with the reassurance that she would take **the curse** on herself. Lest one judge Rebekah too harshly, a major reason for her brazen action was her desire to see the fulfillment of the divine word that she had received during her pregnancy (25:23).

27:14–17 / Jacob carried out his mother's instructions expeditiously. While the food cooked, Rebekah took Esau's **best clothes . . . and put them on Jacob** to make him smell like Esau, a man of the field. Next she **covered his hands and the smooth part of his neck with the goatskins** so that his exposed skin would feel rough to Isaac's touch. **Then she handed** Jacob the savory meat and the bread to take to his father.

27:18–20 / Here begins one of the most dramatic scenes in Genesis. The reader wonders if Isaac will discover that he is being duped by his cunning son Jacob. On entering his father's presence, Jacob said simply, **My father.** When Esau entered, he blurted out, "My father, sit up and eat some of my game, so that you may give me your blessing" (v. 31). Clearly he had a more robust way of communicating with his father than did Jacob.

Isaac responded by asking who was there. Jacob replied, **I am Esau your firstborn.** He did not say "your son," the wording that communicated the affection between Isaac and Esau (v. 32). Also, his use of "firstborn" alerted Isaac to the purpose of his visit. Nevertheless, because he had purchased the birthright from Esau, Jacob stated a legal reality. Reporting that he had **done** as his father had **told** him, he invited Isaac to **sit up and eat some of** the **game so that** he might **give** him his **blessing.** Suspecting that something is amiss, **Isaac asked** how his son had found game **so quickly.** Jacob skillfully dodged this question with a pious reply: "Yahweh **your God gave me success.**"

27:21–26 / Doubting that this voice is Esau's, Isaac asked his visitor to **come near** in order that he might **touch** him, seeking to discover whether this person **really** was his **son Esau.** After touching him, Isaac reflected out loud that **the voice** was Jacob's, but **the hands** were Esau's. Isaac was baffled by the discrepancy between what he heard and what he felt. His expression of perplexity intensified the precariousness of Jacob's situation. Still not convinced that it was Esau, Isaac asked again if he **really** was his **son Esau.** Jacob answered, **I am.** Nevertheless, after these comments about his voice, Jacob spoke few words. Isaac then asked him to **bring** him **some of** the **game** that he might **eat** and then **give** him the **blessing.**

Jacob set the tasty food before Isaac, **and he ate.** Jacob also gave his father **some wine,** which he **drank.** While Isaac ate, Jacob must have wondered if the food would betray him. Given that his father was suspicious, would he figure out that it was truly Jacob in his presence? When would Esau return? Isaac also remained somewhat skeptical. Having finished eating, he asked Jacob to **come** near and **kiss** him, wanting further evidence that this was Esau before pronouncing the blessing. When Jacob bent over, Isaac smelled **his clothes;** being Esau's, they smelled of the field, not the barnyard. Sufficiently persuaded that this person was Esau, Isaac spoke his patriarchal blessing.

27:27–29 / In his blessing Isaac began by referring to his son's love for the field, the open space. He then asked God to **give** him **of heaven's dew.** In Canaan, dew is essential for the summer crops to mature during the rainless summers. Thus dew symbolizes fertility. He also asked God to give **of earth's richness.** The fields would yield **grain and new wine** in **abundance.** Isaac next prayed that **nations** might **serve** him. As leader of a tribe, he would be recognized by his **brothers** as **lord,** and they would **bow down to** him. This promise captures the word that Rebekah had received from God about the children she was carrying (25:23). Isaac concluded the blessing with the standard formula, **May those who curse you be cursed and those who bless you be blessed.** In this setting this last formula was laden with meaning, for as soon as Esau learned of the deception, he became very angry and cursed Jacob. Ironically, that curse placed Esau under the curse attached to the blessing he had lost.

27:30–33 / As soon as Isaac finished the blessing, Jacob left. For him the tension was over. For the reader, however, the suspense increases. What will be the reactions of Isaac and Esau on finding out that a long-cherished dream has been shattered? At the beginning of this scene the narrator identifies Isaac as Jacob's father and Esau as his brother to underscore that Jacob's deception had been against the closest members of his family.

Soon after Jacob left his father's tent, Esau entered, carrying the **tasty food** he had prepared for **his father.** Jubilant, he invited Isaac to **sit up and eat** that he might **give** him his **blessing.** Isaac asked, **Who are you**? He was too grieved and shocked to say "my son." Esau answered emphatically, **I am your son, your first-born, Esau.** This threefold identification made Isaac realize that Esau was before him. By identifying himself as firstborn, Esau gave evidence that he did not admit to himself the full implication of having sold his birthright to Jacob, that legally Jacob was the firstborn. Realizing that he had been betrayed, Isaac **trembled violently.** He felt unnerved at having been cheated out of his long-held dream of blessing Esau. Because he could do nothing to change what had happened, his heart sank.

Helplessly, Isaac asked **who** had **hunted game and brought it to** him, going on to inform Esau that he had just eaten game brought by another and had **blessed** that one. He concluded with the fateful words, **Indeed he will be blessed.** A patriarch's words uttered in such a solemn moment were definitive and final; they affected the cosmic order. No ritual existed to undo a blessing. The power of the blessing was greater than the giver of the blessing. If the recipient of a blessing was other than the one intended, that person still received the blessing. The alteration was attributed to God's design. Isaac thus was powerless to reverse this course of events.

27:34–38 / On learning what had just taken place, Esau **burst** into heavy, **bitter** crying, entreating his father to **bless** him too. Isaac reiterated lamely that his **brother** had come **deceitfully and** taken his **blessing.** Esau lamented that Jacob's name was appropriate, because he had **deceived** him **two times** by taking his **birthright and** his **blessing.** He then asked if there was not **any blessing** for him. He wanted the formal expression of his father's love. Isaac pointed out that he had **made** Jacob **lord over** him and that **all his relatives** were to be **his servants.** He had **sustained him with grain and new wine.** What then could he **possibly do** for his favorite **son**? Esau continued to plead that his father should give him a blessing. He then **wept aloud.** Esau expressed much more concern over the loss of the blessing than he did at the loss of the birthright. It is likely that he had resolved that, having sold his birthright, he would not let Jacob get the blessing. Furthermore, since the blessing was pronounced by his father, he had not foreseen any way that Jacob could get the blessing because of his own close relationship to his father. But Jacob had usurped the deepest expression of that relationship.

27:39–40 / Responding to Esau's pleas, Isaac composed a blessing for him. He said that his **dwelling** would **be away from**

the earth's richness and the dew of heaven. These words indicated that Esau was to find his living in a dry land. This blessing would enable him to survive in such a harsh land and prosper to some extent. He would live by his sword and serve his brother. Esau would have the skill to protect himself from hostile groups. Then Isaac gave him the promise that in time he would throw his brother's yoke from off his neck.

27:41 / With his hatred for Jacob escalating, Esau began to plot to kill his brother after the anticipated period of mourning for their father after his death.

27:42–45 / When Rebekah learned about Esau's plans of deadly vengeance, she devised another strategy for protecting Jacob from harm. She summoned him and informed him that Esau was consoling himself with the thought of killing him. She instructed her favorite son to flee at once to her brother Laban and stay there until Esau's fury had subsided. She anticipated that Esau's anger would cool soon after he forgot what had happened. When it was safe again, she would send word for Jacob to come back home. She underscored her remarks by mentioning the threat of the loss of both sons, for if Esau killed Jacob, a near kinsman would be obligated to kill Esau. Little did Rebekah realize that she would lose the presence of her adored son for twenty years and that in those years Jacob himself would fall victim to cruel trickery.

27:46 / In order that Jacob might travel to Haran openly and honorably, Rebekah needed to persuade Isaac to send him there. She went to him and complained about how irritated Esau's Hittite wives made her. She then pointed out that her life would become unbearable should Jacob marry a Hittite woman. Because of Isaac's fondness for Esau, she concealed the real reason for her request by speaking of an issue that agitated both of them (26:34–35).

28:1–2 / Rebekah persuaded Isaac, for he called for Jacob to give him instructions and to bless him. He told him not to marry a Canaanite woman. Instead he was to go at once to Paddan Aram, to the house of his maternal grandfather. There he was to take a wife . . . from among the daughters of Laban, his mother's brother.

28:3–4 / Isaac then pronounced a blessing of departure on Jacob. Significantly, he pronounced on Jacob the Abrahamic blessing in the name of **God Almighty** (cf. 17:2). He asked God to **bless** him by making him **fruitful**, increasing his **numbers** to a **community of peoples.** Specifically he entreated God to give him and his descendants **the blessing given to Abraham** (12:2–3, 7; 13:15, 17; 22:17). In time he was to **take possession of the land where** he **now** lived **as an alien, the** very **land God gave to Abraham.** Isaac's actions and words made it clear that he had reconciled himself to the fact that it was God's will for Jacob to receive the patriarchal blessing. He thus acted responsibly in blessing Jacob as the seed of promise. That Isaac passed on the Abrahamic blessing at this point, not at the special meal he had set up to bless Esau, informs us that Isaac considered the patriarchal blessing distinct from the special blessing of God to Abraham. It also indicates that he was more concerned with blessing his favorite son for his own purposes than with passing on the special divine blessing given to his father. This brief scene reaffirms that Isaac was a weak spiritual leader to members of his household.

28:5 / A summary statement recounts Jacob's obedience to his mother and father. **Isaac** formally **sent Jacob on his way . . . to Paddan Aram.** There he was to dwell with **Laban son of Bethuel,** whose lineage is given because of its importance in identifying Israel's ancestry.

28:6–9 / **Esau learned that Isaac had blessed Jacob and had sent him to Paddan Aram to take a wife.** He also heard that his father had told him **not** to **marry a Canaanite woman.** Coming to realize **how displeasing the Canaanite women were to his father,** he **married Mahalath, the sister of Nebaioth,** Ishmael's daughter. This marriage gives further evidence of Esau's naïveté. He never took into account the importance of the lineage of the women he married in reference to the possibility of his seed carrying God's promises to Abraham. By highlighting his lack of sensitivity in this critical issue, the account exposes Esau's unworthiness of being the heir of that blessing.

Additional Notes §36

27:39 / The wording of Isaac's blessing for Esau is intentionally vague. One way to read the line is "your abode shall enjoy the fat of the earth and the dew of heaven above" (NJPS). In that case Esau and Jacob were blessed similarly. In support of this reading is the fertility of the western slopes of Mount Seir in Edom, where Esau settled. Another way to read the line is found in NIV: "your dwelling will be away from the earth's richness, away from the dew of heaven." In support of this latter reading are the facts that Edom never had a strong agriculture and that dew does not have a significant role in the agriculture of that region. It is possible that this blessing had a dual thrust, i.e., Esau would enjoy seasons of prosperity mixed with seasons of want.

27:40 / The fact that Esau was to live by the sword had implications for Israel as a nation state. Years later David subdued Edom (2 Sam. 8:11–14). Strife nevertheless continued between the two states. Sometimes Edom was free from Israel's yoke; at other times it was a vassal to Israel. After King Ahaz (715 B.C.), Edom was never again dominated by Judah (2 Kgs. 8:20–22).

28:1 / The discrepancy between Isaac's describing Esau's wives as Canaanites and Rebekah's referring to them as Hittites (27:46) is not a serious problem. "Canaanite" was used broadly for any inhabitants of that area, whereas Rebekah was speaking ethnologically.

28:2 / That Isaac instructed Jacob to "go" instead of "flee," as Rebekah had commanded him, suggests he had not discerned the real reason for Jacob's traveling to Paddan Aram (Sarna, *Genesis*, p. 196).

28:3 / Possibly Isaac did not reprimand Rebekah for having deceived him in the matter of the blessing because he owed her for acting deceitfully in telling Abimelech that she was his sister (Reis, "Take My Wife, Please," pp. 312–13).

28:9 / According to 36:3–4, Esau married Basemath, the daughter of Ishmael. It is possible that these two names were for the same wife, as Jewish tradition holds. But according to 26:34, Basemath was the daughter of Elon the Hittite.

§37 Jacob's Dream at Bethel (Gen. 28:10–22)

In this report of Jacob's dream Jacob rests for the night (vv. 10–11), God speaks to him in a dream (vv. 12–15), Jacob responds (vv. 16–17), he names that place (vv. 18–19), and he makes a vow (vv. 20–22).

28:10–11 / Because of Esau's threats and in order to find a wife, **Jacob left Beersheba and set out for Haran.** It was a long journey, especially by foot. As the sun set, Jacob picked a place to spend the night. The NIV understands the text to say that **taking one of the stones there, he put it under his head.** Since a stone does not make a good pillow, it seems more likely that Jacob arranged these stones to provide protection for his head while he slept on the ground. As far as Jacob knew, that place possessed no special significance. He did not expect anything to happen while he slept.

28:12 / During the night Jacob **had a dream. He saw a stairway resting on the earth, with its top reaching to heaven, and the angels of God were ascending and descending on it. Above it stood** Yahweh, who identified himself to Jacob as Yahweh, **the God of** his **father Abraham and the God of Isaac.** God grounded this self-identification in relationship to those who had followed him, not in terms of this place's being holy.

In the view of the ancients, places where God was thought to have appeared provided direct access to the heavenly realm. Rebekah most likely went to such a place in order to receive a word from God as to why the children in her womb were struggling so fiercely (25:22). People came and lingered at these places in the hope of receiving a special communication from the gods, often through a dream. Such places, being sacred ground, or "houses of the gods," were normally marked by a monument or shrine. No such marker alerted Jacob that he was lying on sacred ground. God chose this place because Jacob was there, not because it possessed any intrinsic holiness. In pagan belief a site was sacred from primordial time, but in Scripture a site never became endowed with sacredness; a particular place was holy only as long as God chose to reveal himself there.

28:13–15 / Yahweh gave Jacob the Abrahamic promises by reiterating three of them (cf. 12:2–3, 7). First, God was going to **give** to Jacob and his **descendants** (seed) **the land on which** he was **lying** (cf. 12:7). In Hebrew "to you," that is, Jacob, stands first to highlight that Jacob was the new recipient of the promise. Next, Jacob's **descendants** (seed) would become so numerous that they would **be like the dust of the earth** (cf. 13:16). They would **spread out** from Bethel, occupying the land in all directions (cf. 13:14–15). In Hebrew "spread out" *(parats)* is literally "burst forth," conveying the coming explosive increase in his offspring. The shift in subject from Jacob to his descendants indicates that through them he was to occupy the full extent of the promised land. Finally, **all peoples on earth** would find blessing **through** him and his **offspring** (seed; cf. 12:3).

Yahweh went on to give Jacob four additional promises that addressed his present predicament. God would be with him (26:3). This is the greatest promise God can make to anyone, and it was especially meaningful to Jacob as he headed by himself to a distant land. God would **watch over** him **wherever** he went, and he would **bring** him **back to this land.** Jacob had no anticipation of being away from Canaan for twenty years. As the years passed, this promise surely grew in importance, keeping alive Jacob's hope that someday he would leave Laban's household to return to his homeland. God asserted that he would **not leave** Jacob until he had completely fulfilled what he had **promised.** While the "until" clause seems to suggest that at some time God might leave Jacob, it is a rhetorical device, an understatement, affirming to Jacob the certainty of God's presence in all circumstances throughout his life.

28:16–17 / **When Jacob awoke from his sleep,** he was full of awe and yet terrified at being in the presence of Yahweh. He declared that the site where he had slept was sacred, identifying it as **the house of God** (Hb. "Bethel"), above which was **the gate of heaven.** Indeed it was the navel of the earth, i.e., the place where there was direct communication between heaven and earth. While Jacob's expression that this was holy ground had roots in polytheistic thinking (v. 12), his amazement reveals that Yahweh, the God of Abraham and Isaac, is not such a God. Yahweh is not tied to a sacred place to which people make pil-

grimages in hopes of receiving a divine word. Rather Yahweh is
the universal God, the one who reveals himself to whomever he
wills and wherever he wills.

Jacob's ecstatic response to this dream contrasts with Abraham's dialoguing with God during such encounters. Whereas
Abraham had an ongoing conversation with God, Jacob's fearful
reaction indicates that he did not have such a relationship with
God and that he had not sought God's guidance for dealing with
the threat of Esau's anger. When he lay down to sleep in that unknown spot, many conflicting emotions must have flooded his
mind: triumph at securing the family blessing from his virile
brother, remorse at having tricked his aging father, relief at being
out of range of Esau's anger, apprehension about the long journey
ahead to Haran, and a deep sense of loneliness for his mother.
God, being aware of Jacob's troubled thoughts and his feelings of
vulnerability, knew that this was not the time to condemn Jacob
for his acts of trickery. Out of compassion God appeared in order
to strengthen Jacob, the bearer of the promises, for the hard years
ahead. He wanted to assure Jacob that the God of his fathers was
directing his way in order that the blessings entrusted to his forefathers would be fulfilled through him.

28:18–19 / Jacob took the stone he had placed about **his
head and set it up as a pillar,** marking the place where God had
appeared. He then **poured oil on top of it,** consecrating this stone
as the place where a person could meet God. Jacob **called that
place Bethel.** Formerly it was **called Luz.** In this account the appearance of God transforms the ordinary into the extraordinary.
Bethel became an important site for Jacob (35:6–7) and later for Israel. During the time of the judges, Israelites came here to worship Yahweh (Judg. 20:18). Centuries later, Jeroboam I made Bethel
one of the crown's sanctuaries, turning that famous site into a
place of illegitimate worship (1 Kgs. 12:28–30).

28:20–22 / In grateful response to God's promises and
in order to cope with the fear of his journey to Haran, **Jacob made
a vow.** In contrast to an oath, a vow is conditional. In making a
vow a person obligates himself or herself to do what is vowed
only if God fulfills the conditions specified. That Jacob, the bargainer, used this approach in dealing with God comes as no surprise. Also it is not surprising, given his disposition, that he
stipulated five conditions. At the beginning and end of the vow, he
laid stress on God's fulfillment of three promises: divine presence,

divine protection, and a safe return to his **father's house.** In the middle he made two conditions that dealt with his immediate needs—namely, God providing him **food** and **clothes.** His request for these basic provisions indicates how apprehensive Jacob was about living in Haran. If God fulfilled these conditions, Jacob committed himself to three standards. Yahweh was to be his God. The **pillar** he had set up was to be the house of God, that is, a marker of the spot where people could meet God. **Of all** that God gave him he would **give** to God **a tenth.** According to the last promise, on his return to Canaan Jacob would give a tenth of all his possessions to God, either at a sanctuary or to a priest (see Abraham's giving a tithe to Melchizedek, 14:20). By making such a contribution a person concretely expressed God's lordship over all one's property. With this comprehensive vow Jacob thus committed himself to serve the God of his fathers.

Additional Notes §37

28:12 / The precise meaning of *sullam* ("stairway"), which occurs only here in the OT, is not known. Some relate it to the root *s-l-l* ("cast up, make a mound") and postulate that it was a ramp. Others relate it to Akk. *simmiltu* ("stairs, ladder"), which suggests that it means a staired ramp like that used in a towered temple such as a ziggurat (11:1–9).

28:18 / People throughout the Near East erected and dedicated stones for a variety of purposes: a memorial of an event, a boundary marker, a marker for a tomb, or a witness of a transaction (e.g., 31:45–54; 35:14, 20). Here Jacob wanted a witness to the promises God had given him in the dream and a marker for the place where one could meet God. Later the law would prohibit the erection of such pillars because of their role in the cults of Israel's neighbors (Exod. 23:24; 34:13; Lev. 26:1; Deut. 16:22).

28:19 / Bethel may have been the name of a sanctuary located on the outskirts of Luz. Thus the two places, though close, were distinct (Josh. 16:2). It is possible that in time the name of the sanctuary became the name of the city.

28:21 / Another way to read "Yahweh will be my God" is as the sixth condition of Jacob's vow (Hamilton, *Genesis: Chapters 18–50,* p. 248). The grammar strongly supports this reading. Theologically, however, this statement about his commitment to God leads to, and is necessary grounds for, his identifying this place as his place of worship and agreeing to pay a tithe.

§38 Jacob Arrives at Laban's House
(Gen. 29:1–14)

This episode is a betrothal type-scene. In such a scene a person travels to a distant place, stops at a well, meets a girl, and draws water for her flock by overcoming some obstacle. The girl's father invites the traveler to stay; eventually the young man marries the local girl (other variations of this type-scene are Abraham's servant and Rebekah in 24:10–61 and Moses and the daughters of Reuel in Exod. 2:15b–21; R. Alter, *The Art of Biblical Narrative,* [New York: Basic Books, 1981], pp. 51–53, 54–56). This account consists of two scenes: Jacob arrives at the well (vv. 1–8) and meets Rachel (vv. 9–14).

29:1–3 / **Jacob continued on his journey and came to the land of the eastern peoples.** Having reached his destination, he stopped at the local **well,** a primary meeting place for shepherds. **Three flocks of sheep** were **lying** about that well, waiting to be watered. A huge **stone** covered the opening **of the well,** protecting the purity of the water and preventing any person or animal from falling into the well. Each day **shepherds** gathered at the well, and when several had assembled, they rolled away **the stone,** watered their flocks, and returned **the stone to its place.**

29:4–8 / Addressing the **shepherds** as **brothers,** Jacob learned that they were **from Haran.** He then asked about the welfare of **Laban, Nahor's grandson.** They pointed to a girl who was leading a flock to the well and informed him that she was **his daughter Rachel.** Suddenly Jacob ordered the shepherds to **water** their flocks and return them **to pasture** since it was still midday. Presumably he wanted to meet Rachel without so many onlookers present. Unmoved by his orders, the shepherds replied that they could not water the flocks until more shepherds gathered and **the stone** was **rolled away from the mouth of the well.**

29:9–14 / While Jacob was contending with these shepherds, Rachel arrived **with her father's sheep.** Excited by her presence, Jacob **rolled the** massive **stone away from the mouth of the well** by himself **and** graciously **watered** her flock. Stones serve as a motif that connects the episodes in Jacob's journey. His great display of strength won Rachel's admiration. Overjoyed that he had arrived safely in his uncle's homeland and that he was now in the presence of a close relative, **Jacob kissed Rachel and began to weep.** He then identified himself as her cousin on her father's side. This manner of recognizing fellow kin is noteworthy, for there are few references in Scripture to a man kissing a woman. Rachel became so excited that she left Jacob standing alone as **she ran** home and **told her father.** On hearing her report Laban ran **to meet** his nephew. **He embraced him and kissed him and brought him to his home. Jacob told** Laban the news about his family, and **Laban** heartily welcomed Jacob into the family by identifying him as his **own flesh and blood** (lit. "my bone and my flesh"). So Jacob dwelt with Laban.

The kiss of kinship frames Jacob's stay with his uncle. At the beginning Jacob kissed Rachel, and Laban welcomed him with a kiss. Years later, however, when Jacob and Laban separated never to meet again, Laban kissed his grandchildren and daughters. But he did not kiss Jacob—evidence of the distance between them (31:55).

§39 Jacob Marries Leah and Rachel (Gen. 29:15–30)

With wide brush strokes this narrative covers fourteen years in which Jacob agrees to labor for marrying Laban's daughter (vv. 15–20) and his marriages to Leah and Rachel (vv. 21–30). Jacob finds himself married to Leah, the unwanted older daughter, powerfully portraying the theme of reaping what one sows. The man who deceived his brother and father is bested by a father-in-law in regard to his wife, his closest companion. Throughout this narrative and the Laban–Jacob cycle two terms are key: "serve, work" (*'abad;* vv. 15, 18, 20, 25, 27, 30; 30:26 [twice], 29; 31:6, 41; *'abodah;* 29:27; 30:26) and "pay or earn" (*sakar;* 30:16 ["hired" in NIV; twice in Hb.], 18, 28, 32, 33; 31:8 [twice] and *maskoret;* 29:15; 31:7, 41). The recurrence of these terms allows the reader to feel the hardships Jacob endured in working for Laban.

29:15–21 / While living with his uncle, Jacob began to work with the flocks. Wanting to have more authority over his nephew, Laban offered to set his wage. We can easily imagine that Laban had noticed Jacob's fondness for Rachel and had come to realize that Jacob had nothing to offer as a bride price. It is surprising that Jacob's parents did not provide him with any resources for a dowry, especially since they had sent him with the hope of finding a bride (28:1–2). Without such resources, Jacob's only option was to offer his labor as a dowry. Shrewdly **Laban** asked Jacob to set his own **wages,** aware that his youth and his being in love would prompt him to state conditions favorable to his future father-in-law.

At this point the narrator adds some vital information to prepare the reader for Jacob's answer. **Laban had two daughters, Leah** and **Rachel.** Leah was known for her beautiful **eyes,** while Rachel was stunning in her beauty. The younger's gaining ascendancy over the older is a common motif in the patriarchal narratives. Since Leah was less desirable, Laban no doubt chafed at the thought of receiving a smaller bride price for her. Jacob eagerly accepted the offer to set his wages because of his love for Rachel. He proposed that he **work . . . seven years** as the bride price for Rachel. Agreeing to these terms gladly, Laban led Jacob to believe that at the end of the seven years he would receive Rachel as his bride. However, it is significant that Laban did not mention Rachel's name in making this agreement, thus allowing himself room to act deviously.

Jacob's intense **love for** Rachel made the **seven years** pass quickly. When the seventh year ended, Jacob went to Laban and told him to **give** him his **wife.** The firmness of his request witnesses to the intensity of his longing for Rachel. Jacob's anxious demeanor heightens the impact of the deception he is about to experience.

29:22–30   /   Responding to Jacob's prompting, Laban prepared a great wedding **feast** and invited **all the people** of that region. In that culture a wedding feast lasted at least a week. On the high day of the feast Laban brought **his daughter Leah and gave her to Jacob.** So excited and so giddy from wine was Jacob that in the night shadows he did not discern that his bride was someone other than Rachel. He consummated the marriage. In the morning the young man who had advanced his way at the expense of his brother found himself jilted by a treacherous deception; his bride was Leah, not Rachel. Again the elder stood in the way of Jacob's desires: in Canaan, Esau; in Haran, Leah.

Shocked and infuriated on discovering that he had spent the night with Leah, Jacob went directly to Laban. After recounting the terms of their agreement, he demanded to know **why** Laban had **deceived** (*rimmah*) him. With this term the narrator makes an ironic point, for it is the same root Isaac used to describe Jacob's usurping the blessing (27:35). Since Jacob had slept with Leah, Laban knew that his plan was beyond reversal and that Jacob was dependent on any proposal he would offer. Laban crafted his response to deflect blame from himself and onto his accuser. He **replied** that it was against **custom** for him **to give the younger daughter** (*hatse'irah*) **in marriage before the older one** (*habbekirah*). His words hit Jacob hard, causing him to recall the way he had manipulated his older brother to gain for himself the privileges of the firstborn (*bekirah*). Jacob was trapped, for he had failed to take into account this custom when he had negotiated the terms of his services. Just as Isaac had no means of renouncing the blessing he had pronounced on Jacob, thinking that he was Esau (27:33, 37), Jacob had no legitimate way to free himself from Leah, thinking she was Rachel. Jacob had to endure disappointment similar to what he had inflicted on his brother.

Acting from a magnanimous posture to appease Jacob and to profit from his labor, Laban offered Jacob his **younger** daughter at the end of the **bridal week ... in return for another seven years of work.** Jacob might have bargained for fewer years since Rachel was the younger and he had already served seven years, but realizing that Laban held the upper hand and having such a longing for Rachel, he agreed to these terms. After the completion of Leah's wedding week, **Laban gave him his daughter Rachel to be his wife.** Since there is no report of a wedding feast for Rachel, Laban apparently provided a place for Rachel and Jacob to live together. Laban's cunning seems to have cost his younger daughter the honor of a formal wedding. Jacob established a marital bond with Rachel. **He loved** her completely. Jacob then **worked for Laban another seven years.**

Following custom, Laban provided each of his daughters with a handmaid. To Leah he **gave Zilpah** and to Rachel, **Bilhah.** These handmaids are named because they are to become mothers of four of Jacob's sons.

Additional Notes §39

29:17 / Leah's eyes were *rak,* "weak (NIV), thin, delicate." Some scholars understand this to mean that her eyes lacked luster (von Rad, *Genesis,* p. 291). Considering that *rak* describes a king's reign as gentle (2 Sam. 3:39) and a woman as delicate (Deut. 28:56; Hamilton, *Genesis: Chapters 18–50,* pp. 258–59), Leah probably had beautiful eyes. Mention of this single trait depreciates her further by faint praise.

29:18 / A laborer's wage was around a shekel a month in the Old Babylonian era. Since Deut. 22:29 sets the highest bride price at fifty shekels for a woman who has been violated, Jacob's offer for Rachel was generous (Wenham, *Genesis 16–50,* p. 235).

Marrying a cousin on the mother's side is a cross-cousin marriage, since the children come from siblings of the opposite sex. Such marriages are common with those who prefer marriages among close relatives, for the wife comes from outside the tribal unit (Hamilton, *Genesis: Chapters 18–50,* p. 234).

§40 The Birth of Jacob's Children (Gen. 29:31–30:24)

This account reports the births of twelve children to Jacob. Each one is named according to the aspiration of the mother. The wordplays made with the children's names, virtually impossible to capture in English, are free and innovative. It is noteworthy that each mother also praises God for his grace through these names. None of the names of the children correlates with the destiny of the later tribes; this fact attests to the antiquity of this narrative.

The narrative is organized according to the order of the births. Four sons are born to Leah (29:31–35), the two handmaids each bear two sons (30:1–13), Leah bears two sons and a daughter (30:14–21), and Rachel finally gives birth to a son (30:22–24).

29:31–35 / **When** Yahweh **saw that Leah was not loved** as much as Rachel, he allows her to conceive. The phrase "God saw" means that, having observed Leah's deplorable position in the family, God acted to comfort her. In those days fertility and infertility were thought to be caused by God. God blessed Leah, and she gave birth to Jacob's first four sons (20:17–18). God was fulfilling the promise to Abraham of numerous offspring (12:2–3).

Leah **named** her first son **Reuben,** meaning "see, a son." With this name she expressed her joy at God's having looked on her **misery** caused by her husband's not loving her. Since she had given Jacob his firstborn son, Leah hoped that he would **love** her **now.** But his attitude did not change. Leah then bore a second son and **named him Simeon,** "one who hears," meaning that God had **heard that** she was **not loved.** The verb "heard" implies that she had been lamenting to God about Jacob's attitude toward her. Leah **again conceived** and bore a third son. **She named** him **Levi** (*lewi,* from the root *lawah,* "be joined to") as an expression of her longing that her **husband . . . become attached to** (*lawah*) her. Again she **conceived** and bore **a son.** This child she **named Judah,** meaning "praise." She looked beyond the distress caused by Jacob's lack of affection and focused on God's fulfilling her desire for children.

With these names Leah revealed her devotion to God, praising God for honoring her with these children. Suddenly Leah's fertility ceased. The ancients interpreted such a change to be the result of God's closing her womb. Two explanations are possible: Leah had become infertile, or Jacob no longer slept with her.

30:1–8 / Distraught at her own infertility and jealous of Leah's fertility, Rachel lashed out at Jacob, demanding that he give her children lest she die. Jacob responded curtly by asking her if he were God with the ability to make her pregnant. Feeling worthless, Rachel decided to provide Jacob with **Bilhah,** her **maidservant,** as a surrogate, in order to **build** her own **family.** Jacob loved Rachel so much that he agreed to her plan without objection. With the words "she shall bear on my knees," rendered in the NIV "she can bear children for me," Rachel asserted that the children borne by Bilhah would be hers (v. 3). Bilhah **bore . . . a son** straightaway. Rachel **named him Dan,** "judge, vindicate," confident that **God** had **vindicated** her. She also said that God had **listened to** her **plea.** This statement shows that she had been lamenting to God as well as complaining to Jacob about the lack of children. Moreover, her naming the child meant that he was legally her son. Bilhah **bore Jacob a second son** whom Rachel **named Naphtali.** The meaning of this name is not clear; possibly it means "I have fought well," signifying Rachel's exclamation of victory over her sister. While polygamy was not forbidden in ancient Israel, it was never romanticized, not even in the family of the patriarch who gave the nation its name. In Scripture, most polygamous families experience deep, bitter conflicts.

30:9–13 / Bilhah's fertility eased Rachel's distress at her own barrenness for a while, but the rivalry between the sisters intensified. No longer fertile, Leah elevated her handmaid **Zilpah** to be a surrogate. Zilpah immediately conceived and bore **Jacob a son.** Leah **named him Gad,** "luck, fortune," in recognition of her **good fortune. Zilpah bore . . . a second son,** and Leah **named him Asher,** "happy," for the increase in her happiness and esteem. These names give further evidence that the center of her life was her children, not Jacob.

30:14–21 / Despite having children by Bilhah, Rachel continued to long for her own children. One day during wheat harvest (May–June), **Reuben . . . brought** home some **mandrakes,** which were symbols of fertility, **to his mother.** It was unusual to find these pleasant-smelling flowers at this time of the year. Because of her great longing for a child, Rachel, humbling herself, politely asked Leah for some of the mandrakes in the hope that they might help her conceive. Her request sparked a caustic complaint from Leah: Did Rachel, who had taken her husband, wish to take her son's mandrakes? Exploiting Rachel's desire for children, Leah made a deal with her sister. She would give her the mandrakes in exchange for Jacob's sleeping with her that night.

That evening **when Jacob came in from the fields,** Leah met him and informed him that she had **hired** his favor for the night **with** her **son's mandrakes.** Jacob obliged her. Although Rachel had acquired an aphrodisiac from her sister, it was Leah who **became pregnant.** Refusing to be manipulated, God opened Leah's womb, not Rachel's. She **named** her fifth child **Issachar,** "hired." In her view **God** had **rewarded** her. Afterward she **bore** another **son** and **named him Zebulun.** The meaning of this name is uncertain; it is apparently related by sound to *zbd* ("endure"). Leah thereby praised God for giving her a precious gift and expressed her hopes that Jacob would **treat** her **with honor.** Some time later she bore **a daughter,** and she **named her Dinah,** "judgment or vindication." The text contains no wordplay on her name. In all, Leah bore Jacob seven children.

30:22–24 / At last God honored Rachel by remembering her. The wording **God remembered** means that God acted on her behalf in light of past commitments. She therefore conceived and **gave birth to a son.** She was overjoyed that **God** had **taken away** her **disgrace.** In the hope and anticipation of more children, Rachel **named** her first son **Joseph,** "add," possibly a short form for **May** Yahweh **add . . . another son.**

Additional Notes §40

29:32 / Leah's acclamation "Yahweh has seen my misery" (*ra'ah yhwh be'onyi*) contains the consonants of the name Reuben (*re'uben*), recalling her acclamation.

29:35 / Judah (*yehudah*) may be a shortened form of a name with a divine element. A. Millard ("The Meaning of the Name Judah," *ZAW* 86 [1974], pp. 216–18) suggests Jehudael (*yehude'el*), "may God be praised." The name Jew derives from his name.

30:14 / Mandrakes have large leaves, violet flowers, and yellow fruit. While ripening, the fruit gives off a strong, distinct smell. The ancients thought that mandrakes had aphrodisiac powers, possibly because the roots resemble the male genitals or because the plant's name, *duda'im,* is similar to Hb. *dod* ("love").

30:18 / There is a variety of explanations for the name Issachar. Possibly it comes from the phrase *yesh sakar* ("there is a reward"). Sarna (*Genesis,* p. 210) traces the original back to *yashaskir* ("may he grant favor/reward"). Another proposal takes it from *'ish sakar* ("a man of hire").

30:24 / Joseph's name comes from either *'asap* ("take away") or *yosep* ("add"). With the former meaning Rachel's shame was taken away; with the latter meaning Rachel expressed her hope for additional children. Sarna believes that both meanings are intended (*Genesis,* p. 210).

§41 The Increase in Jacob's Flocks (Gen. 30:25–43)

In this account Jacob negotiates his wages (30:25–36) and breeds the flocks to his advantage (30:37–43).

30:25–28 / At the end of the fourteen years of labor, Jacob sought Laban's permission to return to Canaan with his **wives and children.** His approach implies that Laban continued to have authority over his daughters' departure from his household. Laban, however, entreated Jacob to **stay** on with him, claiming to have **learned by divination** that his prosperity was the result of Yahweh's blessing him for Jacob's sake (cf. 12:3). The reference to divination may be figurative or literal, but Laban affirmed that the gods had confirmed Jacob's role in his increasing wealth. In a show of apparent magnanimity, he invited Jacob to set his own **wages.** Nevertheless, the following negotiations indicate that Laban sought to keep Jacob on as a hired shepherd, not as a son-in-law.

30:29–43 / Jacob tried to make Laban more inclined to accept what he would propose by stressing how hard he had worked for him and how **greatly** his master's flocks had **increased** under his shepherding. He also pointed out that the extraordinary increase of Laban's flocks was a result of Yahweh's blessing on what his son-in-law was doing. Then he asked what he could do to provide for his **own household.** Taking this question as Jacob's way of asking for a gift, Laban wanted to know what he could give him. Jacob replied that he was not asking for a gift. He would continue on as a shepherd if he could do **one thing,** that is, build his own flocks. The following transaction is described so elliptically that it is necessary to reconstruct what took place. Jacob proposed that he be permitted to **go through all** the **flocks** that day and **remove . . . every speckled or spotted sheep, every dark-colored lamb and every spotted or speckled goat** for his **wages.** Presumably he wanted these members of the flock for breeding more multicolored kids and dark lambs that would then become members of his own flock. Jacob reassured Laban that he could trust him. Any goat in his flock that was not variegated in color and any lamb that was not dark Laban could consider to be stolen from his flocks. That meant Laban could easily get compensation. In the Code of Hammurabi (§69), compensation for stealing a ewe or a ram was six sheep.

These conditions Jacob put forth greatly favored Laban. No wonder he agreed. One of them proceeded to separate out of the flock the multicolored animals, although it is not clear which one did this. However, Laban had the mottled animals taken away, **a three-day journey,** so that Jacob had no chance of using any of them in breeding. Since a flock consisted primarily of white sheep and dark brown or black goats, Laban knew that he had made Jacob's task of building a multicolored flock from sheep and goats of a single color almost impossible—or so he thought. It appears that Laban had again tricked Jacob after the wages had been agreed upon (see 31:7). That is, Jacob had expected to use those animals in breeding his own flocks. Furthermore, Laban anticipated that Jacob's share would be further reduced when at the annual accounting he had to make good any losses suffered during the year out of his own flock (see Exod. 22:12). If things went as he expected, Jacob would become so indebted to Laban over the years that he would end up as one of his permanent shepherds. Ancient records attest that shepherds were often compelled to seek such a course (M. Morrison, "The Jacob and Laban Narrative in Light of Near Eastern Sources," *BA* 86 [1983], p. 161).

From the sheep and goats under his control, however, Jacob was able to breed for himself a sturdy flock of streaked, speckled, or spotted goats and dark-colored sheep, for he had discovered breeding methods for producing such offspring from single-colored animals. The text describes one method he used. He **took fresh-cut branches from poplar, almond and plane trees and made white stripes on them by peeling the bark and exposing the white inner wood.** He set these branches **in the watering troughs** so that females in heat mated in front of them; their offspring were variegated or colored. His methods appear to be close to magic, but there is not sufficient information to understand precisely what Jacob was doing. Apparently he was practicing a type of breeding that allowed the recessive genes to emerge in the healthiest animals. His skill at inducing the strongest females to bear **streaked or speckled or spotted** young caused his own flock to grow much more rapidly than did Laban's. He let the weaker animals that were part of Laban's fold breed naturally.

Contrary to what Laban had expected, Jacob **grew exceedingly prosperous.** "Grow prosperous" *(parats)* is the very term Yahweh used in his promise to Jacob at Bethel in saying that he would "spread out" in all directions (Hamilton, *Genesis: Chapters 18–50*, p. 284). The increase of his flocks at Haran was a foretaste of the fulfillment of God's promise that he would experience in the promised land. From his increasing wealth Jacob was able to acquire **maidservants and menservants, and camels and donkeys.** The deceiver who had been deceived was now besting the person who had deceived him by strictly adhering to the terms of their contract; the irony of Jacob's success is rich.

Additional Notes §41

30:27 / Laban's concession that he had prospered because God was blessing Jacob bears witness to God's fulfilling his promise to Abraham that those who blessed him would be blessed (12:3). Laban had been good to Jacob by providing him wives.

Divination is employed to learn about the future, not the past. Therefore, many propose that there is a second root *nikhesh* in Hb., cognate to Akk. *nakhashu* ("prosper, thrive"), with the meaning that Laban had become rich because of God's blessing on Jacob.

30:40 / This verse may describe producing dark sheep from white ones while earlier verses describe the breeding of goats. Jacob's method of breeding is unclear. A suggestion is that he had the white sheep look at Laban's dark goats while they were mating.

§42 Jacob Departs from Laban's House (Gen. 31:1–55)

Four scenes make up this account, in which Jacob prepares to leave Laban's house (vv. 1–16); Jacob's family flees (vv. 17–24), Laban confronts Jacob (vv. 25–42), and Laban and Jacob make a covenant (vv. 43–55).

31:1–3 / Jacob became aware that **Laban's sons** were disgruntled with him, complaining that he had **gained** much **wealth** at their father's expense. They claimed that he had **taken everything** that their **father owned.** Jacob also **noticed that Laban's attitude toward him** had become more unfavorable. Yahweh used these circumstances to motivate Jacob to leave Laban's household and return to Canaan. Then one day Yahweh told Jacob, **Go back to the land of your fathers.** With these instructions Yahweh gave him the greatest promise, the promise of his presence (28:15). God's instructions to Jacob to leave Haran are similar to his command to Abraham to leave that vicinity (12:1–3).

31:4–13 / In response to Yahweh's instructions, Jacob asked **Rachel and Leah** to join him in **the fields.** There he could speak with them about his plans without fear of being overheard or of arousing Laban's suspicion. He was not sure whether his wives would leave their father's house. Such a step was not only against local custom, but also these women had never lived anywhere else. The fact that Jacob conversed with his wives rather than telling them that they were going to go back to Canaan is evidence that custom required daughters to have their father's permission before leaving.

Jacob introduced the issue to his wives by recounting how their **father's attitude** had turned against him. By contrast, **the God of** his **father** had **been with** him, showing him favor. Jacob thus set a choice before them. They could remain under their father, who was making life hard for their husband. Or they could go to live in the land of his father Isaac, who served the God who had protected Jacob from Laban's wiles. He pointed out how arduously he had worked for their father, yet Laban had tried to cheat Jacob **by changing** his **wages ten times.** "Ten" is a round number for many times. If Laban agreed that Jacob was to receive the **speckled** members of the flock as his wages, **all the flocks gave birth to speckled young.** If he changed the agreement so that **the streaked ones** became his wages, **all the flocks bore streaked young.**

Archaeologists have found ancient contracts between an owner and a shepherd. These contracts were usually renegotiated annually. At the end of each season the owner made an accounting of the flock, and the shepherd received his pay. For the coming season a new contract was agreed on, sometimes several weeks later. Thus Laban probably changed the terms of Jacob's contract in an effort to get terms that would increase the size of his own flocks and limit the growth of Jacob's flock. Nevertheless, God blessed Jacob, and the size of his flocks continued to increase. There was a continual struggle of wit between these two men as they sought to outdo each other.

To convince his wives to leave their father's house, Jacob emphasized that he had survived their father's many devices only because **God** had **not allowed** Laban **to harm** him. God had increased his flock at the expense of their father's flocks. Jacob backed up this assertion by recounting **a dream** he had had during mating season. In that dream he saw **the male goats mating with** those that **were streaked, speckled or spotted.** His implication is that God had shown him how to breed the flocks so that the numbers in his flock would greatly increase. **The angel of God** assured him that the great increase in his flock was compensation for the unmerciful ways **Laban** was treating him. The angel identified himself as **the God of Bethel, where** Jacob had **anointed a pillar and . . . made a vow** (28:11–22). That angel now ordered him to **leave this land at once and go back to** his **native land.** God's promise to bring Jacob back to Canaan was about to be fulfilled. Jacob made it clear to his wives that in leaving their father and returning with him to Canaan they were obeying God.

31:14–16 / Quickly and wholeheartedly, **Rachel and Leah** agreed to depart with Jacob, for they too felt that Laban had mistreated them. Since these two intense rivals were in accord,

Laban's abuse of their husband must have extended to them as well. The sisters had begun to wonder if they still had **any share in the inheritance of** their **father's estate,** for he treated them as **foreigners.** Because Laban had consumed their bride price, nothing was left for either them or their children. His behavior made them feel as though their own father had sold them rather than building their families by getting them a husband. Their reasoning indicates that they valued Jacob's years of service to their father as their bride price. But Laban had never given them their share. Consequently, whatever **wealth God** had taken **from** their **father** in letting their husband build up his flocks while in service to their father was rightfully theirs and their children's.

31:17–21 / Since his wives agreed with his plan, Jacob departed immediately, taking all the members of his family, the **livestock,** and **all the goods he had accumulated in Paddan Aram.** This was an opportune moment for leaving, since **Laban had gone to shear** the **sheep.** That strenuous task required numerous laborers and took several days. Jacob knew that it would be some time before his departure would be detected. In addition, by leaving at the end of the annual contract, he was not under any legal obligations to Laban.

Rachel took advantage of her father's absence to steal the **household gods,** which were small household statues. These gods were thought to bring good fortune and fertility as well as protection during a journey. The one in possession of the family gods was usually the leader in the family and received a larger share of the inheritance, but it is doubtful that these last two factors motivated Rachel. She might have taken them as partial compensation for the losses she had suffered at the hands of Laban, or she might have wanted to have with her some tangible bond with her family as well as the protection of these gods on the journey. In any case this detail is emphasized, for it sets the stage for the final, climactic confrontation between Laban and Jacob.

The narrator comments on Jacob's sudden departure by saying that he **deceived Laban the Aramean by not telling him he was running away.** In this line "deceive," literally "stole the heart" *(ganab 'et-leb),* captures how grievously Jacob broke ancient custom in leaving his father-in-law's home in such a secretive manner. A double offense had been committed against Laban: Rachel had stolen his gods, and Jacob had stolen his heart by taking his daughters. The narrator captures the irony of Jacob's clandestine departure. The deceiver by name must escape the heavy hand of a skilled deceiver in a deceptive way.

31:22–24 / Three days later, Laban was informed that **Jacob had fled.** Immediately he gathered **his relatives** and **pursued Jacob.** After **seven days,** possibly a symbolic number for several days, Laban caught up with Jacob **in the hill country of Gilead,** close to four hundred miles away—a journey of more than seven days for one driving small herds. The night before Laban overtook Jacob, God warned Laban **in a dream,** restricting any hostile action he might be planning. Burning with anger, Laban was intent on pressing heavy charges against Jacob, but God continued to protect Jacob, the heir of the promise, from Laban's aggression.

31:25–30 / Laban and Jacob, the two master deceivers, met face to face. Although neither trusted the other, each knew that he had benefited greatly from their relationship. Laban began with a hard charge, accusing Jacob of having **deceived** him by carrying off his **daughters like captives in war.** Speaking as a heartbroken father in order to win the sympathy of the relatives who were looking on, he complained that Jacob's inconsiderate, deceptive action had deprived him of giving a great, joyful feast for sending off his grandchildren and daughters. He charged Jacob with having **done a foolish thing,** a harsh indictment in that culture. Laban overplayed his outrage, however, witnessing to his own incrimination.

To add force to his accusations Laban asserted that he had **the power to harm** Jacob for contemptuous disregard of family customs. Nevertheless, he admitted that the night before he had been restrained in venting his anger by a warning from **the God of** Jacob's **father,** telling him neither to harm nor to bless Jacob. Only God had more authority than Laban in this family matter. Jacob learned from this revelation that Laban's hostile intent had been tempered and that God was protecting him. Since God had restricted him from dealing with Jacob for leaving his household, Laban accused Jacob of stealing his **gods.** The limitations God had put on Laban did not preclude his exacting compensation for an outright theft by anyone in Jacob's family. Laban was therefore determined to cause Jacob trouble and recover his gods.

The fervor of Laban's desire for getting his gods back stands in stark contrast to his poor treatment of his daughters. These gods had to do with the identity and power of the family, but in valuing the symbols of the family more than members of the family, Laban lost his relationship with his daughters and their children.

31:31–32 / **Jacob answered** Laban's charges forthrightly. To the charge of having stolen Laban's heart he admitted that his hasty departure had violated family custom. Nevertheless, he explained that he had taken this course out of fear that Laban **would take** his wives **away from** him **by force** if he had asked permission for all of them to leave for Canaan. In Jacob's mind, Laban's pattern of behavior had preempted the basis of his claim that he would have given them a joyful send-off. Next, responding to the charge of having stolen his gods, Jacob swore an oath of death against anyone who was found to be in possession of these gods. In this way he staunchly asserted his innocence. His oath indicated that he too viewed the theft as a punishable crime. Knowing that he had taken nothing, Jacob gave Laban permission to search all of his property and to **take** anything he found that belonged to him. The writer adds an editorial comment to heighten the suspense; **Jacob did not know that** his beloved wife **Rachel had stolen the gods.** Would both Laban and Jacob suffer loss with the discovery that Rachel had these gods?

31:33–35 / Laban searched methodically, going from **Jacob's tent** to **Leah's** and then to **the tent of the two maidservants,** but he **found nothing.** The moment of potential discovery arrived as he **entered Rachel's tent.** Only now does the reader learn that Rachel had hidden **the household gods** in **her camel's saddle and was sitting on them.** After Laban had gone through everything in her tent without finding anything, Rachel politely informed him that she was not able to **stand up in** his **presence** since it was the time of her **period.** Her ruse kept Laban from finding the gods. Ancient Israelites would have sensed how strongly the narrative scorns these idols, since for them everything that came in contact with a woman during her period became polluted (Lev. 15:19–23).

31:36–37 / Gaining confidence that Laban was not going to find anything, Jacob vented his anger by pressing his legal advantage. He asked what was his **crime** and what was his **sin,** or more accurately his "offense," that Laban had hunted him **down.** Aware that Laban's search had been futile, Jacob boldly challenged Laban to place whatever he had found in public view so

that their **relatives** might serve as a jury and render a legal decision about the validity of Laban's accusations. In taking this approach Jacob altered Laban's stature from head of the family to
that of a plaintiff before the council (C. Mabee, "Jacob and Laban:
The Structure of Judicial Proceedings [Genesis xxx 25–42]," *VT* 30
[1980], p. 202).

31:38–42 / Seeing Laban's frustration, Jacob delivered
an apology to exonerate himself from having violated family custom in leaving Laban's house without his permission. In this apology he recounted Laban's hard demands and his own faithful
integrity and service to his father-in-law. **For twenty years** he had
shepherded Laban's flocks so skillfully that they had **not miscar-
ried.** He has not taken any **rams from** Laban's **flock** for food.
When any member of the flock was **torn by wild beasts,** Jacob
himself **bore the loss,** even when standard practice did not hold a
shepherd accountable for losses beyond his control. For example,
when members of the flock were torn by wild animals, a shepherd
presented the remnants as proof of the nature of the loss, clearing
himself of any responsibility. Furthermore, a shepherd was accountable for the theft of members of the flock during the day but
not at night, based on the principle that what took place at night
was beyond his control. Laban, however, **demanded payment** for
every lost sheep regardless if the theft took place during the
day or night (Exod. 22:9–13). Jacob added that he had cared for
Laban's flocks during the burning **heat** of the day and the biting
cold at night. He had spent many sleepless nights under harsh
conditions for Laban's benefit. This was how he had worked for
fourteen years for the privilege of marrying his two daughters
and **six years** to build up his own flock. During those years Laban
had changed his wages many times (vv. 6–8). If Laban had his
way, he would have left his household without anything; but his
God, **the God of** his **father,** was watching out for him. Jacob identified God as **the God of Abraham and the Fear of Isaac.** He reminded Laban that this very God had come to him the night
before and made him fearful by rebuking him for Jacob's sake.
Jacob concluded his apology powerfully with the assertion that
God was on his side.

31:43–50 / Laban contradicted Jacob, asserting, **All you
see is mine.** Despite this claim, Laban had lost legally. He could
not prove that Jacob had stolen his gods, and Jacob had given a
good defense for departing so secretly from his house. Laban,

therefore, responded by proposing that their grievances be settled by making a covenant. His patronizing attitude is galling, as he failed to recognize Jacob's role in the increase of his own flocks or his own obligations to Jacob, either as his servant or as his son-in-law. Then Laban conceded his present helplessness with a rhetorical question about what he could do with his daughters and their children. By agreeing to enter into covenant with Jacob, Laban admitted defeat.

Striving to save face, however, Laban proposed to Jacob that they **make a covenant** to delimit the issues between them. Laban wanted to overcome his embarrassment at not being able to substantiate the charges he had made against Jacob. Now he sought to establish a defined border between his clan and Jacob's and to set certain conditions for the protection of his daughters. Laban also appears to have begun to fear Jacob, perhaps on account of Jacob's increasing wealth and power and the possibility that someone from Jacob's family would return to Haran with the family gods and make a claim against his own household, as the use of the term "harm" suggests (v. 52). This pact ended the contact between Abraham's offspring and his father's house in Haran. No one else of Abraham's seed would travel to that area to take a wife.

The report of this covenant between Laban and Jacob is difficult to unravel because it is hard to sort out the duplicate details: two witnesses, two place names, two names for God, two meals, and two purposes, that is, a guarantee of Jacob's protecting the status of Laban's daughters in his house and a boundary marker. These elements in pairs may be understood either as the conflation of two sources or as a rhetorical style for emphasis. Sarna (*Genesis*, p. 221) points out that the twofold nature of the account was to define Jacob's complete separation from Laban and to acknowledge that from this point forward he was a patriarch on the same level as Laban. This covenant was thus both a family agreement and a boundary agreement.

Jacob expressed his agreement by taking **a stone and** setting **it up as a pillar** as was his custom (28:11, 18; 35:14, 20). He also had his relatives **gather some stones.** Their involvement indicates that this covenant was between the clans represented by Laban and Jacob. Eating together beside the heap, the parties solidified the covenant. Each party named the pile of stones "a witness heap" in his own language: **Jegar Sahadutha** (Aramaic) and **Galeed** (Hebrew). Laban explained that the stones were to serve as **a witness**

between them. When they were apart, Yahweh was to **keep watch between** them. Laban added the obligation that Jacob was never to **mistreat** his **daughters** or **take any** other **wives** under the threat that God was constantly **a witness** against him. Such a prohibition is found frequently in marriage contracts from the ancient Near East. Here Laban completed the marriage agreement by formalizing the marriage of his daughters (Morrison, "The Jacob and Laban Narrative," p. 163).

31:51–53 / Laban made an additional statement about the purpose of these stones. They were to be both **a witness** of this covenant and a boundary marker. Neither party was to **go past** them in order **to harm** the other party. Laban confirmed the purpose of these stones with an oath in the name of the God of Terah's two sons, **the God of Abraham and the God of Nahor.** His recognition of more than one god gives evidence of his polytheistic orientation; **Jacob** took his own **oath in the name of the Fear of his father Isaac.** This is the only reference in Genesis to God as Holy, being experienced as Fear or Dread *(pakhad).* Jacob swore by this name in recognition that the God of his father had appeared to Laban the night before Laban met up with him, putting fear in Laban's heart so that Laban would not harm him (v. 42). Jacob knew that his only assurance that Laban would keep the terms of this covenant was Laban's dread of this powerful God.

31:54–55 / Jacob then **offered a sacrifice there in the hill country** to provide **his relatives a** festive **meal,** celebrating the solidarity of his family, now fully and officially on its own. All parties **spent the night** in that place.

Early the next morning Laban arose and bid proper farewell to **his grandchildren and his daughters** by kissing them and by pronouncing a blessing on them. In contrast to his greeting Jacob with a kiss when he had arrived in Haran (29:13), Laban departed with no such display of affection toward his son-in-law.

Additional Notes §42

31:15 / The reference to consuming money occurs in texts from Nuzu that describe a father's holding back part of the dowry

(Selman, "Comparative Customs," pp. 122–23). Because Jacob did not pay any money as the bridal price for either of Laban's daughters, his wives considered Jacob's years of labor to have had a certain monetary value. They felt that their father was obligated to provide them a dowry, recognizing their status and consummating the marriage legally.

31:33 / Von Rad (*Genesis,* p. 309) points out that the determined way that the mighty Laban searched for his powerless images makes him look like a buffoon. To a monotheist this scene is rich in irony.

31:35 / The standards of cultic purity at this early period are unknown. In any case, the Israelites hearing this story after the revelation of Sinai would be amused, for Rachel, in feigning menstruation, was in actuality ridiculing these gods, treating them as worthless (Lev. 15:19–23).

31:42 / Here and in v. 53 the unusual divine name "Fear of Isaac" occurs. Since God's holiness is not stressed in Gen., the use of such a name for God is striking. Working with W. F. Albright's suggestion that the Hb. means "kinsman of Isaac" (*From the Stone Age to Christianity* [2d ed.; Baltimore: John Hopkins, 1957], p. 248), M. Malul ("More on *pakhad yitskhaq* [Genesis xxxi 42, 53] and the Oath by the Thigh," *VT* 35 [1985], pp. 194–96), posits that Hb. *pakhad* comes from an Aram. root *p-kh-d* ("thigh"), which may also be used to symbolize either one's genitals or posterity or family. This title then coincides with the oaths taken in which a hand is placed under the thigh (24:9; 47:29–31). The difficulty with this suggestion is that *pakhad* occurs in a context where a title or an epithet of God is expected. Also, "fear" or "dread" has the advantage of correlating with the limitations God placed on the powerful Laban (v. 24).

31:47 / There is a wordplay on the terms "heap" (*gal*) and Galeed (*gal'ed,* "mound of witnesses").

31:48 / It is possible that there were two stone piles. Laban constructed a heap of stones, and Jacob erected a pillar. Each pile of stones had its own name, Galeed and Mizpah.

31:49 / There is a paronomasia on Mizpah (*mitspah,* "watch post, lookout") and the verb *yitsep* ("may he watch"). Apparently the place had a compound name Mizpah Gilead, i.e., Mizpah in Gilead (M. Ottosson, *Gilead: Tradition and History* [trans. J. Gray; Lund: GWK Gleerup, 1969], pp. 42–47).

§43 Jacob's Enigmatic Wrestling Match
(Gen. 32:1–32)

Before Jacob's wrestling match (vv. 24–30), he has a vision of angels at Mahanaim (vv. 1–2). On the surface this brief report seems to be disjunctive. Nevertheless, several terms tie these two passages into the flow of the Jacob narrative. Jacob meets the angels or messengers of God *(mal'ake 'elohim)*, and he sends "messengers" *(mal'akim)* to meet Esau. There is a play on "camp" *(makhaneh;* 32:2, 8, 10, 21) and "gift" *(minkhah;* 32:13, 20; 33:8, 10). Two terms for grace reverberate the sounds from these last two words: *khanan* ("give graciously," 33:5) and *hen* ("favor," 33:8, 10). Throughout this story "face" *(panim)* is a key term (32:19–20, 30; 33:10; also used in a preposition in 32:17; 33:3, 14). It conveys Jacob's deep anxiety as he anticipates seeing Esau's face. After the wrestling match Jacob claims to have seen God face to face; therefore he names that place Peniel ("face of God," 32:30). Then, seeking to appease Esau (lit. "soothe his countenance" [face]), he gives him an enormous gift so that Esau might receive him honorably (lit. "lift his face," 32:20). There is also a wordplay involving the three terms "wrestle" *(ye'abeq),* "Jacob" *(ya'aqob),* and "Jabbok" *(yabbok).* Another wordplay is with the term "cross over" *('abar).* After his camp has crossed over (32:22), Jacob causes his family and possessions to "cross over" the ford or crossing *(ma'abar)* of the Jabbok (v. 23). Later Jacob himself "crosses over" from Peniel (v. 31). When Esau arrives, Jacob "crosses over" in front of his family to meet Esau first (33:3).

In the three parts of this passage, angels appear to Jacob (vv. 1–2), Jacob makes elaborate preparations to meet Esau (vv. 3–23), and Jacob wrestles with a "man" (vv. 24–32). The second part contains the longest prayer in Genesis as Jacob earnestly prays for God's help (vv. 9–12).

32:1–2 / Approaching Canaan, Jacob was full of anxiety at the prospect of meeting Esau. At this critical moment Jacob received a special visitation from God: **the angels of God met him.** He then **named** that place **Mahanaim,** meaning "two camps." The term suggests a temporary encampment used by angels as they went about doing God's bidding on earth. "Two camps" may mean that the angels were in two camps, or it could refer to the angels' camp and Jacob's camp. Because Jacob was traveling at God's instruction (31:11–13), God encouraged him by revealing to him the heavenly army that accompanied him on his journey (Ps. 34:7). As in the visitation from God he had experienced at Bethel (ch. 28), Jacob saw angels and named the place.

32:3–5 / Jacob next sought to make contact with his brother Esau, who had settled **in the land of Seir** *(se'ir),* better known by the wider geographical term **Edom** *('edom).* These place names recall the day when Esau, the hairy one *(se'ir),* sold his birthright for some red pottage *('adom;* 25:30). Although Esau now lived far from central Canaan, Jacob feared that Esau was still so angry at him that on learning of Jacob's return he would seek retaliation for the losses of the birthright and the patriarchal blessing. To mollify Esau, Jacob **sent messengers ahead of him,** instructing them to tell Esau about his sojourn **with Laban** and his wealth. In these instructions Jacob called his brother his **master,** indicating that he now looked on his brother with respectful deference. By mentioning his wealth, he informed Esau that he no longer had any desire for or need of anything that was his brother's. He might also have been indicating that he was able to pay any reparation Esau might demand.

32:6–8 / These messengers returned much sooner than Jacob anticipated. They reported that Esau was approaching with **four hundred men.** This report caught Jacob by surprise and raised his fears. Having no clue as to Esau's intent, Jacob was troubled by wild thoughts of what his brother intended to do. Therefore, he divided his company—**people . . . , and the flocks and herds and camels—into two groups.** His action was in accord with what he saw at Mahanaim (v. 2). Jacob sought to make it possible for at least some of his group to escape an attack from Esau.

32:9–12 / Jacob then prayed earnestly for God's help. He addressed God using three names: **God of my father Abraham, God of my father Isaac,** Yahweh. These names God used for himself when he spoke to Jacob in the dream at Bethel, when he was fleeing from Esau (28:13). In the patriarchal period God was best known as the God of one's fathers. At the outset of his prayer Jacob, the bargainer, reminded God of two things: because he was following God's orders, he now faced this crisis; and God had promised to **make** him **prosper.** Jacob then praised God for **the kindness and faithfulness** shown to him, humbly acknowledging that he was unworthy of God's blessing. Specifically he praised God for the abundance of his children and flocks. When he had left Canaan he had only his **staff,** but on his return he possessed so much that they made up **two** camps. Humbly and devoutly Jacob identified himself as God's **servant.** That God was directing such an insignificant person gives evidence that he is accomplishing his design away from the power structures of the great civilizations. Next Jacob simply and frankly asked God to **save** him **from** Esau's power as he mentioned his fear of an attack from his brother. This is the basic pattern of prayer found in Scripture, the call for deliverance from difficult or oppressive circumstances. Jacob strengthened his petition by recounting to God the promises of prosperity and descendants that God had given him in terms of the Abrahamic blessing. He wanted to impress on God that the divine purposes were at stake in his meeting with Esau.

32:13–21 / Having resolved to spend **the night** in that place, Jacob prepared an enormous **gift for his brother Esau: two hundred female goats and twenty male goats, two hundred ewes and twenty rams, thirty female camels with their young, forty cows and ten bulls, twenty female donkeys and ten male donkeys.** The size of this gift demonstrates that Jacob acknowledged that he had inflicted great damages on Esau by having usurped the birthright and the blessing. Apportioning these animals into several companies under **the care of his servants,** he ordered them to **go ahead** of him, keeping **some space between the herds.** The companies were to station themselves at different locations along the road on which Esau was approaching. When Esau arrived at a particular station, Jacob's servant was to tell him that these were Jacob's flocks and that they were **a gift** for him. Each servant was to address Esau as **lord** and to refer to Jacob as **servant.** Jacob sought to **pacify** Esau by having him receive all these gifts, accompanied by words of Jacob's deference, in several stages. He hoped the repetition would soften Esau's anger so that he would **receive** his younger brother. The text reads literally, "I will see his face, and perhaps he will lift up my face" *(nasa' panim).* "Face" captures the critical issue. If the anger was removed from

Esau's face, Jacob hoped that he might see his brother's face and that Esau would look on his face with respect. Intent on meeting Esau face to face as he owned up to his past vile behavior, Jacob resolved not to flee, hide, or trick his brother. To prepare himself for the meeting Jacob stayed behind, spending **the night in the camp.**

32:22–23 / Deeply troubled and unable to sleep, Jacob **got up** and forded his family and remaining **possessions** across **the Jabbok.** There are two possible reasons for his doing this after dark. The next morning he did not want to be involved with getting his family across the Jabbok when Esau arrived. Or perhaps he had a strong inner need to spend the night alone in meditation and prayer.

32:24–28 / **Jacob was left alone,** feeling safe from attack during the night. But before dealing with Esau, Jacob had to deal with God. Divine encounters frame Jacob's time away from Canaan. When Jacob left Canaan, God appeared to him at Bethel, promising to be with him (28:10–22). Now before he reentered Canaan, God met him again. Whereas in the first encounter Jacob had a euphoric dream, this time he had to wrestle long and hard with "a man" before winning a divine blessing. In God's judgment Jacob's struggle was against his own deceptive, cunning, self-serving ways rather than against Esau. What took place that night would determine the character of Jacob's meeting with Esau. While Jacob prayed for God's help, **a man wrestled with him till daybreak.** The description of this wrestling match is intentionally enigmatic. The reader never finds out the identity of the wrestler. Furthermore, the ambiguous use of the pronouns in the Hebrew text deliberately conceals the course of the fight so that the reader feels with Jacob the deep mystery of his struggle with an ominous foe. Whose thigh was injured? Who wanted to end the fight? Who asked for the blessing? Although we come to suspect that Jacob was struggling with a heavenly being, possibly the angel of Yahweh, the narrator identifies the opponent simply as "a man" to stress that Jacob was fighting a real opponent.

Throughout the night Jacob put up a fierce struggle. Neither wrestler was able to overpower the other. As dawn began to break, one of the wrestlers exerted a great effort in an attempt to end the match. That wrestler attacked the other's leg so hard that he **wrenched the socket of** his opponent's **hip.** Only later does it become clear that Jacob was wounded. Nevertheless Jacob held on, refusing to surrender.

Exhausted, the wrestlers turned to a verbal contest. The man pleaded with Jacob, **Let me go, for it is daybreak**; he did not want the light to reveal his identity. Taking advantage of his opponent's desire to depart, Jacob refused, saying he would not **let** him **go unless** he blessed him. The term "bless" means that Jacob sought some vital power, perhaps greater physical stamina so that he would prosper in Canaan or possibly the power of destiny that would guarantee success in dealing with Esau. In blessing him the heavenly being would speak words to direct Jacob's destiny for good. The opponent responded by asking for his **name. "Jacob," he answered.** In speaking his name, Jacob ("finagler") confessed that his disposition was to deceive others for personal gain. The wrestler responded that his **name** would **no longer be Jacob, but Israel, because** he had **struggled with God and with men and** had **overcome.** Israel means "God fights"; it may be emblematic for "you have fought with God." This account is vital for the people who bear the name Israel; it records that their identity was defined in a special encounter with God.

The changing of Jacob's name reveals the power this opponent had over Jacob as well as his heavenly role, for in giving him a new name he altered either his character or his destiny. As the narrative will reveal, the change for Jacob was a change of character. In the accounts that follow, Jacob never again resorts to deceit as the means to get his own way. Rather, he places his relationship with God above all personal gain. Jacob, the one who had deceived and used others, thus became the one who struggled with God until God molded him into the vessel he desired. The reference to his prevailing with men points to his prevailing over Laban and Esau.

His new name, however, does not shield Jacob from the obstacles and tragedies of life. He will continue to have dealings with people who deceive him, causing him great pain. The two most agonizing incidents are when his sons use circumcision as a ruse to slaughter the inhabitants of Shechem because of the rape of Dinah, forcing Jacob to leave the place where he had bought some land (ch. 34), and when his ten sons lead him to the false conclusion that Joseph, his favorite son, has been killed (ch. 37). Jacob bears these griefs rather than striking back at those who harm him.

The claim that Jacob won the wrestling match, as underscored by his name Israel, raises a troubling question. How could his foe declare that Jacob overcame in this struggle, since he suffered a disabling blow? The answer is threefold. First, Jacob fought until he persuaded "the man" to bless him. This blessing empowered the promises to Abraham with which Jacob had ended his prayer (v. 12). What he had taken from his father by deceit was now his by honorable struggle. If these promises were operative, Esau was powerless to harm his family, since Jacob's seed held that promise. Second, Jacob persisted in fighting until the man changed his name from one that implied a negative character trait to a glorious name with spiritual overtones. Third, Jacob saw God face to face (v. 30). Out of that meeting he gained confidence to face Esau. When Esau arrived, Jacob met him first rather than last as he had planned. By settling accounts with God Jacob won reconciliation with Esau. Jacob learned that his real struggle was with God, not with his brother.

32:29 / Gaining confidence, Jacob asked his opponent to tell him what his **name** was, desiring to match his opponent verbally as he had physically. To learn a person's name provides access to that person. Skillfully the wrestler avoided giving his name by asking why Jacob wanted to know it. With this question the heavenly being refused to make himself accessible to Jacob. Despite denying Jacob's request, he **blessed** him and departed. Brueggemann offers significant insight into this struggle: "Israel is not formed by success or shrewdness or land, but by an assault from God . . . Jacob is not consulted about his new identity. It is given, even imposed. When daylight comes . . . there remains only Israel . . . blessed and named. Israel is born in the combat where he had asked about God's name" (*Genesis*, pp. 269–70).

32:30 / Having seen **God face to face,** Jacob named that place **Peniel,** meaning "face of God." "Face to face" indicates that he had been in direct contact with God, not that he had looked on God's face. Jacob thereby acknowledged that his opponent was more than one of the heavenly messengers. In light of other divine-human encounters reported in the book of Genesis, this man most likely was "the angel of Yahweh" (16:7).

32:31–32 / As **the sun rose,** Jacob crossed the Jabbok and joined his family. Because of the blow inflicted during the wrestling bout, he walked with a limp. Ironically, having won a blessing from God, Jacob was weakened physically. In gaining position with God, he surrendered standing among people. Every day his limp reminded him that he was to rely on God rather than on his own conniving.

Several concrete details mark the dramatic change in Jacob's character: change of name, change in a physical trait, the naming of the place Peniel, and the initiation of a food regulation (W. Roth, "Structural Interpretations of 'Jacob at the Jabbok' [Genesis 32:22–32]," *BR* 22 [1977], p. 55). In memory of the wound Jacob suffered, **the Israelites do not eat the tendon attached to the socket of the hip,** that is, the sciatic muscle. Jacob's hip or thigh is closely identified with Jacob's offspring, who are those who come out of the thigh of Jacob (46:26: Exod. 1:5; S. Geller, "The Struggle at the Jabbok: The Uses of Enigma in a Biblical Narrative," *JANESCU* 14 [1982], p. 50). These tangible details anchor this mysterious event to reality; Jacob had a real encounter with a real celestial being. He was not just dreaming.

Additional Notes §43

32:1 / Similarly, Joshua saw angels before entering the promised land (Josh. 5:13–15).

32:2 / Mahanaim had an important role in Israel's history. After Saul's death, his son made this place the capital (2 Sam. 2:8). Later, during Absalom's revolt, David fled to this city and ruled from it for a short time (2 Sam. 17:24). Under Solomon it served as the seat of a district (1 Kgs. 4:14).

32:9 / This way of referring to God contrasted with that of Israel's neighbors, who referred to their gods in relationship to a place; e. g., Baal Ekron was Baal of the town Ekron.

32:22 / The Jabbok runs from the Transjordan plateau westward into the Jordan River. Dropping several thousand feet in a short distance, it cuts a deep gorge in the hillside.

32:28 / The meaning of "Israel" is popularly interpreted as "he fought with God." There is no scholarly consensus on the meaning of this name based on an exact etymology. If it is taken from the root *sarah* ("fight, contend"), a rare word in the OT, it means "God contends or fights." It is also possible to take it from either *sarar* ("rule," Hos. 12:4) or *sarah* ("rule"), to mean "God will rule" or "may God rule." Scholars have also offered numerous other explanations. One suggestion is that it may originally have been *Ishrael*, meaning "God is right"; the root then is *y-sh-r* ("be straight, right, just," O. Margalith, "On the Origin and Antiquity of the Name 'Israel,' " *ZAW* 102 [1990], pp. 225–37). Another suggestion is to take it from *s-r-y* or *y-s-r* ("cut" and by extension "judge"), to mean "God judges" (R. Coote, "The Meaning of the Name *Israel*," *HTR* 65 [1972], pp. 140–41).

Although in the Abraham narrative the text consistently uses the new names God gave Abraham and Sarah, such is not the case with Jacob. In the following narratives he is most often referred to as Jacob, not Israel. The crucial point is that his offspring become known as the people of Israel.

32:31 [MT 32] / MT has Penuel (a note in NIV), the more usual spelling of this place name (also Judg. 8:8–9 and in 1 Kgs. 12:25) instead of Peniel. The latter spelling may have been used in v. 30, for it captures the wordplay on God's face better.

32:32 / As is usual in cultic matters, this food prohibition has been greatly expanded to encompass the entire area around this nerve.

§44 The Reunion of Jacob and Esau (Gen. 33:1–16)

At last Jacob meets Esau face to face. The character of their meeting catches the audience off guard.

33:1–3 / Finally Jacob saw his brother **Esau coming with his four hundred men.** Wounded from the wrestling bout, he was powerless before Esau's entourage. To welcome Esau, Jacob had arranged his family, placing the mothers with their children and then ordering them according to their standing: first **the maidservants and their children,** next **Leah and her children,** and last **Rachel and Joseph.** This arrangement was not for self-protection as previously Jacob had done (32:7–8), but for receiving Esau as a prince. Emboldened by his victory with God, Jacob moved past his family to greet Esau, bowing **down to the ground seven times.** Ordinarily bowing once was sufficient, but, wishing to show complete deference to his brother as well as remorse for his deception, Jacob bowed seven times, the number symbolizing completeness.

33:4–7 / By contrast, **Esau ran to meet Jacob, embraced him . . . and kissed him.** Welcoming close relatives and friends with a kiss was a common practice throughout the Near East. The embrace caused deep, complex emotions to overflow. Both brothers wept. Their fear and anger dissolved in the flow of tears. **Then Esau** inquired about **the women and children.** Identifying himself as Esau's **servant** (also in v. 14) Jacob answered that these were **the children** whom **God** had **graciously given** him, acknowledging thereby that God had been with him in Paddan Aram. He then formally introduced them to Esau; each group came forward and respectfully bowed before Esau.

33:8–11 / **Esau asked** the meaning of **all** the **droves** of animals that he had passed. Jacob answered directly, admitting that they had been placed along the way in order that he might win his lord's **favor.** Relishing Jacob's deference (Jacob addresses him as lord also in vv. 13, 14 [twice], 15), Esau declined the gifts, saying that he had **plenty.** Among peoples of the Near East it was not proper to accept a large present without strongly protesting. Jacob countered by pressing him to **accept this gift.** "Accept" carries the idea that the gift be received for the purpose it was given. Jacob added that for him seeing Esau's **face** was **like seeing the face of God.** This statement shows that Jacob's struggle with "a man" had laid the foundations for resolving his alienation from Esau. Although he never saw the face of his divine opponent, Jacob saw God in the face of his brother. In the moment of reconciliation, Esau represented God to Jacob. Reconciliation is one of the fruits of the blessing Jacob had wrestled from his divine foe. That Esau did not mention the wrongs he had suffered at Jacob's hands confirmed his unconditional forgiveness of his brother.

Jacob **insisted** that Esau take these gifts, referring to them as a "blessing" (*berakah;* NIV "present"). With this term he made Esau aware that accepting them was compensation for his having stolen their father's blessing (27:27–29). Jacob sought to persuade him by stressing that this wealth came from God's graciousness to him. Esau therefore could take these gifts without any sense of depriving his brother. More significantly, in accepting the gifts Esau would affirm that God's blessing was on his brother's life and that God had intended the blessing of Abraham to go with Jacob. **Esau** yielded to Jacob's pressure and **accepted** the gifts. In this act Esau humbled himself, for he honored Jacob's desire and relinquished any claims he had against Jacob. This gift sealed a bond between them, a bond that had not existed in their youth.

33:12–16 / Enthusiastically Esau stated that both of them needed to resume their journey. He offered to **accompany** Jacob on his **way.** His men would go in front to provide Jacob protection as they traveled to Seir. He thus invited Jacob to live with him there. Jacob protested that the fast pace of Esau's company would be hard on his young **children** and **for the ewes and cows that** were **nursing their young.** Jacob, however, was headed for Canaan, not Seir. Possibly he was apprehensive that if they traveled together friction might arise between the two groups. Jacob therefore suggested that Esau **go on** his way, leaving him to travel at his own pace. Eventually he would meet him **in Seir.** Since there is no evidence that he ever planned to go to Seir, this comment is puzzling. Many scholars interpret it as another example of Jacob's use of deception. It is better understood, however, as a polite refusal of Esau's offer with both brothers realizing that Jacob would never make it to Seir. Nevertheless, Esau extended his invitation to his brother again, offering to **leave some of** his **men** to assist Jacob. But Jacob continued to demur. It was crucial for him to withstand Esau's friendly overtures in order that he might return to and settle in the land of Canaan in accordance with God's promises to Abraham. Realizing Jacob's determination to go his own way, Esau **started** out for **Seir.**

This reunion demonstrates remarkably that a desired outcome of making peace with God is to win reconciliation with a brother, even a brother deeply offended. When these two brothers parted, no boundary stone had to be erected, as was the case with Laban (31:51–54). While the two brothers had reconciled, they were not yet ready to establish a warm relationship. The only report of their meeting again is at the funeral of Isaac, their father (35:29).

Additional Note §44

33:4 / The narrative does not address the reason for Esau's conciliatory attitude. Although he did get very angry, there is no evidence that he bore grudges. More importantly for the narrator, the outcome of Jacob's struggle with the angel paved the way for reconciliation with Esau. Because Jacob had wrestled *('abaq)* with God (32:24–25), Esau embraced *(khibbeq)* him instead of attacking him. The similarity in the sound of the two Hb. words captures this connection (S. Geller, "The Struggle at the Jabbok," p. 42).

§45 Jacob Settles in Canaan and the Rape of Dinah (Gen. 33:17–34:31)

A number of years after Jacob settled in the vicinity of Shechem, a man named Shechem, the son of Hamor, rapes Dinah, Jacob's daughter. The approaches of the two parties to resolving this offense reveal the deep conflict between two different ways of life: shepherds in conflict with urban dwellers and worshipers of one God in conflict with polytheists. Several acrid terms in the story convey the brothers' outrage at Shechem's act of passion against their sister: violated (*'innah,* 34:2), defiled (*timme',* 34:5, 13, 27), a disgrace (*kherpah,* 34:14), and an act of folly (*nebalah;* 34:7; NIV "a disgraceful thing"). The last term is the strongest Hebrew word for folly; it describes bold, arrogant behavior against honor.

Several persuasive speeches distinguish this narrative. In chapter 34 Shechem presses Hamor, his father, to secure Dinah as his wife (v. 4). Hamor then negotiates with Jacob and his sons in order that Dinah might become Shechem's wife (vv. 8–10). At that meeting Shechem delivers an appeal to Jacob's sons (vv. 11–12), and Jacob's sons offer a detailed counterproposal (vv. 13–17). Hamor and Shechem move the local assembly to enter into agreement with Jacob's family (vv. 20–23). A sharp exchange between Jacob and his sons Simeon and Levi over the devastation of Shechem brings the narrative to a close (vv. 30–31).

This passage recounts that Jacob settles at Succoth (33:17–20); Shechem rapes Dinah (34:1–7); Hamor and Jacob negotiate (34:8–17); the citizens of Shechem decide to make a covenant with Jacob's family (34:18–24); and Shechem is pillaged (34:25–31).

33:17 / Jacob journeyed to **Succoth,** where he settled and made **shelters for his livestock.** There is a play on the name of this place and "shelters" *(sukkot).* Given that Succoth was a common name, a reliable identification is difficult. It is most often identified with Deir ʾAllah (*P. Šeb.* 9:2), not far from Peniel. Sarna (*Genesis,* p. 231) suggests that Jacob stayed there for a season or two in order to replenish his flocks, depleted by his large gift to Esau.

33:18–20 / After an unspecified length of time Jacob continued his journey to the promised land and **arrived safely at Shechem.** "Safely" communicates that God had fulfilled the conditions of Jacob's vow about returning to Canaan (28:21). God had been faithful to Jacob through the many trials he faced in Paddan Aram. Jacob encamped close to the city of Shechem, which was Abraham's first stopping place in Canaan (12:6).

Desiring to settle in this area, **for a hundred pieces of silver, he bought from the sons of Hamor, the father of Shechem, a plot** of land **where he pitched his tent.** Since the value of this unit of silver cannot be determined, it is difficult to know how expensive this field was. Like Abraham before him, Jacob came to own a plot in the land of promise as a foretaste of the promise that his descendants would occupy the land. He expressed his devotion to God by setting **up an altar and** calling **it El Elohe Israel.** By building an altar instead of setting up a pillar, as was his custom, he intentionally emulated Abraham. Nevertheless Jacob's imprint is on the report of this act of devotion, for the verb used is "set up" *(hitsib)*, a term in accord with setting up a stone pillar, not with building an altar (28:18, 22; 31:45; 35:14, 20). In naming the altar El Elohe Israel, "God, the God of Israel," Jacob identified El (God), the name of the supreme Canaanite god, with the God who had revealed himself and changed Jacob's name. That is, the local god El was in fact the God of Jacob. With the use of his new name, Israel, Jacob enthusiastically heralded his new relationship with God and fulfilled his earlier vow to worship God (28:21).

34:1–4 / Some time later, a tragic incident took place. **Dinah,** Jacob's **daughter** by **Leah, went out to visit the women** of that area (compare Lot's attraction to Sodom, 13:10–13). Her behavior went against custom, for girls of marriageable age in small shepherd clans were not permitted to go about unescorted. **Shechem son of Hamor . . . saw her.** Drawn by her beauty, he raped her. Afterward he longed for her to become his wife. His lust appears to have turned to love, for he **spoke tenderly** to Dinah in order to win her affection. Since in that society a marriage had to be negotiated, Shechem pressured **his father,** Hamor, **the ruler of that area,** to take the necessary steps to get her as his **wife.** To do that Hamor had to go to Jacob, the offended father, and win his consent to this marriage.

34:5 / **When Jacob heard that his daughter Dinah had been defiled, he kept quiet,** especially since **his sons** were some distance from home tending the flocks. Jacob's mild reaction to the abuse of his daughter may indicate that he was not overly fond of Leah's children. It is also noteworthy that after wrestling with a man (ch. 32), Jacob acted more patiently, relying on God to work out a resolution when he faced trouble. But given the shame inflicted on Dinah, Jacob should have been more proactive.

34:6 / **Hamor** with Shechem spoke **with Jacob,** hoping to persuade Jacob to give his daughter as a bride to his son.

34:7 / When her brothers heard that their sister had been raped, they returned from the fields, furious at what happened. They called this wrong an act of blatant folly, seeing it as an act of outrageous depravity that threatened the fabric of their clan's existence. God used their anger to deliver Dinah from Shechem.

34:8–12 / In conversation Hamor addressed both Jacob and Dinah's brothers. Without offering an apology and avoiding any direct reference to the abuse of Dinah, he informed them that **Shechem,** his **son,** had **his heart set on** Dinah and requested that they might **give her to him as his wife.** Hamor strengthened his request by offering Jacob's clan the opportunity to enter into a pact with the town of Shechem. The pact would permit any of Jacob's children to negotiate marriages with the local people. It would also open all the surrounding territory for grazing his flocks, and his family would be able to **trade and . . . acquire property.** Aware that Jacob had bought a plot of land (33:19), Hamor appealed to his longing for ownership of land in Canaan. Since Hamor's position and power greatly exceeded Jacob's, he thought he could easily entice Jacob and his sons into an alliance.

Shechem, his son, spoke up (vv. 11–12), hoping to move Jacob and his sons to agree to the proposed accord. He assured them that his heart was set on Dinah by offering to give them any price they asked for Dinah's becoming his bride. He encouraged them to set **the price** high as long as they truly permitted the marriage. Although Shechem did not admit that he had done any wrong to Dinah, he essentially offered compensation to Jacob's family for the damages he caused them. Only later does the audience learn that these two men were negotiating from the advantage of having Dinah under their control (v. 26). Inexcusably, these two Shechemites displayed no remorse or any hint of contrition for the grave wrong that Shechem had done. Their cavalier attitude increased the fury of Dinah's brothers.

34:13–19 / Aggravated by Hamor's patronizing approach and yet desiring to recover their sister, the sons of Jacob answered **deceitfully.** The author discloses their pretense in order to prepare the reader for the tragic outcome. In the Jacob narrative "deceit" *(rmh)* is a crucial term. It describes Jacob's stealing the blessing from Esau (27:35). It is the term Jacob used to accuse Laban for giving him Leah instead of Rachel (29:25). This time Jacob's sons resorted to deceit as the way to rescue their sister and to take revenge on these city dwellers.

The shift in the identification of Dinah from "his daughter" to "sister" signals that the brothers have taken the responsibility for her recovery. Cunningly they responded to Hamor's offer by making a condition designed to provide them a tactical advantage against the inhabitants of Shechem. They stated firmly that they could not consent to Dinah's engagement to Shechem or to giving their daughters in marriage to any who were uncircumcised, for such unions among them would be **a disgrace.** However, if the Shechemites circumcised **all** their **males,** they would agree to intermarriages and to **settle among** them **and become one people.** If the Shechemites did not accept this condition, they would **take** their **sister** and depart. Their use of "disgrace," a potent term in societies structured around the concept of honor, is readily understood as a nonnegotiable condition by Hamor and his son. The approach of these brothers should have alerted Hamor to their anger at the dishonor and outrage that had been done to their sister by his son. In the same vein, it is important to notice that in the counterproposal Jacob's sons avoided Shechem's encouragement to bargain about the bride price and the gift for Dinah. They spoke only about entering into a treaty on the basis of principle. Their emphasis on principle should also have warned Hamor that the sons of Jacob were more interested in their sister's honor than in material gain. The fact that Jacob's sons made no reference in their counterproposal to trading and buying land, the two motivating factors that Hamor had set forth, further supports this. Not picking up on these incongruities, Hamor and Shechem blindly accepted their terms.

This episode illustrates the dangers that the seed of Abraham faced any time they entered into a pact with the inhabitants of Canaan. A cornerstone for accommodation between two groups was intermarriage; entering into such unions for Jacob's small family, however, held the likelihood that they would be assimilated into the larger group. Over time they would lose their identity as the seed of Abraham. In advocating intermarriage Hamor was also laying the basis for the Shechemites to gain the property and animals belonging to Jacob (34:16, 23).

The narrative reports that Shechem had himself circumcised, indicating how favorably disposed he and his father were to entering into a pact with Jacob's family. It also anticipates the circumcision of the Shechemites (v. 24). As the story unfolds it becomes evident that Shechem must have been circumcised with the other men. Otherwise he would have recovered and been able to resist the attack by Jacob's sons.

34:20–24 / **Hamor** and **Shechem went to the gate of their city** to address the public assembly about entering into a formal agreement with Jacob's family. With great diplomatic skill, Hamor delivered a powerful speech. Informing the citizens that these new settlers were **friendly toward** them, he assured them that there was **plenty of room** for Jacob's family to **live** and **trade** among them. This agreement would open new markets, increasing their wealth. Intermarriage would also guarantee peaceful relations. Shrewdly, Hamor omitted any mention of granting Jacob's family the right to buy land. Then he brought up the difficult condition of circumcision required by Jacob's sons. To overcome any objection the citizens might have to submitting to such a painful operation, Hamor used a rhetorical question to focus the assembly on the great economic windfall that would be theirs by entering into this agreement, namely, their gaining access to the **livestock, . . . property and . . . animals** of Jacob's family. In addition to the issue of honor, this narrative treats settlement and accommodation (Brueggemann, *Genesis,* pp. 272–73). Skillfully Hamor played on the pride and greed of the Hivites as he pictured them dominating the new alliance. He ended his speech with a fervent plea that they all **consent** to this condition. Being persuaded, the assembly willingly **agreed** to the proposal. In preparation for the treaty ceremony all the men of Shechem were **circumcised.**

34:25–29 / **Three days** after the rite of circumcision, **Simeon and Levi, Dinah's brothers,** entered the city. Taking advantage of the painful, feverish condition of the men of Shechem and of their sense of security, they killed **every male,** including

Hamor and Shechem, and rescued **Dinah from Shechem's house.**
While the city was in confusion, the rest of **the sons of Jacob
looted the city** and **seized** the **flocks and herds and donkeys,**
along with the **women and children.**

34:30–31 / On hearing of his sons' treacherous raid,
Jacob reprimanded **Simeon and Levi,** claiming that they made
him **a stench to the Canaanites and Perizzites.** He feared that
these people living nearby might be so angered that they would
join forces and avenge the Shechemites by destroying his **household.** By giving only the reason of self-preservation and by failing
to address the abuse of Dinah or his sons' blatant misuse of the
sign of the covenant, Jacob discloses his absorption with his own
survival and his lack of adequate concern for Leah's children. His
sons challenged their father's complaint with a poignant rhetorical question: How should they have responded to their sister
being **treated . . . like a prostitute?** Even though Jacob failed to
react strongly enough to the rape of Dinah, the narrator casts her
violation as a terrible act of violence that leads to even greater violence in the pillage of Shechem.

The question leaves open the interpretation of this tragic
episode. It was necessary to hold those who had abused Dinah accountable, but the extent of the destruction her brothers inflicted
on the offenders far exceeded the crime. On top of that, Jacob's
sons had used the symbol of the covenant as a ruse for pillaging a
people. Although Jacob addressed the serious consequences of
his sons' vengeful action, he was not able to enlighten them as to
how they should have carried out their moral responsibility. Jacob's lack of response to the harm done to his daughter also becomes a mark against him. That the behavior of Simeon and Levi
increased Jacob's sorrow is discovered in his harsh words for
them in his final testament (49:5–7). Such repugnant behavior
against the local citizens by the bearers of God's promises made it
necessary for God to direct the course of events to keep Jacob's
household from suffering retaliation from the neighboring villages, as will be seen in Jacob's move from Shechem.

Additional Notes §45

33:18 / Another reading of the text takes *shalem* as the name of a place in the plain east of Shechem rather than "safely." Then Shechem may be understood as either a person's name or the name of the city.

34:7 / The phrase "he had done folly in Israel" defines the abuse of Dinah as a repulsive, abhorrent act. This phrase was applied to various repulsive deeds in Israel's history (Deut. 22:21; Josh. 7:15; Judg. 20:6, 10; 2 Sam. 13:12; Jer. 29:23). Its occurrence here results from a later interpretation of this event, for "in Israel" requires the existence of Israel as a people.

After reentering the promised land, Jacob follows in the steps of Abraham. His moving from Shechem to Bethel and then south toward Hebron parallels Abraham's initial journey through the land of promise. At Bethel God blesses Jacob with the Abrahamic blessing. The imprint of Abraham continues when Jacob and Esau inter their father Isaac in the Cave of Machpelah, the only plot of land in Canaan owned by Abraham (35:27–29).

This portion of the Jacob narrative contains three sections: Jacob's pilgrimage to Bethel (vv. 1–7), the report of Deborah's death (v. 8), and God's blessing Jacob (vv. 9–15).

35:1 / While Jacob was apprehensive that the local inhabitants would take vengeance on his family for their violent raid of Shechem, **God** told him to **go up to Bethel and settle there, and build an altar there to God** in commemoration of God's faithful guidance during his years of living outside of Canaan. God identifies himself as the one who **appeared** to him when he left Canaan, **fleeing from . . . Esau.** This pilgrimage symbolizes Jacob's complete repatriation in the promised land and completes the fulfillment of his vows, to worship God and recognize Bethel as God's house, made on leaving Canaan (28:20–22). This is the only place in Genesis that God commands someone to build an altar.

35:2–4 / Responding to God's orders, **Jacob** immediately instructed **his household** and others who had joined him to prepare themselves for a religious pilgrimage to Bethel. Careful preparations had to be made to protect everyone from the possibility of God's breaking forth against anyone who was not ritually pure. Specifically Jacob commanded those of his house to **get rid of the foreign gods,** indicating that some continued to worship various deities. Some gods or idols may have been brought from Haran; others might have been taken from the pillage of the Shechemites. The report of this command accounts for the removal of the teraphim Rachel had stolen from her father's house (31:19). Jacob also ordered his company to **purify** themselves so that they could be in the presence of God without danger. Ritual purification included bathing, shaving, and putting on clean clothes. It symbolized the removal of all that was unclean and sinful. In an exhortation Jacob told his entire household that they were going **up to Bethel, where** he would **build an altar to God,** who had helped him in his **distress** and who had **been** present **with** him throughout his long journey. The mention of God's being with Jacob establishes a connection to the vow he had made at Bethel long ago (28:20).

The people responded willingly by giving **Jacob all the foreign gods they had and the rings in their ears.** These earrings must have had religious significance; possibly they were amulets. Jacob disposed of all the idols and rings he had collected by burying **them under the oak at Shechem.**

35:5 / As Jacob's company traveled along the road to Bethel, God put his **terror . . . upon the towns** around Shechem (Exod. 15:14–16). This means that a heavy sense of fear of Jacob's house settled over the local inhabitants, restraining them from taking vengeance. Their plunder of Shechem had aroused such hatred in the local population that Jacob and his family needed God's special protection to travel in safety.

35:6–7 / Jacob arrived at **Luz** (28:19), and **built an altar. He called the place El Bethel,** literally "the God of the house of God," in remembrance of God's self-revelation to Jacob **when he was fleeing from** Esau. This name signals that Jacob focused on the God who had revealed himself to him rather than viewing the place as inherently holy. Jacob's understanding of God was deepening.

35:8 / At this point the narrative reports that **Deborah, Rebekah's nurse, died and was buried under the oak.** They called that place **Allon Bacuth,** meaning "the oak of weeping," a memorial to commemorate this great matriarch. Throughout these narratives, honor is accorded the matriarchs. They stand alongside the patriarchs as playing a key role in fulfilling God's promises to Abraham. This death report is surprising, for rarely does the Hebrew Bible recount the death of a woman, especially a handmaid, and nowhere else does it introduce a person by a death report. This report is also important for bringing closure to

Jacob's relationship with Rebekah, his mother, who had orchestrated the events that had forced him to flee Canaan. The patriarchal narratives contain no further references to Rebekah after Jacob fled Canaan. This omission is particularly amazing in light of the long account of Sarah's death (23:1–20). Apparently Rebekah had died while Jacob was in Haran, and the account was lost to the tradition. This report about Deborah, her nurse, compensates in some measure for the absence of an account of Rebekah's burial and the need to honor this matriarch. In attending to the burial of Deborah, Jacob participated vicariously in the burial of his mother.

35:9–13 / **God appeared to** Jacob **again and blessed him.** Given the preceding report of Deborah's death, this appearance of God must have come some time after Jacob built the altar. Since Jacob's name had been changed outside the promised land, God reaffirmed the change of Jacob's name to **Israel** (32:28) in the land of promise. God then blessed him in terms of the blessing spoken to Abraham at the covenant renewal (17:4–8). Identifying himself as **God Almighty,** the name he used before renewing the covenant with Abraham (17:1), God enjoined Jacob to **be fruitful and increase in number.** Similar language occurs in God's command to Adam (1:28) and in Isaac's blessing Jacob (28:3). In that Jacob already had eleven sons and at least one daughter, this command was a general blessing that was to be realized in his children's fruitfulness. His offspring were to be so numerous that they would develop into **a nation;** also **kings** would **come from** his **body** (17:6). **The land** that God had promised **to Abraham and Isaac,** his forefathers, God promised to **give** to Jacob and his **descendants** (seed; 17:8). God then left.

35:14–15 / In response to God's appearance **Jacob set up a stone pillar.** Either he erected a new stone or he rededicated the stone he had set up earlier (28:18–19). He consecrated this pillar first by pouring **out a drink offering on it** and then by pouring **oil on it.** Jacob named that **place Bethel,** "the house of God." Just as God had reaffirmed the promises to Jacob, Jacob reaffirmed his commitment to God by setting up a pillar. Just as God had restated that Jacob's new name was Israel, so Jacob again named that site Bethel as he had done when God had first appeared to him there.

Additional Notes §46

35:1 / The Eng. term "settle" suggests more permanence than Jacob understood in God's instructions. A better translation of the Hb. root *y-sh-b* might be "stay." This time Jacob was free to remain there as long as he wanted, in contrast to his first visit when he was fleeing from Esau (Sarna, *Genesis,* p. 234). These orders from God parallel those his mother gave him before leaving Canaan (27:43; Wenham, *Genesis 16–50,* p. 323).

35:6 / The use of the name Luz is surprising since the reader is already aware of Bethel's former name (28:19). Its usage here is a strong indication that this account circulated independently before it was connected with other accounts of Jacob's life.

35:14 / This is the only reference in Gen. to a drink offering, a ceremonious pouring out of wine to God.

§47 The Birth of Benjamin and the Deaths of Rachel and Isaac (Gen. 35:16–29)

This section contains small vignettes in the context of Jacob's moving south from Bethel to Mamre. Jacob loses his beloved wife Rachel as she gives birth to Benjamin (vv. 16–20). Reuben sleeps with Bilhah (vv. 21–22a), and there is a list of Jacob's children (vv. 22b–26). Isaac dies (vv. 27–29). These vignettes, framed by the burial scenes of Rachel and Isaac, conclude the core Jacob narrative. Jacob, however, continues to live and reemerges in the story of Joseph to bless Joseph's sons (ch. 48) and his own twelve sons (ch. 49).

35:16–20 / Having left **Bethel** and **still some distance from Ephrath,** most likely located in the territory of Benjamin, **Rachel** was stricken by excruciating birth pangs. Her **midwife** sought to comfort her by saying, **Don't be afraid, for you have another son.** Rachel had expressed her longing for more children in naming her firstborn Joseph, "adding" (30:24). At last that longing was being fulfilled—at the cost of her life. **She named her son Ben-Oni,** "son of my sorrow." Mindful of the importance of a name in defining either one's personality or one's destiny, Jacob quickly renamed him **Benjamin,** meaning "son of the right [side]," that is, "my good fortune" (Deut. 27:12–13; Matt. 25:33). Jacob then buried Rachel beside the road leading **to Ephrath** and **set up a pillar over her tomb.** This, the fourth pillar he erected (28:18; 31:45–50; 35:14), reveals the great honor in which he held Rachel. It also gave her a perpetual memorial in the land of promise.

35:21–22a / **Israel** journeyed on and **pitched his tent beyond Migdal Eder,** "the tower of the flock." There **Reuben . . . slept with his father's concubine Bilhah.** This wording suggests that Bilhah complied with Reuben's advances. While the narrative offers no explanation for Reuben's act, he undoubtedly wanted to influence leadership in the clan. Perhaps he did not want Bilhah, Rachel's maid, to become the matriarch of the family in place of Leah, his mother (Sarna, *Genesis,* p. 244), especially since Leah had never received from Jacob the affection she desired. Another interpretation posits that Reuben asserted his leadership over the family by taking advantage of his father's sorrow. In either case, Bilhah was reduced to living widowhood, because she could not be legitimately joined to a man again (2 Sam. 15:16; 16:22; 20:3; Sarna, *Genesis,* p. 244). When Jacob learned of the incident he took no definitive action, similar to his response to the rape of Dinah (ch. 34). His containing his anger bears additional witness that his character had indeed been changed at Peniel. He no longer resorted to trickery to retaliate against those who had offended him. That Reuben's act deeply offended him, however, is discovered in his last testament (49:3–4; 1 Chron. 5:1).

35:22b–26 / At the close of the Jacob narrative there is a list of his twelve sons. Leah's sons and those of Zilpah, her handmaid, frame this list. At the center are the sons of Rachel and Bilhah, her handmaid. All of his children, save Benjamin, were born in Paddan Aram. The compiler of the list was concerned not with that exception but with the important fact that all of Jacob's sons were now living in the land of promise.

35:27–29 / The narrative reports Isaac's death, signaling the close of the main portion of the Jacob narrative. Isaac's death also coincides with Jacob's traveling to the south. This report prepares for the genealogies of Esau (ch. 36) and Jacob (37:1–2). The location of this report indicates that the chronology of the vignettes assembled here may not be linear. **Jacob came home to his father Isaac in Mamre,** which was **near Kiriath Arba,** later named **Hebron.** Isaac died at **a hundred and eighty years,** being **old and full of years** (25:7–11). On the basis of this age, he lived approximately twelve years after Joseph was sold into servitude in Egypt (Sarna, *Genesis,* p. 368a, n. 17). The phraseology "old and full of years" means that he had lived a long, happy life under God's blessing. **His** two **sons Esau and Jacob buried** their father in the Cave of Machpelah (49:29–32). Reconciled, the two brothers joined in honoring their father with a proper burial (25:9).

Additional Notes §47

35:16 / Scholars dispute the location of this Ephrath. The traditional site is located a mile north of Bethlehem, supported by v. 19 and 48:7. The problem with this identification is that Rachel died shortly after Jacob left Bethel, suggesting a site north of Jerusalem. Accounts that place Rachel's tomb in the territory of Benjamin support this latter location (1 Sam. 10:2; Jer. 31:15; Ramah being a site five miles north of Jerusalem). At one time the border of Benjamin appears to have reached to Jerusalem (Josh. 15:8; 18:15–17). This text says that the company was still some distance from Ephrath, so it is possible that the site here is the same as in 1 Sam. 10:2. However, as Sarna observes (*Genesis,* p. 408), Jacob traveled on to Migdal Eder, a site in the vicinity of Jerusalem. If he had gone as far south as Bethlehem, he would have had to turn back north, which seems unlikely since he was moving to the south. Thus the original location of Rachel's tomb was most likely in the territory of Benjamin, north and/or west of Jerusalem.

35:18 / Various proposals have been made for Benjamin's two names. Ben-Oni could be "son of my wickedness" and Benjamin "son of the oath." Another suggestion for Benjamin is "son of my days," referring to Jacob's old age (*T. Benj.* 1:26). The name could also mean "son of the south." In texts from Mari there is a tribe known as "son of the south." The connection between that tribe and this Benjamin is debated, but the biblical account does not offer any basis for connecting these two peoples.

§48 The Descendants of Esau (Gen. 36:1–43)

Following the report of Isaac's death (35:27–29), the narrative records the genealogy *(toledoth)* of his two sons, Esau (36:1–43) and Jacob (37:1–2). As with Ishmael (25:13–18) and Isaac (25:19–20), the genealogy of the son who is not the direct heir of God's special promises to Abraham appears before that of the son who is the heir of that promise.

These lists contain seventy personal names, including five women. The names are Semitic. Five different lists are divided into two groups marked by the repetition of the *toledoth* formula. The repetition of this formula (vv. 1 and 9) is most unusual, suggesting that these two lists are to be read in tandem. "Esau, father of Edom" (vv. 9, 43) frames the second *toledoth* section, which contains four separate lists of the sons of Esau (vv. 10–19), sons of Seir, the Horite (vv. 20–30), kings of Edom (vv. 31–39), and chiefs from Esau (vv. 40–43). Overall, the political movement is from the extended family (vv. 1–8) to the tribal organization (vv. 15–19, 29–30) then to the monarchy (vv. 31–39; C. Westermann, *Genesis 12–36: A Commentary* [trans. J. Scullion; Minneapolis: Augsburg, 1985], p. 568). These lists function to establish the legitimacy of these rulers in Edom. In addition, they witness to the fulfillment of God's promise that kings would come from Abraham's sons (17:6).

Remarkably, the list presents Esau's genealogy three times, in verses 2–5, 9–14, and 15–19. This repetition suggests that varying traditions have been assembled and that no editor sought to harmonize the information. In contrast to Western approaches to official lists, the ancients were not troubled by such apparent contradictions, as they treasured the diverse traditions as part of their rich heritage. If the core material comes from Edom, it has been adapted to the style of Genesis, for the pattern is similar to that of other genealogical lists in Genesis. Wenham (*Genesis 16–50*, p. 336) argues that the tight structure of these lists indicates that they were assembled in block.

The preservation of this long, complex genealogy honors Esau and his descendants as offspring of Abraham. Indeed, the number of his offspring and their rise to leadership witnesses that God honored Isaac's blessing of Esau (27:39–40). These lists also attest to God's continued interest in the welfare of Isaac's offspring through Esau. While the line of promise moves through Jacob, it does not follow that God casts off Esau. In accord with this chapter, Deuteronomy 23:7 says, "Do not abhor an Edomite, for he is your brother." Even after Edom, the nation that arose from Esau's seed, became a hated foe of Israel, these lists were neither expunged nor altered to cast Esau in a bad light. Their inclusion witnesses to the powerful force that tradition had in ancient Israel. It also placed "a check on over-zealous understanding of election" (Brueggemann, *Genesis*, p. 287). Given the hostility between Israel and Edom during the kingdom period, this material must have been incorporated into Genesis either early or late (Obad.; Ps. 137:7–9).

36:1–5 / The basic genealogy of Esau is oriented to his three Canaanite wives: **Adah . . . the Hittite, Oholibamah . . . the Hivite,** and **Basemath,** the Ishmaelite (26:34; 27:46; 28:1, 6, 8–9). His wives bore him five children: **Eliphaz, Reuel, Jeush, Jalam and Korah.**

36:6–8 / Under his own initiative **Esau** took **all** of his family and **settled in the hill country of Seir,** or Edom (Deut. 2:4–6, 12, 22; Josh. 24:4). Thereby he officially separated **from his brother Jacob,** for he did not think that the land of Canaan was able to **support . . . both** of their clans. This step portrays Esau as an insightful person, taking steps to avoid conflict. Esau's settling in Edom is paralleled with Jacob's settling in Canaan (37:1). This note gives the reason Jacob could settle there unhindered by the size of Esau's family and herds, thus avoiding the need for them to separate as did Abraham and Lot (13:5–6).

36:9–14 / This list presents Esau's children for three generations, except for the descendants through his wife Oholibamah. Without Amalek, the son of a concubine, the result is a twelve-tribe league, a political unit favored in Genesis in the families of Nahor (22:20–24), Ishmael (17:20; 25:13–16), and Jacob/Israel (35:23–26).

36:15–18 / The list of **chiefs among Esau's descendants** introduces each grandson as the chief of a clan. This list is almost identical to the genealogy in verses 11–14; the variations are that **Gatam** and **Kenaz** are in different positions and **Amalek** is raised to be on par with the sons. **Eliphaz** has an additional son named **Korah.** It is possible that these differences reflect changes in the standing of tribes in Edom (Sarna, *Genesis,* p. 250).

36:19 / This summary statement binds together the list of Esau's sons (vv. 10–14) and the list of chiefs from Esau (vv. 15–18).

36:20–30 / This is the genealogy of three generations of **Seir the Horite** (vv. 20–28) to which a list of **Horite chiefs,** bearing the same names as Seir's sons, has been attached (vv. 29–30). Thus "family history is succeeded by tribal history" (Westermann, *Genesis 12–36,* p. 565). These were the occupants of Mount Seir prior to Esau's arrival. The genealogy mentions one daughter, **Oholibamah.**

The list preserves a legendary story about this Anah (v. 24), distinguishing him from his uncle (vv. 20, 25). While he **was grazing the donkeys of his father,** he came on some **hot springs.** Such stories about the origin or discovery of important places and customs often became part of a genealogy. The finding of water in such a dry region was noteworthy.

36:31–39 / These eight **kings . . . reigned in Edom** before Israel had a king. Since their succession was not by genealogy, Edom apparently did not have a dynasty. After performing a heroic act of deliverance, such as Hadad's defeat of the Midianites (v. 35), a leader was invested with authority similar to that of the judges in Israel, but by contrast he was called a king. Then that king ruled from his own town. The mention of a second Hadad (v. 39) leads to the conjecture that there was an attempt to establish a dynasty (Westermann, *Genesis 12–36,* p. 565). This latter Hadad may be the king of Edom whom David subdued (2 Sam. 8:11–14).

36:40–43 / This is another list of chiefs who trace their lineage back to Esau. How this list is to be compared with the list in verses 15–19 is unclear. Seven names occur for the first time while the following four—Timna, Oholibamah, Kenaz, and Teman—appear earlier. Since these names also serve as place names, this list may reflect administrative districts in Edom (Wenham, *Genesis 16–50,* p. 340).

Additional Notes §48

36:2–3 / In earlier references, Esau's three wives are Judith, daughter of Beeri, the Hittite; Basemath, daughter of Elon, the Hittite (26:34); and Mahalath, daughter of Ishmael (28:9). While only Basemath's name occurs in both lists, the identity of her father and her ethnic origin differ. One solution to these variations is the conjecture that each woman had two names; another solution is that Esau had five or six wives (Sarna, *Genesis*, p. 248). A third possibility is that varying traditions have been preserved.

36:11 / Some names, like Teman (v. 34), have as a referent both a person and a place. Teman was the name of a city and by extension of a district in Edom (e.g., Amos 1:12; Ezek. 25:13). It was also used as a metonymy for Edom (Jer. 49:7, 20). Kenaz could be connected with Caleb, the hero who captured Hebron, for he is called a Kenizzite (Num. 32:12; Josh. 14:6, 14). A study of the texts in which Caleb is mentioned leads J. Milgrom to postulate that Caleb belonged to an Edomite clan that joined the tribe of Judah (e.g., *Numbers* [JPS Torah Commentary; Philadelphia: Jewish Publication Society, 1990], pp. 391–92).

36:12 / Amalek was a bitter enemy of Israel (Exod. 17:8–16). The command not to abhor an Edomite did not extend to the Amalekites (Deut. 25:17–19).

36:16 / Since the Sam. Pent. omits the name Korah, it is possible that its inclusion here is a secondary development.

36:20 / One etymology identifies Horite as the word for "cave," i.e., the Horites were cave dwellers. While this explanation may be too simplistic to be accurate for a racial group, the region of Seir is full of caves.

36:24 / What Anah found is uncertain because the Hb. term *yemim* is unknown. Suggestions include "water," "fish," "geyser," "mules," and "mirage." This note may have been included to distinguish this person from an uncle with the same name (Wenham, *Genesis 16–50*, p. 339).

36:31 / According to Num. 20:14, Edom had a king when Israel was still in the wilderness.

36:33 / Bozrah, also the name of the ancient capital of Edom (Isa. 34:6; 63:1; Jer. 49:13, 22; Amos 1:12), is identified with the present-day Buseirah, which is located in northern Edom on the King's Highway, thirty-five miles north of Petra (S. Hart and U. Hübner, "Bozrah," *ABD* 1:775).

§49 Joseph's Dreams and His Sale into Slavery (Gen. 37:1–36)

The Joseph narrative (37:1–50:26) begins here and concludes with Joseph's death at the end of Genesis. (See the Introduction for a general overview of the Joseph narrative as a unit.) Joseph comes to the fore as the son of Jacob through whom God is going to direct the clan's destiny. Both Jacob and God favor Joseph. Jacob gives him an elegant cloak, and God gives him exalted dreams. These favors arouse the jealousy of his brothers. When an opportune occasion presents itself, the brothers rid themselves of their troublesome brother and his annoying dreams by selling him to traveling merchants. They in turn sell him to an important Egyptian official. The brothers conceal their hideous deed from their father by leading him to believe that a wild animal has killed Joseph.

This passage gives accounts of Jacob's family (vv. 1–2), Jacob's love for Joseph and Joseph's dreams (vv. 3–11), the sale of Joseph into bondage (vv. 12–28), the brothers' concealing the sale of Joseph from Jacob (vv. 29–35), and the selling of Joseph to Potiphar (v. 36).

37:1 / Jacob **lived** or settled in **Canaan,** near Hebron where his father **had stayed.** His settling in Canaan parallels Esau's settling in the hill country of Seir (36:6–8). Whereas Abraham and Isaac had only stayed or sojourned (*gur*) in the land of Canaan (35:27), Jacob settled down (*yashab*).

37:2 / The *toledoth* of Jacob introduces the Joseph narrative. Typically, reference to the father of the main character heads a new section (cf. 2:4a). This wording also reinforces that the following material concerns Jacob's whole family, not just Joseph, and permits the drama about Judah to be an integral part of this narrative. A brief report about Joseph characterizes his aloofness from his brothers. At the age of **seventeen** he was shepherding

with his brothers; he served as the assistant to his step-brothers by his father's concubines. When they returned home, Joseph gave his father **a bad report about them.** In light of the developing hostility of all the brothers toward Joseph, Joseph must have spoken ill of all his brothers, not just those by the concubines. This incident suggests that Joseph continually influenced his father's attitude negatively toward his brothers.

37:3–4 / The Joseph narrative begins with an illustration of Israel's deep love for Rachel's firstborn. He lavished on Joseph **a richly ornamented robe** or cloak. The upper class wore this type of garment; its design precluded manual labor (von Rad, *Genesis,* p. 351). Immediately becoming a symbol of Joseph's favored position, this coat so aroused his brothers' jealousy that they could no longer say anything **kind to him.**

37:5–11 / God likewise favored Joseph, giving him two dreams. Joseph recounted these dreams to his family, possibly in a flaunting manner; he was heedless of the negative effect this had on his brothers. In the first dream Joseph saw all members of his family **binding sheaves of grain out in the field.** His **sheaf rose and stood upright;** then the other **sheaves gathered around** his and **bowed down to it.** Angered by Joseph's youthful arrogance, **his brothers** asked him if he was going **to rule** over them. Their question contains the dream's interpretation. The clarity with which Jacob's family understood Joseph's dream sharply contrasts with Pharaoh's inability to find an interpretation for his dreams (41:8). Despite the growing animosity of his brothers, Joseph related a second **dream. This time the sun and moon and eleven stars were bowing down to** him. Besides increasing his brothers' fury, Joseph's recounting his dream exasperated Israel so much that he **rebuked** Joseph. "Rebuke" *(ga'ar)* stands for a stern reprimand aimed at putting an end to an activity by the force of the words uttered. Nevertheless, out of his love for his son Israel **kept** the dreams **in mind,** pondering the destiny God had for Joseph.

37:12–22 / Some time later, Jacob's sons were shepherding the flocks in the good pastures in the vicinity of **Shechem,** some distance from **the Valley of Hebron.** Concerned about their welfare, Israel sent Joseph to visit them and bring back news. The fact that they were shepherding in the vicinity of the town they had pillaged might have heightened his concern for his sons (ch. 34). Joseph had not accompanied his brothers, either because they had prevented him or because Jacob did not want him to be away from home for a long time.

Joseph did not find his brothers around Shechem, and a man informed him that they had moved **to Dothan.** When Joseph approached his brothers near Dothan, they recognized him **in the distance** because of his elegant cloak. They began to plot how they might get rid of this troubling dreamer and his threatening dreams. Since the ancients believed that dreams held the future, the most effective way to put an end to an undesirable future foreshadowed by dreams was to put an end to the dreamer himself. The brothers plotted **to kill** Joseph and dispose of him by throwing his body into one of the **cisterns** that dotted the hill country of Canaan. They planned to cover up their grisly deed by reporting that **a ferocious animal devoured him.** But **Reuben,** the oldest, felt responsibility for his young brother and exhorted them not to **take his life.** To gain some time for figuring out a way to rescue Joseph, Reuben ordered them to **throw him into** the **cistern** without harming him.

37:23–28 / As soon as Joseph arrived, the brothers grabbed him, gleefully stripped off his **ornamented** cloak, the symbol of his favored position, **and threw him into** a dry **cistern.** While eating and scheming about what to do to Joseph, they **saw a caravan of Ishmaelites coming from Gilead,** a region in northern Transjordan, on their way **to Egypt. Their camels were loaded with spices, balm, and myrrh.** The Egyptians prized these items, which they used for medicines, perfumes, embalming, and worship. In Reuben's absence **Judah** proposed that they **sell** Joseph to these traders since there was no **gain** in killing their **brother,** their **own flesh.** When **the Midianite merchants came by,** the **brothers sold** Joseph to them **for twenty** pieces **of silver.** These merchants continued on their way with Joseph, taking **him to Egypt.**

37:29–30 / On returning, **Reuben** passed by **the cistern.** To his dismay he discovered that **Joseph was** gone. Furious, **he tore his clothes, went back to his brothers,** and poured out his anguished feelings.

37:31–35 / The account jumps to the brothers' efforts to cover up their vile deed. After retrieving **Joseph's** cloak, they slaughtered **a goat and** dipped the cloak **in the blood.** They hastened back to Hebron and handed the garment **to their father,** saying that they had **found** it on the way. With feigned innocence they asked him to **examine it to see** if it belonged to Joseph. Recognizing it immediately, Jacob concluded that **some ferocious animal** had torn his son to pieces. His sons had succeeded in covering up their dastardly deed.

Full of anguish, Jacob **tore his clothes** and **put on sackcloth,** that is, clothes made out of old, rough cloth. He **mourned** for Joseph **many days. His sons and daughters** were unable **to comfort** their father. He told them that he would grieve the loss of his son until he died. Jacob, the deceiver of his own father and brother, suffered another terrible blow by being deceived about the fate of his most loved son. The sequence of events in Jacob's life forcefully portrays the theme of retribution.

37:36 / It is reported that **the Midianites sold Joseph to Potiphar, one of Pharaoh's officials, the captain of the guard.**

Additional Notes §49

37:2 / For the Hb., which has two distinct sentences, the NIV has one, placing "the sons of Bilhah and the sons of Zilpah" in apposition to "his brothers." However, in the Hb. the second sentence reads "he was a helper (*na'ar,* lit. 'a youth,' which may mean here 'servant boy' [Wenham, *Genesis 16–50,* p. 346]) with the sons of Bilhah and Zilpah."

37:3 / The precise meaning of *ketonet passim,* rendered in NIV "a richly ornamented robe," is uncertain. It may have been a long coat with long sleeves (2 Sam. 13:18–19, as Josephus understood it [*Ant.* 7.8.1]). Based on the LXX and Vg., it may have been a cloak of many colors. There are Egyptian pictures of Semites wearing long, multicolored robes.

37:23–28 / The use of two names for these merchants, "Ishmaelites" and "Midianites," is puzzling. An old rabbinic explanation says that Joseph was sold to various groups. A better explanation is that the Midianites were members of a tribal league known as Ishmaelites (25:13–17; Judg. 8:22).

The identification of these products is imprecise. Spices may be "gum tragacanth" from *Astragalus* shrubs, and balm a resin having medicinal value from storax trees (Jer. 8:22; 51:8). Myrrh could be ladanum, a resin-like substance from the leaves of cistus shrubs. These materials were used for incense and as medicines and fragrances. Gilead was a good source of these gums and resins.

37:28 / In Lev. 27:5 a male from the age of five to twenty was to pay a tax of twenty shekels. The Code of Hammurabi also attests this price for a slave (§§116, 214, 252).

37:32 / A variant reading has the brothers sending the robe through a messenger. Either reading is possible, but it seems unlikely that they would have involved an outside party lest their plot be uncovered.

§50 Judah and Tamar (Gen. 38:1–30)

The account of Judah and Tamar is set as an interlude in the Joseph narrative. It adds to the suspense of the Joseph story, as the reader wonders what is going to happen to Joseph. The action takes place in four scenes: the failure of Judah's sons to have an heir (vv. 1–11), Judah's relationship with a supposed prostitute (vv. 12–23), Tamar's vindication (vv. 24–26), and Tamar's bearing twins (vv. 27–30).

Although this account appears to interrupt the long, closely knit Joseph narrative, several reasons account for its inclusion at this point. First, it further identifies Judah, a central figure in the Joseph narrative. In the preceding chapter he persuaded his brothers to sell Joseph instead of killing him (37:26–27). In the following episodes with Joseph, Judah will emerge as the leader of the clan in dealing with the severe famine (43:3–5, 8–10; 44:14–34; 46:28). Second, this account gives Judah's lineage for three generations, vital information for the future line of Davidic kings. Although Judah was the fourth born, he became heir to the role of leadership in Israel because of his older brothers' failures (49:3–7). Third, this account could not have been placed prior to chapter 37, for Judah was not yet old enough, and it could not have been inserted later since the setting of the Joseph narrative shifts from Canaan to Egypt.

Significant literary connections between this account and the Joseph narrative indicate that it was crafted for this setting in Genesis. The narrative opens with Judah's going down (*yrd*) to Adullam, and the next episode about Joseph opens with his having been brought down (*yrd*, Hiphil) to Egypt (39:1). Crucial to the plot of each story is the recognition of an identifying object. After beholding Joseph's coat, Jacob recognized it and mistakenly concluded that Joseph had been killed (37:32–33). Here Tamar asks Judah to examine certain objects in order to identify the man who impregnated her (38:25–26). Both narratives employ several literary devices, "disguise, mistaken identity, sudden reversal of misfortune, rescue from disaster, and reversal of expectations" (S. Mathewson, "An Exegetical Study of Genesis 38," *BSac* 146 [1989], p. 375).

Furthermore, this story serves as an apology for the length of the nation of Israel's sojourn in Egypt. In pursuing accommodation with the Canaanites, Judah threatened his house with loss of identity as a member of Jacob's family. The implication of Judah's conduct is that if Jacob's sons had settled in Canaan, they would have assimilated with the local population and lost their identity as a nation united under God's promises to Abraham. Thus God isolated them in a region of Egypt while they increased in numbers to become a nation.

38:1–5 / Leaving **his brothers,** Judah traveled to the south of Bethlehem and then west into the low hills of the Shephelah in search of a place to stay. Two notes prepare for the following incident: he made friends with **Hirah,** a citizen of **Adullam,** and **married** a woman from that town. The narrative never gives his wife's name and identifies her solely as **the daughter of a Canaanite man named Shua.** She bore him three sons, **Er, Onan,** and **Shelah.** The last son was born **at Kezib,** usually identified with Achzib, a site southwest of Adullam. All of Judah's children were thus born in the territory that will belong to his tribe.

38:6–10 / When **Er** grew up, Judah secured for him a Canaanite **wife** named **Tamar.** Er died suddenly. The text is enigmatic in saying that Yahweh **put** Er **to death.** The statement that God killed someone is very unusual. This language probably means that Er suffered a tragic death, either for having done something quite wicked or for having an incorrigible character. Another possibility is that the text describes his having met a tragic, inexplicable fate. The standards of levirate marriage required that a man raise up a line of a near relative who had died without children through that one's widow (Deut. 25:5–10). Accordingly, **Judah** instructed his next oldest son, **Onan,** to cohabit with Tamar, his **brother's wife to fulfill** his **duty to her as a brother-in-law.** But Onan rejected his responsibility. Whenever he had sexual relations with Tamar, he withdrew before climaxing, thus refusing to impregnate her. Using Tamar without owning up to his responsibility in regard to her and his deceased brother was an affront to Yahweh. As a result, Yahweh **put him to death,** possibly by a tragic accident.

38:11 / **Judah** then asked **Tamar** to remain **a widow in her father's house until Shelah,** his youngest **son,** had grown **up.** Tamar agreed and **went to live in her father's house.** While Judah had expressed his commitment to fulfill the obligations of levirate marriage, his subsequent actions reveal that over time his commitment had waned. Perhaps he feared that if he married his youngest son to Tamar, that son too might face a tragic death. Living at her father's house, Tamar was in danger of being bypassed despite Judah's promises to her.

38:12–14 / Some years later, **Judah's wife ... died.** At the end of the period of mourning, Judah **went up to Timnah** with **his friend Hirah** to visit **the men who were shearing his sheep.** Hard work and joyous festivities characterized the time of sheep shearing. Hirah's accompanying him reveals that Judah was identifying with the Canaanites. **Tamar** learned of Judah's journey to Timnah. Since **Shelah had grown up,** she had come to suspect that Judah no longer intended to keep the obligations of levirate marriage. Tamar therefore decided to take matters into her own hands. Putting aside **her widow's clothes,** she dressed up, put on **a veil,** went out, and **sat down at the entrance to Enaim,** a town **on the road to Timnah.**

38:15–19 / When **Judah** passed by that place in the road, he noticed a woman sitting at the entrance to the gate, and he took her to be **a prostitute.** His strong sexual drive led him to turn aside and visit (lit. "come to") her. Both "turn aside" and "come to" establish a connection with Judah's initial settling in Adullam (vv. 1–2). Both of these actions become definitive for Judah's destiny. He was unaware that this prostitute was Tamar, his daughter-in-law. Tamar, being in full control of the situation, asked Judah what he was willing to pay for her **to sleep with** him. She wanted to able to implicate her father-in-law convincingly whenever the occasion arose. Since Judah did not have any money with him, he promised to **send** her **a young goat from** the **flock,** a very generous offer. But Tamar shrewdly asked him for **a pledge.** Unwittingly, he allowed her to remain in control by asking her to define the pledge. She requested his **seal ... cord,** and **staff.** A seal was usually a small precious stone in the form of a cylinder on which were inscribed a person's name along with some symbols that were closely connected with that person. When it was rolled over a soft clay tablet, the seal imprinted the owner's name and symbol. Many of these seals had a hole through the center for a cord so that it could be worn around the neck. Other seals were in the form of a ring. Tribal leaders carried a staff, which often had carved heads depicting the symbol of that tribe. These three items unmistakably identified their owner. Judah was so filled with desire that he handed over these personal items to her, apparently without any second thoughts. He slept **with her,** and Tamar conceived. Tamar **left** that place, went home, **took off her veil and put on her widow's clothes.** Having no intention of living as a prostitute, she performed this one desperate act to address the protracted wrong against her and Er, Judah's firstborn.

38:20–23 / When Judah returned home, he sent Hirah to pay the woman *('ishah)* the kid and retrieve **his pledge.** The term "woman," used here to describe Tamar, often means "wife" and captures Tamar's motivation for acting in this way, for she had not been given to Shelah as a wife (M. E. Andrew, "Moving from Death to Life: Verbs of Motion in the Story of Judah and Tamar," *ZAW* 105 [1993], p. 264). Hirah made inquiry as to the whereabouts of **the shrine prostitute,** literally "a holy woman." But the men of Enaim did not know about any shrine prostitute's having visited that area. The friend returned to Judah and told him that he was unable to find the woman. He also said that the local men knew of no shrine prostitute in that area, meaning that there was little likelihood that this woman could be found.

Fearful that he might be disgraced for not having kept his pledge, Judah attempted to clear himself of failing to keep a pledge by making a formal pronouncement that he had sent this young goat, but Hirah could not find the woman. A play is made on the term "pledge." Judah sought to pay his debt to a prostitute (Tamar), even though he had failed to keep his more important pledge of arranging for his widowed daughter-in-law (Tamar) to marry Shelah. Ironically, in trying to cover a small disgrace he was unaware that a much greater disgrace was being exposed—his disregard of levirate marriage. Tamar thwarted Judah's attempt to pay his small pledge because she had been thwarted by his failure to keep his pledge of marriage to his youngest son.

38:24–25 / **About three months later Judah** was informed that his **daughter-in-law Tamar** had acted as a prostitute and was **now pregnant.** It is instructive to note the shift in terms these men use for a woman who provides sexual gratification for a fee. When they want to dignify their hiring such a woman, they identify her as "a holy woman," but when they want to cast her in a bad light or place the blame for such activity on her, they refer to her as "a harlot." On hearing this report, Judah was outraged at the flagrant behavior of his daughter-in-law. Reference to Tamar as Judah's "daughter-in-law" reminds the reader of his obligations toward her. Judah ordered that she be brought out and **burned to death** (Lev. 20:10; Deut. 22:22). He was so angry that he decreed her sentence without providing her either a trial or even a chance to speak. The fervor of his outrage heightens his own culpability. Judah did not realize that the events would take an unexpected turn and that Tamar held the upper hand. Tamar conducted herself calmly and forthrightly. **As she was being brought out** to be put to death, **she sent a message to** Judah, **her father-in-law,** informing him that she had become **pregnant by the man who owns these** items. In this shrewd way she called Judah, her accuser, to account by asking him if he recognized the seal, cord, and staff. These objects immediately revealed to all the bystanders who had impregnated her.

38:26 / Recognizing the objects, Judah admitted his involvement, humbly conceding that Tamar was **more righteous than** he because of his failure to give her to Shelah. Yet he did not take her as a wife. How may Tamar's act of harlotry be considered a righteous act? As is typical of an ancient narrative, the focus is on the major issue of offspring in the line of Judah and honoring his deceased sons. In this account motives are accorded higher moral value than are actions. Although Tamar had committed an illicit act, she acted out of the highest motives. True to her word she had kept herself for marriage to Shelah, but Judah had failed to keep his promise to her. To fulfill her responsibility of having a child for her deceased husband Er, Tamar humbled herself in order to hold Judah accountable for failing to keep his word. That is, her behavior placed the value of the lineage of a clan in Judah over an illicit sexual act. As a result, a Canaanite woman held Judah, a male Israelite, accountable to the standards that protected the continuance of the line of his eldest son. In God's providence her line led to the birth of David (Ruth 4:12, 18–22; Matt. 1:3–6). Thus both Judah and Tamar were vindicated: Tamar by reason of Judah's concession and her giving birth to twins, and Judah by admitting that Tamar had acted more righteously than he had.

38:27–30 / The outcome was joyous. Tamar gave birth to **twin boys.** During labor one child **put out his hand,** and **the**

midwife took a scarlet thread and tied it on his wrist. He drew
back his hand, and his brother came out first. The latter Tamar
named Perez, meaning "a breaking forth," that is, life has burst
forth. This child symbolized a wonderful triumph for her because
her former experiences of sexual union had resulted in the deaths
of her partners. Then the boy with the scarlet thread on his wrist
came out and was named Zerah, meaning "brightness." The tribal
unit that had been threatened with extinction once again had a
bright future.

Additional Notes §50

38:8 / Middle Assyrian and Hittite laws attest levirate marriages. A major distinction between levirate marriage as described in this
narrative and that prescribed in the laws of Deuteronomy is that here the
father-in-law takes the initiative to have his sons accept their obligation,
while in Deuteronomy the brother-in-law bears the responsibility. The
law also contains an escape for a brother who does not want to accept his
burden, but in this narrative there appear to be no grounds for escaping
the obligation.

38:14 / There is no known town in Cisjordan with the name
Enaim. Some scholars identify it as Enam, located in the Shephelah (Josh.
15:34). Some render the phrase *bepetakh 'enayim* as "a fork in the road"
(e.g., NEB, JB). Hamilton (*Genesis: Chapters 18–50*, p. 440) suggests that the
phrase indicates a woman who makes herself available to men. The term
may have a double meaning. In such a case it explains why Judah considered Tamar, sitting at that location, to be a prostitute.

§51 Joseph in Potiphar's House (Gen. 39:1–23)

Joseph goes from favorite son to bondservant and from chief steward to prisoner. Although Joseph appears prone to bad luck, the narrator makes it clear that God is directing Joseph's destiny, including his setbacks, to his ultimate destiny of ruler as anticipated in his boyhood dreams.

A key term in this episode is "hand" (*yad*). It captures the trust Joseph inspires and plays a key role in his fall. Potiphar places all things in Joseph's "hand" (vv. 3, 4, 6, 8, 22, 23). But in the incident with Potiphar's wife Joseph flees her grasp, leaving his cloak in her "hand" (vv. 12, 13). Her hand holds the evidence that leads to his being cast into prison.

This episode depicts Joseph's rise in Potiphar's house (vv. 1–6), his resistance to the advances of Potiphar's wife (vv. 7–20), and Joseph's responsibilities in prison (vv. 21–23).

39:1–2 / Joseph arrived in Egypt, and **Potiphar, one of Pharaoh's officials, the captain of the guard, bought him from the Ishmaelites.** This wording establishes a connection with the last verse of chapter 37 in order to resume the Joseph narrative. From the outset the narrator asserts that Yahweh's presence was the unseen force directing Joseph's life. God's presence empowered him to prosper (also vv. 21, 23), and he became a successful person (*'ish matsliakh;* v. 2; compare vv. 3, 23). Through God's blessing on Joseph, Potiphar's house prospered (12:3).

39:3–6 / Recognizing that God causes everything Joseph does to flourish, Potiphar made him **attendant,** or head administrator, of all that is done **in the house and in the field.** Potiphar trusted Joseph so completely that he put all details and duties **in his care.** He kept only his own **food,** or his private matters, under his own control. Joseph matured into a **well-built, handsome** man.

39:7–9 / Joseph's success and position attracted the attention of Potiphar's wife. She began to lust after him. Eventually, she became so aggressive that she entreated him to go **to bed** with her. Joseph **refused**, saying that he had been **entrusted** with everything **in the house** of his master **except** her. He tried to dissuade her with a rhetorical question, asking **how** he **could do such a wicked thing and sin against God.** Joseph understood well that doing wrong to another human is not only a crime but also a sin against God. His fear of God guarded him against being caught by such a tempting offer.

39:10–12 / Passing off Joseph's refusal, Potiphar's wife continued to entice him to lie with her. **One day** when Joseph entered **the house** to work, she was the only one present. Taking advantage of the occasion, she became aggressive, grabbing **his cloak** and pleading with him to **come to bed with** her. Terrified at the possibility of having his integrity compromised, Joseph pulled away. Leaving **his cloak in her hand,** he **ran out of the house.**

39:13–15 / Distraught that she failed to seduce Joseph and seeing **his cloak in her hand,** Potiphar's wife instantly contrived a plan for humiliating Joseph because of his rebuff. She summoned **her household servants** in order to make them witnesses to her accusation against Joseph. According to her version, this Hebrew had come **in to sleep with** her; she **screamed,** and he fled, leaving **his cloak beside** her. She portrayed Joseph as disrobing before her in order to force himself on her. She won the servants over by showing them Joseph's cloak and by defaming him with racial slurs: **this Hebrew has been brought to us to make sport of us!** Her assertion that she had screamed was critical, for it served both as evidence that she had been surprised by Joseph's attempt to rape her and as proof of her lack of compliance with Joseph's intended action (Deut. 22:25–27).

39:16–20 / Potiphar's wife **kept** Joseph's **cloak beside her** to show her husband. When he returned, she told him her account of the incident, slurring Joseph's high standing with Potiphar by calling him a **slave** and a **Hebrew.** Boldly, she even implicated her husband by saying that it was he who **brought** in this slave. She then cleared herself by emphasizing that she **screamed for help.** On hearing his wife's report, Potiphar became very angry. The text does not identify the object of his **anger.** Perhaps he was angry at the whole situation that forced him to lose the best attendant he had ever had (Sarna, *Genesis,* p. 275). He took immediate action against Joseph, putting him in **prison** in the section of Pharaoh's **prisoners.** That Potiphar did not have him executed shows that he still favored him. Either he did not fully believe his wife's accusation or Joseph had defended himself convincingly. Regardless, Joseph's descent from overseer to prisoner was another hardship on his path to becoming a leader.

39:21–23 / The prison was under Pharaoh's control (40:3, 7). There Yahweh continued to be with Joseph, blessing whatever he did. After **the warden** noticed Joseph's trustworthiness and his success, he **put** him **in charge of all** the prisoners and whatever **was done there.** He felt no need to supervise him. Truly Yahweh **was with Joseph,** guiding his destiny in even the most dismal circumstances.

Additional Note §51

39:20–22 / The reference to a prison reflects an Egyptian setting, for Egypt had prisons long before other countries in the ancient Near East did.

§52 Joseph Interprets the Dreams of Pharaoh's Servants (Gen. 40:1–23)

Joseph is now about twenty-eight years old (Sarna, *Genesis*, p. 276). While he has been in Egypt for at least eleven years, the number of years he has spent in prison is uncertain. God nevertheless continues to direct events from behind the scenes. Two things happen in prison that will prove to be crucial for Joseph's future rise to power. He makes contact with Pharaoh's personal servants, and he displays his skill at interpreting dreams.

During his time in prison Joseph meets Pharaoh's servants (vv. 1–4), Joseph interprets their dreams (vv. 5–19), and the dreams are fulfilled (vv. 20–23). At the center stands Joseph's plea for someone to ask Pharaoh to release him from prison (vv. 14–15). The dramatic action makes a play on the phrase "lift up the head." Favorably this phrase portrays the butler's restoration to position (vv. 13, 20), and unfavorably it describes the baker's death by hanging (vv. 19, 22).

40:1–4 / Two of Pharaoh's closest servants, the chief **cupbearer** and the chief **baker, offended** him. Since they served Pharaoh his food, these servants had ready access to Pharaoh and were his advisors. Suspected of being behind some deed that greatly angered Pharaoh, both of them were thrown into prison. They were being detained while the matter was investigated so that the appropriate punishment could be rendered. In God's providence these officials were confined in the same prison as Joseph and were assigned to him.

40:5–8 / One night both the cupbearer and the baker had dreams. Dreams made ancient Egyptians uneasy, for they believed that the gods used dreams to alert them of impending situations. Because they could not discern the meaning of their dreams, these men became troubled about their fate. And since they were in prison, they could not go to an interpreter. Noticing the dejection of these two men, Joseph made inquiry. They reported that during the night each of them had dreamed, but there was no interpretation for either of their dreams. God had given these dreams to pave the way for Joseph's eventual release from prison. Joseph assured these two high court officials that **interpretations belong to God,** implying that he possessed divine powers for interpreting dreams. Joseph's approach encouraged them to tell him their dreams.

40:9–13 / Taking courage, **the chief cupbearer** related his dream about **a vine** with **three branches.** The vine blossomed and produced clusters of grapes. He **took** some of these **grapes** and **squeezed them into Pharaoh's cup and put the cup in** his **hand.** Joseph explained the dream. **The three branches** stood for **three days.** Before **three days** passed **Pharaoh** would "restore the head," that is, restore him to his former high **position** in Pharaoh's service.

40:14–15 / Wishing to improve his own lot, Joseph asked the cupbearer to **remember** him after his restoration to Pharaoh's service. He vividly described how he had been **forcibly carried off** (lit. "stolen") **from the land of the Hebrews** and that he had **done nothing** in Egypt **to deserve being put in a dungeon,** literally "pit" *(bor).* He lamented that he had been taken from one "pit" in Canaan and put in another "pit" in Egypt. The use of this loaded term bears witness to the depth of Joseph's anguish at having to bear such ill fate. He was trying to impress the cupbearer so that he would **show** him **kindness** by speaking to Pharaoh in a way that would get him **out of this prison.**

40:16–19 / Taking heart at the interpretation of the cupbearer's dream, **the chief baker** related his dream **to Joseph.** He saw **on his head three baskets of bread; in the top** one **were all kinds of baked goods for Pharaoh.** On his way to the palace **birds were eating** the baked goods. Joseph interpreted his dream. **The three baskets** likewise stood for **three days.** In three days **Pharaoh** was also going to "lift up his head." In an ironic twist, this phrase means that Pharaoh would have him hanged. Instead of being buried, his body would be exposed for the birds to consume his **flesh.**

40:20–23 / Three days later Pharaoh threw a great **birthday** party. As part of the activities he had both the chief cupbearer and the chief baker brought from prison. He **restored the cup-**

bearer to his position, but he hanged the chief baker. Joseph's interpretations proved to be right on target. Unfortunately for him **the cupbearer** was so enthralled with being restored to high position that he failed to **remember** him. Joseph continued to languish in prison.

Additional Note §52

40:19 / Such a death would be the worst indignity for an Egyptian, because the Egyptians mummified the deceased.

§53 Joseph Interprets Pharaoh's Dreams and Rises to Power (Gen. 41:1–57)

Clothing, a motif throughout the Joseph story, plays a particularly prominent role in this account; it marks Joseph's transition from prison to the honor of standing before Pharaoh and then his investiture with authority. In this account we read about Pharaoh's dreams (vv. 1–7), his need for an interpreter (vv. 8–16), Joseph's interpretation of the dreams (vv. 17–32), his counsel to Pharaoh concerning the coming crisis (vv. 33–38), Joseph's installation into office (vv. 39–45), the years of plenty (vv. 46–49), the birth of Joseph's two sons (vv. 50–52), and the beginning of the famine (vv. 53–57).

41:1–7 / Since Pharaoh's power was directly related to the fertility of the Nile, years of poor crops weakened the throne. One night Pharaoh received two dreams in succession. In the first dream he saw seven **cows, sleek and fat** grazing **among the reeds** along the Nile. **After them, seven other cows, gaunt and ugly, came up out of the Nile and ate up the seven sleek, fat cows.** In the second dream Pharaoh saw **seven heads of grain, healthy and good, . . . growing on a single stalk.** Afterward **seven other heads of grain sprouted—thin and scorched by the east wind.** The thin **heads of grain swallowed up the seven healthy** ones. When **Pharaoh woke,** he realized that he had been dreaming.

41:8 / The next **morning** Pharaoh was agitated, aware that his dreams carried an ominous word about Egypt's future. He summoned to the palace **all the magicians and wise men,** cultic leaders who were especially skilled in interpreting dreams. Pharaoh recounted **his dreams** to these trained diviners, but none of them could give him an acceptable interpretation. It is easy to imagine that some of the interpreters tried unsuccessfully to impress Pharaoh with an explanation.

41:9–13 / Amid the tense atmosphere at court **the chief cupbearer** stepped forward and told Pharaoh how Joseph had interpreted his dream and that of **the chief baker.** He emphasized that Joseph, **a young Hebrew** who was serving **the captain of the guard,** was skilled at interpreting dreams.

41:14–16 / **Pharaoh** immediately **sent for Joseph. He was quickly brought from the dungeon** (lit., "pit"; 40:15). At last Joseph was being rescued from the pit. In order to stand **before Pharaoh,** Joseph **shaved and changed his clothes.** After proper introductions, Pharaoh informed Joseph that no one had been able to interpret his dreams. Joseph assured Pharaoh that though he could not interpret dreams in his own power, **God** would **give Pharaoh the answer.** In making this claim Joseph was speaking boldly, for in Egypt Pharaoh was a god. His confidence before Pharaoh testifies to his communion with God during his years in prison. He was ready to face the challenge before him, assured of God's help. Since Joseph had proven to be a person of integrity under very trying and disheartening conditions, God would be able to work through him in order to bring deliverance both to Egypt and to his own family during the coming crises.

41:17–24 / Pharaoh recounted his dreams to Joseph. In retelling them he made minor changes, underscoring the ominous aspects. He also connected the two dreams in a way that indicates he thought they had a single meaning. However, in muddling the balanced symmetry between the details in the descriptions of the two opposing pairs within each dream and between the dreams, Pharaoh contributed to the failure of the Egyptian diviners to interpret the dreams (M. Sternberg, *The Poetics of Biblical Narrative: Ideological Literature and the Drama of Reading* [Bloomington, Ind.: Indiana University Press, 1987], pp. 399–400).

41:25–32 / Insightfully, **Joseph** began by informing **Pharaoh** that his two dreams had a single meaning. He added confidently that **God** was revealing **to Pharaoh** what was about to take place in Egypt. **The seven good cows** and **the seven good heads of grain** stood for **seven years** of bumper crops throughout Egypt, while **the seven lean, ugly cows** and **the seven worthless heads of grain** represented **seven years of famine.** The seven years of famine would **be so severe** that they would consume all the surplus produced during the seven years of bumper crops. God had shown Pharaoh the future **in two** different **forms** because **the**

matter had **been firmly decided by God** and the cycle was about to begin. A variety of texts from Egypt and Mesopotamia attest that one of the fates the ancients dreaded was a seven-year drought. Conversely, seven years of plenty symbolized the richest blessing. Sternberg (*The Poetics of Biblical Narrative*, p. 400) points out that despite the way Pharaoh had blurred the details in recounting the dreams, Joseph's ability to reconstruct the symmetry of details led him to interpret them correctly.

41:33–36 / Joseph proved to Pharaoh that he was a skilled wise man, wiser than all those in Egypt, by ably interpreting his dreams. Joseph then boldly ventured to counsel Pharaoh about the best course of action for dealing with the coming famine. He advised the monarch to select **a discerning and wise man** and appoint him as manager of agriculture. That person, along with **commissioners** appointed by Pharaoh, would collect and store **a fifth of the harvest of Egypt during the seven years of abundance.** Then **during the seven years of famine this food** could be distributed so that the throne of Egypt would not be threatened by riots during the long drought.

41:37–40 / **Pharaoh** and **his officials** welcomed Joseph's counsel. They also recognized that for this position there was none wiser than Joseph **in whom was the spirit of God.** The reference to God's spirit affirmed Joseph as having extraordinary wisdom (Prov. 1:7, 23). The ancient Egyptians, being very religious, venerated those who had clairvoyant powers. They had no difficulty believing that God was working through someone. However, they would not accept any claim that there was only one God, nor would they submit to the authority of this one God when that God's will was in conflict with the will of the Pharaoh (as the account of the exodus attests). Deeply impressed by Joseph's counsel, Pharaoh appointed him head over his **palace, and all** his **people.** This was one of the highest positions in Egypt's government. But Pharaoh made it clear that the **throne** was still **greater than** Joseph.

41:41–45 / Pharaoh invested Joseph with official power. He removed his **signet ring,** used to make documents official, and **put it on Joseph's finger,** thus empowering him as his personal officer. Next Pharaoh elevated him in the eyes of the people by having him outfitted with **linen** garments, that is, clothes of the finest material, and by putting **a gold chain around his neck.** He provided Joseph **a chariot** and forerunners to announce his arrival. Joseph's chariot was to follow Pharaoh's in the procession. Also Pharaoh gave him an Egyptian name, **Zaphenath-Paneah,** insuring his acceptance as an integral member of the court. To make him a full member of Egyptian society Pharaoh arranged for him to marry **Asenath, daughter of Potiphera,** a **priest** in the city of **On,** the center of the worship of the sun god Re. The city is also known as Heliopolis, which is Greek for "sun city."

41:46 / Joseph's rise to this high position in a foreign government at the young age of **thirty** testifies that God watched over him during the hardships he had endured. Joseph's youthful dreams were remarkably fulfilled by this appointment. Joseph went to work, traveling **throughout Egypt** to gain a sense of the preparations that needed to be taken for the coming famine.

41:47–52 / The land produced abundantly for the next **seven years. Joseph collected** grain and **stored it in the cities.** The surplus of grain became so great that it was beyond counting. During this time Asenath bore Joseph **two sons.** The **firstborn** he **named Manasseh, . . . because God** had **made** him **forget all** his **trouble and all** his **father's household.** It is not that Joseph no longer remembered his family or the hard times but that the bitterness of that memory had been eased. His **second son he named Ephraim, . . . because God** had **made** him **fruitful in the land of** his **suffering.** The meanings of these names illustrate Joseph's attitude toward the hard years he had endured and foreshadow the way he would relate to his brothers.

41:53–57 / **Seven years** later, as God had forewarned Pharaoh, the **famine began.** It proved to be a terrible famine, spreading well beyond Egypt's borders. When the Egyptians **cried to Pharaoh,** Pharaoh directed them to follow Joseph's instructions in order to buy grain from the **storehouses.** Peoples from other lands, also suffering from the famine, **came to Egypt to buy grain from Joseph.** The stage was set for Joseph to meet his brothers again.

Additional Notes §53

41:40 / Many scholars believe that Joseph became vizier, the highest official in Egypt after the Pharaoh (Exod. 7:11, 12; 8:3–4), but the duties Joseph undertook do not correspond to those of that office. Further, since there was a vizier when Joseph arrived at court, it is doubtful that Pharaoh replaced that person with Joseph. It is more likely that Pharaoh created a new position for Joseph. One of Joseph's responsibilities was minister of agriculture: the Egyptian title was "Overseer of the Granaries of Upper and Lower Egypt." He had a powerful role in Pharaoh's house, possibly "lord of all his household" (45:8); this title would make him minister of the possessions of the crown (de Vaux, *Early History of Israel*, pp. 298–99). That it was possible for a Semite to rise to such a high position in the Egyptian government is well attested. Under Pharaoh Akhenaton a Semite named Tutu held power over special tasks and reported directly to the Pharaoh. There is a painting of Tutu riding away from the palace in his chariot and the people bowing before him (de Vaux, *Early History of Israel*, p. 299).

41:45 / The precise meaning of Zaphenath-Paneah is debated. K. Kitchen proposes the meaning "(Joseph) who is called (I)pi-'ankh," a common name in early second millennium B.C. ("Genesis 12–50 in the Near Eastern World," in *He Swore an Oath: Biblical Themes from Genesis 12–50* [ed. R. Hess et al.; Cambridge: Tyndale House, 1993], pp. 80–84).

§54 Jacob's Sons Buy Grain in Egypt (Gen. 42:1–38)

The scene shifts to Canaan, where Jacob's family feels the full brunt of the famine. Their hope for survival rests on the availability of grain in Egypt. Therefore Jacob sends his sons to Egypt (vv. 1–4); the brothers negotiate with Joseph (vv. 5–25) and then return to Canaan (vv. 26–38).

42:1–4 / To cope with the crisis of the famine the mournful Jacob reasserted his leadership. Having **learned that there was grain in Egypt,** Jacob called **his sons** together, scolded them for inaction, and instructed them to **go down** to Egypt to **buy** grain so that they might **live. Ten** of his sons went to Egypt; they are identified as **Joseph's brothers** to build the anticipation of their meeting Joseph. Jacob did not let **Benjamin,** the younger son of Rachel, go along because he feared **that harm might come to him.**

42:5–17 / Israel's sons **arrived** in Egypt. The brothers **bowed ... with their faces to the ground** before **the governor ... who sold grain.** Unbeknownst to them, they had met Joseph. He **recognized** his brothers immediately. Considering that these were ten brothers dressed as Semites, it was not difficult for him, and he would have recognized their voices. The brothers had no awareness that they were talking to anyone other than a high Egyptian official. Excited and wanting to learn as much as possible about his family and their attitude toward him, Joseph spoke to them with stern authority. He immediately threw them off guard by accusing them of being foreign **spies** intent on learning Egypt's weakness. Fearfully, the brothers responded with great deference, stating that the purpose of their visit was **to buy food.**

As an irate interrogator Joseph repeated the charge of spying. The brothers defended themselves by identifying themselves further, offering Joseph the information he longed for. To keep them on the defensive Joseph challenged them to prove their

innocence by having one of them go back to Canaan and bring the
youngest brother to Egypt while the rest waited **in prison.** The arrival of the youngest brother would prove their story. To impress
on them the precariousness of their situation, Joseph **put them all
in custody for three days.** Joseph was giving his brothers a taste of
the hardship and sense of helplessness he had suffered during his
years as a prisoner in a foreign land. At the same time he was seeking to discover the present disposition of his half-brothers toward
the sons of Rachel in addition to trying to devise a plan that
would reunite him with his father and full brother.

42:18–20 / **On the third day, Joseph** summoned his
brothers and informed them what he required of them. They
were to **take grain back** to their family members who were **starving,** as long as **one** of them stayed behind **in prison.** Then they
were to return with their **youngest brother.** Only then would Joseph believe that they were not spies worthy of the death penalty.
By keeping one of them in Egypt, Joseph assured their return.

42:21–25 / The brothers discussed Joseph's plan without seeking privacy, for they did not imagine that the Egyptian
overseer could understand Hebrew. As they spoke it became apparent to Joseph that they were heavily burdened with guilt for
having sold him into slavery. **Reuben** reminded them that he had
warned them **not to sin against the boy.** Their remorseful attitude so overwhelmed Joseph that he **turned away from them and
began to weep,** giving vent to years of distress resulting from the
harm they had done to him. He also recognized the mercy of God
in putting him in a position where he could deliver his father's
household from this severe famine. After speaking some more to
them, he **had Simeon taken from them and bound before their
eyes.** Then he ordered that **their bags** be filled **with grain** and that
their money be **put in** the sacks. He also gave them additional
provisions for their journey.

42:26–28 / The brothers **loaded** their sacks of **grain on
their donkeys and left. At the place where they stopped for the
night one of them opened his sack to get feed for his donkey.**
He was startled to find his money. The text does not state Joseph's
reason for returning their money. Perhaps he wanted to make
sure that they had sufficient money to return to Egypt to buy
grain. This gesture, however, increased his brothers' consterna-
tion, especially in light of the overseer's charges. While they

knew that they were innocent of spying, they were apprehensive about not being able to defend themselves before an accusation of theft when they had the money. This fate convinced them that they were meeting such pitfalls for having sold their brother.

42:29–35 / Back home, the brothers reported their adventures in Egypt. Not wanting to heighten Jacob's fears, they did not report everything. They had to tell him enough to account for Simeon's absence and the requirement of taking Benjamin with them whenever they returned to buy more grain. They emphasized how **harshly** the overseer in Egypt had spoken to them and his outrageous charge that they were spies. The overseer had demanded that they **bring** their **youngest brother** as evidence that they were **not spies.** In the meantime, he had let them return with food for their families as long as they left one of them behind in an Egyptian prison. When they had convinced him of their honesty, he would release Simeon and let them **trade in the land.** After telling their father of their experiences in Egypt, **they** emptied **their sacks;** each of them was frightened as he found his money in his sack. Since they must have opened their sacks on the journey back to Canaan, it is doubtful that this is when they made this discovery. A solution to this apparent discrepancy, proposed by Sarna (*Genesis,* p. 296), fits the character of Jacob's sons. Not wanting to explain the return of their money, they staged this discovery in Jacob's presence so that he would be as surprised as they were. Sternberg, however, thinks that Jacob's fear was rooted in his suspicion that the money came from his sons having sold Simeon (*The Poetics of Biblical Narrative,* p. 298).

42:36–38 / Jacob mourned that he had lost Joseph and Simeon. He felt that **everything** was **against** him. Their taking Benjamin along to Egypt was a higher risk than he was willing to permit. **Reuben** proposed that if he did **not bring** Benjamin **back,** his own two **sons** could be put **to death.** But Jacob was not persuaded. He steeled himself against letting Benjamin go to Egypt. Having lost two sons, **only** Benjamin was **left.** Should Benjamin meet an accident on that trip, Jacob would go **to the grave** with great **sorrow** in his heart. So his family had to endure the famine as long as possible without returning to Egypt to get more grain.

Additional Note §54

42:22   /   It is possible that Joseph detained Simeon, the second born, because he had learned that Reuben had tried to save his life (Wenham, *Genesis 16–50*, p. 409).

§55 Jacob's Sons Return to Egypt
(Gen. 43:1–45:28)

With the supplies of grain almost gone, Jacob finally accepts the reality that his sons must return to Egypt to buy more grain. After they arrive in Egypt, Joseph orchestrates a sequence of incidents that moves to the climactic moment when he makes himself known to his brothers. This, one of the most powerful accounts in history, has seven scenes. Jacob's family discusses the need to return to Egypt (43:1–14). When they arrive in Egypt, the brothers attempt to return the money to Joseph's steward (43:15–23). During the meal at Joseph's house (43:24–34), Joseph recognizes Benjamin and feasts with his brothers. Later the brothers are detained under suspicion of stealing the overseer's divining cup (44:1–13); they defend their integrity before Joseph (44:14–34). Joseph then identifies himself to his brothers (45:1–24), and the brothers return to Canaan (45:25–28).

43:1–7 / Since their supply of grain was depleted, Jacob ordered his sons to return to Egypt to **buy food.** Judah reminded him that the Egyptian overseer would not let them buy food unless Benjamin was with them. **Israel** angrily **asked why** they had brought **this trouble on** him **by telling** this Egyptian that they **had another brother.** His sons defended themselves by recounting how the overseer had **questioned** them **closely** about their family. In answering him honestly the brothers had no intimation that he would demand that they **bring** Benjamin to Egypt. This discussion provides a glimpse into the distress the loss of Joseph caused in Jacob's household. It also emphasizes that neither Jacob nor his sons had any inkling that the Egyptian overseer was Joseph.

43:8–10 / **Judah** sought to persuade **Israel** to let Benjamin, his youngest son, accompany them to Egypt by personally guaranteeing Benjamin's **safety.** Judah underscored his argument by noting that they should **have gone** to Egypt for food **twice.**

43:11–14 / Jacob relented and then instructed them on how to deal better with the Egyptian overlord. They were to give him a present of some choice items from Canaan, including **balm, honey, spices, myrrh, some pistachio nuts and almonds.** Possibly Jacob had stored these delicacies to help alleviate the drab, meager diet during the famine. Or perhaps they produced small amounts of these food items during the famine. Jacob reasoned that this gift should encourage the overseer to treat these Hebrews more favorably since they were sharing treasured foods during a time of scarcity. Furthermore, they were to **take double the amount of** money, to buy the new grain and to pay back the money that **was put** in their **sacks** by **mistake.** Full of emotion and resolve, Israel commanded them to **take** Benjamin and **go back to the man** in Egypt. Then he invoked **God Almighty** (17:1; 28:3) to **grant** them **mercy before the man so that he** would **let** their **other brother,** Simeon, and **Benjamin come back** to Canaan. Having consented to his sons' going to Egypt and having prayed, Israel braced himself to accept whatever happened.

43:15–16 / With **the gifts,** the money, **and Benjamin,** the brothers **hurried down to Egypt.** On arrival **they presented themselves to Joseph. When** he **saw Benjamin with them,** he gave orders to have **these men** brought to his **house . . . to eat with** him **at noon.**

43:17–23 / The brothers were alarmed when they learned that they **were** being **taken to** Joseph's **house.** They anticipated that the overlord was preparing to punish them for the money they had found in their **sacks.** They were so apprehensive that they imagined that the Egyptians were going to confiscate their donkeys and make them slaves of the state. Their fears were similar to Joseph's when he was detained in the cistern. To prevent their worst fears' being realized, the brothers went straight to **Joseph's steward** and reported how they had found their money in their **sacks.** They offered to return the **exact** amount due the treasury. The steward, however, reassured them that he had **received** their money and encouraged them by saying that it was their **God** who had given them this **treasure. Then he brought Simeon out** of prison.

43:24–31 / **The steward took** all of them **into Joseph's house.** He **gave them water to wash their feet** and **fodder for their donkeys.** While waiting for dinner, **they prepared their gifts** for the overseer. **When Joseph** arrived, **they presented to him the gifts . . . and bowed down before him to the ground.** In so doing, they were fulfilling Joseph's youthful dreams in his own house.

Joseph **asked** about their well-being and the well-being of their **aged father,** no doubt worried about his father's ability to survive the famine. They answered that their **father** was **still alive and well.** Joseph next inquired about their **youngest brother. At the sight of his** own **brother** he became so overwhelmed with emotion that he **hurried out** of the dining hall, **went into his private room and wept** joyfully. **After he had washed his face,** he returned and ordered the servants to **serve the food.**

43:32–34 / The brothers were seated at the table according to their birth order. This arrangement astonished and puzzled them, for in their minds no foreigner, especially an Egyptian, would have any idea of their birth order. Joseph had arranged for them to sit in that order both to keep his brothers off guard and to give them significant evidence that would establish his true identity whenever he chose to reveal himself to them. The other Egyptians sat at a separate table, because of Egyptian custom. Joseph had a fivefold portion set before Benjamin. They all ate and **drank freely.**

44:1–2 / After the meal Joseph ordered his **steward** to **fill the men's sacks** to the brim and to **put each man's silver in the mouth of his sack.** In the mouth of Benjamin's sack he was to **put** Joseph's **silver cup along with** Benjamin's money. Joseph was planning a confrontation with his brothers in which they would be beholden to him and in which they would reveal their true attitude to the sons of Rachel. Also, by having his cup put in Benjamin's sack Joseph gave none of his half-brothers any reason to argue that Joseph had singled him out for retaliation. If Joseph had chosen another brother for this ploy, that brother might have always doubted his standing with Joseph (50:15).

44:3–5 / At the first light of dawn the brothers **were sent on their way.** Before they had traveled very **far,** Joseph commanded **his steward** to **go after those men.** When he overcame them, he was to ask **why** they had **repaid good with evil** by taking the master's **cup** that he used **for divination.** This special use of

the cup made it irreplaceable. The theft of such a prized possession attached to the royal office was a brash affront against one
who had shown them hospitality. Whether or not Joseph practiced divination is open to question. While such practice was condemned by the law (Lev. 19:26b; Deut. 18:10b), Joseph was not
under that law. However, since God endowed Joseph with wisdom, he might have had this cup solely to accommodate himself
to Egyptian custom.

44:6–9 / After overtaking these Semites, the steward accused them of theft as Joseph had directed. Protesting vociferously, the brothers proclaimed their innocence with an argument
and an assertion. By pointing out that they had sought to return
the money they had **found inside** their **sacks,** they claimed it
would be unlikely for them to **steal silver or gold from** the overseer's **house.** They went on to assert that if the cup should be
found with any of them, that one would **die** and **the rest** of them
would **become slaves** to the overseer. Putting oneself under such
an outrageous penalty was a rhetorical device aimed at convincing the steward of their innocence (cf. 31:32).

44:10–13 / The steward answered by reasserting what
the overseer had stipulated: only the one who had the cup would
become the overseer's **slave** and **the rest** would be **free.** He began
the search, moving from **the oldest** to **the youngest.** One can
imagine the anxiety of each of these brothers as his sack was
searched and then his relief when the cup was not found in it.
When Benjamin's turn came, the anxiety of all of them rose. Although they were confident that Benjamin had not taken the cup,
they were very worried because of all the strange things they had
been experiencing in dealings with the Egyptians. **The cup was
found in Benjamin's sack.** Filled with terror and driven by a
sense of urgency, the brothers **tore their clothes, loaded their
donkeys and returned to the city.**

44:14–17 / The brothers went straight to Joseph's house
and found him **still** there. With Judah at their head, **they threw
themselves to the ground before him,** fulfilling in even greater
measure the dreams of Joseph's youth. Taking advantage of the
moment, Joseph heaped shame on them by asking why they had
dared to do such a wrong in light of his ability to **find things out
by divination.** The atmosphere was ripe for his discovering the
true character of his brothers and the sincerity of their acceptance

of Benjamin. Would they heap blame for their present precarious fate on another son of Rachel? Or would they defend Benjamin, thereby giving convincing proof that they had changed? Having separated Benjamin from his brothers, Joseph had reconstructed a situation similar to that in Dothan. They could let Benjamin be sent into slavery while they returned to their father. Did Jacob's sons still have such hatred for a son of Rachel that they would abandon him for their own benefit?

Speaking for the group, **Judah** conceded that their situation was hopeless, knowing of no way to **prove** their **innocence.** He admitted that they were in this quandary because **God** had **uncovered** their **guilt,** thereby admitting that they had sinned in selling their brother into slavery. He went on to concede that all of them were **slaves** to the overseer. Joseph rejected his capitulating offer by reasserting that **only the man who** was **found to have the cup** should **become** his **slave. The rest** of them could return in peace to **their father.** Joseph was testing the extent of their resolve to defend Benjamin.

44:18–34 / **Judah** stepped forward and politely asked the overseer for permission to **speak.** His appeal for Benjamin's release is the longest speech in Genesis. From Egyptian texts like *The Eloquent Peasant,* we discover that the Egyptians were moved by long, eloquent speeches. Judah was therefore employing the best tactic for seeking to keep Benjamin out of slavery. He began by recognizing the status of the one he was addressing as **equal to Pharaoh.** Then he pleaded for the overseer's mercy, recounting what had transpired between them on their first visit to Egypt. He focused on the overlord's demand that they **bring** their youngest brother to Egypt despite their protest that it would cause their father grief and possible death should something happen to him. With great reluctance their father had consented to Benjamin's coming along to buy grain. He mentioned how their father Israel had described the **misery** he would experience should Benjamin not return. Judah pointed out how he had **guaranteed** the safe return of his brother to ease his father's anxiety. He concluded by entreating the overseer to make him a **slave** in Benjamin's **place** so that **the boy** could **return** home **with his brothers.** He underscored his offer with the passionate plea that he not be made to **see the misery that would come upon** his **father.**

In this speech Joseph learned how grievously his father mourned his absence. Judah was demonstrating the complete change in his attitude to his younger brother; he was willing to submit himself to a hard situation in order to protect a son of Rachel from becoming a slave. Joseph witnessed that the brother who had proposed his sale now vigorously defended Benjamin.

45:1–2 / **No longer** able to **control** his emotions, Joseph ordered all his attendants to leave. He wanted privacy for making himself known to his brothers. Furthermore, being alone with his brothers, he could speak with them unofficially. When all the servants had left, Joseph **wept . . . loudly,** full of joy at their reunion and remorse over the years of separation. His weeping was so loud **that the Egyptians heard him.** The report of what was happening in Joseph's house reached **Pharaoh's household.**

45:3–8 / In one of the most dramatic moments in Scripture, Joseph identified himself, saying simply, **I am Joseph!** He then asked if his **father** truly was alive; this was his compelling concern. The brothers were so astounded and fearful that they **were not able to answer him.** Joseph's being alive altered the family dynamic. That realization, coupled with the fact that Joseph was one of the most powerful officials in the Egyptian empire, made them tremble at the prospect of his vengeful wrath. Sensing their alarm, Joseph asked his brothers to approach him.

When they had drawn near, he identified himself again as the **brother** whom they had **sold into Egypt.** He enjoined them **not** to **be distressed** nor to **be angry** by emphasizing that what they had done was used by God **to save lives.** He went on to inform them that in addition to the past **two years** of **famine, five** more **years** were to come without any productive farming. Thus **God** had **sent** him to Egypt **ahead of** them in order that he might **preserve** them as **a remnant** and keep them alive **by a great deliverance.** He sought to alleviate his brothers' anxiety by stressing that not they **but God** had **sent** him to Egypt. God had ordered the course of his life so that he had become **father to Pharaoh, lord of his entire household and ruler of all of Egypt.** "Father to Pharaoh" means he was Pharaoh's counselor (see 2 Kgs. 13:14), and "ruler of all Egypt" means that his particular authority extended throughout the land of Egypt. In selling him they had merely been agents of God's will.

45:9–13 / Joseph next enjoined them to return to his **father** and tell him what they had learned: Joseph was alive and **God** had **made** him **lord of all Egypt.** They were to give Israel the command to **come down to** him without **delay.** When he arrived in Egypt, he would **live in . . . Goshen** and **be near** his son. Joseph made it clear that there was room for the whole family, **children, grandchildren, flocks and herds,** and all their possessions. Jacob's family, threatened by death from the fierce famine, had found a genuine savior—the lost son and brother. Those who had been surviving on meager rations would now have access to the riches of Egypt. During the coming five years of famine Joseph would provide for them in abundance. To persuade Israel to come to Egypt, Joseph instructed his brothers to rehearse before his father **all the honor accorded** him **in Egypt** and all that they had **seen.**

45:14–15 / Joseph then embraced **Benjamin and wept, and Benjamin** wept on his neck. **He kissed all his brothers and wept over them.** Reconciliation between Joseph and his brothers had begun. Regaining some composure after the shock of this dramatic revelation, they began to speak with each other.

45:16–20 / A report went out to **Pharaoh's palace that Joseph's brothers had come** to Egypt. **Pleased** with this news, **Pharaoh** enjoined them to **return to the land of Canaan and bring** their **father and** their **families** to Egypt. He promised them **the best of the land of Egypt.** He made **carts** available to them for moving their families and their **father** to Egypt.

45:21–24 / Joseph **gave them carts, as Pharaoh had commanded,** and **provisions for their journey.** He also gave **to each of them . . . new clothing. To Benjamin he gave three hundred** pieces **of silver** and **five sets of clothes.** Having tested his brothers' attitude toward Benjamin, Joseph knew that the favoritism he showed Benjamin would not produce jealous retaliation. For his father he **sent ten donkeys loaded with the best things of Egypt.** Also he sent an additional **ten female donkeys loaded with grain and bread and other provisions for his journey** to Egypt. Joseph had his brothers take back such a huge amount of supplies not so much to meet the family's needs as to provide evidence to support the incredible report that Joseph was alive and a high official in Egypt. He concluded by ordering his brothers not to **quarrel on the way.** His gentle admonition reminded them that his living in Egypt was a result of their quarreling in the past. Certainly Joseph did not want them to delay in bringing his father to Egypt because of a difference of opinion. It is also possible to read the line, "do not be agitated on the way" (Wenham, *Genesis 16–50*, p. 430); that is, they were not to become apprehensive about returning to Egypt.

45:25–28 / On reaching Canaan, the brothers reported to Jacob that **Joseph** was **alive** and that **he** was **ruler of all Egypt. Stunned,** Jacob **did not believe them.** They continued to seek to persuade him by telling **everything Joseph had said to them.** When **he saw** the many **carts Joseph had sent,** Jacob's **spirit . . . revived,** and he was **convinced** that his **son Joseph** was **still alive.** He then declared his determination to **go and see him before** he died.

Additional Note §55

44:5 / In Egypt, counselors used such cups for divination. They would pour a variety of liquids, such as oil or wine, into water standing in the cup and then read the future by the configuration of the resulting designs.

§56 Jacob and His Family Move to Egypt (Gen. 46:1–47:12)

This account of Jacob's family's settling in Egypt contains seven sections: Jacob offers sacrifices at Beersheba (46:1–4), the journey to Egypt (46:5–7), a list of Jacob's family (46:8–27), Jacob meets Joseph (46:28–30), Joseph prepares his brothers to meet Pharaoh (46:31–34), the audience with Pharaoh (47:1–10), and Joseph's provisions for his father and brothers (47:11–12).

46:1–7 / Several elements common to the experience of the patriarchs are present: God appears to Jacob, Jacob stops along the way to worship God, and the reference to God as the God of the fathers (26:24; 28:13). **Israel set out** for Egypt, traveling from Hebron by way of **Beersheba,** where both Abraham and Isaac had lived for a time. This site marked the southern boundary of the promised land (2 Sam. 24:2). Before leaving the land of promise, Israel **offered sacrifices to the God of his father Isaac** (26:23–24; 28:13). God honored him by speaking to him **in a vision,** affectionately calling his name twice (22:11; Exod. 3:4; 1 Sam. 3:10). Identifying himself as **the God of** his **father,** God enjoined Jacob not to fear about going **down to Egypt.** He reaffirmed his promise to **make** him **a great nation there.** The command "not to fear" is a word of assurance whereby God promises a person or a group deliverance from endangering circumstances (15:1; 21:17). Jacob required confirmation of God's approval in order to leave the promised land for what turned out to be a very long stay in Egypt. Critically, this word from God provided his descendants with the assurance that their living in Egypt was part of the divine design and that the Abrahamic promises were still operative (12:2). God supported this word of salvation with the promise that his presence was going **down to Egypt with** him (26:24; 28:15, 20; 31:3–5). God also assured him that he would **bring** him **back,** that is, for his burial, adding the tender promise that Joseph would place his **own hand** on his **eyes,** meaning that his beloved son Joseph would attend to his burial. Jacob's worship of God at Beersheba completed his retracing of Abraham's initial journey through the promised land upon his return from Haran.

Jacob and his entire family, with their **livestock** and **possessions, left Beersheba** and went **to Egypt in the carts** provided by **Pharaoh.**

46:8–27 / This list gives the names of Jacob's offspring up to the third generation and identifies all who went to Egypt and increased into the tribes of Israel. The children and grandchildren by Leah come first, followed by those of Zilpah, Leah's handmaid; they total **thirty-three** and **sixteen** respectively. Next are the offspring of Rachel and then those of Bilhah, Rachel's handmaid, numbering **fourteen** and **seven** respectively. Seven and its multiple fourteen, being sacred numbers, honor Rachel as the favored matriarch. The total number in Jacob's family was **seventy** persons. Seventy is a crucial number in the OT, being the product of ten (a round number for a group larger than just a few; ten persons became the number required to form a congregation) times seven (the number of perfection). It symbolizes an ideal, complete unit, such as the Sanhedrin. The list of Jacob's seventy children at the end of the patriarchal era parallels the seventy nations at the close of the primeval narrative (ch. 10).

46:28–30 / **Judah** went ahead to meet with **Joseph** to learn where they were to settle in **Goshen. Joseph went to Goshen** in his **chariot.** On meeting **his father,** he embraced him and **wept for a long time.** The only way Israel could respond was to say that he was **ready to die,** having been comforted in seeing Joseph again.

46:31–34 / Joseph informed his whole family that he was going to report their arrival to Pharaoh. He then instructed them on what to say to Pharaoh, especially about their **occupation.** They were to mention that they had been shepherds since their youth. In that way they would assure Pharaoh that they did not intend to seek work done by Egyptians. On hearing their report, Pharaoh would grant them permission **to settle in the region of Goshen,** since **shepherds** were **detestable to the Egyptians.**

47:1–6 / **Joseph** took along his father and **five of his brothers** to meet with Pharaoh. After proper introductions **Pharaoh asked** about their **occupation. They replied** that they were **shepherds** and that they had **come to live** in Egypt as temporary residents **because** of the **famine.** They then asked permission to **settle in Goshen.**

Speaking to **Joseph, Pharaoh** welcomed his family and graciously said that they could dwell **in the best part of** Egypt, specifically **Goshen.** Pharaoh granted these Semites official permission to become resident aliens in Egypt. He also authorized Joseph to appoint those especially skilled among them to oversee the royal flocks. The crown often employed foreigners to take care of its livestock.

47:7–10 / **Joseph** then introduced **his father** to **Pharaoh. Jacob blessed Pharaoh;** that is, he greeted him with a word that promoted his well-being. The great monarch of Egypt displayed genuine deference before such an elderly patriarch. **Pharaoh asked him** his age. Jacob responded that he was **a hundred and thirty** years old and that his **years** had **been few and difficult.** Jacob's words markedly contrast the usual saying of an aged patriarch that one had lived to a good old age, full of years (25:8). The schemer and manipulator of God's will had to bear many hardships through the years because of his scheming. He had served Laban for twenty years for his wives and flocks. He had been deceived about the two people he loved most, Rachel and Joseph. Jacob also lamented that his life span would not reach that of his forefathers. On departing **Jacob blessed Pharaoh** again, expressing his gratitude to Pharaoh for providing them grain and a place to reside. The Abrahamic blessing that those who blessed his seed would find blessing was operative in this setting (12:3). Egypt blessed Jacob's family by providing food and a place to live, and God blessed Pharaoh through Jacob's son Joseph as he guided Egypt to survive this long natural catastrophe.

47:11–12 / **Joseph settled his father and brothers in Egypt and gave them property** in Goshen, identified as **the district of Rameses.** Since the term for "property" (*'akhuzzah*) implies permanent residence, Joseph's family was given permission to stay in Egypt indefinitely. **Joseph also provided** them **food,** supplies, and feed for their livestock. Jacob's family no longer had to fear starvation.

Additional Notes §56

46:8–27 / A few comments about this list: Dinah should be added (v. 15); Er and Onan (v. 12) had died in Canaan; Joseph and his two sons (v. 20) were already in Egypt. Thus the list has been constructed to make sure it was a list of seventy.

46:17 / More women accompanied them than the text mentions. The reason Serah was singled out is unknown.

46:21 / Ten sons of Benjamin are listed, but Num. 26:38–40 and 1 Chron. 8:1–2 mention only five, and 1 Chron. 7:6 only three. Perhaps this list includes grandchildren in anticipation of their birth (Kidner, *Genesis*, p. 209).

46:34 / Egyptian texts do not support the claim that Egyptians despised shepherds. What Joseph might have meant is that Egyptians did not like foreign shepherds moving about, especially given the scarcity of arable land in Egypt. It is possible that Semitic shepherds, accustomed to moving about, did not sufficiently control their flocks around farm land, thus provoking strong antipathy from the Egyptians.

47:11 / Goshen is identified as the region of Rameses, the name of Pharaoh in the nineteenth dynasty (thirteenth century B.C.). Rameses II built Tanis in the northeastern delta and put his capital there. This name appears to be a later editorial addition, for Joseph preceded Rameses by several centuries.

§57 Joseph's Administration of the Famine (Gen. 47:13–27)

Joseph is pictured as a wise, shrewd, and compassionate administrator, loyal to Pharaoh as well as concerned for the people. During the harsh famine he displays great administrative skill in distributing the stored food in a way that meets the needs of the people and strengthens the crown. He prudently prepares for the land to return to production at the end of the famine.

47:13–17 / The Egyptians and the inhabitants of Canaan groaned beneath the unending famine. After the Egyptians had paid **all** their **money for grain** and Joseph had **brought it to Pharaoh's palace,** they began to cry out to Joseph for **food.** Joseph agreed to **sell** them f**ood in exchange for** their **livestock—their horses,** their flocks, **their cattle and donkeys.**

47:18–26 / The next year the people informed Joseph that they had **nothing left** for buying food except their **bodies** and their **land.** They begged him to **buy** them and their **land** and make them Pharaoh's servants **in exchange for food.** In that society the crown had complete sovereignty, and servitude was a common way of handling debt to avoid becoming destitute. Joseph showed mercy to the people by allowing them the dignity of paying for the grain. He **bought all the land in Egypt for Pharaoh.** Only **the land of the priests he did not buy,** because Pharaoh had apportioned to them **a regular allotment** of food. The priesthood in Egypt was a powerful force in government.

Since the people were now tenant farmers, Joseph allotted them **seed** for planting the fields, an indication that the famine was about to end. Under this agreement, they paid twenty percent of their **crop . . . to Pharaoh.** Texts from the ancient Middle East attest that the interest rate for seed was often much higher, many times at forty percent. According to ancient standards, Joseph thus acted graciously toward the people. He stressed that the rest of the crop was theirs for **seed** and for **food.** The people gladly accepted the agreement, knowing that they had been spared from death.

47:27 / During these hard times **the Israelites** lived peacefully in **Goshen.** They were blessed and **increased greatly in number.**

Additional Notes §57

47:13–17 / There is insufficient information from ancient Egypt about the crown's land holdings with which to compare this report.

47:18–26 / Although making the citizens servants of the state is unacceptable from today's political perspective, Joseph acted prudently in his role as administrator of the food supply in order to keep the people from starving. God had not commissioned Joseph to be a social reformer. Even if Joseph had not wanted the citizens to become servants of the state, there was no ideological basis for a more progressive approach to dealing with the terrible social threats posed by such a long, hard famine. Joseph is a model of those servants of God who act wisely for the good of the community within the social patterns of their time and setting.

47:21 / Joseph's reason for moving the people to cities is an enigma, for the people were needed to work the land after the famine was over. Therefore NIV reads "and Joseph reduced the people to servitude" based on Sam. Pent. and Gk. Many commentators follow the variant because the reading in MT does not make sense and the variant accords better with the context.

§58 Jacob Prepares for His Death (Gen. 47:28–31)

Because Jacob's death marked the end of the patriarchal age, the preparation for it is given much attention and is treated three times (also 48:21–22; 49:29–32). **Jacob lived in Egypt seventeen years,** reaching the age of **a hundred and forty-seven.** Sensing that his death was approaching, **he called for his son Joseph.** The right of attending to the burial of the father normally belonged to the oldest son, but Israel entrusted Joseph with this responsibility because of his love for this son and because of Joseph's high position in Egypt. He asked Joseph to swear by putting his **hand under** his **thigh** (24:2, 9) that he would **not bury** him **in Egypt.** Instead he was to bury him in the Cave of Machpelah, where his fathers were **buried.** Joseph took the oath. **Israel** then **worshiped,** comforted by knowing that his last request would be honored.

§59 Jacob Blesses Joseph and His Sons (Gen. 48:1–22)

On learning that Jacob has become very ill, Joseph and his sons Manasseh and Ephraim go to visit him. On this occasion Jacob blesses both Joseph and his sons. Significantly, he raises Joseph's two sons to the level of his own children. This account carries great weight, for it modifies Israel's tribal structure.

Throughout the account there are abrupt shifts that disturb the narrative flow. Joseph introduces his sons to Jacob (vv. 8–9) even though Jacob has already spoken about them (v. 5). Later, the heading to Jacob's blessing of Joseph's sons reads "he blessed Joseph" (vv. 15–16). Joseph objects about the position of his father's hands on his sons' heads (v. 18), but this objection appears to be after the fact (v. 14). In addition, the text does not include the blessings spoken to Manasseh and Ephraim. The fact that these blessings may have circulated independently of this narrative may help account for the unevenness in the narrative. Headings in the text set the blessings off for liturgical usage (vv. 15, 20). All Israelites will speak blessings in the name of Ephraim and Manasseh (v. 20), for these sons of Joseph will be so blessed that the other tribes will want to share in their blessing.

In five scenes we read that Joseph visits his ailing father (vv. 1–2); Jacob recounts the history of the blessing he received (vv. 3–7); Joseph formally introduces his two sons (vv. 8–12); Israel blesses Joseph, Ephraim, and Manasseh (vv. 13–20); and Israel gives Joseph a special inheritance in Canaan (vv. 21–22).

48:1–2 / On learning that his father was seriously **ill,** Joseph went to him, taking along **his two sons Manasseh and Ephraim.** When Joseph's arrival was announced, Jacob **rallied his strength and sat up on the bed.**

48:3–4 / Jacob recounted how **God Almighty** had **appeared to** him **at Luz,** that is, Bethel (28:19; 35:9–11). God had promised **to make** him **fruitful** and **increase** his **numbers,** to **make** him into **a community of peoples,** and to **give** him **this land as an everlasting possession to** his **descendants after** him. Jacob thus joined the specific promises God gave him at Bethel to those from his father Isaac (28:3). Although the motif of an increasing family occurs three times and that of land only once, the strategic importance of the latter is borne by the wording "an everlasting inheritance" and by its placement at the climax of the blessing. Jacob looked to the day when his descendants would occupy the land God had given him. Emphasizing God's great faithfulness, Jacob did not refer to himself or brag about his own achievements. His attitude and faith witness to the transformation of his character from finagler to one who placed his trust in God. In recounting how he had been blessed, Jacob was asserting his authority for passing on that blessing to his sons before he died.

48:5–7 / Jacob then formally recognized Joseph's **two sons,** Ephraim and Manasseh, who had been **born . . . in Egypt,** as his own sons. By the words "they **will be . . . mine,**" he officially elevated them to the same standing as his sons by birth. Since this transaction redefines the position of Joseph's sons among Jacob's children, a conditional clause is included: should Joseph have **any** more **children,** their inheritance would **be reckoned** as Joseph's children, not as Jacob's. At this point Jacob reminisced about their grandmother Rachel's death and burial in **Canaan** (35:16, 19). In Jacob's memory her death was associated with God's blessing, since she died shortly after God had conferred on him the Abrahamic promises at Bethel (35:11–12). Jacob was recounting some family history for his two grandsons.

48:8–9 / **Israel saw the sons of Joseph** and **asked who** they were. This question disrupts the flow of the narrative. While it might be evidence that two accounts of this blessing were blended, another view takes the question as serving a legal purpose: the precise identification of the two children standing before Israel as Joseph's. Joseph's father is called Israel here since Joseph's sons were being numbered among the tribes of Israel. Joseph identified his sons as **the sons God** had **given** him, thereby praising God for them. Israel then instructed Joseph to **bring them** near that he might **bless them.**

48:10–12 / Jacob's eyesight had faded in his old age. This detail alludes to Isaac's dim eyesight that had enabled Jacob to steal Esau's blessing (27:1), and it prepares for the confusion over whose head he should place his right hand on. **Joseph brought his sons close to** his father. Israel **kissed them and embraced them,** rejoicing that he had lived for this high ceremony. He stated that he had **never expected to see** Joseph **again,** but **God** had **allowed him to see** even his son's **children.** Then Joseph took his sons from **Israel's knees and bowed down . . . to the ground,** honoring both Israel his father and the God who had guided their lives. Despite his own exalted position in the government, Joseph was recognizing Israel's leadership in the family.

48:13–14 / Joseph and his sons rose in preparation for the blessing ceremony. Joseph stationed his two children close to his father, with **Ephraim on his right** and **Manasseh on his left** so that Israel would naturally put his right hand on Manasseh, the firstborn. Joseph was making sure that the older received the greater blessing. Israel, however, crossed his hands so that he put **his right hand . . . on Ephraim's head** and **his left hand on Manasseh's head.** The text also labors this point in order to emphasize precisely whom Israel identified as leader.

48:15–16 / Israel **then blessed Joseph.** This introduction is problematic since Israel was supposed to be blessing Joseph's sons. Possibly a blessing on Joseph stood before that of his sons, but it seems more likely that in blessing his sons Israel was simultaneously blessing Joseph. Jacob began by elaborately identifying God as **the God before whom** his **fathers Abraham and Isaac** had **walked.** "Walk" means "conduct," as in God's command to Abraham that he walk before him and be blameless (17:1). This **God** had **been** his **shepherd** throughout his **life to this day.** "Shepherd" conveys that God had led and cared for him compassionately and protectively throughout the complex journey of his life (49:24; Ps. 23). Above all, as shepherd God had guided his destiny to this moment of blessing Joseph's offspring. He further identified God as **the Angel who** had **delivered** him **from all harm.** In the accounts of Jacob, "angel" and "God" are used interchangeably (e.g., 31:3, 11, 13); the term "deliver" (*ga'al*), however, only appears here in Genesis. It identifies one who acts as next of kin in rescuing a close relative from trouble. In Paddan Aram, Jacob had no blood kinsmen to help him with the difficulties he faced. His next of kin was God himself, present as the angel of the Lord.

Next Israel prayed that this God might **bless these boys,** who would be called by his **name** Israel and **the names of** his **fa-**

thers **Abraham and Isaac,** and that **they** might **increase greatly upon the earth.** The increase of their offspring would contribute to the fulfillment of God's promise that Jacob would increase (v. 4). A father usually divided his estate into shares so that the oldest son received two portions. Through Israel's blessing on Joseph's two sons, Joseph received the double portion of his father's inheritance. Jacob elevated Joseph, the firstborn of Rachel, over Reuben, the firstborn of Leah.

48:17–19 / Joseph **was displeased** at **his** father's **placing his right hand on Ephraim's head** since he was the younger. Therefore, he **took hold of his father's hand to move it . . . to Manasseh's head,** asserting that Manasseh was **the firstborn.** Israel, however, rejected Joseph's effort, pointing out that he was fully cognizant of what he was doing. Israel was determined to establish Ephraim as the head in Joseph's family. He might have been so set on taking this course since he himself was not the firstborn. He pointed out that Manasseh **too** was to **become a people** and to **become great.** Nevertheless, Ephraim, the younger, was to be **greater than** he, and **his descendants** (seed) would **become a group of nations.** Mention of Joseph's displeasure establishes beyond doubt that Israel acted knowingly and purposefully in elevating Ephraim.

48:20 / Israel **blessed them,** proclaiming that even their names would become a term of blessing in Israel: **"May God make you like Ephraim and Manasseh."** That is, all the tribes were to be blessed through Joseph's two sons.

48:21–22 / At the end of the ceremony Israel informed Joseph that he was **about to die.** He encouraged him by saying that God's presence would continue to **be with** all of them. He boldly asserted that God would **take** them **back to the land of** their **fathers,** thereby expressing his confidence in God's promise to give the land of Canaan to Jacob's seed. During the ensuing hard years of Egyptian bondage, Jacob's word gave his descendants hope that they would one day return to Canaan. In recognition of his great love for Joseph, Israel bequeathed to him a certain **ridge of land** that he had taken **from the Amorites with** his own **sword and . . . bow.** The report of this battle has not been preserved. Since the term "ridge" *(shekem)* literally means "shoulder," it may designate a portion of land given as an inheritance rather than being the name of a place. Tradition identified this piece of land with Shechem (Josh. 24:32).

Additional Notes §59

48:16 / This is the only reference to God's acting as next of kin in Genesis (Job 19:25; Ps. 19:14). It conveys how deeply Jacob appreciated God's help during the difficult times of his life. This term became attached to God's redeeming Israel from Egyptian bondage (Exod. 6:6; 15:13). Isaiah later used it to proclaim God as the one able to rescue Israel from exile (43:14; 48:17; 49:26).

48:20 / These two tribes became the economic and political core of northern Israel. Ephraim's prominence led to the use of his name as a synonym for northern Israel (e.g., Isa. 7:2, 5, 8–9, 17; Hos. 5:3, 5, 9, 11–14).

48:22 / The location of this ridge is debated. It is reported that Jacob bought a field in Shechem (33:18–19). The only recorded battle involving Jacob was his sons' defeat of the Shechemites (ch. 34), but there is no indication that they gained any land from that battle, and Jacob disapproved of their contentiousness. Since Joseph was buried at Shechem (Josh. 24:32), Jacob must have had in mind a plot of land in that area.

§60 Jacob's Last Testament (Gen. 49:1–28)

Just before his death, Jacob, the patriarch whose name Israel will become the name of the nation that will develop from his children, delivers his last testament, focusing on the destinies of his twelve sons. Since God has appeared to Jacob from time to time, he has the authority to describe the character of each tribe in regard to its future settlement in the promised land. This testament is a complex piece, for it is the composite of three genres: deathbed blessing, farewell address (Josh. 23), and tribal poem (Deut. 33; Sarna, *Genesis*, p. 331). It makes rich use of paronomasia, alliteration, and metaphors. Several of its lines are obscure because of the antiquity of the language, unusual grammar, and elliptical phrases.

The testament is organized according to the birth order of Jacob's sons with the respective mother (cf. 29:31–30:24). Leah's six sons come first in the order of their births, with the exception that Zebulun precedes Issachar. Next are the children of the two concubines, the children of Bilhah framing those of Zilpah: Dan, Gad, Asher, and Naphtali. In final position are the beloved children of Rachel, Joseph and Benjamin. The longest sayings are oracles about Reuben, Simeon, Levi, Judah, and Joseph, all prominent figures in the Jacob and Joseph cycles. The brief words regarding the other sons are aphoristic tribal sayings. Jacob curses the oldest three sons, Reuben, Simeon, and Levi. These curses preclude classifying this document as a blessing.

The literary style here is quite distinct from the other passages in Genesis. This suggests that it originated in a different setting and circulated independently before being incorporated into Genesis. Nevertheless, this testament is closely tied to Genesis, for numerous details are intelligible only in light of the preceding narratives. First, the order of the sons of Jacob is in accord with the order of their births in Genesis 29:31–30:24 and the list in 35:22b–26. Second, Jacob curses Reuben for lying with Bilhah, his concubine (35:22). Third, Jacob curses Simeon and Levi for their brutal sack of Shechem (ch. 34). Jacob's curses against the three oldest sons can be accounted for only in light of their blunders as reported in Genesis. Fourth, Judah's exaltation as leader harmonizes both with his leadership role in dealing with the famine and with the narrative that recounts the birth of his grandchildren (ch. 38). Finally, the emphasis on Joseph corresponds to his delivering the family from the harsh famine and to his high position in Pharaoh's court.

These descriptions of the tribes correspond best to the early days of Israel's settlement, the second half of the second millennium B.C. The Hebrew found here is ancient, as is evidenced by the ambiguity of several terms, the obscurity of the wordplays, and the uncertainty of the meaning of many metaphors. It also correlates to the style found in texts from Ugarit (from the middle of the second millennium B.C.). The tribes are settled in the land but loosely connected, as they were in the early days of the settlement, according to the book of Judges (H. Seebass, "Die Stämmesprüche in Gen 49 3-27," *ZAW* 96 [1984], pp. 333–50). By the time of the monarchy, the destinies of the tribes were markedly different from those given here. Furthermore, in speaking of his sons as tribes Jacob builds a bridge from the patriarchal era to the league of twelve tribes. He does this in order to show how God would fulfill through each of them the promises to Abraham. That is, his seed would become a great nation (12:2), and they would live in the promised land (12:7).

Jacob's sayings played a powerful role in ancient Israel, for the ancients believed that the patriarchs heard from God and that their final words held the destiny of their offspring. Thus this testament united the tribes by placing all of them on the same footing as sons of Jacob. Furthermore, it prepared them for the fact that the future of the twelve sons would vary markedly. Some, like Dan, would experience great hardship, while others, especially Judah and Joseph, would be richly blessed. If the kernel of these sayings goes back to Jacob, it is easy to imagine that over time the sayings as we have them grew and developed. Nevertheless, that growth was minimal since the text includes the curses on the first three sons and the negative traits mentioned in the sayings of Zebulun and Asher. Most of the additions took place in the blessings of Judah and Joseph. This is seen in their length and content—the lauding of Judah's leadership and the prominence of Joseph, which fit best with the era of the united monarchy.

49:1–2 / **Jacob** summoned **his sons,** asking them to **gather around** him as he delivered his final testament about **what** would **happen** to them **in days to come.** Energetically he exhorted them to **listen** to him.

49:3–4 / Jacob spoke first about **Reuben,** his **firstborn.** By position Reuben represented Jacob's **might** or virility, **excelling in honor** and **in power**—qualities essential for the tribal leader. As firstborn he had a right to a double portion of the family inheritance (Deut. 21:15–17). However, motivated by anger that had been simmering for years, Jacob proclaimed that Reuben would **no longer excel** because he had acted as **turbulent . . . waters** in defiling his **father's bed** when he slept with Bilhah, Jacob's concubine (35:22; 1 Chron. 5:1–2). By underscoring the term "bed," Jacob expressed the shame he felt because of what Reuben had done. This act was so repulsive that Jacob took away from Reuben the rights of the firstborn—leadership of the family and a double share of the inheritance. In the settlement Reuben occupied land in the central Transjordan (Josh. 13:15–23). This tribe was the first to disappear from the league, even before the rise of kingship in Israel.

49:5–7 / Jacob addressed **Simeon and Levi** as **brothers** or allies, condemning them for their use of **swords** as **weapons of violence.** He was outraged at their having used circumcision, the sign of the covenant, to gain a tactical advantage for plundering Shechem (34:25–30). Their cunning ploy had led them to kill **men in their anger and** hamstring **oxen** randomly. Jacob therefore dissociated himself from ever sitting in **their council** (Ps. 1:1); **cursed be their** fierce, cruel **anger.** Like a prophet, Jacob quoted a word from God in saying that God would **scatter them** among the tribes of **Israel.** It is important to note that Jacob cursed a trait of these sons, not the sons themselves. The tribe of Levi, as priests, received no specific allotment of land, only selected cities dispersed throughout Canaan. Simeon disappeared from the league very early, apparently being absorbed by the tribe of Judah (Josh. 19:1; 1 Chron. 4:24–43). Neither the Blessing of Moses (Deut. 33) nor the Song of Deborah (Judg. 5) mentions the tribe of Simeon.

49:8–12 / Jacob blessed **Judah,** raising the next in line to leader. Judah would be **praised** by his **brothers** and acclaimed as leader for having decisively defeated his **enemies.** Jacob lauded Judah's strength by comparing him with **a lion,** embellishing this image with three terms for this majestic animal: **cub** *(gur)*, **lion** *('aryeh)*, and **lioness** *(labi'*; Num. 23:24; 24:9). This text is the origin of the messianic title the Lion of the tribe of Judah. Rulership would be the right of this tribe as the symbols, **the scepter** and **the ruler's staff,** indicate. No one would be able to vie with him. His power would be over his brothers, or those in the tribal league, as well as over other nations. This blessing anticipated the Davidic kingdom; David, in turn, became the type of the Messiah. In that way this blessing looked to the reign of the Messiah. It expressed a way that God would fulfill the Abrahamic blessing; other nations would come under the rule of the house of Judah and thus participate in the Abrahamic blessing (12:2–3).

A set of beautiful metaphors lauded Judah's stately position and abundant riches in verses 11–12. His vines were to grow so lush that he would not hesitate tying **his donkey . . . to the choicest branch,** unmindful of his donkey's devouring everything in its reach. This tribe's harvests would be so bountiful that the people would **wash** their **garments in wine.** His having dark **eyes** and sparkling white **teeth** attest either the stately nobility of the leader or the rich produce of flocks and fields that this tribe would enjoy.

49:13 / **Zebulun** was to dwell **by the seashore** and have a good port (Deut. 33:19); **his border** would reach **toward Sidon,** a major Phoenician city. This latter reference suggests that Zebulun would either learn sea trade from the Phoenicians or be employed by them in their commercial adventures. A difficulty arises from the fact that Zebulun's allotment was not along the Mediterranean Sea (Josh. 19:10–16). It is possible that during certain periods, perhaps very early in the settlement, Zebulun's territory extended into the Bay of Acco, which offers a fair seaport. Wenham (*Genesis 16–50,* pp. 479–80) proposes, by taking *shakan* to mean "dwell" in tents, or temporary settlements, that in some periods this tribe camped along the sea.

49:14–15 / **Issachar** was **a rawboned donkey lying down between two saddlebags.** "Lying down" symbolizes either exhaustion from work or stubbornness. A rabbinic tradition, however, took it as a description of the geography of Issachar's allotment. Although receiving a fine inheritance, this tribe became forced laborers to the Canaanites. They worked hard, waiting for the time when they would have full control of their heritage (Judg. 5:15).

49:16–17 / **Dan** was to be a force for **justice** within Israel. A play is made on the name Dan *(dan)* and "judge, provide justice" *(din)*. "Provide justice" may mean "rule or take vengeance"; Dan's acts for justice would benefit the entire league. Jacob compared Dan with **a serpent** or a horned **viper** that hides in the sand along the side of the road. When it strikes at a horse passing by, that horse rears up, throwing off **its rider.** This imagery suggests that this small, weak tribe would use stealth tactics to overcome stronger foes.

49:18 / At this point Jacob inserted a brief prayer asking for Yahweh's **deliverance.** Perhaps, after the word regarding Dan, he felt the need to express his desire that God would deliver the weaker tribes through the obstacles they were to face.

49:19 / **Gad** would have to deal with attacks **by a band of raiders.** But he would be able to stand them off and then pursue them as they fled. Since this tribe settled in Gilead in the Transjordan, it felt the first brunt of most raids against Israel in the days of the judges. Four of these six words are a play on Gad's name *(gad)*. The first line reads *gad gedud yegudennu*, literally "Gad—a band will attack him," and the second line has *yagud*, "he will attack." This picture accords with Gad's fame for its warriors (Deut. 33:20–21; 1 Chron. 5:18; 12:8).

49:20 / **Asher,** a skilled farmer, would grow a **rich** variety of luscious produce **fit for a** king's table. Possibly this refers to exporting choice produce to foreign kings. His tribal allotment, which reached from the Jezreel Valley north along the coast, was among the most fertile areas in Canaan.

49:21 / **Naphtali** was to be **a** freed **doe,** symbolic of grace, agility, speed, and shyness. Being fertile, she would **bear** numerous **beautiful fawns.** Naphtali left its roving to settle in the rich Huleh Valley, between the Lebanon mountains to the west and Bashan to the east. In Judges (4:6, 10; 5:18b) this tribe was praised for its efforts to help the other tribes defeat their enemies.

49:22–26 / Joseph received the longest blessing, for Jacob chose him to receive the blessing of the firstborn. He was to be **a fruitful vine,** planted by **a spring;** thus its roots would always have water. Its **branches** would **climb over a wall** (Ps. 80), meaning that Joseph was to be prosperous and occupy its heritage fully. When **attacked** by a ruthless army of **archers,** he would be brave, not shrinking from the battle. **His bow** would be **steady** because the power of **the Mighty One of Jacob** was with him. The battle could refer either to attacks on the center of Israel during the era of the judges or to the troubles Joseph faced from his brothers.

A series of titles for God captures God's presence with the tribe of Joseph, sustaining, helping, and delivering: **the Mighty One of Jacob, Shepherd, the Rock of Israel, father's God, the Almighty.** In this blessing Jacob gave exuberant expression to God's guidance, care, and blessing in his own life and in the life of his favorite son. God would bring **blessings of the heavens above** and **the deep below.** That is, Joseph would have an abundance of water, both from rain and from springs, and thus he would have bumper harvests. This was a very rich blessing for those living in a land that often lacked sufficient water. The next verse amplifies this blessing as it describes the greatness and the bounty of his inheritance with the metaphors of **the ancient mountains** and **the age-old hills.** These ancient landmarks symbolize endurance and abundance. The productivity of this tribe's inheritance provided a solid basis for the economy of the tribal league. The **blessings of the breast and womb** empowered Joseph's family to become numerous. Jacob asked for this blessing to **rest on Joseph,** whom he identified as **prince** *(nazir)* **among his brothers.** Because of Joseph's high position in Egypt many interpreters identify this prince as Joseph himself, rather than as a future leader coming from his tribe. But given that the time orientation of these blessings is toward the early days of the settlement, this saying must be looking further into the future.

49:27 / **Benjamin** was **a ravenous wolf;** that is, a fierce fighter. He would defeat his foes **in the morning** and joyfully divide **the plunder** among his people **in the evening.** The play on "morning and evening" conveys the speed with which he would defeat his foes. Ehud, one of the first judges, was a Benjamite (Judg. 3:15–30). In a gruesome incident at Gibeah in the territory of Benjamin during the era of the judges, the Benjamites proved themselves skilled, fierce warriors (Judg. 19–21; 1 Chron. 8:40; 12:2).

49:28 / This verse is a summary statement.

Additional Notes §60

49:1 / "In days to come" is lit. "in the last days." In the prophets it is a technical phrase for the end of time (e.g., Isa. 2:2), but in this early text it means "the future."

49:6 / Hamstring means to cripple an animal by cutting tendons in its legs.

49:10 / This famous crux, *shiloh,* has defied explanation. Of the many proposals, three prominent ones follow. First, NIV renders it "until he comes to whom it belongs," based on reading the consonants as *she lo.* This line then refers to the owner of the scepter who comes to rule, i.e., the Davidic dynasty or the Messiah. This reading is attested at Qumran. However, there is no good way to explain its becoming *shiloh,* nor does this reading accord well with the preceding line. Second, others take it as Shiloh, a city in Ephraim, where the ark of the covenant was kept during much of the era of the judges. Judah's coming to Shiloh means that this tribe would extend its rule over the northern tribes. It is difficult, however, to determine why this town was singled out, for when David rose to rule Israel, it lay in ruins. Furthermore, the normal spelling of this town is different (*shilōh,* with variants *shilô, shîlô*). Third, the entire line may be repointed to read *yuba' shay loh,* "until tribute is brought to him" (according to some ancient rabbinic sources). In support of this reading Wenham argues that it fits the context, offers a good parallel to the last line of the verse, and amplifies the theme of Judah's rule over the nations (*Genesis 16–50,* p. 478). Each of these alternatives sees a reference to a dynasty from the house of Judah ruling Israel.

Many interpreters have taken these words as a reference to an ideal king coming from Judah to achieve God's high hopes for Israel. It must be kept in mind that the original intent of these words concerned the role of Judah in the tribal league. Nevertheless, changing historical situations cause texts to be read differently. After the fall of the Davidic dynasty, many Jewish groups, and later Christians, came to find in this line a messianic promise, especially since David became the ideal model for the Messiah.

49:14 / Other proposals for the obscure term rendered saddlebags *(mishpetayim)* are "sheepfolds" and "hearth" (Sarna, *Genesis,* p. 339).

49:17 / Some scholars see here the exploits of Samson (a Danite) against the Philistines (Judg. 14–16).

The use of horses in battle was not common until the end of the second millennium B.C.

Dan was unsuccessful in taking territory allotted to it in the Shephelah between Judah and Benjamin. Therefore, this tribe migrated to the northernmost part of the promised land (Judg. 17–18).

49:21 / For "doe" (*'ayyalah*) various suggestions have been made, such as "mountain goat" or reading *'elah* ("terebinth"; Gk.).

The meaning of the phrase *'imre-sheper,* rendered "beautiful fawns," is obscure. Of the many other proposals two of the best are "beautiful words" and "goodly boughs"; i.e., Naphtali would become a courier of good news, or this tribe was being compared with a terebinth with lovely branches.

49:22 / The firstborn son had a right to a larger share of the inheritance (Code of Lipit Ishtar §§24, 31 (36) and Code of Hammurabi §§165–70). One practice was to divide the inheritance into shares according to the number of sons plus one, i.e., for a family of five sons there would be six shares; the oldest son then received two of these shares. In that Joseph received a special share in regard to Shechem (48:22) it appears that his father regarded him as the firstborn (de Vaux, *Early History of Israel,* p. 251).

"A fruitful vine" *(porat)* is a pun on the name Ephraim (*'eprayim;* Sarna, *Genesis,* p. 343). Another way to render *porat* is "a wild colt" (NIV margin). Hamilton favors "wild she-ass," connecting it with Ugar. *prt* "cow, heifer" (*Genesis: Chapters 18–50,* p. 678). This rendering coincides with the animal metaphors used for other tribes. Nevertheless, in the OT the vine serves several times as a metaphor for the settlement of Israel in the land (e.g., Ps. 80:8–11). This reading is supported by Gk. and Tg. Both views have weaknesses; so given the obscurity of the Hb., it is better to follow the ancient tradition.

Joseph's story may serve as a basis for the blessing. He began with abundance (v. 22), suffered great hardship as a prisoner and servant (v. 23), maintained his bearing during these hardships (v. 24), and rose to fame and riches under God's guidance (vv. 25–26).

49:28 / In tribal lists Joseph represents either one tribe (here) or two (Ephraim and Manasseh; Num. 1:10, 32–35), sometimes depending on whether or not Levi is a member of the list.

§61 Jacob's Death and Funeral
(Gen. 49:29–50:14)

This report offers the assurance that Jacob was truly buried in the Cave of Machpelah. More importantly, this recounting of Jacob's death looks ahead to his children's going out of Egypt to return to the land of promise. This unit has three sections: Jacob's death (49:29–33), the mourning for Jacob in Egypt (50:1–3), and Jacob's burial in the Cave of Machpelah (50:4–14).

49:29–33 / Jacob instructed all of his sons, presumably assembled for his last blessing, to **bury** him **in the cave** of Machpelah (47:27–31; 48:21–22), identified by its purchase **from Ephron the Hittite** and by its occupants, **Abraham, Sarah, Isaac, Rebekah,** and **Leah.** At the end of Genesis this registry functions as a review of the main characters. Jacob **breathed his last and was gathered to his people** (25:8, 17; 35:29).

50:1–3 / **Joseph** solemnly mourned his father's death. He **threw himself upon his father and wept over him and kissed him.** Afterward Joseph ordered Egyptian **physicians . . . to embalm** Israel. The preparation of a mummy took **forty days.** Because of Joseph's high status, the whole nation **mourned for** Jacob **seventy days.**

50:4–6 / At the end of the time of **mourning, Joseph** asked **Pharaoh's court** for permission to bury his father in Canaan, stressing his desire to carry out the **oath** he had sworn to his father to **bury** him **in the tomb** he had **dug.** The Egyptians placed the highest importance on providing a person of honor with a proper burial. Joseph emphasized that he would **return** after the burial, making it clear that he did not intend to use this occasion to resettle in his homeland. Out of regard for Joseph, **Pharaoh** granted him permission to **bury** his **father** in Canaan.

50:7–9 / **Joseph, his brothers,** and their extended family, with an entourage of Egyptian **dignitaries,** traveled to Canaan with their father's mummy. A military guard of **chariots and horsemen** accompanied them, both to assist and to provide security. It was a grand procession. The young **children** and the **flocks** of Jacob's family, however, stayed behind **in Goshen.** Their remaining in Egypt guaranteed the return of Joseph and his brothers.

50:10–14 / When they arrived at **the threshing floor of Atad,** located beyond **the Jordan,** the entourage held a great public memorial ceremony for Jacob. The mourning lasted **seven** days. **The Canaanites,** observing the ceremony, were so impressed with the large number of Egyptians present that they called that place **Abel Mizraim,** or "mourning of Egypt." At the end of the week of mourning **Jacob's sons carried** their father to Hebron and **buried him in the cave in the field of Machpelah.** The interment ceremony itself was thus a family matter. After the burial, the entire procession **returned to Egypt.**

Additional Notes §61

50:2–3 / Integral to their strong belief in the afterlife, the Egyptians sought to preserve the body close to its living form so that when, as they believed, the spirit and/or the soul (the Egyptian *ka* and *ba*) of the deceased returned to the tomb, it would recognize its original habitation.

According to Herodotus, the process of preparing a mummy took seventy days. But Egyptologists studying the process of embalming have discovered that seventy days would be too long, for too much damage would be done to the body. They discovered that the dehydration of the body takes forty days; this time corresponds to the time specified in this text (J. Hamilton-Paterson and C. Andrews, *Mummies: Death and Life in Ancient Egypt* [New York: Penguin, 1978], p. 43). Perhaps Herodotus had in mind the time for the funeral.

50:4–5 / Custom may have prevented Joseph from going to Pharaoh himself. Joseph said to Pharaoh's court that Jacob had dug a grave, but if he was to be buried in the Cave of Machpelah, digging a grave would not have been necessary. Joseph likely used this terminology in his request to bury his father so that the Egyptians, who prepared their graves long before death, would understand (C. Westermann, *Genesis 37–50: A Commentary* [trans. J. Scullion; Minneapolis: Augsburg: 1986], p. 200).

50:10–11 / Atad has not been identified, and the precise location of "beyond the Jordan" (*'eber hayyarden;* NIV "near the Jordan") is debated. Usually the latter phrase is taken for the Transjordan. That identification is doubtful here, because it requires the account to read that the cortege crossed Sinai, traveled north through the Transjordan, recrossed the Jordan, and climbed the hills to Hebron to reach the Cave of Machpelah. This phrase could refer to the Cisjordan, given the orientation of the person using this term (e.g., Deut. 3:20, 25). A reconstruction of the journey provides another explanation for this toponym. Most likely this cortege traveled to Canaan on the coastal road. In Canaan they took a spur leading northeast to Hebron. Atad was the site on the border between Egypt and Canaan, and Abel Mizraim was Nahal Mizraim, i.e., the wadi that defined the border between Canaan and Egypt (A. Demsky, "The Route of Jacob's Funeral Cortege and the Problem of *'eber hayyarden* [Genesis 50:10f.]" in *Minkhah le Nakhum* [ed. M. Brettler and M. Fishbane; JSOTSup 154; Sheffield: JSOT Press, 1993], pp. 54–64). Demsky also identifies Jordan with a city in the Negev, present-day Khirbet Irq, some eighteen miles from Gaza. *'eber* then refers to "a crossing" at this location. If these identifications are correct, the procession took the main highway to Canaan and did not go through the Transjordan. At a site near the border between Canaan and Egypt they held a public mourning for Jacob.

§62 Joseph's Care of His Brothers (Gen. 50:15–21)

After the burial of Jacob, the brothers are anxious about how Joseph might treat them. Their anxiety offers insight into the persistent fear that accompanies guilt over a harmful act against another, especially against a family member. Only full and genuine reconciliation removes that anxiety. This story is important, for it recounts the establishment of true solidarity among Jacob's twelve sons in a foreign land.

In this account Joseph's brothers send word to him (vv. 15–18), and Joseph and his brothers achieve full reconciliation (vv. 19–21).

50:15–17 / Without the security of their father's presence and fearful that Joseph might seek revenge, the brothers felt the need to define their relationship with Joseph. Not sufficiently confident of Joseph's forgiveness to approach him directly, the **brothers sent word to Joseph** pleading for his forgiveness. They claimed that his **father, before he died,** had instructed Joseph **to forgive . . . the sins and the wrongs** of his brothers that they had committed **in treating** him **so badly.** By identifying Jacob as "your father," they appealed to the special relationship between Joseph and Jacob, the very relationship that had spurred them to treat Joseph so cruelly. They admitted that their selling Joseph had been a gruesome deed by the use of three strong words: "sin or transgression" (*pesha'*), "wrong or misdeed" (*khatta't*), and "bad or evil" (*ra'ah*). They then petitioned Joseph to **forgive the sins of the servants of the God of** his **father.** They strengthened their petitions by pointing out that they had not only the same earthly father but also the same God.

On receiving **their message,** Joseph **wept,** overcome with emotions as he remembered the pain of sitting in the dark, dismal cistern awaiting death, being sold into slavery, and spending years in Egyptian prisons. He wept at the guilt and anxiety his brothers still felt. He wept for joy that they had been reunited and expressed true remorse for their transgression against him. His weeping demonstrated that his concern for them was genuine.

50:18 / When they learned about Joseph's response to their request, the **brothers came** to him, bowing to the ground **before him.** Submissive, as Joseph had dreamed in his youth (37:5–11), they asserted that they were his **slaves.**

50:19–21 / **Joseph** addressed their fears directly and forcefully by saying twice, **Don't be afraid.** This is the word of assurance God himself gives to those facing harsh, threatening circumstances (15:1). This word provides the basis on which to build a new relationship. Joseph added three affirmations. He reminded them that he did not take **the place of God** for them and thereby renounced any right to take vengeance on them. He emphasized the vast difference between God's way of working and human planning. Whereas his brothers had planned to do him **harm,** God had used their plans **for good** (see 45:5–8). Throughout the ordeal God had led him and protected him, elevating him to leadership in the Egyptian government at a crucial time, thereby enabling him to save their lives and those of numerous peoples throughout that region. This view of divine providence accords with the teaching of wisdom literature. Humans make plans, but God determines the outcome (Prov. 16:9; 19:21). As God directs the course of human affairs, he brings good outcomes out of acts of evil. God can handle every situation for those who trust him, no matter how complicated or foreboding, to bring good out of human hate, greed, and jealousy.

Joseph also promised that he would continue to **provide for** them and their **children.** They would have plenty of food, and their flocks would have sufficient fodder, so they could shepherd their flocks in security. This promise is concrete evidence of his forgiveness. Whereas Lamech had hoped that Noah would bring comfort to humans (5:29), Joseph comforted (NIV **reassured**) his brothers with his forgiveness and care for them.

Joseph's words spoke directly to their fears and brought relief (for other occurrences of "spoke kindly," *wayedabber 'al-libbam,* see 34:3; Judg. 19:3; Ruth 2:13). Joseph used the same words God later used to comfort *(n-kh-m)* Israel in captivity, informing them that their exile had ended (Isa. 40:1; 49:13; 51:3, 12, 19; 61:2).

§63 Joseph's Death (Gen. 50:22–26)

50:22–23 / Joseph lived **a hundred and ten years.** For the Egyptians, this age symbolized a long and full life. Joseph saw his grandchildren to the third and fourth generation. The ancients viewed such a privilege as the reward for righteousness.

50:24–25 / Before his death Joseph wished to give his extended family a word of promise that would sustain and guide them as long as they remained in Egypt. He reiterated the promise that **God** would **surely** bring them **out of this land to the land** that God had sworn **to Abraham, Isaac and Jacob.** The God of Israel is especially known as the God of these three patriarchs (e.g., Exod. 3:6). Joseph had his brothers **swear an oath** that they would **carry** his **bones up from this place** when **God** came **to** their **aid** in Egypt.

Genesis closes with a reference to the great promises God gave Abraham (12:1–3), for they contained the destiny of the children of Israel. Since Jacob's entire family lived in Egypt, the hope of these promises had to be accepted by faith. This faith would have to be kept alive throughout the long, dark years of bondage.

Joseph was not raised to the level of his forefathers. His blessing of his children is not recorded, for they had been blessed by the great patriarch Jacob (ch. 48). Although Joseph had enabled the children of Israel to survive the terrible famine, he remained one brother among the twelve, honored as the firstborn by having received a double inheritance through the elevation of his two sons to the level of his brothers.

50:26 / The Egyptians **embalmed** Joseph and **placed** him **in a coffin in Egypt.** The coffin is mentioned in anticipation of its being carried to Canaan when the Israelites leave Egypt. After the conquest, the Israelites fulfilled this oath by burying Joseph at Shechem (Josh. 24:32). This act symbolized that the offspring of Abraham now rightfully occupied the land of promise.

For Further Reading

Commentaries

Alter, R. *Genesis: Translation and Commentary.* New York: Norton, 1996.

Brueggemann, W. *Genesis.* Interpretation. Atlanta: John Knox, 1982.

Cassuto, U. *A Commentary on the Book of Genesis.* Vol. 1: *From Adam to Noah: A Commentary on Genesis I–VI 8.* Translated by I. Abrahams. Jerusalem: Magnes, 1961.

———. *A Commentary on the Book of Genesis.* Vol. 2: *From Noah to Abraham: A Commentary on Genesis VI 9–XI 32.* Translated by I. Abrahams. Jerusalem: Magnes, 1964.

Gowan, D. E. *From Eden to Babel: A Commentary on the Book of Genesis 1–11.* ITC. Grand Rapids: Eerdmans, 1988.

Gunkel, H. *Genesis.* Translated by M. Biddle. Macon, Ga.: Mercer University Press, 1997.

Hamilton, V. *The Book of Genesis: Chapters 1–17.* NICOT. Grand Rapids: Eerdmans, 1990.

———. *The Book of Genesis: Chapters 18–50.* NICOT. Grand Rapids: Eerdmans, 1995.

Janzen, J. *Abraham and All the Families of the Earth: A Commentary on the Book of Genesis 12–50.* ITC. Grand Rapids: Eerdmans, 1993.

Kidner, D. *Genesis: An Introduction and Commentary.* TOTC. Downers Grove, Ill.: InterVarsity, 1967.

Leibowitz, N. *Studies in Bereshit Genesis: In the Context of Ancient and Modern Jewish Bible Commentary.* Translated by A. Newman. 4th ed. Jerusalem: Publishing Department of Jewish Agency at Alpha Press, 1981.

Rad, G. von. *Genesis: A Commentary.* Translated by J. Marks. Rev. ed. OTL. Philadelphia: Westminster, 1972.

Rashi. *Pentateuch with Targum Onkelos, Haphtaroth, and Rashi's Commentary.* Translated by M. Rosenbaum and A. Silbermann. Jerusalem: Silbermann Family, 1973.

Sailhamer, J. "Genesis." Pages 3–284 in vol. 2 of *The Expositor's Bible Commentary with the New International Version of the Holy Bible.* Edited by F. E. Gaebelein. 12 vols. Grand Rapids: Zondervan, 1990.

Sarna, N. *Understanding Genesis.* New York: McGraw-Hill, 1966.

_____. *Genesis.* The JPS Torah Commentary. Philadelphia: Jewish Publication Society, 1989.

Speiser, E. *Genesis: Introduction, Translation, and Notes.* AB. New York: Doubleday, 1964.

Wenham, G. *Genesis 1–15.* WBC 1. Dallas: Word, 1987.

_____. *Genesis 16–50.* WBC 2. Dallas: Word, 1994.

Westermann, C. *Genesis 1–11: A Commentary.* Translated by J. Scullion. Minneapolis: Augsburg, 1984.

_____. *Genesis 12–36: A Commentary.* Translated by J. Scullion. Minneapolis: Augsburg, 1985.

_____. *Genesis 37–50: A Commentary.* Translated by J. Scullion. Minneapolis: Augsburg, 1986.

Literary, Religious, and Historical Issues

Albright, W. F. *Yahweh and the Gods of Canaan: A Historical Analysis of Two Contrasting Faiths.* Garden City, N.Y.: Doubleday, 1969.

Alter, R. *The Art of Biblical Narrative.* New York: Basic Books, 1981.

Anderson, B. *From Creation to New Creation.* OBT. Minneapolis: Fortress, 1994.

_____, ed. *Creation in the Old Testament.* Issues in Religion and Theology 6. Philadelphia: Fortress, 1984.

_____. "From Analysis to Synthesis: The Interpretation of Genesis 1–11." *JBL* 97 (1978), pp. 23–39.

Brenner, A., ed. *A Feminist Companion to Genesis.* Sheffield: Sheffield Academic Press, 1993.

Clines, D. *The Theme of the Pentateuch.* JSOTSup 10. Sheffield: University of Sheffield, 1978.

_____. *What Did Eve Do to Help? and Other Readerly Questions to the Old Testament.* JSOTSup 94. Sheffield: JSOT Press, 1992.

Coats, G. W. *Genesis, with an Introduction to Narrative Literature.* FOTL 1. Grand Rapids: Eerdmans, 1983.

_____. *From Canaan to Egypt: Structural and Theological Context for the Joseph Story*. CBQMS 4. Washington: Catholic Biblical Association, 1976.

_____. "The Joseph Story and Ancient Wisdom: A Reappraisal." *CBQ* 35 (1973), pp. 285–97.

Cross, F. *Canaanite Myth and Hebrew Epic: Essays in the History of the Religion of Israel*. Cambridge, Mass.: Harvard University Press, 1973.

Dever, W., and W. Clark. "The Patriarchal Traditions." Pages 70–148 in *Israelite and Judean History*. Ed. J. Hayes and J. Miller. Philadelphia: Westminster, 1977.

Fishbane, M. *Text and Texture: Close Reading of Selected Biblical Texts*. New York: Schocken, 1979.

Fokkelman, J. *Narrative Art in Genesis: Specimens of Stylistic and Structural Analysis*. 2d ed. The Biblical Seminar 12. Sheffield: JSOT Press, 1991.

Fox, E. "Can Genesis Be Read As a Whole?" *Semeia* 46 (1989), pp. 31–40.

Garrett, D. *Rethinking Genesis: The Sources and Authorship of the First Book of the Pentateuch*. Grand Rapids: Baker, 1991.

Gordon, C. H., and G. Rendsburg. *The Bible and the Ancient Near East*. 4th ed. New York: Norton, 1997.

Gunkel, H. *The Legends of Genesis*. Translated by W. Carruth. New York: Schocken, 1964.

Harran, M. *Temple and Temple Service in Ancient Israel*. Oxford: Oxford University Press, 1978.

Hendel, R. *The Epic of the Patriarchs: The Jacob Cycle and the Narrative Traditions of Canaan and Israel*. HSM 42. Atlanta: Scholars, 1987.

Hess, R., and D. Tsumura. *"I Studied Inscriptions from before the Flood": Ancient Near Eastern, Literary, and Linguistic Approaches to Genesis 1–11*. Sources for Biblical and Theological Study 4. Winona Lake, Ind.: Eisenbrauns, 1994.

Hess, R., P. Satterthwaite, and G. Wenham, eds. *He Swore an Oath: Biblical Themes from Genesis 12–50*. Cambridge: Tyndale House, 1993.

Kikawada, I., and A. Quinn. *Before Abraham Was: The Unity of Genesis 1–11*. Nashville: Abingdon, 1985.

Kitchen, K. *Ancient Orient and Old Testament*. Chicago: InterVarsity, 1968.

_____. *The Bible in Its World: The Bible and Archaeology Today*. Downers Grove, Ill.: InterVarsity, 1977.

_____. "Genesis 12–50 in the Near Eastern World." Pages 67–92 in *He Swore an Oath: Biblical Themes from Genesis 12–50.* Edited by R. Hess et al. Cambridge: Tyndale House, 1993.

Kselman, J. "The Book of Genesis: A Decade of Scholarly Research." *Int* 45 (1991), pp. 380–92.

Longacre, R. *Joseph: A Story of Divine Providence.* Winona Lake, Ind.: Eisenbrauns, 1989.

Mann, T. "'All the Families of the Earth': The Theological Unity of Genesis." *Int* 45 (1991), pp. 341–53.

McCarter, Jr. P. "The Historical Abraham." *Int* 42 (1988), pp. 341–52.

Millard, A., and D. Wiseman, eds. *Essays on the Patriarchal Narratives.* Winona Lake, Ind.: Eisenbrauns, 1983.

Moberly, R. *The Old Testament of the Old Testament: Patriarchal Narratives and Mosaic Yahwism.* OBT. Minneapolis: Fortress, 1994.

Moor, J. de. *The Rise of Yahwism: The Roots of Israelite Monotheism.* BETL 91. Leuven: University Press, 1990.

Morris, P., and D. Sawyer. *A Walk in the Garden: Biblical, Iconographical and Literary Images of Eden.* JSOTSup 136. Sheffield: JSOT Press, 1992.

Niditch, S. *Underdogs and Tricksters: A Prelude to Biblical Folklore.* New Voices in Biblical Studies. San Francisco: Harper & Row, 1987.

Patte, D., ed. *Genesis 2 and 3: Kaleidoscopic Structural Readings.* Semeia 18. Chico, Calif.: Scholars, 1980.

Rad, G. von. "The Joseph Narrative and Ancient Wisdom." Pages 292–300 in *The Problem of the Hexateuch and Other Essays.* Translated by E. Dicken. New York: McGraw-Hill, 1966.

Redford, D. *A Study of the Biblical Story of Joseph (Genesis 37–50).* Leiden: E. J. Brill, 1970.

Renckens, H. *Israel's Concept of the Beginning: The Theology of Genesis 1–3.* New York: Herder & Herder, 1964.

Rendsburg, G. *The Redaction of Genesis.* Winona Lake, Ind.: Eisenbrauns, 1986.

Santmire, H. "The Genesis Creation Narratives Revisited: Themes for a Golden Age." *Int* 45 (1991), pp. 366–79.

Sasson, J. "'The Tower of Babel' As a Clue to the Redactional Structuring of the Primeval History (Gen. 1–11:9)." Pages 211–19 in *The Bible World: Essays in Honor of Cyrus H. Gordon.* Edited by B. Rendsburg et al. New York: KTAV Publishing House, 1980.

Steinberg, N. "The Genealogical Framework of the Family Stories in Genesis." *Semeia* 46 (1989), pp. 41–50.

Sternberg, M. *The Poetics of Biblical Narrative: Ideological Literature and the Drama of Reading.* Bloomington, Ind.: Indiana University Press, 1987.

Stratton, B. *Out of Eden: Reading, Rhetoric, and Ideology in Genesis 2–3.* JSOTSup 208. Sheffield: Sheffield Academic Press, 1995.

Thompson, T. *The Historicity of the Patriarchal Narratives: The Quest for the Historical Abraham.* BZAW 133. Berlin: Walter de Gruyter, 1974.

_____. *The Origin Tradition of Ancient Israel: I. The Literary Formation of Genesis and Exodus 1–23.* JSOTSup 55. Sheffield: JSOT Press, 1987.

Trible, P. *God and the Rhetoric of Sexuality.* OBT. Philadelphia: Fortress, 1978.

Van Seters, J. *Abraham in History and Tradition.* New Haven, Conn.: Yale University Press, 1975.

Vaux, R. de. *The Early History of Israel.* Translated by D. Smith. Philadelphia: Westminster, 1978.

Westermann, C. *The Promises to the Fathers.* Translated by D. Green. Philadelphia: Fortress, 1980.

Wilson, R. *Genealogy and History in the Biblical World.* New Haven, Conn.: Yale University Press, 1977.

Wolde, E. van. *Stories of the Beginning: Genesis 1–11 and Other Creation Stories.* Translated by J. Bowden. London: SCM, 1996.

_____. *Words Become Worlds: Semantic Studies of Genesis 1–11.* Biblical Interpretation Series 6. Leiden: E. J. Brill, 1994.

Subject Index

Abel, 78–81, 86; meaning of his name, 79

Abimelech, 8, 9, 10, 20, 31, 140–41, 192–96, 202–4, 240–42

Abraham, 1, 16, 18, 20, 21, 22, 23, 26, 31, 33–34, 35, 91, 128, 202, 225, 235, 239, 240, 243, 298, 306, 309, 343, 352, 363, 368; portrayed as a king/sheik, 8–9, 139, 217; as a prophet, 9, 154, 194, 196; a military commander, 9, 147–51; an intercessor, 9, 20, 181–83, 189, 194, 196; his righteousness and his obedience to God, 8, 33–34, 131–34, 156–57, 159, 162, 175, 181, 189, 190, 196, 198, 207–10, 213, 240; evidence of God's blessing on him, 139–41, 142, 173–74, 194, 196, 198–99, 202–4, 217, 222, 225, 231; his trials, 8; his building an altar, 31, 135, 239, 243; God's call, 6, 8, 49, 130, 131–34; going down to Egypt, 139–41; returning to Canaan and separation from Lot, 142–46; the rescue of Lot from the kings of the East, 147–48; blessed by Melchizedek, 149–51; entering into covenant with God, 8, 22–23, 154–61; taking Hagar as surrogate wife, 164–68; God renews covenant and changes his name to Abraham, 23, 169–76; interceding for Sodom, 177–84; his dealings with Abimelech, 140–41, 192–97, 239, 241; birth of Isaac and expulsion of Hagar, 198–201; covenant with Abimelech 31, 202–4; binding of Isaac, 8, 34, 205–15; purchase of the Cave of Machpelah, 25, 216–20; getting a bride for Isaac, 221–29; his death and burial 30, 230–31

Abrahamic: narrative, 1, 3–4, 6–9, 16, 36, 130–232; promises, 11, 15, 18, 23, 24, 33, 130, 132–34, 140–41, 144–45, 158–59, 161, 171–72, 180–81, 200, 210, 213, 231, 240, 243, 247–48, 253, 256, 282, 285, 298, 300, 345, 351, 356, 358, 368

Adah, 85

Adam, 6, 59, 71, 72, 78, 79, 86, 91, 92

Admah, 119, 147

Adoption, 26, 31

Adullam, 12, 36, 315

Africa, 116, 118, 121, 122

Albright, W. F., 26, 279, 370

Altar, 21, 31, 105, 135, 142, 145, 208, 239, 243, 292, 298–99

Alter, R., 259, 369, 370

Amalekites, 148, 152, 308

Ammonites, 189, 189–90

Amorites, 27, 116, 119, 145, 148, 160, 163, 175, 353

Amraphel, 147, 151

Ancestral narratives, reliability of, 29–32, 37

Anderson, B., 107, 370

Andrew, M. E., 317

Andrews, C., 364

Angel of God (Yahweh), 10, 13, 166–67, 168, 174, 183, 200, 209–10, 226, 272, 283, 285

Angel(s)/messenger(s), 96, 181, 185–89, 223, 280, 281, 286, 352

Animals, 6, 47, 49–50, 54, 58, 59, 61–62, 74, 89, 98, 103, 105, 107, 109, 159, 203, 288, 295, 311, 312

Aqhat, 52, 88

Arabia, 120, 121, 122–23, 215, 233

Ararat, 104, 108

Ark, 6, 101, 102–4, 108

Asenath, 28, 329

Asher 356, 359; meaning of his name, 265

Assyria, 118, 122

Astour, M., 152

Atrahasis, 54, 106, 114

Baal, 27, 46, 88, 153, 286

Babel/Babylon, 35, 36, 118, 121, 124, 126

Babylonian Creation Epic, 41, 43, 127

Scripture Index